Early childhood studies

Early Childhood Studies

An Holistic Introduction

Edited by

Jayne Taylor BSc, RGN, RHV, Dip N (Lond), Cert Ed
Director, Nursing and Midwifery,
University College Suffolk

Margaret Woods MA, BA, Dip Ed
Director, Early Childhood and Behavioural Studies,
University College Suffolk

A member of the Hodder Headline Group
LONDON • SYDNEY • AUCKLAND

First published in Great Britain in 1998 by
Arnold, a member of the Hodder Headline Group
338 Euston Road, London NW1 3BH

http://www.arnoldpublishers.com

British Library Cataloguing in Publication Data
A catalogue record for this book is available from the British Library

Library of Congress Cataloging-in Publication Data
A catalog record for this book is available from the Library of Congress

ISBN 0 340 61388 2

Publisher: Clare Parker
Production Editor: Wendy Rooke
Production Controller: Bob Allen

Composition in 10/13pt Palatino by J&L Composition Ltd, Filey, North Yorkshire
Printed and bound in Great Britain by JW Arrowsmith Ltd, Bristol

Contents

List of contributors   vii

Preface   ix

Introduction
Margaret Woods   1

Chapter 1   **Early Childhood Studies – first principles**
Margaret Woods   10

Chapter 2   **New beginnings: factors affecting health and well-being in the infant**
Catherine Forsdike   32

Chapter 3   **Growth and development**
Val Thurtle   45

Chapter 4   **Personal, social and affective development**
Carolyn Silberfeld and Clare Robinson   72

Chapter 5   **Child in society**
Val Thurtle   85

Chapter 6   **Social policy: the state, the family and young children**
Erica Josyln, Christine Such and Cath Dixon   105

Chapter 7   **Children's relationships**
David Rutherford   124

Chapter 8   **Child health**
Jayne Taylor   143

Chapter 9   **Play, language and learning**
Anne Greig   154

Chapter 10   **Child protection, welfare and the law**
Kevin Pettican   172

Chapter 11   **Early childhood education in pre-school settings**
Margaret Woods   199

Chapter 12   **Multidisciplinary care of sick children in the community**
Val Thurtle   225

Chapter 13   **Children in developing countries**
Jayne Taylor   243

Chapter 14   **Perspectives on early childhood research**
Jayne Taylor   **260**

Chapter 15   **Managing self and others**
Caroline Jeffree and Graham Fox   **273**

Chapter 16   **Working with young children and their families**
Jayne Taylor   **289**

Index   **298**

List of Contributors

Catherine Dixon BA, PGDip, RGN, RHV, RHVT
Health Visitor Practitioner Researcher in East Anglia (formerly Senior Lecturer in Health Visiting, University College Suffolk, Ipswich)

Catherine Forsdike RGN, SCM, ADM, PGCEA, BA
Senior Lecturer in Midwifery, Directorate of Nursing and Midwifery, University College Suffolk, Ipswich

Graham Fox BA, MIMgt, MIPD, DMS
Senior Lecturer in Training and Personal Development, Directorate of Post-graduate Management and Technology, University College Suffolk, Ipswich

Anne Greig PhD, MA, DipEd
Senior Research Associate, Department of Social Work, University of East Anglia, Norwich

Caroline Jeffree BA, RGN, Diploma of Nursing, London
Formerly Senior Lecturer in Nursing Studies, University College Suffolk, Ipswich

Erica Joslyn MSc, BA, RM, RGN
Principal Lecturer in Social Policy, Directorate of Early Childhood and Behavioural Studies, University College Suffolk, Ipswich

Kevin Pettican MA, CQSW, DMS
Senior Lecturer in Social Work, Directorate of Social Work, Education and Counselling, University College Suffolk, Ipswich

Clare Robinson MA, BEd
Early Years Teacher, formerly Lecturer in Early Childhood Education, University College Suffolk, Ipswich

David Rutherford BA, MSc
Principal Lecturer in Social Psychology, Directorate of Early Childhood and Behavioural Studies, University College Suffolk, Ipswich

Carolyn Silberfeld BSc, PGCEA, RN, RSCN, RM, RHVT, CPT
Senior Lecturer in Child Health and Research, Directorate of Early Childhood Studies, University College Suffolk, Ipswich

Christine Such, MA, BSc
Lecturer in Social Policy, Directorate of Early Childhood and Behavioural Studies, University College Suffolk, Ipswich

Jayne Taylor BSc, RGN, RHV, DipN(Lond), Cert Ed
Director of Nursing and Midwifery, Directorate of Nursing and Midwifery, University College Suffolk, Ipswich

Val Thurtle MA, BSc, RGN, RHV, RM, Cert Ed
Senior Lecturer in Early Childhood Studies, Directorate of Early Childhood and Behavioural Studies, University College Suffolk, Ipswich

Margaret Woods MA, BA, DipEd
Director of Early Childhood and Behavioural Studies, University College Suffolk, Ipswich

Preface

The area of early childhood has been ripe for study at undergraduate and postgraduate level for some years. Early years professionals and parents recognise the value of actively promoting the development of young children, and the consequent benefit to children of quality early years provision is well known. Integral to this are well qualified, up-to-date reflective professionals.

In 1992 at University College Suffolk the work commenced on developing the BA (Hons) course in Early Childhood Studies as a route in the Modular Degree Programme. The course team was composed of teachers, children's nurses, health visitors, social workers, psychologists and researchers and was a truly multidisciplinary group of professionals and academics with different skills, roles, responsibilities and knowledge. By co-operating and working together in the multidisciplinary team their shared understanding and expertise have enabled the development of their work in early childhood practice to create the undergraduate programme of Early Childhood Studies.

Following successful validation of the degree, the seed was sown for this text, in which the holistic philosophy of the child within the context of family and culture, is the central, underlying and unifying theme.

Each chapter is complete and can be read in isolation from the rest, although it would be the wish of the team that the complete book be used by early years practitioners regardless of their particular sphere of practice. It is hoped that the book will interest and excite readers and encourage them towards a fuller understanding of young children and their families.

Marilyn E. Watsham
Head of School of Health and Social Work
University College Suffolk
Ipswich

Introduction

Margaret Woods

Welcome to the academic study of early childhood.

If you have taken the trouble to delve into this book, you are undoubtedly one of the many enthusiasts who enjoy the company of children and have a keen intention to increase your knowledge and understanding of childhood. Whatever your particular involvement in the early years might be – as a professional from the health, education or social services, as a day-care practitioner or as a member of a voluntary organisation, an undergraduate or Higher National Diploma student on one of the new Early Childhood Studies courses, or possibly as a paediatric nurse, health visitor, teacher training or Advanced Diploma in Childcare and Education (ADCE) student – our holistic introduction to early childhood may well be of interest and use to at least some aspects of your studies or practice.

The academic study of early childhood is, at this point in time, a relatively new concept. There is much cause for celebration in the early years professions, because it does appear that Early Childhood Studies is on the way to being acknowledged as a respected academic subject in its own right. Early Childhood Studies Degrees and Higher National Diplomas are offered in several institutions of higher education, and apparently 'university departments often appear to have bent over backwards to suit the degrees to workers in the early years field' (O'Grady, 1996, p.12). Further validity is evident with most of the first ever Early Childhood Studies graduates in 1995 quickly obtaining relevant and status-appropriate posts. Moreover, a significant number of the 1996 graduates have been accepted on to Early Years Postgraduate Certificate in Education (PGCE) courses (teacher training) in universities all over the UK.

Prior to the establishment and even the conception of these courses, there had existed for several years, and indeed centuries, considerable academic and altruistic interest in the early childhood life-stage. As long ago as the fourth century BC, Plato (427–347 BC) claimed that children were a form of 'riches', and advocated that they be valued and nurtured because they would become the future leaders and guardians of their society. In *The Republic* (a treatise on education), Plato succinctly encapsulated his belief in the importance of the early years of childhood and the significance of children's education and environment with the statement '*the beginning is the important part of any work, especially in the case of a young and tender thing*' (Jowett (translation), 1875, p.376)

Nearly 350 years ago, Joan Amos Comenius (1592–1670), a Czech bishop and educationist, similarly emphasised the importance for their future citizenship within society of the right start in life for children. He envisaged this as being provided within a compulsory education system which would enable individuals to develop their natural abilities, and in which teaching would be appropriate to children's or young people's age and abilities. Comenius consequently proposed a universal education structure which should include a nursery school for children up to the age of 6 years. In this nursery, play was actually recommended as one of the most significant means of learning.

Another of the early years pioneers was Robert Owen (1771–1858), who was manager of his father-in-law's cotton mill in New Lanark in Scotland, as well as being a social philosopher and reformer of some repute. He limited the employment hours of young children in his mill, but is better known for opening what is regarded as the first infant school in Britain, in New Lanark in 1816, for the millworkers' children. While this reform could be open to imputations of improving his own profits, Owen does appear to have strongly believed that children's experiences in their early years are extremely influential with regard to their later development and well-being. Much in accord with the views of Plato and Comenius, infant education was for Owen a certain way to ensure good citizens in the future.

Friedrich Froebel (1782–1852), one of the most famous and influential early years educational philosophers, also regarded early childhood as an extremely important life-stage. Froebel contributed greatly to our thinking about how children learn. He claimed that children's intellectual development begins as soon as they are born and advocated play as an excellent medium for learning. The term 'kindergarten', which implies the 'fostering of a child's nature . . . drawing on it, guarding it, tending and cultivating it like a good gardener tending a young plant ' (Liebschner, 1992, p.25) was of course one of his most illustrative and enduring concepts.

The philosophy underpinning much modern nursery-school practice has its origins in the open-air nursery of Margaret and Rachel McMillan, which was started in Deptford in London in 1911. The McMillan sisters were particularly concerned to provide a rich nurturing childhood experience which would counteract the disadvantage stemming from the impoverished and unhealthy home environments that characterised the daily existence of many children and which, if left unchecked, would undoubtedly impair their adult lives. This emphasis on promoting good health (with the setting up of clinics, open-air camps and nursery school) emanated from the McMillans' firm belief that children's learning and all-round development were unlikely to be maximised and their self-esteem and self-confidence adequate if the children remained sickly and frail. Their nursery education was planned to promote all aspects of children's development along with their good health, happiness and respect and thought for others. Such characteristics were deemed necessary by the McMillans to ensure children's well-being in adulthood and to produce a just and caring society. Bradburn (1989) is a compelling and unforgettable text on Margaret McMillan, if you wish to read further on her remarkable achievements.

More recently, much public attention has been given to early childhood. Newspapers, professional journals, popular magazines and television programmes regularly include commentaries or debates on early years issues. Nursery vouchers and the teaching of basic literary skills were being given much media consideration at the time of the writing of this book. A significant amount of this publicity, substantiated by the strengthening base of early childhood research and also by the increasingly numerous early childhood publications, reflects the growing recognition of the value of promoting children's development and well-being by raising early education standards and providing high-quality parenting and child-care services. The rigorous longitudinal research emanating from the American High Scope Project of the 1960s is probably the most famous study illustrating the positive long-term social and personal outcomes resulting from quality educare in the pre-school years (Schweinhart *et al.*, 1993). You can read a little more about this study in Chapter 11.

Two crucial tenets have emerged from much of the recent research, and feature prominently in many current texts. They have also been incorporated into reports and legislation such as *The Rumbold Report* (Department of Education and Science, 1990) and *The Children Act 1989* (Department of Health, 1991). These findings were that significant benefits to children and their families were forthcoming when:

- children's needs, development and experiences were considered, conceptually and practically, from an holistic viewpoint; and
- there was strong liaison between, or some degree of integration of, health, education and social services – in other words, a multidisciplinary or co-ordinated approach by the early years professions was advocated.

A new term – *educare* – was coined (e.g., David, 1990) to embrace the precept that care and education should be combined and are in fact inseparable.

The aspirations of early years professionals and parents for children were consequently raised. This manifest interest, proven need and increased demand for appropriate provision naturally required serious deliberation on exactly what quality educare with its holistic philosophy and concomitant training should look like.

One well-known set of recommendations about this more integrated form of training came from a group of early years experts convened under the auspices of the famous National Children's Bureau. They produced an influential discussion paper entitled 'The Future of Training in the Early Years' (National Children's Bureau, 1992). This document reinforced the wisdom of co-ordinated provision, and proposed a framework for a graduate-level academic/professional qualification to head the early childhood career structure – Early Childhood Studies Degrees.

At the same time, three such Early Childhood Studies Degrees were being developed at higher education institutions. These progammes were envisaged as precursors to postgraduate professional courses such as Early Years PGCE and Diploma in Social Work and also as a form of in-service training for early years professionals wishing to 'top up' their existing qualifications in order to enhance their knowledge and understanding of young children as well as improve their career opportunities. Progression for nursery nurses was also anticipated. Certainly there were very many enthusiastic potential students and practitioners (e.g., ADCE/Diploma in Post Qualifying Studies (DPQS) diplomates, experienced nursery nurses, paediatric nurses, health visitors, early years advisers and teachers) imploring college and university staff to develop just such a degree specialism.

Thus was Early Childhood Studies created, its inauguration as a university subject setting it on the road to academic credibility. It was hoped that such graduates would become articulate professionals, skilled in research methodology and able to rationalise and promote quality practice in an endeavour to enrich the experiences and improve the life chances of young children and their families. It was also anticipated that, in many instances, they would become the pioneers and leaders within the early years academic and professional arenas.

What does Early Childhood Studies actually involve?

Very simply and obviously Early Childhood Studies involves studying early childhood – but what exactly is that? What is the specific focus of this recently evolved academic and professional subject?

As you will be well aware, children are the young of the human species and childhood is the actual state of being a child. In contemporary Western society early childhood is usually considered to extend from birth until 8 years. It is, therefore, the initial stage of life outside the womb. Human beings pass through early childhood as they progress towards and through middle childhood and adolescence and eventually into adulthood. Usually in childhood humans are viewed and treated differently to adults and in a manner deemed, in their particular culture, to befit the perceived child character, status and needs.

In an holistic and broad-ranging study of this period of life, such as that contained within an Early Childhood Studies Degree programme or, as in this particular case, within an Early Childhood Studies textbook, intellectual attention will be focused on issues that are relevant to the familial, social and cultural realities of children's lives. The research and learning involved will be concerned with children's physical growth and development, with their personalities, cognitive abilities, health, social relationships and emotional well-being, and with some of the more significant policies, legislation and services relating to young children and their families. Strategies to develop the effectiveness of early years professionals must be considered, and the nature and possible impact of a number of the more typical experiences, problems and challenges of childhood investigated. In summary, Early Childhood Studies involves a study of the child within some form of family grouping that is in turn set within the wider social and cultural contexts.

Of course we must keep firmly in our minds that childhood is what is termed a 'social construct'. It is a label that society has created for young people in the early part of their lives. Consequently, childhood can have different connotations within different cultures and in different periods of history. This leads to a variety of child-rearing practices emanating from the customs and beliefs of the particular time and place.

Agiobu-Kemmer (1992), for example, explains that in contemporary rural African society children are regarded as the 'essence or sap of life' and as the 'clothing and adornment for their parents' (p.5). They are viewed very much as a status symbol in whose education and welfare much should be invested in order that they may provide for their parents in old age.

It is also interesting to note the attitudes towards children of the contemporary !Kung peoples, whom Melvin Konner lived with and studied for 2 years. They apparently treat their children with considerable gentleness and generosity. They are exceedingly responsive to their children's needs and do not advocate any form of punishment, believing that children's mental immaturity is responsible for any behaviours that are deemed undesirable. Education is for real life; learning is genuinely through play and by observation and imitation of adults as they tackle their daily tasks (Konner, 1991). Interestingly, such practices have recently been rationalised and advocated by Singer (1996) as being more effective in terms of children's learning than modern nurseries which tend to create a 'separate children's world'.

When we delve briefly into the history of childhood, Bryans and Wolfendale (1981) describe parents in medieval times as regarding their children in terms of the contribution they could make to the family economy and survival. In Tudor times, the children of the wealthy were well provided for educationally, while the children of the poor were often tied into harsh apprenticeships and forced to beg for money or food.

Bryans and Wolfendale (1981) also mention the high child mortality rate, the general ambivalence towards children and their exploitation by commerce and industry in previous generations. De Mause (1974) also presents a depressing historical picture of the considerable physical abuse to which children have been subjected from earliest times. According to his research and interpretations, many children were obviously not regarded as worthy of care, attention or respect.

In the so-called religious mortality or evangelical period of the eighteenth century, epitomised by Susanna Wesley in letters to her sons John and Charles, it is evident that the prime concern of parents was to save children's souls early in their lives because of the high expectation of death in childhood. This strongly held minority view recommended that children be brought up in an atmosphere of fear, extreme godliness and harsh physical punishment. Sangster (1963, p.75), however, does wonder to what extent this evangelical discipline was a generally held view, and whether in practice it was quite 'as rigorous as its reputation'.

Another somewhat extreme, but again not necessarily universal, historical perspective is that of the hygienist movement of the 1920s and 1930s, when children were considered to be in need of strict discipline, and cleanliness was of prime consequence. We are already aware that the McMillan sisters, especially Rachel, who was a sanitary inspector, were justifiably concerned with the hygiene aspects of children's upbringing. We must remember, however, that this was within a warm and caring nursery environment created to counteract the desperately impoverished and unhealthy conditions of the period. The publicly available hygienist advice to parents and practitioners was to inculcate into children, in not too kindly a fashion, the 'virtues' of self-control, strict obedience, recognition of authority and respect for elders. Recommendations were given that children were not to be picked up when they cried, and not to be hugged and kissed by their parents. Watson (1928) advocated that parents should shake hands with their children in the morning and give them a pat on the head if they had accomplished some task extraordinarily well! Newson and Newson (1974) tell us that apparently a few conscientious, well-meaning, very often intelligent and well-educated parents actually followed such guidelines explicitly, although many others felt unhappy about this somewhat harsh and regimented treatment of children.

If you are interested in the history of childhood, there is a list of relevant publications at the end of this chapter. There is also a further discussion of childhood as a social construct in Chapter 5.

As you will realise, it is important to bear this cultural relativism in mind when studying childhood. Since societies, cultures and indeed families differ or change over time, concepts of children, childhood and the ensuing child rearing practices and expectations of children differ and change accordingly.

Why might we study early childhood?

We have reflected briefly on what the study of early childhood might involve. Now, in the manner of the true early years professional, we should consider why we might be studying this fascinating subject. It is always a wise precept to be able to rationalise the undertaking of a particular course of action, whether it involves embarking on an Early Childhood Studies Degree programme, organising a specific art and craft activity in an infant class or a paediatric ward, or selecting an appropriate story for a group of nursery children. Ascertaining, justifying and articulating our ultimate objectives as well as our modest, short-term aims can make our actions more confident and focused. We may, therefore, be enabled to work towards our specified goal with greater purpose and meaning. Success then becomes a more likely outcome.

Many readers will know exactly why they wish to increase their knowledge and understanding of childhood, but let us consider some of the more typical reasons – academic, philanthropic or pragmatic. Some students may wish to:-

- fulfil a desire to do something worthwhile for children and their families;
- discover how children become the people they eventually will be or, as Konner (1991, p.7) observes, 'always will be becoming';
- establish what the main influences on children's holistic development are considered to be;
- appreciate how children might develop and account for differences and similarities between children;
- understand how to provide the environment and experiences most conducive to promoting children's happiness, well-being and optimum all-round development;
- become more sensitive and responsive to the diverse needs of young children and their families.

Many professionals and researchers also study early childhood because their findings can constitute a rich source of information on human beings in general. In addition, they may believe that we can improve aspects of adult life by using the results of our research to enrich the quality of childhood. We might, for example, ascertain how best to protect children against abuse, to supply a well-balanced diet, to encourage a love of learning, or to provide social and emotional stability in childhood and so create a more stable foundation for adulthood.

We must not, of course, regard childhood only as a preparation for adult life. Early childhood is also studied because, as Pugh (1992) tells us, it is a very significant life-stage in its own right, as well as being critical in terms of children's future well-being and development. Pugh summarises the significant achievements of this period, being the time when children make considerable developmental strides:

> It is now well established that a high percentage of children's learning takes place in the first five years of life, and that this is the time when attitudes are formed, when first relationships are made, when concepts are developed, and the foundations of many skills and later learning are laid.
>
> It is also the time when children begin to develop a concept of self, of self-value and self-esteem.

(Pugh, 1992, pp.2–3)

Certainly for many people these are appealing and exciting reasons for opting to work with children. They do, however, illustrate the tremendous responsibility of parents and early years professionals to provide the optimum support and appropriate experiences necessary to promote young children's development. Surely in-depth study becomes absolutely crucial, as does ensuring that prospective practitioners are of the highest calibre and integrity.

The holistic approach to the study of early childhood

Since this book is among the first to offer an holistic perspective on early childhood, it is necessary to clarify the term 'holistic'. This is particularly important since the philosophy of holism sustains and unifies our text.

The approach is commended or assumed in many of the books and research papers mentioned in the reference sections at the end of each chapter. An extremely readable account of its origins, rationale and implications for educare policy and practice is provided by Hazareesingh *et al.* (1989).

Holism goes hand in hand with advocacy of greater co-operation and collaboration between early years professionals, e.g. teachers, nursery nurses, health visitors, social workers, playgroup supervisors and paediatric nurses.

This philosophy is reflected in the many strong recommendations for greater liaison between education, health and social services, and also in the trend towards integrating under-eights services, e.g. in Strathclyde, Manchester, Sheffield, Leeds, Humberside, Kirklees, Camden, Hackney, Islington, Lewisham, Newham and Southwark. Similar organisation can also be found in other countries, e.g., Spain, New Zealand and Denmark.

This holistic ideology values the whole child and endeavours to understand each young child as an individual within the context of his or her family, community and culture. In the best early years provision, holism does not separate care and education, but rather combines the two to produce the term we mentioned earlier in the chapter, namely 'educare'.

With this approach, professionals endeavour to be sensitive and responsive to all of a child's needs and aspects of development, i.e. physical, intellectual, social, emotional, cultural, moral and spiritual. Ideally they would strive to avoid promoting or prizing one area of development over and above, or at the expense of any of the others. Early years practitioners also realise that children's needs and developing abilities are closely inter-connected and very much intertwined with the needs and circumstances of each child's family.

In addition, all aspects of a child's welfare and development are viewed as part of a co-ordinated system and are seen as growing alongside, influencing and interacting with each other. Naturally, specialism in or study of one aspect of a child's development (e.g. education or health) is feasible within an holistic framework which recognises the existence of all aspects.

Professionals who adopt this holistic stance would be strongly committed to equality of opportunity for each child regardless of race, class, gender or ability. They would also recognise the many factors that are influential in a child's life, and work towards integrating the diverse and unique experiences of each child's life into a meaningful whole.

Of course such a philosophy is very much easier to write and talk about than to put into practice. Hopefully by reading this book, which is strongly supportive of the principle of holism, you will be able to extract some ideas for its practical implementation. While initial and in-service training and academic study with a more multidisciplinary or at least integrated perspective will certainly help to promote realisation of the tenet of holism, only by early years enthusiasts working collaboratively towards and publicly disseminating the approach can we hope to come anywhere close to such a high ideal.

References

Agiobu-Kemmer, I.S. (1992): Child Survival and Child Development in Africa. *Bernard Van Leer Studies and Evaluation Paper Six.* The Hague: Bernard Van Leer Foundation.

Bradburn, E. (1989): *Margaret McMillan: Portrait of a Pioneer.* London: Routledge.

Bryans, T. and Wolfendale, S. (1981): Changing Attitudes to Children – A Comparative Chronicle, *Early Childhood*, **2**, 4–7.

David, T. (1990): *Under Five – Under-educated?* Milton Keynes: Open University Press.

De Mause, L. (Ed) (1974): *The History of Childhood.* London: Bellen.

Department of Education and Science (1990): *Starting with Quality: Report of the Committee of Inquiry into the Education Experiences offered to Three and Four Year Olds (Rumbold Report).* London: HMSO.

Department of Health (1991): *The Children Act 1989: Guidance and Regulations. Vol. 2. Family Support, Day Care and Educational Provision for Young Children.* London: HMSO.

Hazareesingh, S., Simms, K. and Anderson, P. (1989): *Educating the Whole Child.* London: Building Blocks Educational.

Jowett, B. (1875): *The Republic of Plato.* Oxford: Clarendon Press.

Konner, M. (1991): *Childhood.* London: Little, Brown & Company.

Liebschner, J. (1992): *A Child's Work.* Cambridge: Lutterworth Press.

Liddiard, M. (1928): *The Mothercraft Manual.* London: J&A Churchill.

National Children's Bureau Early Years Training Group (1992): *The Future of Training in the Early Years.* London: National Children's Bureau.

Newson, J. and Newson, E. (1974): *Cultural Aspects of Childbearing in the English-speaking World.* In Richards, M.P.M. (ed.), *The Integration of a Child into a Social World.* Cambridge: Cambridge University Press, 53–82.

O'Grady, C. (1996): Graduating Through Early Childhood. *Co-ordinate* **52**, 11–13.

Pugh, G. (1992): *An Equal Start for all our Children* (Times Educational Supplement/Greenwich Lecture 1992) London: Times Educational Supplement.

Sangster, P. (1963): *Pity my Simplicity.* London: Epworth Press.

Schweinhart, L.J., Barnes, H.V and Weikart, D.P. (1993): *Significant Benefits.* Ypsilanti, MI: The High/Scope Press.

Singer, E. (1996): Prisoners of the Method. *International Journal of Early Years Education*, **4**, 28–40.

Watson, J.B. (1928): *Psychological Care of Infant and Child.* New York: W.W. Norton.

Further Reading

Aries, P. (1982): *Centuries of Childhood: a Social History of Family Life.* London: Cape.

Hoyles, M. (1979): Childhood in Historical Perspective: In Hoyles, M. (ed.), *Changing Childhood.* London: Writers and Readers Co-operative, 16–29.

Sears, R.R., Maccoby, E. and Levin, H. (1957): *Patterns of Child Rearing.* Evanston, IL: Row Peterson.

Walvin, J. (1982): *A Child's World: a Social History of English Childhood.* Harmondsworth: Penguin.

1 Early childhood studies – first principles

Margaret Woods

This chapter aims to:

- introduce the study of early childhood, with particular emphasis on observation and assessment;
- provide an overview of child development perspectives;
- consider some values and principles underlying early years theory and practice.

In the introduction we considered what we meant by the terms *early childhood* and *Early Childhood Studies*. We also reflected on possible reasons for our interest in this fascinating topic. The philosophy of holism as it relates to early childhood was examined, and we noted that this was the ideology underpinning and integrating our series of essays. In this chapter we shall deliberate on a few of the basics or first principles of the study of early childhood.

Early Childhood Studies, as readers will already be aware, has only relatively recently been regarded as an academic discipline in its own right. It has assimilated many of the methodologies, perspectives, theories, concepts and debates from other academic disciplines; psychology, sociology, paediatrics, education, genetics and social policy are among the most obvious sources. These varied origins do make it imperative that we investigate the generally accepted ways in which the scientific study of childhood is being approached.

Making an academic study of early childhood

Mastery of any subject is more likely if students have acquired the standard academic study skills. Extending and improving reading strategies and note-taking capabilities will be especially important as will becoming familiar with the layout of, and resources offered by, the nearest academic library. A greater chance of success either in studies or in a profession is likely if techniques for remembering and revising information are developed, and if students can become competent at essay and report writing. Borrowing a good study skills guide is highly recommended, and there are many available.

In Early Childhood Studies students must certainly undertake a great deal of reading, and the research reports and textbooks produced by the growing band of early years researchers and professionals will be especially important. With this ever-widening research base the rather exciting problem faced by early years enthusiasts is actually finding the time to delve into the multitude of publications currently available. Whatever students' particular areas of interest within the realm of early childhood may be, they must read deeply and acquire a sound understanding of developmental psychology; without doubt this will provide a strong and advantageous basis for other aspects of the field of study. Chapter 3 discusses in greater detail the considerable value to early years students and professionals of acquiring this deep knowledge of child development.

Enormous benefit can also be gained from acquaintance with many of the major theories within the field of study. Students need to reflect on these theories, question their validity and usefulness and discuss them with fellow students, early years professionals and tutors. They must strive always to be objective, rational and critically evaluative in their thinking.

Very importantly, Early Childhood Studies students must work with and learn to observe children of different ages in a variety of social contexts, and particularly within their everyday or natural social environments, when accurate assessments are more likely to be made. They should always endeavour to be circumspect in their choice of observation technique and selection of data. Evidence used to substantiate judgements should be stated, and interpretations of any evidence should be cross-referenced to increase validity.

As students of early childhood become more experienced, they may possibly deepen their understanding of children by undertaking formal research; indeed, some students may be required to plan and implement their own research project. Initially this must be with tutor guidance and, at all times, with careful regard to the ethics of conducting research involving children. Chapter 14 on early childhood research will provide the necessary introductory support and guidance should readers wish to further their studies by embarking on such an exciting academic venture.

At this preliminary stage of study we shall confine our discussion to three important topics. The first is an overview of the principal theoretical perspectives underpinning many of the psychological theories that will be encountered later in this book. The second is the vital process of observing and assessing young children. Such skills are fundamental and absolutely indispensable for early childhood students, professionals and researchers. Finally we shall deliberate on some values and principles which might usefully support studies or practice relating to the early years.

Overview of the main theoretical perspectives on early childhood

Most psychological theories derive from three main stances or premises. Richardson (1988) defends the use of the formal academic terminology to describe those three perspectives as rationalism, associationism and constructivism. He argues that it is necessary for students to understand these three 'poles, ideas or sets of pre-suppositions' (p.viii) before they can make sense of most of Western psychology or, in our case, early childhood studies.

It is often helpful to imagine these three belief systems as being positioned along a spectrum. At one end is rationalism, or as it has come to be called today, nativism, for example by Eysenck (1994) and Bruce (1987). Bee (1995) refers to this perspective as 'the nature side of the equation' (p.5).

Originally, rationalism entailed the belief that knowledge and concepts were innate and, in some mysterious way, present in the newborn child. Individual differences, e.g. in intelligence, were deemed to be biologically determined or inherited. Today this perspective involves the concept of children being pre-programmed to develop or mature in certain ways. Bruce (1987) suggests that this nativist stance has often been considered to be a 'dominant influence in the early childhood tradition' (p.5). The practitioner provides an 'appropriate' environment but does not intervene or force a child's development or learning. Chomsky's (b1928) theory of language acquisition, which is discussed in Chapter 9, is probably the most well-known contemporary example.

However, evidence substantiating the influence of experience on children's behaviour and development is now available from much research to challenge such rationalist/nativist assumptions. We shall come across a few examples of this later in the book.

At the other end of the spectrum is associationism. Eysenck (1994) and Bruce (1987) allude to it as empiricism, and Bee (1995) terms it 'the nurture side of the equation' (p.7). This perspective encapsulates the view that children's knowledge and behaviour stem from their experiences and environments. The child is seen as somewhat passive in his or her own learning and development. Parents and early years professionals can have a powerful role in determining which experiences children ought to have; they educate and possibly mould their charges into socially conforming beings by rewarding or reinforcing learning and behaviour which they wish to develop in the child. The behaviourism of B. F. Skinner (1905–1990) is probably the most extreme set of ideas within this perspective. Of course most of us are engaging in mild behaviourist practices when we praise children for doing something we deem worthwhile in order to encourage repetition of that desirable behaviour.

The main and very significant criticisms of the traditional behaviourist ideology, expressed for example by Richardson (1988), are its over-simplification of the learning process and its failure to provide an acceptable explanation for human creativity and originality of thought.

Not surprisingly, therefore, Bee (1995) explains how recently this side of the nature-nurture debate has become much more complex than one particular aspect of the environment shaping a child's behaviour and development. She identifies research which illustrates that the timing of experiences can be significant in children's development and also how individuals interpret, and react to, the same experience differently. In addition, she discusses how the wider social and cultural context, extending well beyond a child's family (e.g. the type of nursery a child attends, or the employment status or cultural background of his or her parents), can have considerable implications for the individual child growing up.

Bronfenbrenner (1979) captures the essence of this latter thinking with his 'ecological approach'. The model of this concept is intended to portray the complex, interactive and interdependent nature of the many and varied environmental influences on a child; it is often graphically depicted as a series of concentric circles. The innermost environments, that is, those closest to the child (and there can be several), contain the family, nursery, playgroup and school. These are referred to as the *microsystems*, and they are enclosed within the *mesosystem*, which is the layer providing the links between these more immediate settings (that might be, for example, the communication or relationships between home and nursery). *Exosystems,* such as the parents' workplace and network of friends, are contained within the next environmental layer or circle, those aspects not being experienced quite so intimately by the child. The outer circle contains the *macrosystems*, e.g. social class, ethnicity, cultural values, the type and state of the national economy, famine, and war, all of which are deemed to impact on the other environments of the child and family.

With neither the rationalist nor the empiricist perspective even adequately explaining children's learning, behaviour and development, the two were combined to form the constructivism conceived by Kant in his *Critique of Pure Reason* (1781). Nowadays it is often referred to as interactionism (Bruce, 1987; Bee, 1995).

Understanding the interplay of internal/biological factors with external/ experiential influences is unfortunately no easy task – even though it may seem a simple compromise. Implicit are the ideas of qualitative changes taking place within a child's cognitive structures and of the child being active in the construction of his or her knowledge and development. Bee (1995) informs us that there are two ways in which this interaction is currently studied. The first is by investigating how innate skills are altered by particular experiences or environments. The other approach is by examining the ways in which children with different innate properties can respond differently to the same environment. Readers may well be able to identify similarities here with the contemporary research which Bee (1995) described as emanating from dissatisfaction with the radical behaviourist theories.

Interactionism within the role of early years professionals implies supporting the child's natural development within a suitable environment, and also being proactive in promoting development and learning with appropriate and stimulating experiences. Bruce (1987) refers helpfully to 'the notion of reciprocity – that is, sometimes the child leads, sometimes the adult' (p.7). Elder *et al.* (1993, p.11) tell us that contemporary 'child developmentalists are increasingly receptive to the interactive view of developmental domains and to the concept of *multiple* processes for the explanation of developmental change'.

The most famous constructivist theory of cognitive development is undoubtedly that of Jean Piaget (1896–1980) which is explained in greater depth in Chapter 9. Piaget was a Swiss genetic epistemologist, i.e. he studied the development of knowledge. The constructivist theory currently most favoured in the world of early childhood is that of Lev Vygotsky (1896–1934), a Russian academic and psychologist. His brand of constructivism was much more social than Piaget's. Vygotsky believed that social interaction with more knowledgeable others and cultural systems such as language were dominant influences in a child's cognitive development. More details of his theory are also provided in Chapter 9.

We shall return several times within this text to these three viewpoints, albeit in different guises. Hopefully students' understanding of the famous nature-nurture debate will accordingly be enhanced.

Observing and assessing young children

Chapter 14 considers the observational method as a research technique. In this section, however, we shall provide initial guidance on observing and assessing young children. This information and the associated practice (the latter is vitally important) will support students by enabling them to gain further insight into the world of childhood and deepen their knowledge of child development.

Observation is an essential and integral aspect of the role of every early years professional and student. We should regularly observe the children for whom we have (or intend to have) responsibility. Sometimes we observe for a very specific purpose – perhaps to ascertain the level of a child's language development or performance on a predetermined task. At other times we may observe in order to achieve broader knowledge and understanding of an individual child or group of children – perhaps to ascertain how they might be settling into nursery (Figure 1.1). Mostly we shall observe children in their usual day-to-day activities and environments, although occasionally we may set up a particular activity for observation in what we term a 'controlled setting', e.g. in a quiet room free from the distractions of normal nursery activities.

We should always reflect on and make a reasoned analysis and interpretation of our observations. Whenever possible we should share our thoughts and assessments with respected colleagues, fellow students, tutors and/or

Figure 1.1   We observe in order to achieve a broader knowledge and understanding of children.

children's parents or carers. It is this shared discussion and evaluation, as well as pooling of our joint knowledge of children, which can help to ensure that our conclusions are valid. This process of cross-referencing the perspectives and interpretations from different sources is more formally known as triangulation.

What can be gained from competent observation and assessment?

Through the processes of regular observation and justifiable and valid assessment we can gain much greater insight into:

- individual children's all-round development, needs, health and well-being;
- individual children's capabilities and the extent of their knowledge and skills;
- children's interaction with other children and with adults;
- typical patterns of all-round childhood development;
- typical childhood behaviours;
- what is unique about each child;
- the very different experiences and familial, social and cultural environments of individual children and groups of children;
- the possible consequences of these different backgrounds.

As professionals it is of course most important to act on the information we have acquired and use it to inform our planning and practice. With the insight from the observations and their assessments, we are better equipped to:

- devise optimum environments to promote the holistic development of each child and respond to his or her needs;
- take appropriate action if any aspect of a child's development, behaviour, health or well-being causes us concern and does not appear to be within the range typical for his or her age;
- interact more sensitively with children and form happy relationships with them;
- monitor, evaluate and improve the provision we make for children, i.e. the care we give, the curriculum we devise and the outcomes we achieve.

For students, competence in observation and assessment also promotes the integration of theoretical knowledge of childhood with practice; much theory can be vividly illustrated for us. In addition, we can begin to build our own theories about children and their development, behaviour and needs.

What might we observe?

In order to increase our holistic knowledge and understanding of young children and help us progress with our study of development in early childhood, we might usefully make observations and assessments of the following:

- characteristics of children's physical growth and development (e.g. appearance, height, weight, co-ordination, fine and gross motor skills, general physical activity);
- development of children's communication skills (e.g. non-verbal, language, speech, understanding, listening, reading and writing, emergent literacy and numeracy skills);
- development of children's cognitive skills (e.g. memory, understanding, thinking, reasoning, discrimination, knowledge, formal learning skills, concentration);
- evidence of emotional development and expression (e.g. aggression, regression, shyness, tantrum, excitement, distractibility, concentration, fear, confidence, independence, feeding and sleeping problems, obsessive tendencies, reactions to new situations);
- typical and atypical childhood behaviour revealed in different experiences (e.g. reaction to the arrival of a new baby, starting school, dad's arrival home, mum going into hospital, in the home corner, etc.);
- development and different types, stages and patterns of play;
- evidence of children's social development and relationships (e.g. social interaction in a variety of situations and with different people, evidence of

social skills and socialisation, particularly in different cultures, in play, in reactions to strangers, on visits, and at social events);

- children engaged in specific activities (e.g. art and craft, music, drama, leisure activities, school work);
- children's learning capabilities (e.g. within the context of the National Curriculum or the Early Years Curriculum, of the gifted child, or of the child with learning difficulties);
- behaviour occurring within the daily routine (e.g. at story-time, mealtime, arrival at nursery, playtime);
- behaviour of groups of children (e.g. differing abilities, varying reactions, different levels of involvement, etc., within a group);
- identification of children with special needs (e.g. children for whom English is a second language, with physical or mental disability, or with learning difficulties);
- children in hospital or who are unwell;
- children during screening procedures or Standard Assessment Tasks (SATs).

Embarking on the process of observation

Please note that the advice given here is especially directed at students new to the study of early childhood.

First we must decide:

- what in particular we need to observe about a child or group of children (*i.e. our aim*);
- how we will negotiate access;
- who will give us permission (*e.g. parent, carer, educator, manager, committee, governors. We must remember to promise confidentiality/anonymity at this stage, and keep that promise*);
- when and where we will undertake the observation;
- which observation technique will be most suited to our purpose;
- what organisation and preparation we need to make;
- with whom we shall share and discuss the information obtained;
- how we shall facilitate the preservation of confidentiality and/or anonymity (*e.g. by using a child's first name, an alternative name, or the initial of his/her first name*).

The next stage of selecting the most suitable observation technique is of prime importance. It will be helpful at this initial stage to review several techniques which could be most useful to students in the early days of their studies.

Figure 1.2   Evidence of children's social development and relationships can be gained through observation.

NARRATIVE REPORT

This is probably the most illuminative if also fairly time-consuming technique. If well done, it can vividly capture a child's behaviour, actions, stage of development, personality, mood, etc.

It involves reporting in prose, in the greatest detail possible, a child's actions, utterances (verbal and non-verbal), facial expressions, head and eye movements, and use of toys, objects and play materials. Naturally we should concentrate on the written detail of the behaviours which have particular relevance to our aim and which may be significant in increasing our understanding of the child.

The written description should provide a valid and true representation of the child's actions and activities. Great care must therefore be taken to record only what is seen and heard e.g. *'John rubbed his eyes'* and *not* any thoughts, beliefs and opinions, e.g. *'John is tired'*.

Within the observation report we also strive to *avoid*:

- value judgements and jumping to conclusions, e.g. *'Mary is good at drawing'* or *'Jane is looking unhappy'*;
- labelling children, e.g. *'Henry is a naughty boy'* or *'Justine is a nice little girl'*;
- generalisations, e.g. *'As always the girls are tidying up'*.

In endeavouring to report as objectively as possible, it is often helpful to think of ourselves as a camcorder and consider how the camcorder would record the incident. In the case of Mary drawing it would have depicted the precise movements of the hand holding the pencil, Mary's facial expressions, any verbal or non-verbal utterances and the development of the final product (the drawing).

Mention of a child other than the focal child or an adult should be kept to a minimum. We record only what is necessary about the actions of others to enable us to make sense of the focal child's behaviour.

The narrative report technique can provide a particularly graphic illustration of critical incidents (significantly informative events or children's activities) and vignettes (short and typically characteristic descriptions of children and their actions). It is always best to write up the full report from rough notes as soon as possible after undertaking your observation.

Possible topics might include:

- observing the nature of a child's interaction within home corner play;
- observing a child's imaginative role play;
- observing a child having a tantrum.

The resulting assessments of these three observations would enable us to make individualised and hopefully more beneficial provision for each child, or to deal more effectively with the next tantrum – probable reasons for undertaking the observations in the first place.

TIME SAMPLING

With this technique a clear focus is necessary. We note, at regular intervals, what a child is doing (or children are doing). A variety of formats is possible, and either descriptive or coded recording of data may be used. Intervals of time are selected (e.g. every minute, every 10 minutes, every half an hour) which best suit your purpose, provide maximum information and accord with the total observation time. Obviously it would be rather impracticable to record an observation every 30 seconds for 3 hours! A timer or watch with a second hand is recommended.

Possible topics might include:

- observing a child's participation in nursery activities. He or she might be observed every 5 minutes for 1 hour when he or she is free to choose play materials and activities. (The resulting assessment here would help us to understand the child better. Learning more about his or her interests, motivation and abilities would again enable us to plan more relevant and individualised experiences for that particular child in order to achieve optimum outcomes);
- observing a child during playtime in order to note his or her level of social interaction/friendship patterns or type and stage of play, or perhaps even instances of him or her being bullied.

Figure 1.3 provides a further example of time sampling. Headings are included to aid the presentation of observations for course assignment purposes.

NAME:	Henry (H)	**DATE:**	15–19 January 1996
AGE:	4 years 2 months	**GENDER:**	Male

BACKGROUND INFORMATION:	Henry has recently seemed to spend much time on the sidelines, not participating in nursery activities. This is not his usual behaviour. *(Here the observation is a way of verifying (or otherwise) staff's impression and concern. This would contribute to a more informed assessment of Henry's behaviour)*
AIM:	To observe Henry's participation in nursery activities during the time when children have freedom of choice
CONTENT:	Nursery playroom and outdoor play area. *(Children may move freely between these areas)*
OBSERVATION TECHNIQUE:	Time sampling, descriptive recording every 5 minutes for 1 hour over 5 days

DAY ONE **TIME STARTED:** 9.15 a.m. **TIME COMPLETED:** 10.15 a.m.

Time	Area of nursery	H's activity/language/interaction	Social group
09.15	Entrance hall doorway	Standing, looking round playroom	H and father
09.20	Sand tray	Standing at side of tray, looking at toys in sand, listening to NN[a]	H, NN and 2 children
09.25	Sand tray	Digging in sand	Alone
09.30	Sand tray	Digging in sand	Alone
09.35	Middle of playroom	Walking across room	Alone
09.40	Outside home corner	Looking in home corner window	Alone
09.45	Bookcorner	Sitting on floor, listening to story read by NN, looking at NN	H, NN and 3 children
09.50	Bookcorner	Answered question from NN, 'It's a zebra'	H, NN and 3 children
09.55	Bookcorner	Sitting on floor watching other children say a rhyme	H, NN and 3 children
10.00	Bookcorner	Standing looking at bookshelves	Alone
10.05	Outside home corner	Looking in home corner window	Alone
10.10	Outside home corner	Putting on bus driver's hat	Alone
10.15	Outside home corner	Sitting in box pretending to drive bus, 'Broom, broom'	Alone

[a]NN, nursery nurse.

Figure 1.3 Example of time sampling

EVENT SAMPLING

This is a convenient method of collecting what is called frequency data. It involves recording on a check-list each time a particular behaviour occurs. As with time sampling, the data collected may provide the necessary baseline evidence to inform future action. The event sampling could also be repeated after any ameliorative programme has been completed, in order to assess its level of success or otherwise.

Possible topics might include:

- recording each time a child for whom English is a second language, and who does not appear to be integrating into nursery, interacts with another child or adult. (We would distinguish between occasions when the child is initiating or responding to conversation.This would give precise information about the nature/extent/absence of interaction, and again would inform strategies for supporting the child in the future);
- recording each time a child, whose behaviour is deemed aggressive, behaves aggressively and, if possible, identify any causal factors (see Figure 1.4). (By recording this information we may ascertain possible causes or triggers and, in the future, be enabled to pre-empt the aggression. Alternatively, the data may help us to cope more effectively with a future outburst of aggression).

NAME: Amy (A)   **DATE:** 3–7 June 1995

AGE: 3 years 9 months   **GENDER:** Female

BACKGROUND INFORMATION: Amy is often considered to behave aggressively. It is necessary to verify this behaviour and note any possible provocation in order to justify and underpin any programme designed to counteract such a tendency

AIM: To record each instance of, and any observable provocation for, behaviours identified as aggressive

CONTEXT: Nursery playroom

OBSERVATION TECHNIQUE: Event sampling

DAY ONE   TIME STARTED: 09.15 a.m.   **TIME COMPLETED:** 12.00

Time	Behaviour deemed aggresive	Location	Possible provocation	Social grouping	Number of event
09.03	Kicked NN[a]	Sand tray	Asked to share toys	A,NN and 2 children	1
10.15	Pushed child to floor	Homecorner	Wanted child to be baby but he did not want to	A and 2 other children	2
10.25	Threw doll across floor and stamped feet	Homecorner	Wanted another doll which child was cuddling	A and 2 other children	3
11.50	Pushed lego construction from table to floor	Lego table	None evident	Alone	4

[a]NN, nursery nurse.

Figure 1.4 Example of event sampling

CHECK-LISTS

Check-lists are often a simple and reasonably fast method of collecting and presenting data from observations. A child may be observed in the course of his or her usual daily activities, or possibly in a contrived situation. Occasionally it may not be possible to observe some aspect of the child's behaviour or development, and we may therefore have to ask the parent or main carer to provide the information. In such instances we must beware of bias on their part (as well as on our own!).

Completed check-lists can often constitute helpful baseline data:

- for guiding future observations (e.g. suggesting a detailed focus or an aspect of behaviour causing concern);
- for planning nursery activities (perhaps to enhance an aspect of development, or which we realise a child would particularly enjoy);
- for selecting a course of treatment (e.g. physiotherapy).

We must, however, always bear in mind that check-lists can miss crucial contextual information, and may provide only a superficial picture of the child's behaviour and development.

When this method of observation is used to assess a child's development, data is usually collected on the basis of standardised developmental norms, e.g. Sheridan's (1975) Stycar Sequences or The Denver Developmental Screening Test (Frankenburg and Dodds, 1967). These give greater validity to assessments.

Possible topics might include:

- collecting data on the play and interaction emanating from different nursery activities during one nursery session;
- focusing on a specific aspect of a child's development e.g. physical development (using standardised developmental norms);
- gaining a comprehensive picture of a child's development (again using standardised developmental norms).

For an example from an extract of a developmental check-list based on Sheridan (1975), see Figure 1.5. Readers might find it good practice to devise appropriate headings (name, age, aim, etc.) and to complete this example of a check-list for a 6-month-old baby.

Figure 1.6 provides another example of a check-list which was used to explore the use of four nursery activities/areas during a period of free choice

Activity/behaviour	Yes	No	Almost	Additional information
Posture and large movements				
Can s/he raise from pillow when lying on back?	✓			
Can s/he sit with support in cot or pram?	✓			
Does s/he hold arms up to be lifted?	✓			only to mother
Does s/he kick strongly, with legs alternating?	✓			
Can s/he roll over from front to back?			✓	

Figure 1.5 Extract from a developmental check-list for an infant of 6 months based on the developmental norms of Sheridan (1975)

Learning areas/activities	Number of children using area/activity	Types of play observed	Interaction
Home corner/dressing up	1111111111111111 1111	Exp, IP, IP, RP, IP, RP, EP, IP, RP, RP	CC, CCC, CC, CC, CC, CCC, CA, AC, CCC, CC, CC, CCC, CC, AC, AC
Outdoor area	111111111	PP, PP, ExP, IP, PP,	CC, CC, CCC, CA
Sand tray	1111111	ExP, ExP, IP, HP,	CCC
Construction toys	111	CP, CP	

KEY

Types of play (BAECE, 1994)

ExP, exploratory play;
HP, heuristic play;
EP, epistemic play;
IP, imaginative play
RP, role play;
CP, constructive play;
PP, physical play.

Interaction

CC, 2 children talking
CCC, 3 children talking;
CA, child and adult talking, child initiated;
AC, adult and child talking, adult initiated.

The data from this check-list would of course be summarised for formal presentation in an assignment or research project.

Figure 1.6 Extract from nursery activity check-list, completed during 1 hour of free choice of activities

for the children. Coded recording is used, and a key is included to explain the codes. The results would enable us to assess the popularity of nursery activities. As a consequence we might enhance an infrequently used corner/activity to ensure it is more often utilised by the children. If children are not experiencing all of the nursery activities, an aspect of their development may be hindered. With our holistic approach we cannot allow that to happen.

VERBATIM REPORTING

This involves recording word for word a conversation between two or more children, or between a child or children and an adult. Writing this by hand can prove to be quite a difficult procedure. Tape-recording and then transcribing the text is likely to provide a more accurate account, but one risks distortions in the speech; moreover, being recorded can alter the behaviour of some participants. Positioning the microphone can sometimes be problematic, but small personal radio microphones attached to children's and adults' lapels are a very helpful alternative.

Transcription from a tape recording is a notoriously time-consuming process. However, it can be tremendously worthwhile because it allows repeated listening to a conversation and consequently considerable insight into a child's language development and possibly even his or her thinking and logic.

DIARIES/FIELD NOTES

These are notes pertinent to an observation focus, written as and when appropriate, necessary or possible over a period of time. They may be notes on children's behaviour, reactions, development, learning, social skills, aspects of health or emotional well-being. Critical incidents in early years settings can also be recorded in this manner.

Diaries/field notes are usually written as narrative descriptions, although the inclusion of codes and drawings can often save time and energy. However, there should be sufficient detail to create a vivid memory of the event or behaviour several months later. Thus diaries and field notes can provide rich illuminative data and capture the complexities of a child's nature or situation. They constitute a fruitful basis for analytical reflections which can often usefully inform and improve early years practice. Worthwhile analysis of what can be a mass of data can, of course, be daunting and does require a sound knowledge of relevant theory. Evidence for inferences and interpretations must be obvious in the notes.

A possible topic might include recording over a term any significant activities, thinking and conversations of a child whom it is believed might be gifted. Figure 1.7 provides an extract from just such a diary. By the way, it is a true incident!

Date	Significant incident	Analysis
3 May 1996	R after listening in to a group of 7-year-olds having a lesson on multiplication stated, 'If I counted the squares down this side of the tennis racquet and if I could multiply like these big children, I could tell you how many squares there are altogether.'	R has grasped the concept and function of multiplication immediately and at a very young age – evidence of advanced logico-mathematical thought.

Figure 1.7   Extract from diary/field notes: R is aged 4 years 10 months.

Analysing Our Observations

Having completed our observation using the appropriate technique for successful collection of data, we now come to the all-important task of analysing and utilising that data. This topic will be covered in more detail in Chapter 14.

In the analysis we discuss the significance of our observation with particular reference to our stated aim. In other words, we consider what we set out to observe in relation to what we actually did observe. This analytical process will often involve application of relevant theory, e.g. we might refer to a particular theory of learning to help us to understand how a child is making sense of his or her world. Alternatively, as was stated earlier, we may find it appropriate to refer to standardised norms for a child's age, e.g. we might undertake a development check-list to assess a child's level of development against what is considered typical for his or her age according to the selected norms. At other times we may compare a child's present and previous performances on a task or set of tasks in order to ascertain whether he or she is making progress. This is called ipsative assessment.

Such reflective analysis within an appropriate framework of theory and research should enable us to make reasoned interpretations and assessments of a child's development, progress, behaviour, knowledge, abilities, skills, experience, attitudes, interests, etc. We must take very great care to avoid making tactless, discourteous, stereotypical, inappropriate or sweepingly judgemental assessments of children, the adults involved, their practices and the observation context. We are more likely to make rational and professional judgements if we ensure that we have clear-cut evidence for our conclusions and if we have acquired a sound knowledge base from our in-depth study of early childhood; the latter competence provides us with a wide range of theory to which we may apply our data. Sharing our data and comparing our analysis with that of early years professionals, tutors or fellow students will also add greatly to the credibility of that analysis and assessment.

The procedure for observation analysis generally consists of three elements, although the ways in which these may be linked can vary dramatically. We shall consider two very straightforward examples. Do not worry if they seem a little mechanistic in being taken out of context, but rather try to concentrate on the different order in which the three elements are incorporated within each example.

EXAMPLE 1

For 15 minutes we have undertaken an observation of Aznan (aged 7 months) sitting on the carpet playing with a small piece of loofah; we have used the narrative report technique. This is part of an assessment of his overall development.

1. Refer to the aspect of observation data to be discussed. For example:

   Aznan was engaged in heuristic (discovery) play – finding out about the properties of the piece of loofah. He frequently grasped hold of it using a palmar grip, peered at it and put it in his mouth.

2. Refer now to relevant theory. For example:

   Bee (1995, p.196) affirms that play at this age includes 'exploring and manipulating objects using all the sensorimotor schemas in her repertoire'. This exploratory play behaviour is also confirmed as typical of infants around 6–7 months by Sheridan (1975) and Goldschmied and Jackson (1994). The latter theorists tell us that 'by sucking, mouthing and handling (objects), babies are finding out about weight, size, shapes, texture, sound and smell' (p.88), as well demonstrating considerable levels of concentration.

3. We now bring stages 1 and 2 together to make a reasoned assessment. For example:

We can, therefore, see that Aznan's play is typical for his age and he is learning much about objects from within his environment. He is also learning to concentrate for increasing periods of time.

This three-stage process would naturally be repeated with any other aspect of the observation which it is necessary to analyse in order to achieve the holistic assessment.

The next very important step is to consider future action to support Aznan's development. For example:

It would seem to be appropriate now to introduce Aznan to the 'treasure basket' of Goldschmied and Jackson (1994, pp.86–100). This should contain a 'wide variety of different objects (natural materials) to engage (his) interest and (further) stimulate (his) developing senses and understanding' (p.97).

Of course an observation such as this one on Aznan would not necessarily be transmitted to paper. It would probably occur as part of a competent and experienced professional's daily reflections and forward planning.

EXAMPLE 2

Marian (aged 4 years 4 months) is happily settled at nursery, but staff have concerns about her level of language development. Over a period of 4 weeks, we have noted in a diary instances of her spoken language, responses and understanding. We have also made a 30-minute tape recording of her engaged in a game/conversation. There is much evidence for analysis.

1. On this occasion we might start with the assessment. For example:

We have collected considerable evidence to suggest that Marian's language development is not yet at the standard typical for her age. This is a cause for concern amongst the nursery staff.

2. We next need to cite examples to substantiate our claim. For example:

Marian's speech is indistinct and largely consists of one-word or two-word phrases with only the occasional three-word phrase – 'Me come', 'No want', 'Where goin (going)?', 'Me pay (play) house', etc. She finds difficulty in following some instructions and responding to some questions, etc.

3. Now we should give an indication of the evidence which, combined with the examples, helped us to reach an informed judgement. For example:

> Browne (1996) tells us that most children of 3 years 'begin to construct longer, more complex sentences'(p.3) and Bee (1995) confirms this acquisition of 'complex and difficult sentence form' at around 4 years. Indeed, Marian's frequent use of such phrases is, according to Bee (1995, p.236) and Sheridan (1975), more typical of a 2-year-old child.

Once again action to promote Marian's linguistic development must be discussed and planned. For example, we might implement a particular plan of action. This might include:

- setting aside time to talk *with* (not to) Marian each day;
- ascertaining her interests and using this knowledge to stimulate conversation with her;
- ensuring that she is not rushed but rather given time to speak – of course with staff listening carefully and responding appropriately to what she says;
- asking open-ended questions which encourage discussion;
- working in partnership with her parents.

If there is no improvement within a certain time-scale, then the intervention of a speech therapist should be sought.

For professionals who have acquired a rich theoretical understanding of childhood and child development and gained wide experience of children, this interlinking of theory and observation becomes a very natural and indeed quintessential aspect of providing sensitive educare. This is, of course, only possible when the valid and reasoned interpretations and assessments from our observations are used to inform our planning and underpin our future practice with children. It is this which will enable us to make more appropriate or relevant provision or to enrich or amend the experiences we offer in order to foster each child's all-round development, learning, health and well-being. We might, for example, devise particular activities, draw up learning programmes or consider alternative forms of support or treatment. This whole process is in fact referred to as *reflective practice* – the hallmark of a genuine professional.

On some occasions we might realise that, before we can actually make any recommendations concerning a child, we need more data. We must therefore undertake further observations in order to collect specific information to improve our knowledge and understanding of the child. In addition, if we are a novice to the technique of observation, it would be wise to reflect critically on the technique that we used. Was it appropriate for our purpose? Did it provide sufficient information? Is it possible that another technique could have been more helpful?

Much practice in observation and assessment, and discussion of the results of that practice with experienced early years professionals, will greatly improve students' and practitioners' skills of observation and assessment.

Ethical issues relating to observation of children (and the study of early childhood)

There are principles relating to professional standards of conduct which apply to all early years professionals, and are equally important to students of early childhood. These ethical issues need to be clearly understood and must be addressed before we commence observations of children, and indeed a study of childhood.

One of the first ethical issues which students will encounter is negotiating access to a child or children. For students, this entails asking and gaining permission from the child's parents, guardians and/or professional carer or educator. The purpose, method, envisaged outcome and uses of your observation(s) must always be explained. It is inadvisable to proceed if one parent is unhappy about this. Sometimes parents have genuine concerns about their child being observed, perhaps concerning an aspect of his or her development or behaviour They may, of course, simply not like the idea, or feel that they do not have the time or the appropriate home environment. Be sensitive to such feelings, and do not be too upset if permission is not granted.

We seek adult agreement for childhood observations because it is unlikely that we would ever gain fully informed consent from the young children concerned; they cannot be entirely cognizant of the implications of being observed and assessed. Fine and Sandstrom (1988) advocate that children be told as much as they are able to understand, and emphasise that their age should not diminish their rights. Not all researchers do in fact seem to ask children's permission or discuss their intent to observe. If asked by children what we are writing, it is probably best to be truthful and matter-of-fact in our response. For example, we might explain that we should like to write about some of the interesting things he or she and other children do in the nursery and give an honest reason to which they can relate, e.g. 'This is my homework', and ask if that is all right with them. Most children are usually satisfied with this approach, and there is seldom much obviously distorted behaviour resulting from such a request and explanation.

It is also essential to be aware of our responsibilities as an observer. Students should not be in charge of a child or children. Nevertheless, the safety of the child or children must take precedence over completion of observations. We may also need to consider what to do should we see or hear something an adult is not meant to and/or which causes us concern – perhaps a suggestion that a child is being abused, or a plan being made to bully a child.

Hopefully there will be a tutor or early years professional with whom students may discuss such worrying situations.

Confidentiality and anonymity are extremely important issues. Parents/professional carers must be assured that any data collected will be treated in the strictest confidence and it *must be treated thus*. Never be tempted to disclose details gleaned professionally or under the promise of confidentiality and anonymity to anyone; this includes parents, boy-, girl- or best friends, partners, neighbours, sons or daughters. Be a true professional.

If information is to be disclosed, perhaps in a project or shared in a seminar, this must be explained and agreed in advance. Within a student group, discussion or reporting of an observation or incident must be anonymous. Use only a child's first name, the initial letter of his or her first name or a pseudonym. Refer to professionals as 'teacher', 'nursery nurse' and 'health visitor', and to parents as 'mother' and 'father'. Be very careful to omit the names of early years settings and schools, and instead use terms such as the playgroup, nursery class, class 1R, etc.

Our obligations as professionals or potential professionals also require us, in all interactions, to behave in a courteous and unobtrusive manner. We should be sensitive to the needs of the child or children and to the demands made on the practitioners and the parents or carers. Students should always arrange visits and observations at the convenience of the family, nursery, school or ward, and fit in with the routine of the setting.

Fine and Sandstrom (1988) mention one further issue that is significant at this early stage in our text and studies, and that is consideration of the extent to which we, as adults, can re-enter a child's world and truly understand and interpret his or her behaviour and viewpoint. It is often difficult for us to take ourselves back into the world of childhood and adopt that perspective and reasoning. We must, therefore, remain open-minded to a variety of possible interpretations and explanations and a range of influential factors.

Readers who have not had the opportunity to observe young children in a variety of contexts should use this new-found guidance to begin their acquisition of the skills of observation and assessment. A great deal of detailed and helpful advice about these processes can be found in Bentzen (1993). Ethical issues that arisewhen undertaking research are discussed fully in Chapter 14.

Values and principles for students of early childhood

We considered in the introduction just a little of how values and principles differ between cultures and have changed over time. Certainly we must be continually conscious of this cultural relativism, and supportive of children and families from other cultures. As well as taking account of these factors, we must also be well aware of the values and principles which constitute our own beliefs and underpin our own practices and theories. Students new to the study of early childhood may still be in the process of formulating their own beliefs and values. Contact with children and their families, reading relevant publications, examining research reports and engaging in discussions with early years professionals, tutors and fellow students can aid the development and consolidation of these professional values and principles. Being able to articulate these is vital, because they will guide thinking, studying and practice as a student and early years professional. They will also be exceedingly influential in the aims and policies developed now or in the future.

The National Children's Bureau provides a statement of the values and principles which reflect their strong commitment to children and determine their policies and the direction of the excellent work they undertake on behalf of children and their families. These are set out in Figure 1.8, and it is worth taking the time to examine each of them. Consideration might be given to whether they match the readers' own beliefs, and to the ways in which they might influence present or future practice with young children and their families. In addition, they may provide a helpful starting point from which to begin, or continue, to develop a personal set of values and principles.

Values

- Children are individuals in their own right
- All children are of equal worth, whatever their race, ability, gender, sexual orientation, social class or religion
- Children should be seen as the responsibility of society as a whole, as well as of their parents and family
- Society has a responsibility to promote children's welfare and development, and to protect them from physical and emotional harm, deprivation or disadvantage
- Society has a responsibility to ensure that children can achieve their full potential
- Children should occupy a more central position as valued participants in our society, and should have the opportunities and information to enable them to do so
- Children should be encouraged to accept, as they mature, increasing responsibility for themselves and towards others
- Society should recognise the needs and characteristics of children at different stages and respond appropriately to them
- Society should recognise the value of children's own views and perceptions and should ensure that they are fully taken into account

Principles

- The National Children's Bureau sees children's needs as a whole rather than from the viewpoint of education, health or social services
- We consult and support children, parents families, other carers and professionals
- We draw attention to the needs and interests of children and seek to influence policy and practice
- We celebrate the richness and diversity of childhood, including the different strengths deriving from ethnic background, culture, ability, age and gender
- We attempt to eradicate prejudice and discrimination against children as a group or because of race, disability, gender, sexual orientation, social class or religion
- We are committed to hearing and responding to the views of children
- Through research and in other ways, we identify and promote the best conditions for children, whatever their circumstances whether living with their families or apart
- We foster co-operation, collaboration and effective communication between all those who with and for children

Figure 1.8   National Children's Bureau statement of values and principles. Reproduced with kind permission of the National Children's Bureau, 8 Wakley Street, London EC1V 7QE.

CONCLUSION
In this chapter we introduced approaches to the study of early childhood. An overview of the main theoretical perspectives was presented, and the essential processes of observation and assessment were examined and recognised as vital skills for effective early years practitioners. The chapter then concluded with the provision of a set of values and principles to underpin competent educare practice.

References

Bee, H. (1995): *The Developing Child*, 7th edn. New York: Harper Collins.

Bentzen, W.R. (1993): *A Guide to Observing and Recording Behaviour*. New York: Delmar Publishers Inc.

Bronfenbrenner, U. (1979): *The Ecology of Human Development*. Cambridge, MA: Harvard University Press.

Browne, A. (1996): *Developing Language and Literacy 3–8*. London: Paul Chapman Publishing.

Bruce, T. (1987): *Early Childhood Education*. London: Hodder and Stoughton,

Elder, G. H., Modell, J. and Parker, R.D. (1993): Studying Children in a Changing World. In Elder, G. H. Modell, J. and Parker, R. D. (eds), *Children in Time and Place*. Cambridge: Cambridge University Press, 3–21.

Eysenck, M. (1994): *Perspectives on Psychology*. Hove: Lawrence Erlbaum Associates.

Fine, G.A. and Sandstrom, K.L (1988): *Knowing Children: Participant Observation with Minors*. London: Sage Publications.

Frankenburg, W.K. and Dodds, J.B. (1967): Denver Developmental Screening Test. *Journal of Paediatrics*, **71**, 181–91.

Goldschmied, E. and Jackson, S. (1994): *People Under Three: Young Children in Day Care*. London: Routledge.

Richardson, K. (1988): *Understanding Psychology*. Milton Keynes: Open University Press.

Sheridan, M. (1975): *From Birth to Five Years*. London: Routledge.

2 New beginnings: factors affecting health and well-being in the infant

Catherine Forsdike

This chapter aims to:

- consider the nature and impact of processes and experiences which might influence the future health and well-being of infants;
- note the development of the fetus *in utero*;
- discuss the role of the early years professional.

Introduction

Birth is just one stage in the development of the child. By gaining an understanding of the processes before, during and in the early period following birth we can consider the impact that these may have on future health, growth and development.

In this chapter we shall explore some of our earliest life experiences and consider the extent to which they are beneficial or detrimental to health – not just health in the newborn, but the ongoing health of the child. The significance of early experience is reflected in the growing interest in this period of the child's life.

Consider the following dialogue which takes place in some form at hundreds of birth every day:

> Midwife: It's a girl!

> Mother: Thank goodness – is she all right?

> Midwife: She's fine.

From this dialogue the mother is reassured that she has given birth to a healthy baby. Yet if we examine the dialogue more closely, it becomes apparent that the mother may not be aware of the complexity of her question or the superficial nature of the midwife's answer.

In effect, the mother is asking two questions. First, she is asking if the baby has suffered any ill effects from the experience of the labour and delivery, and secondly she is asking whether her baby is normal and healthy.

From a superficial glance at the baby it is possible to assess his or her condition at birth and to ascertain whether there are any gross abnormalities. Around 5 per cent of all babies born in England and Wales have a congenital or other developmental defect (Office of Population Censuses and Surveys, 1995). Some of these are immediately apparent at birth, e.g. cleft lip, while others become apparent during the first few days or weeks of life, and yet others only become apparent later, e.g. cerebral palsy. Consequently it is not possible to answer the mother's apparently simple question so easily.

In the first place, the question 'What is health?' raises a number of issues. Health may be considered to be the absence of disease, a state of well-being or, as the World Health Organisation (WHO) (1946) defined it 'a complete state of physical, mental and emotional well-being, and not merely the absence of disease and infirmity.'

The WHO definition may be seen as an idealistic concept, but when considering the health and well-being of the newborn it is relevant to address the broader definition, rather than to concentrate solely on the absence of disease and abnormality.

This widens the scope of this chapter, which will consider preconception and prenatal influences on health, as well as factors relating to the delivery and period immediately following birth. In addition to identifying influences on the health and well-being of the child, strategies to enhance outcome and the relevance of this period to the early years professional will be considered.

Life does not begin at birth. The individual is already 9 months old when he or she is born. It takes three to make a birth day – the mother, the father and the newborn baby. The mother and father will each contribute to the unique genetic composition of the baby by virtue of their own genetic make-up. The whole process of embryonic and fetal development is dependent on genes, and abnormal genes can cause abnormality and disease in the newborn. The life-style of the parents before and during pregnancy will have an impact on the health and development of the fetus. In turn, social, cultural and environmental factors will influence the childbearing process. None of these factors stands alone – their integration and the interplay between them will all contribute to the early experience of the child.

From conception to birth

The development of the embryo is a unique and amazing process. Our knowledge of this complex process is increasing with advances in embryological and genetic research, yet there is still only partial understanding of the early period of human experience. To understand why the period before birth is so significant, and to appreciate the potential impact of factors such as drugs and infections on development, it is necessary to describe briefly the developmental timetable from conception to birth.

The human gestation period is approximately 38 weeks from conception or 40 weeks from the onset of the last menstrual period. The gestation period is divided into two phases.

- *The embryonic phase* commences with conception and continues until the end of the eighth week. It is a period of rapid growth and development, and during this phase all of the major organs of the body are formed. The first 3 weeks following conception are sometimes referred to as the pre-embryonic period.
- *The fetal phase* comprises the remaining 30 weeks of gestation. It is characterised by growth and further development of the organs and systems established in the embryonic phase.

An individual's development commences at fertilisation when the sperm enters the egg. As soon as fertilisation has taken place, the new cell starts to change. Cells are the basic unit of life. Human beings are composed of about 350 specialised cells, such as red blood cells and muscle cells (Wolpert, 1993). The embryonic cells are initially less specialised, but all cells have basic characteristics and activities. The activities which we need to consider here are cell multiplication, cell differentiation and cell movement.

The process of cell multiplication begins about 30 minutes after fertilisation, when the egg starts to divide into two cells. The cells continue to divide, and by day 4 there is a solid ball of cells known as the morula. The morula enters the uterus and changes into a blastocyst, which is a fluid-filled sphere containing a group of cells known as the inner cell mass. The inner cell mass will become the embryo, and the trophoblastic cells will form the placenta. Approximately 7 to 8 days after ovulation the blastocyst will become embedded in the wall of the uterus.

By the third week after ovulation the inner cell mass has become a disc differentiated into three different types of cells. It is from these cells that the different structures of the body will evolve. Four weeks after fertilisation the cells have developed to form an embryo 0.5 cm long which has curved in on itself with a head and tail fold. Most of the body systems are now present in a rudimentary form; there is a neural tube which will form the brain, lung buds which will develop into a respiratory system, and primitive eyes, nose and ears. By this stage the heart is beating. The changes have been achieved not just by cell differentiation but also by cell movement which transforms the flat embryonic disc so that the basic body plan is laid down.

At the end of the embryonic phase of development, the embryo is covered with a thin skin. The head has increased greatly in size and is nearly as large as the rest of the body, and the facial features are more distinct. The embryo is making some movements, but at this stage they are not strong enough for the mother to feel them. There is no visible difference between male and female embryos at this stage.

Twelve weeks after fertilisation the fetus has eyelids which are fused. The kidneys secrete urine, the fetus swallows amniotic fluid, and the external genitalia have developed sufficiently for it to be possible to determine the sex of the fetus.

At 20 weeks the fetus looks distinctly human. The body is beginning to be covered by fine hair and a thick greasy substance known as vernix caseosa which protects the skin from the macerating effects of the amniotic fluid. The fetal movements are now strong enough to be felt by the mother.

By 24 weeks the fetus weighs 550–700 g. The organs have developed and matured to such an extent that the fetus may survive with medical assistance if the birth takes place prematurely. The fetus responds to light, sound and touch, and has developed a sense of taste. It has also developed the ability to feel and respond to pain.

During the remaining weeks of pregnancy the fetus accumulates fat stores and maturation continues. The lungs, in particular, continue to develop and prepare for function. At birth, the normal baby weighs between 3.0 and 3.5 kg. Although birth is a stage in the developmental process, and rapid changes take place within the baby as it adapts to life outside the uterus, birth does not represent the end of development. Many organ systems do not develop into their final form until puberty or later.

From the above description it can be seen that important milestones are reached very early in the embryonic period. At this early stage the embryo is vulnerable to harm from a variety of sources, yet many women are unaware that they are pregnant when this crucial stage of development is occurring.

Factors affecting the health and well-being of the baby

The factors that are likely to affect the health and well-being of the baby vary from the genetic inheritance to parental health and environmental influences. Some of these factors may be more significant at particular stages of development, e.g. rubella infection during the first 24 weeks of pregnancy (Wang and Smaill, 1990). Others may be of ongoing significance, e.g. parental smoking may have a preconception influence, it may affect growth and development during intrauterine life (Lumley and Astbury, 1990), or it may be a risk factor for sudden infant death (McGreal, 1995).

When congenital malformation or developmental defects arise this may be due to mutant genes or chromosomal abnormalities, environmental factors, or a combination of both. However, in 60 per cent of abnormalities the cause is unknown. Bearing this in mind, let us now consider some of these potential influences on the health of the baby in more detail.

Parental influences

Parental health and well-being make an important contribution to the development of the fetus and baby. It is clearly desirable that a couple are in optimum health before embarking on a pregnancy. This is also true when there is a pre-existing medical condition. For example, diabetes mellitus in the mother may seriously complicate a pregnancy. This is particularly significant if the condition is poorly controlled, as there is an increased likelihood of congenital abnormality and problems for the newborn. However, if the condition is well managed both before and during pregnancy, the risks are decreased.

For some women, problems arise during pregnancy itself. There are many risk factors to be considered during the antenatal period, and it is important that maternal health and well-being are carefully monitored. This includes measuring the blood pressure, as pregnancy-induced hypertension may result in the baby having a low birth weight or being born prematurely.

Embryonic and fetal development may also be affected by infections which cross the placenta from the mother to the baby. In some cases the mother may not feel particularly ill, but the effects on the fetus can be considerable.The acronym TORCH is used to denote those infections which may affect the developing infant:

- *Toxoplasma gondii* – a protozoon present in cats' faeces and raw meat. it can cause damage to the nervous system and mental retardation. If it is diagnosed and treated in pregnancy the chance of damage is reduced;
- Other – including sexually transmitted disease such as human immunodeficiency virus (HIV), gonorrhoea and syphilis;
- Rubella – a virus which inhibits cell division and causes defects in the organs that are developing at the time of the infection. It affects the eyes, ears, heart and brain. The earlier an infection occurs, the more severe the problems are likely to be;
- Cytomegalovirus – which may affect the baby at any stage during pregnancy, and may cause growth retardation or preterm delivery. Complications may lead to mental retardation;
- Herpes simplex – in the early stages of pregnancy this can result in abortion. The baby is particularly vulnerable during delivery, and may develop a range of illnesses at the newborn stage.

In addition to infections and complications during pregnancy, other parental factors play a part. It is necessary to consider the age of the parents, since there is an increase in morbidity and mortality rates at the extremes of reproductive age. Adolescent mothers are more likely to have small babies, which may be linked to their nutritional status. Mothers over 35 years of age are more prone to chromosomal abnormalities such as Down's syndrome. Some chromosomal abnormalities are linked to increasing paternal age (Wildschut, 1994).

As well as chromosomal abnormalities, there are also many genetic abnormalities and with advancing knowledge it is becoming possible to screen couples for risk, and to make a diagnosis of some chromosomal and genetic abnormalities during pregnancy. This enables parents to decide whether to terminate the pregnancy or to continue and prepare for the birth of the baby. Triple screening for Down's syndrome has been introduced to estimate the probability of the fetus being affected. Women who are shown to be at high risk are then offered amniocentesis in order to make a diagnosis. On the one hand this may seem to be a positive step to reduce the incidence of the condition, but on the other it is now becoming apparent that there is heightened anxiety in the pregnant population, as well as poor understanding of the nature of the test. It has been suggested by Katz Rothman (1988) that amniocentesis during pregnancy may disturb the developing relationship between the mother and her unborn child. As yet there has been no research to determine whether there are long-term consequences for the mother–child relationship and the emotional well-being of the child.

Parental life-style

Parental life-style may have an influence throughout pregnancy. Many substances will cross the placental barrier. This includes prescription drugs, over-the-counter drugs and illegal substances, and some of these will have a teratogenic effect. Alcohol consumed during pregnancy also influences development and can cross the placenta. High levels of alcohol consumption can cause a condition known as fetal alcohol syndrome. Babies born with this condition may have physical abnormalities and suffer from delayed intellectual development and behavioural problems. There is considerable debate about the dangers of drinking at different stages of pregnancy. It is known that high levels of alcohol consumption are harmful, but it is difficult to determine the effects of moderate consumption, as studies to date have been inconclusive (Hepburn, 1992). The patterns of alcohol consumption among women have been poorly researched, and it is difficult to obtain a clear picture of alcohol consumption during pregnancy (Miles, 1991). As a result, the precise effects of alcohol are difficult to ascertain, especially since alcohol consumption is often associated with tobacco smoking and poor nutrition.

Tobacco smoking should be discouraged during pregnancy, as there is clear evidence that it causes harm to the fetus. Birth weight decreases with increasing number of cigarettes smoked, and preterm labour is more likely. Tobacco smoking is also associated with poorer nutritional status.

There is increasing interest in the role played by diet and nutrition in promoting the health of the mother and fetus prior to and during pregnancy. The effects of the mother's nutritional status on fetal growth and development are not clearly understood, and of necessity some of the evidence is circumstantial, owing to the ethical and moral implications of manipulating the diet of pregnant women.

It has been postulated that poor nutrition in the later stages of pregnancy affects fetal growth, whilst poor nutrition in the early stages affects embryological development. This hypothesis is supported by the statistical evidence from the Dutch Hunger Winter of 1944–1945. Prior to the famine conditions the mothers had been relatively well nourished. It was found that babies exposed to the famine during the latter half of pregnancy showed the greatest reduction in birth weight. Conversely, there was a higher incidence of congenital abnormality and stillbirth in babies conceived during the course of the famine (Worthington-Roberts and Williams, 1993). This aspect is discussed further in Chapter 13.

The long-term effects of poor nutrition *in utero* and during the first year of life are also attracting interest. In one study in Hertfordshire birth records from the early part of this century were examined and a follow-up study of the adults between 59 and 70 years of age was carried out. It was discovered that low birth weight was related to an increased risk of heart disease, raised blood pressure and non-insulin-dependent diabetes in adult life. It was not clear from the birth records whether the low birth weight was due to growth retardation or prematurity. However, it seems likely that the low birth weight was due to undernutrition of the fetus, since the records showed that the children who were still underweight at 1 year also showed an increased risk of developing the above conditions (Barker, 1992).

The environment in which the parents live and work may also adversely affect fetal health and development. Radiation has long been known to damage the fetus. The so-called 'Gulf War syndrome' has prompted concerns about the cocktail of drugs and chemicals to which armed forces personnel were exposed both prior to and during the conflict.

However, parental life-style cannot be isolated from the overall social context. Lower socio-economic status may, for example, affect the ability to purchase a healthy diet. The stress and strain of unemployment, poor housing and homelessness may create additional burdens for the pregnant woman. The incidence of smoking and alcohol consumption has increased among the female population, and may be a strategy employed to cope with adverse social circumstances.

It is difficult to separate the factors that affect the health and development of the fetus and newborn infant. Figure 2.1 illustrates the interrelationship between them. The characteristics of the newborn itself, in terms of sex, birth order or whether it is a singleton or multiple birth, are also significant. For babies who are born prematurely, of low birth weight, or who are ill following delivery, advances in neonatal intensive care have increased the likelihood of survival. However, the old adage that prevention is better than cure holds true, and this will now be considered.

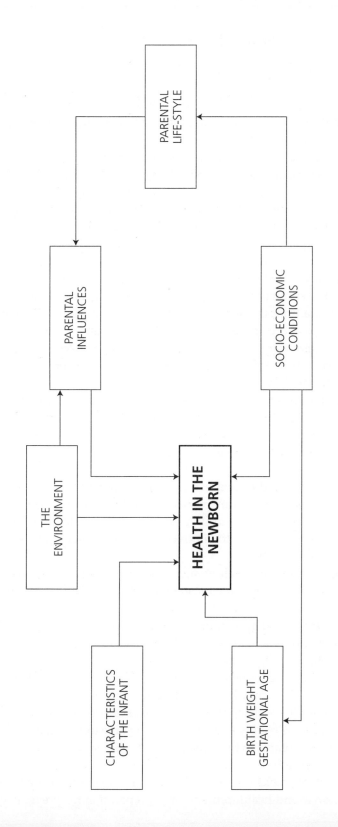

Figure 2.1 Interrelationship between factors that influence health and well-being in the newborn infant.

Strategies to optimise health and well-being in the newborn

It has been demonstrated that the factors which influence health in the new-born are many, and that they are interrelated. As a result, a variety of strategies is required to reduce risk and promote health. By the end of the embryological phase of development, most major structural anomalies that affect the fetus are already determined (Moos, 1989). A major challenge, therefore, is to provide education about the potential effects of life-style choices and health status on the developing embryo. Yet many people are unaware of the relationship between preconceptual health and pregnancy outcome. Helping people to prepare for pregnancy is a strategy known as preconception health promotion and care.

The media may be a powerful means of raising general awareness among the population. Media campaigns may address either general issues or a specific factor. For example, the importance of folic acid supplementation prior to conception was promoted by advertising in the newspapers and on television. Leaflets and posters were available from a variety of sources to reinforce the message. Slogans such as 'Think Folic Before you Frolic' captured the imagination! Despite this high-profile campaign, many women considered their diet to include a sufficient intake of folic acid without supplementation. However, it is becoming apparent that diet alone does not provide the level required to protect against neural tube defect. It has been suggested that more foods could be fortified with folic acid in order to overcome this problem (McGrath, 1995).

Good health and sex education in schools is an essential part of preconception care. Teachers and health care professionals should work together to provide accurate, relevant and sensitive advice so that children can make informed choices with regard to contraception, pregnancy and parenthood (House of Commons, 1991).

Family-planning clinics, well-woman and well-man clinics all provide opportunities for preconception education. In one study of women attending family-planning clinics it was found that over 50 per cent of women were taking prescribed drugs, and approximately 30 per cent smoked cigarettes, used over-the-counter drugs and drank alcohol, all factors which may have an adverse effect should pregnancy occur (Moos, 1989).

In addition to raising general awareness, preconception clinics are available in some areas. They may be situated in GP surgeries or health centres, or be 'drop-in' clinics in local shopping precincts. For preconception care to be effective, it needs to be readily accessible and sensitive to the needs of the local population and acceptable to the wide range of religious and cultural groups in contemporary society.

Preconception care consists of two elements. The majority of clients require advice on life-style and health promotion in preparation for pregnancy. In its evidence presented to the 1991 House of Commons Health Committee investigating the maternity services, the Royal College of Midwives outlined a variety of approaches to be taken in the provision of preconception care. In the first place it is necessary to take a detailed family and obstetric history in order to determine whether any specialist referral is required. Screening for infections can be carried out. Rubella immunisation is offered for all children, but in some cases immunity is not achieved. If the woman is not immune, then vaccination can be offered as part of preconception care. Advice on life-style may consider weight, nutritional status and the adverse effects of smoking and alcohol consumption. Opportunities should be provided for those contemplating pregancy to talk about the implications of parenthood and to discuss their fears and anxieties.

Specialist preconception advice should be available for women with preexisting medical conditions. Genetic counselling may be required by couples if there is a family history of genetic disorder, or if they have previously had affected children. Genetic counselling involves providing information about the level of risk, describing the options open to the parents, and providing support for the couple through the choices they make as a result of that information.

If preconception care is to be effective, then the needs of a local population must be identified and strategies formulated to meet local need in an acceptable form. For example, many Asian women have not been immunised against rubella. This is significant, since Asian women are more susceptible to rubella than non-Asian women, and they are also less likely to seek diagnostic investigations. Setting up a preconception clinic will not necessarily reach these women, and it may be necessary to consider alternative approaches. The Asian Mother and Baby Campaign was set up with the aim of improving the antenatal and postnatal care given to Asian women, and to inform Asian families about the importance of early antenatal care (Rocheron, 1991).

Whether preconception clinics are providing a broad range of services or meeting the specific needs of couples at increased risk, the intention should be to provide sufficient information for people to make informed choices about conception. Care must be taken to ensure that all advice is non-judgemental and non-directive, so that reproductive decisions are taken by the woman or couple, and not by the health care professional. Equally, it should be recognised that preconception care has not failed if the clients do not act on the advice that they receive.

Looking forward to pregnancy, preconception clinics also provide the ideal opportunity for educating the woman about the importance of antenatal care and the decisions that she may need to make during pregnancy. *Changing Childbirth* (Department of Health, 1993) emphasises the rights of women to exercise choice and control during childbearing. The mother should be able to choose whether the midwife, the General Practitioner or the obstetrician will act as the main co-ordinator of her care, and make choices relating to the type of care provided. Women are confronted with the need to make decisions about whether to have screening tests early in the pregnancy. It may be helpful to spend time considering the nature of these tests and the implications of choosing to have them before pregnancy occurs.

Preconception care may be provided by a variety for sources. It could be argued that it is especially relevant for the maternity services and in particular midwives to provide preconception care and advice. At present there is a potential gap between preconception and antenatal care. The third aim of *Changing Childbirth* is continuity of care. If the maternity services provide preconception clinics, then the woman will be seen by the same health care professionals throughout the childbearing process. This can promote ongoing and consistent advice and support which is sensitive to the needs of the woman and her partner.

The process of childbearing is a time of great psychological and physiological change. It is also a normal physiological event, and in the majority of cases the end result is a healthy mother and baby. Antenatal care was first introduced in 1915 as a means of improving the health of the mother and baby. The broad aims of antenatal care are to promote fetal and maternal well-being, to detect and treat deviations from normal, and to prepare the woman and her partner for labour and parenthood. As with preconception care, there is a significant health education element to enable informed choice during the antenatal period. The diagnostic and technical facilities used in the care of the mother and baby have become increasingly sophisticated, and it is now being questioned whether all women require frequent supervision. Identifying the at-risk cases for whom more supervision is required may be a more realistic and valuable use of resources. It is also being questioned whether antenatal care is sufficient to override the problems caused by social deprivation.

The period following delivery also offers opportunities to screen the newborn for a variety of disorders, and to instigate treatment at an early stage in order to reduce or prevent the potential for harm. Again there are opportunities to teach parents about caring for their babies, including advice on infant feeding (a theme that is discussed in detail in Chapter 3), how to recognise when the baby is ill, and how and when to seek help.

Like pregnancy, the postnatal period may bring joy and excitement, but it is also a time of major adjustment to new roles and responsibilities. An important aspect of care is the emotional and psychological support of the mother and the family. Few women escape the transitory 'three-day blues' following delivery, but 3–25 per cent of women will go on to develop postnatal depression, which can adversely affect the ability to cope with the demands of motherhood and interfere with the developing relationship between the mother and her baby (Niven, 1992).

Social support mechanisms are important for enhancing the mother's own coping strategies. In addition to family support, the National Childbirth Trust, Meet-a-Mum schemes and postnatal support groups may be vital sources of contact for new parents. Jean Ball (1987) has identified how all of these factors are interrelated in promoting the well-being of the mother in the early months of parenthood, which increases confidence in meeting the needs of the baby, and thus promoting physical and social well-being in the child.

Information about health in childbearing should be part of general health promotion and education work, so that women and their partners can make informed choices. It is unrealistic to expect that individuals will address all risk factors, but even small improvements in life-style may prevent complications for the mother or the fetus. However, it is also unrealistic to believe that improvements in pregnancy outcome can be achieved by health promotion alone. There needs to be an improvement in social conditions such as poverty, poor housing and inadequate diet. Without such an improvement, a significant proportion of the population will remain vulnerable during pregnancy.

Implications for early years professionals

As stated earlier, the period surrounding birth is attracting interest not just in relation to the health of the newborn baby, but also with regard to the presence of disease in later life. The promotion of health begins before we are born, and subsequently it is within the family that the first messages about health are given. The early years professional has opportunities to reinforce positive health messages and to offer alternatives to negative messages. By providing information, a vital part of the preconception care of the next generation is instigated.

Whilst this may be an aspect for the early years professional to consider, it is also important that there is understanding of the early holistic influences on the children in their care. This understanding may then lead to greater insight into meeting the needs of children who have a congenital abnormality, have been born prematurely or of low birth weight, or have been born into poor socio-economic conditions.

CONCLUSION

This chapter has focused on the factors influencing the health and well-being of the newborn baby. It has been suggested that some influences play a part before conception, whereas others arise during pregnancy and the period following birth. The factors are often interlinked and there is a danger of blaming the victim if the wider social and environmental factors are ignored.

Health promotion and advice have been emphasised, rather than the more medical aspects of preconception and pregnancy care. This has been intentional, so that an overview of early experience can be gained. It is hoped that this chapter will act as a springboard for the reader to follow up areas of personal interest to him or her, and which are relevant to his or her particular area of early years work.

References

Ball, J., (1987): *Reactions to Motherhood: the Role of Postnatal Care*, Cambridge: Cambridge University Press.

Barker, D.J.P. (ed), (1992): *Fetal and Infant Origins of Adult Disease*. London: British Medical Journal.

Department of Health (1993): *Changing Childbirth*. London: HMSO.

Hepburn, M. (1992): *Socially Related Disorders: Drug Addiction, Maternal Smoking and Alcohol Consumption*. In Calder, A. and Dunlop, W. (eds), *High Risk Pregnancy*. Oxford: Butterworth Heinemann, 263–88.

House of Commons (1991): *Health Committee Fourth Report. Maternity Services: Preconception Care*. London: HMSO.

Katz Rothman, B (1988): *The Tentative Pregnancy: Prenatal Diagnosis and the Future of Pregnancy*. London: Pandora.

Lumley, J. and Astbury, J. (1990): *Advice for Pregnancy*. In Chalmers, I., Enkin, M. and Keirse, M. (eds), *Effective Care in Pregnancy and Childbirth*. Oxford: Oxford University Press, 16–20.

McGrath, P. (1995): Planning for Pregnancy. *Practice Nurse* **9**, 193–7.

McGreal, I. (1995): Smoking and the Pregnant Woman. *Midwives* **108**, 218–21.

Miles, A. (1991): *Women, Health and Medicine*. Milton Keynes: Open University Press.

Moos, M. (1989): Preconceptual Health Promotion: a Health Opportunity for all Women. *Women and Health* **15**, 55–68.

Niven, C. (1992): *Psychological Care for Families: Before, During and After Birth*. Oxford: Butterworth Heinemann.

Office of Population Censuses and Surveys: (1995), *The Health of our Children: Dicennial Supplement*, London: HMSO.

Rocheron, Y. (1991): The Asian Mother and Baby Campaign: the Construction of Ethnic Minorities Health Needs. In Loney, M. *et al*. (eds), *The State or the Market*, 2nd edn, London: Sage Publications, 184–205.

Wang, E. and Smaill, F. (1990): Infection in Pregnancy. In Chalmers, I., Enkin, M. and Keirse, M. (eds), *Effective Care in Pregnancy and Childbirth*. Oxford: Oxford University Press, 89–100.

Wildschut, H. (1994): Sociodemographic Factors: Age, Parity, Social Class and Ethnicity. In James, D.K. *et al*. (eds), High Risk Pregnancy. London: W B Saunders Co Ltd, 35–49.

Wolpert, L. (1993): *The Triumph of the Embryo*. Oxford: Oxford University Press.

World Health Organization (1946): *Constitution*. Geneva: World Health Organisation (cited by **Seedhouse, D.** 1986 *Health – the Foundations for Achievement*. Chichester: John Wiley & Sons, 31).

Worthington-Roberts, B and Williams, S. (1993): Prenatal Nutrition – General Issues. In Worthington-Roberts, B. and Williams, S. (eds), *Nutrition in Pregnancy and Lactation*, 5th edn. St Louis, MO: Mosby, 87–172.

Growth and development

Val Thurtle

This chapter aims to:

- consider why early years professionals study child development;
- investigate health and growth screening in early childhood;
- reflect ways of meeting the physical needs of young children.

Why study child development?

Most professionals who come into contact with children, be they teachers, nurses or social workers, are likely to have studied child development during their basic education and training. The study of their prospective clients is seen as a 'good' thing, and there is an understanding that there are rules and patterns in the progression of all children that can be discovered, described and perhaps understood. Reflecting on the purpose of studying child development, it can be viewed as an extremely interesting area of academic study in its own right. More practically, psychoanalytical thinking has encouraged the view that the 'child is father of the man'. What has happened in childhood is seen as being influential in adulthood, and therefore must be worth exploring.

By setting up a taxonomy of norms, milestones or stages that the majority of children are likely to reach by a certain age or point, children can be compared to that norm. Much of the developmental screening conducted by health professionals is done in this way, and Standard Assessment Tasks and Attainment Targets within the National Curriculum set up such norms. The measurement of a child's development against such norms is not, however, for its own sake, but as already mentioned in Chapter 1, to support and advance the potential of the individual child. This may mean identifying the limitations of a child so that appropriate diagnostic measures can be taken and appropriate remedial input be directed to the child. Child development is important not only for the child with 'difficulties', but also for all children so that the early years worker can define appropriate care, stimulation and education for the needs of any one child according to his or her physical, emotional, social and intellectual development.

Although it perhaps sits uneasily in this text, it can be argued that powerful professionals want to see into all areas of life, extending their influence. The study of child development is an example of the web of surveillance extending into all parts of society, reaching into private areas of an individual's world, so that children, like other sectors of society, can be controlled and manipulated (Nettleton and Bunton, 1995). This is not a belief that early years workers are likely to espouse, but it is a valid view of which they should be aware.

The rationale for inclusion of child development in most programmes is that it underpins sound professional practice in early years provision. The study of child development facilitates the worker's understanding of the child and how he or she is likely to progress.

Health for all children

Until recently, the emphasis in child health care has been on the detection of abnormalities. Specific norms – competencies that would be expected to be achieved by a certain age – have been outlined, and children have been compared with this standard. Recent good practice has redefined child health as much broader, encompassing activities that prevent ill health and promote good health (Hall, 1996)

Nevertheless, the early detection of difficulties is often referred to as screening, but we might want to query whether the monitoring of children's development is true screening.

The Hall Report (Hall, 1996) quotes the American Commission on Chronic Illness (1957) as saying that screening is:

> *the presumptive identification of unrecognised disease or defect by the application of tests, examinations, and other procedures which can be applied rapidly. Screening tests sort out the apparently well persons who do have a disease from those who probably do not. A screening test is not expected to be diagnostic.*

(Hall, 1996, pp. 82–83)

Screening, therefore, will be for a significant health problem and treatment should be available. It will be economically worthwhile; in other words, screening should be:

- simple;
- acceptable;
- accurate;
- repeatable;
- sensitive;
- specific.

To what extent does monitoring of children's progress fit these criteria? The distraction test carried out on babies aged approximately 8 months was at one time seen as sorting those who were and were not hearing adequately, using a method which is simple and acceptable to most parents. Variation in facilities and the quality of staff training have led to serious reservations about the sensitivity of the test (Hall, 1996), and therefore its validity as a screening procedure. On the other hand, neonatal blood screening at 8 days of age for phenylketonuria and congenital hypothyroidism appear to fit the screening criteria, and their value is accepted.

Some observations and direct questions asked of a parent might be seen as a screening procedure. 'Is the child walking by a certain age?' is such an example, but with much of a child's development it is difficult to say 'yes, this child is progressing normally' or 'this child needs further investigation' on the basis of one simple test.

Virtually all pre-school children in the UK have access to child health programmes, but the majority of health and developmental difficulties will be picked up in the very early weeks of the child's life, or by parents, friends and professionals who come into contact with the child in other contexts. Their concerns may then be taken to health workers who can pursue avenues of referral which may or may not lead to health interventions.

To be able to do this, all early years practitioners need to be working in partnership with the parents and to have good professional relationships with each other. This is the multidisciplinary approach referred to in Chapter 1. Communication skills are clearly vital, as is a detailed and interpretative knowledge of children's development, behaviour and play.

Acquiring child development knowledge

Students and practitioners who come into contact with children need to have some idea of what can be expected of children at particular ages, or stages. For thousands of students of children this need has been met by Sheridan's *Birth to Five* (Sheridan, 1975). This slim volume sets out what large numbers of children of various ages have been found to have achieved in terms of posture and gross movement, vision and fine movement, hearing, speech, social behaviour and play. As it is based on research carried out on in the 1950s, one might question the validity of the findings and their relevance to practice in the late twentieth century. Sheridan's sample has been criticised as not being representative even at the time of data collection, with a bias toward children with a middle-class background. Child-rearing patterns have changed, as have the opportunities offered to many children.

While the way in which Sheridan's schedule was constructed may have limitations the more significant constraints of the schedule lie largely in the way it is viewed or used. If it is seen as a fixed entity it does not allow for variety in the progression of individual children. The majority are likely to follow the pattern outlined, but possibly at different rates.

The Denver Development Screening test (Frankenburg and Dodds, 1967) set out to take account of this. It identifies the ages by which 25 per cent of children have achieved the developmental point in question, the point at which 50 per cent have achieved it, and so on. Bax's study of children at various ages (Bax *et al.*, 1990) also identified the many variations in developmental achievement.

Development scales of a check-list type cannot take into account the variety in the child's progression, influenced as it is by a host of factors, including genetic make-up, birth history, family background, nutritional state, socioeconomic status and cultural setting, to name just a few.

Schedules would appear to be of limited value, yet there is little doubt that effective early years practice needs to be based on a sound knowledge of child development. The novice will need to learn the key developmental milestones of early childhood with at least approximate ages. A condensed framework is reproduced in Table 3.1 to act as a simple starting point.

As students synthesise material from a variety of disciplines (particularly developmental psychology) with their own observations in practice, they will be able to interpret their findings by applying developmental knowledge based on experience of many children to one child in particular.

Children will not conform to pre-set lists of what they can and cannot do. When the student feels that he or she is coming to grips with a milestone approach to child development, they should consider the following childhood scenarios:

- absence of a social smile at 6 weeks;
- 9-month-old child not taking weight on his or her legs;
- a clinging 1-year-old who refuses to be separated from his or her parent;
- a 3-year-old who is incomprehensible to outsiders;
- a 4-year-old with no co-operative play;
- a 5-year-old who has never been dry at night.

Although these examples are all taken out of context, we can reflect upon those which might generate concern.

Schedules may give some indication if behaviours are within expected norms, but such scenarios should generate more questions than they answer. Inquiries related to the child's health, family history and social setting need to follow. The reader will be able to generate further examples of children's development that do not necessarily fit into existing schedules.

Physical growth and centile charts

So far we have been considering general all-round development – that is, how the child progresses through various stages. One aspect of development which is largely concerned with size and the rate of its change is physical growth. The weight and growth of the baby have assumed an importance that

Table 3.1 'Quick' developmental assessment (reproduced with kind permission of the publisher from Moreton, J. and Macfarlane, A. 1991: Child health and surveillance, 2nd edn. Oxford: Blackwell Scientific Publications)

Age[a]	Gross motor	Visual motor	Language	Social
1 month	Raises head slightly from prone, makes crawling movements	Has tight grip, follows to midline	Alerts to sound (by blinking, moving, standing	Regards face
2 months	Holds head in midline	No longer clenches fist tightly, follows object past midline	Smiles after being stroked or talked to	Increasingly alert
4 months	Sits well when propped	Grasps with both hands co-ordinated, touches cube placed on table	Orients to voice *5 months*: turns head to bell, says 'ah-goo'	Enjoys looking
6 months	Rolls from back to front, sits well, puts feet in mouth in supine position	Reaches with either hand, transfers, using raking grasp	Babbles *7 months*: waves bye-bye *8 Months*: 'dada/mama' inappropriately	Recognises strangers; plays pat-a-cake
9 months	Creeps, pulls to feet, likes to stand	Uses overhand pincer grasp, probes with forefinger, holds bottle, finger feeds	Imitates sounds *10 months*: 'dada/mama' appropriately *11 months*: one word	Starts to explore environment
12 months	Walks with hands held or alone, pivots when sitting, co-operates with dressing	Uses pincer grasp, throws objects, lets go of toys	Follows one-step command with gesture, uses two words *14 months*: uses three words	Imitates actions, comes when called, co-operates with dressing
18 months	Runs, throws toys from standing position without falling	Turns 2–3 pages at a time, fills spoon and feeds	Knows 7–20 words, points to named part of body, uses mature jargoning with intelligible words	Copies parents (e.g. in sweeping, dusting). plays with other children
2 years	Walks up and down steps without help	Turns pages one at a time, removes shoes, pants, etc.	Uses 50 words, 2-word phrases, pronouns, names objects in pictures	
3 years	Pedals tricycle, alternates feet when going up steps	Partial dressing and undressing, dries hands if reminded	Tells stories about experiences, knows his or her sex	Shares toys, takes turns, plays well with others
4 years	Hops, skips, alternates feet when going downstairs	Buttons clothes fully, catches ball	Knows all colours, recites song or poem from memory	Tells 'tall stories', plays co-operatively

[a] These are approximate ages. Sometimes a child may skip a stage, such as crawling, and walk at 13 months, or 'bottom shuffle' instead of crawling and not walk until 18 months or later. Each child is an individual, and parents sometimes need reassurance when they try to compare their child's development with that of others.

is perhaps out of proportion to their value in British culture. The first question asked by relatives and friends after the birth of the baby concerns its weight, and regular weighing has been seen to be part of good mothering. However, measurement of a child's weight, length or head circumference, is of little value unless such measurements can be adequately interpreted and compared to the norm for children of that age.

Regular weekly weighing of half-clothed children on uncalibrated scales is arguably of little benefit. However, accurate measurement of children with careful plotting of these measurements on an up-to-date centile chart, can lead to the early detection and monitoring of conditions such as growth hormone insufficiency, coeliac disease, and organic and non-organic failure to thrive. For the majority of parents of infants, accurate measurements and plotting will be a source of reassurance that their child is growing at an appropriate rate, although there is a risk that too frequent recording of weight will lead to parental anxiety.

Measurements should be made at birth and when there is contact with health professionals The introduction of parent-held records allows measurements taken by health visitors and general practitioners to be plotted on the same chart. The child, when measured, should be naked and weighed on regularly calibrated scales. The practice of converting from imperial to metric weight increases the chance of error and should be avoided. Head circumference is measured around the occipito-frontal diameter prior to hospital discharge. It should be measured at 6–8 weeks and, unless there is concern, later measurement is unnecessary. Accuracy is vital, as errors can lead to anxiety for both parent and professional.

The measurement of length is potentially difficult. Fry (1993) maintains that it is of value and that the infant should be measured in the supine position upon a calibrated mat, and from 18 months onward should be measured in an upright position. He argues that growth is fastest in the first 18 months and should therefore be monitored. Hall (1996) comments that more errors arise when infants are supine, but this does provide useful information. Height measurements should be made as soon as the child can stand. Despite the existence of guidelines variations in practice continue.

Measurements are then plotted upon a centile chart (Figure 3.1). This is a device based on a 'bell' distribution that allows for the variation in height, weight and head circumference across a population. Current charts are based on the serial and cross-sectional measurements of large groups of infants and children in the indigenous UK population, and include pre-term measurements. The most recent are the 1993 United Kingdom Child Growth Standards, which replaced earlier charts published initially in the 1960s. With advances in computerisation, the plan is to update 'the standard' whenever growth surveys indicate shifts in growth patterns. Measurements need to be plotted accurately, with the correct calculation of the child's age in weeks and the readings plotted at the appropriate point allowing for prematurity and post-maturity.

Deciding whether the measurements are of concern is where interpretation becomes significant. Little can be concluded from a single reading, and measurements should be considered over a period of time. Interpretation also needs to take into account the condition of the child – is he or she happy and alert, or pale and unresponsive? Weight, in particular, is only one aspect of

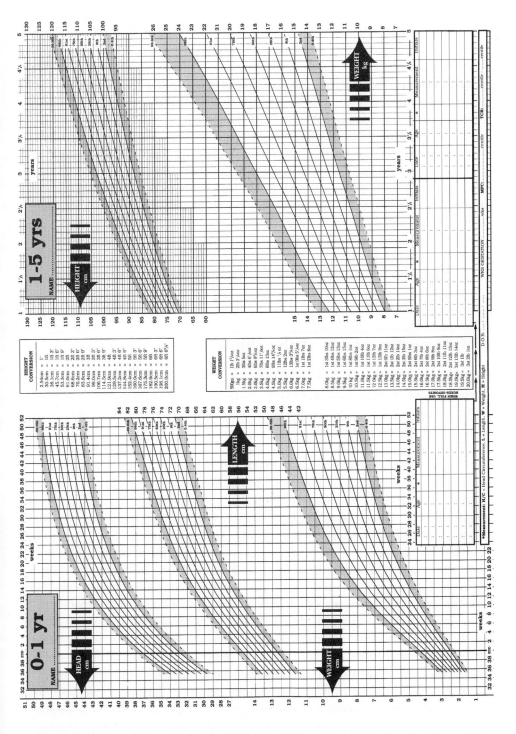

Figure 3.1 Child growth chart. Copyright Child Growth Foundation. Reproduced with permission.

infant and child well-being. Ideally, the child should grow approximately along a centile line, and the head circumference and weight will usually be on a similar centile. Some infants, especially those with inter-uterine growth retardation, may take several months to settle on to 'their' line. Significant crossing of centile lines should raise concerns – the first being the accuracy of measurement and plotting. Measurements outside the 99.6 or 0.4 centile should be queried and referred, although with a bell distribution some children will fit into this category. Parental stature should also be considered.

While crossing of centile lines may be the first sign of an organic problem, one of the commonest causes of failure to gain weight in the young child is underfeeding. A discussion with the carer as to what and how the child eats is likely to prove valuable. Persistent concerns about the growth of a child need to be discussed with the health visitor, general practitioner and ultimately the paediatrician. However, most parents regard their parent-held centile chart as a source of reassurance and a sign of their partnership in the health care of their child.

Such charts can be obtained from Harlow Printing, Maxwell St, South Shields, NE33 4PU, (Tel 0191 455 4286).

Meeting the needs of the child

In a sense this whole volume is concerned with discovering and meeting the holistic needs of the child. Maslow's classic hierarchy of needs (1970) (Figure 3.2) is a useful way of conceptualising the needs of the child at various developmental stages.

The essence of the hierarchy is that the lower-level needs must be met before the individual can move on to the higher-level order needs. This model would therefore imply that raising a child's self-esteem by plenty of positive handling will be of little value if his or her very survival is at risk, e.g. from hypothermia. Indeed he or she is unlikely to benefit at the higher levels if the basic needs of survival, safety and security are not being met.

Using this framework, it is useful to explore what the needs of a child will be at, for example, 6 months of age and 4 years of age. In terms of physical needs, both require adequate nutrition and hygiene, but these needs will be met in ways appropriate to each child's developmental stage. The 6-month-old needs breast milk or a modified substitute. He or she needs to move on to solid food in order to acquire the skills of chewing and to ensure an adequate iron intake, and foods will need to be puréed or at least mashed. The 4-year-old also requires a balanced diet, has mastered the skills of chewing, is at a much reduced risk of choking, can usually handle cutlery, and will have his or her own opinions about food preferences. In terms of warmth, the 6-month-old is totally dependent upon the carer to add or subtract clothing, communicating temperature discomfort in an unspecific way. The fit 4-year-old, in contrast, can move around to generate heat, can communicate his or her

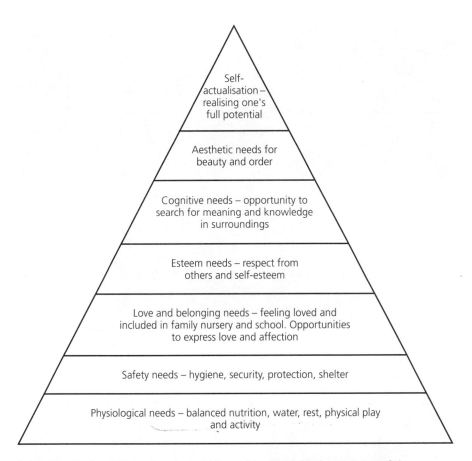

Figure 3.2   Maslow's hierarchy of needs. Reproduced with kind permission of the publisher from Maslow, A.H. 1970: Motivation and personality, 2nd edn. New York: Harper & Row.

perception of temperature in words, and can remove clothing as necessary. The 4-year-old still requires observation, and is unlikely to be able to control the wider environment in this respect, but this child's developmental stage allows him or her to take some responsibility for his or her own warmth.

Safety and security can be discussed in terms of protection from disease, protection from accidents, and the security of loving relationships which over-flows into love and belonging. The 6-month-old requires a high standard of hygiene precautions. Feeding implements need to be sterilised and drinking water must be boiled. Hygienic nappy routines are vital, but the onus is on the carer. The 4-year-old will largely adopt the hygiene practices of the rest of the household. While able to toilet independently, he or she will need reminders about hand-washing and contact with pets. Both will need protection from disease via immunisation and vaccination.

The 6-month-old will gain much security from firm confident handling from a small number of care-givers. Security for the 4-year-old is grounded in relationships with the significant people in his or her life.

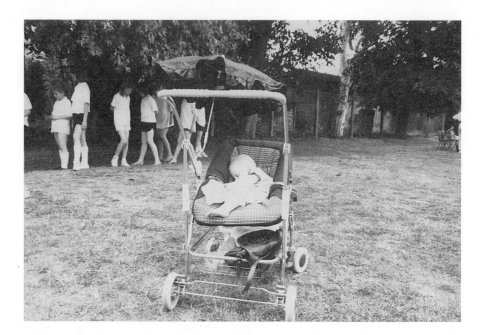

Figure 3.3

Figure 3.4

Figures 3.3–3.6 The needs of children of different ages are met in different ways.

Figure 3.5

Figure 3.6

Both need a safe environment in which to play and explore. Many childhood accidents in the home are a result of the usual play behaviour for a particular developmental stage. Such accidents are likely to occur in a home setting, particularly in the case of children up to 5 years old. After this age, children feature more extensively in road accidents (Thomas, 1993). Accident prevention for the under-fives can be increased by using developmental knowledge to anticipate what skills and movements a child might acquire next. For example, the parent may not previously have seen the child roll over – to do so for the first time over the edge of a changing table when left unattended contributes to the high rate of falls in the under-ones. The 4-year-old will appear confident, with practised motor skills of running, jumping and bike-riding. A desire to hone these skills and to imitate or keep up with his or her siblings, particularly in outside areas, puts him or her at risk (Thomas, 1993).

The love and belonging needs of each child are met by attachments to a stable group of carers. The 6-month-old is still forming such attachments, and these are likely to be limited to a small nucleus of individuals – the mother, father, and perhaps a child-minder and grandparents. The 4-year-old has wider social horizons, forming relationships outside the family group with other adults, and friendships with his peers. He knows he belongs to his nursery, finding security in established routines and practices. Both children will respond to attention, but again it needs to be developmentally specific. The 6-month-old will respond to handling, songs and speech, whereas the 4-year-old has extended his or her repertoire into conversation participation, rhymes, songs, games and a host of other activities.

It is this growth in ability and confidence that gives the developing child self esteem. Such children need to be aware that they are valued and that their achievements are noted and appreciated. Their cognitive needs will be met by the activities with which they are presented, and by their own exploration and interaction with the environment. These will, of course, be specific to each child's developmental stage.

Aesthetic needs of children are often ignored, but are met by the beauty and order of the child's world. Self-actualisation is difficult to discuss for any of us. Perhaps it is a case of getting in touch with ourselves, knowing who we are and how we fit into the world around us. This is a lifetime's work, which in the early years is facilitated by appropriate stimulation, human contact and play.

The meeting of all of these needs by any one individual or agency, is probably an ideal. It may, in fact, be easier to identify situations when these needs are not met, e.g. illness of the child or within the family, poverty, lack of knowledge of how to respond to a child, and outside pressures upon the family. Such situations may lead to difficulties in providing for basic needs where there is a lack of material resources or differences in priorities as carers cope with other issues.

In an ideal world all children would have a high proportion of their needs met. In reality it may be a case of professionals in the form of health visitors, social workers, therapists, educationalists and family-centre personnel work-ing with parents to meet as many needs as possible.

The developmental progress of the child and the meeting of his or her needs are influenced by a host of factors related to health, socio-economic sta-tus of the family, culture, child-rearing practices and disciplinary practices. It is impossible to pick out any one of these as being more significant than the others. Yet, according to Maslow's hierarchy, the contribution of the basic needs for survival must be met first. For that reason, and also because other aspects of childhood development are discussed elsewhere in this text, the rest of this chapter will focus upon nutrition, which is itself influenced by many different factors.

Infant feeding: breast or bottle?

Generations of midwives, health visitors, nursery nurses and mothers have been told that 'breast is best'. While they can outline the advantages of breast-feeding, in practice only 64 per cent of women in 1990 in England and Wales commenced breast-feeding, and breast-feeding at 4 months of age is very much a minority activity, with a prevalence of 25 per cent (White et al., 1992). The knowledge base of mothers and professionals does not always match their emotional response, which is in turn influenced by their own experi-ences, that of women close to them, and the social setting in which they live. Women express their reluctance to breast-feed citing embarrassment, lack of privacy, inconvenience, a desire to return to work, and lack of enthusiasm from family members as reasons. The high number who commence breast-feeding and then cease may reflect pressure from health professions in the antenatal period, but is more likely to demonstrate a lack of support, both practical and emotional, during the early weeks of motherhood. Authors such as Palmer (1988) see the ambivalent attitude towards breast-feeding more caught up with Western societies' perceptions of sexuality, and a male fear of an exclusively female power.

WHY BREAST-FEEDING IS PROMOTED

The anatomy and physiology of lactation is well explained elsewhere (Ben-nett and Brown, 1993; Verrals, 1993) However, it is worth exploring why breast-feeding is promoted. This can be seen in terms of milk composition, anti-infective properties, long-term benefits to both mother and child, and practical advantages to the mother.

COMPOSITION

Essentially, breast milk is seen as an ideal food for infants, ideally balanced for their needs as well as adapting to meet the child's requirements. This adap-tation occurs both over time and within the feed. Colostrum, the substance secreted in the early days, is quite different in content to mature milk. In mature milk the fore milk will satisfy the infant's thirst, while the hind milk contains more fat to satisfy the child.

Table 3.2 shows the difference in composition of cow's and human milk, although of course few children are now offered cow's milk in the early weeks of life.

Cow's milk contains a higher proportion of protein, which increases the risk of solute overload on the immature kidneys. The casein-whey ratio is

Table 3.2 Composition of human milk and cow's milk: compositional guidelines for infant formula and follow-on formula (per 100 ml) (reproduced with permission of HMSO from Department of Health 1994: Weaning and the weaning diet. London: HMSO.

		Mean values for mature human milk[a]	Mean value for whole cow's milk	Infant formula[b]	Follow-on formula[b]
Energy	(kJ)	293	284	250–315	250–335
	(kcal)	70	68	60–75	60–80
Protein	(g)	1.3[c]	3.3	1.2–1.95	1.5–2.9
Carbohydrate	(g)	7	4.9	4.6–9.1	4.6–9.1
Fat	(g)	4.2	4.0	2.1–4.2	2.1–4.2
Vitamins					
A	(µg)(RE)	60	57	39–117	39–117
D	(µg)	0.01	0.03	0.65–1.63	0.65–1.95
E	(mg) and (TE)	0.35	0.09	≥0.33	≥0.3
K	(µg)	0.25	0.6	2.6	ns[e]
Thiamin	(µg)	16	31	265	ns
Riboflavin	(µg)	30	175	39	ns
Niacin	(µg)	620	802	163	ns
equivalent[d]		620	802	163	ns
B_6	(µg)	6	62	22.8	ns
B_{12}	(µg)	0.01	0.4	0.07	ns
Total folate	(µg)	5.0	6	2.6	ns
Pantothenic acid	(µg)	260	361	195	ns
Biotin	(µg)	0.8	2.0	1.0	ns
C	(mg)	3.8	1.0	5.2	5.2
Minerals					
Sodium	(mg)	15	57	13–39	ns
Potassium	(mg)	60	144	39–94	ns
Chloride	(mg)	43	103	32.5–81	ns
Calcium	(mg)	35	119	19.5	ns
Phosphorus	(mg)	15	95	16.3–58.5	ns
Magnesium	(mg)	3	11	3.3–9.8	ns
Iron	(µg)	76	62	325–975	650–1300
Copper	(µg)	39	tr[f]	13–52	ns
Zinc	(µg)	295	412	325–975	325
Iodine	(µg)	7	15	3.3	3.3

[a] Data on nutrition levels in cow's milk provided by MAFF.
[b] EC Directive: the acceptable range (one value only indicates minimum permissible values). Calculated from EC Directive for a product containing 65 kcal/100ml.
[c] True protein = 0.85 g/100 ml (excludes non-protein nitrogen) although a proportion of the non-protein nitrogen is used for the maintenance and growth of infants.
[d] Of this. 720 mg/100ml is derived from trytophan.
[e] ns, not specified.
[f] tr, trace.
D of H 1994.

quite different in the two milks, with a lower proportion of casein in breast milk. Casein curds are more difficult to digest, which means faster gut transit, resulting in less growth of pathological bacteria. The fatty acids in human milk are appropriate for human brain development. In addition, human milk contains vitamins, antibodies, phagocytes and lymphocytes and a multitude of trace elements, hormones and enzymes, some of which have known functions, while the roles of others are unknown.

ANTI-INFECTIVE PROPERTIES

Perhaps the most obvious anti-infective property of breast milk is that it is sterile and is delivered to the infant without any intervening processes, so reducing the chance of bacteria being introduced during a feed. Also important are the contents of breast milk in this respect. Immunoglobulins help to control pathological bacteria in the gut, reducing the prevalence of gastro-enteritis. Macrophages cells that 'gobble up' invading bacteria are active, and antibodies destroy pathogens such as the polio virus. Lacto-ferrin binds to iron, which inhibits the action of *E. coli*, staphylococci and thrush, all causative agents of potentially severe illness. Human milk contains a growth factor for *Lactobacillus bifidus* which colonises the gut with non-pathogenic bacteria, while the breakdown of lactose to lactic acid inhibits the growth of pathogens.

While the nutritional content of breast milk can in part be replicated by the formula manufacturers, the same cannot be said of its anti-infective properties. The breast-fed child is likely to have less gastro-enteritis and nappy rash. In the western world this can generally be rectified by medication and health care, whereas in a developing country the choice between breast-feeding and bottle-feeding may be a question of life or death (see Chapter 13 for further discussion).

LONG-TERM BENEFITS

Various long-term benefits have been claimed for breast-feeding, some of which have not stood the test of time. It seems probable that the breast-fed child is less likely to be over fed, as the infant has more control of intake. To say that the breast-fed infant cannot become an obese child is an over-generalisation, although the child may have a different pattern of weight gain to his or her bottle-fed peer, gaining a significant amount of weight in the early months. Until recently, centile charts have been based on a predominantly bottle-fed population of infants, and may not reflect the growth patterns of the breast-fed child. The breast-fed infant has been said to show fewer allergic responses (Saarinen and Kajosaari, 1995), particularly if breast-fed exclusively. Other benefits may include a higher IQ, less chance of sudden infant death, and less coronary heart disease in later life (Minchin, 1985). The mother of the breast-fed child seems to be less at risk of carcinoma of the breast (UK National Case Control Study Group, 1993). All of these statements are of course subject to the interaction of other factors.

ADVANTAGES TO THE MOTHER

The advantage of breast-feeding most frequently cited by mothers is economic. With infant formula costing more than £3.50 for a 450 gram tin, breast-feeding must be cheaper, and unless the mother's diet is extremely deficient, expensive supplements are not necessary. Some women find breast-feeding convenient, as it removes the chore of sterilising and making up bottles with the milk always ready to feed. Breast-feeding holds out the hope of facilitating the return to a pre-pregnant figure, as fat deposits are utilised, and in the early days it aids the involution of the uterus. Changed hormone levels during lactation reduce fertility – a significant factor in birth control world-wide (Palmer, 1988). However, the limits western women place, or are made to place, on their breast-feeding make it a less than efficient form of contraception for them. Many women feel that breast-feeding gives them a sense of psychological satisfaction – in that they are doing something only they can do for their child – and it thus strengthens the relationship or bond between mother and child. It may even be that breast-feeding has emotional benefits for the child.

CURRENT BREAST-FEEDING SITUATION

With so much to commend breast-feeding it may be surprising that more women do not choose to feed their children in this way. *Infant Feeding 1990* (White *et al.*, 1992) demonstrates that the incidence of breast-feeding in England and Wales rose from 51 per cent in 1975 to 67 per cent in 1980, and then levelled out at 65 per cent and 64 per cent in 1985 and 1990, respectively. The incidence of breast-feeding showed regional differences, with an incidence of 74 per cent in London and the South East and an incidence of 50 per cent in the North, the incidence being even lower in Scotland and Northern Ireland. Commencement of lactation was found to be strongly correlated with social class (as defined by last occupation of husband or partner). Of those from social class I, 87 per cent commenced breast-feeding as compared to 42 per cent of mothers from social class V. Those who reported having no partner showed only a 45 per cent incidence of breast-feeding . The prevalence of breast-feeding over time has been commented upon, with 39 per cent of all mothers breast-feeding their children at 6 weeks, 21 per cent at 6 months and 12 per cent at 9 months. Government publications advocate the continuing of breast-feeding until at least 4 months (Department of Health, 1994), so clearly there is much room for improvement.

Links were also found between birth order, with fewer women feeding subsequent children. Age of completing full-term education was also significant with earlier cessation of schooling linked with a lower incidence of breast-feeding. The mother's age also affected the mode of feeding, with younger mothers being less likely to breast-feed. Whether a mother was in paid employment made little difference when the results were controlled for class (White *et al.*, 1992).

The prevalence of breast-feeding in the UK has changed very little since 1985. The significant minority of women who choose not to breast-feed, making their decision early in pregnancy, and the number of women who choose to breast-feed but cease before 8 weeks raises questions for health professionals. The situation varies considerably around the world – for many children, to be breast-fed means a much higher chance of reaching 5 years of age. That is not necessarily so in western countries, and the twentieth century has seen a decline in lactation in the UK and the USA. However, New Zealand has seen an increase in its incidence of breast-feeding over the last 20 years, and over 90 per cent of mothers now initiate breast-feeding. Regional and socio-economic and ethnic differences exist within New Zealand, but 89 per cent of mothers with less than 11 years of schooling commence breast-feeding (Alison, 1992). There is a fall-off in feeding, particularly in the first week of life, but by 8 weeks only 15 per cent of those who commenced it have ceased breast-feeding. Compared to the UK situation these are impressive statistics. Why such international differences exist, particularly between cultures that share some common features, is unknown. The increased education of the population, the activities of Plunket nurses, the long-term influence of Truby King and the work of La Leche league may have been instrumental in achieving this situation, but these factors in general have parallels in the UK where they have not had the same marked influence.

Women's lack of enthusiasm for breast-feeding has been mentioned, with the most commonly cited reasons for ceasing to breast-feed being sore nipples and insufficient milk. The booklet by the Royal College of Midwives (1988) entitled *Successful Breast-Feeding – a Practical Guide for Midwives* explains ways in which these and other difficulties can be addressed. Perhaps the activities and procedures carried out by health care professionals are not conducive to breast-feeding. Care-givers have not always followed optimum practice, separating mother and baby on the first night and giving infants water or formula (Beeken and Waterston, 1992). Making hospitals more 'baby friendly' by changing attitudes to breast-feeding, altering practices and co-operating with voluntary groups such as the National Childbirth Trust and La Leche League would certainly help (Waterston and Davies, 1993). Important as these are, changes would also seem to be desirable in wider society. Leach (1994) points out that, while not encouraging breast-feeding, modern western society does not value children, and its structures need to change in order to support family life and value those who care for young children.

WAYS OF ENSURING THAT THE BOTTLE-FED CHILD DOES AS WELL

The reader is likely to have identified a bias in the author's enthusiasm for breast-feeding. Two breast-fed infants and 15 years of extolling the value of breast-feeding have left their mark. However, all women will not share this stance, and early years professionals must be able to provide information and support for these mothers without heaping on the guilt. If the new mother is not going to breast-feed, for whatever reason, how then does she proceed? She can rely on her professional advisers, who may themselves be influenced by manufacturers' advertisements, or she can consider the array of formula milks available in any chemist or supermarket. Few if any neonates would commence on cow's milk. It is are now recommended that children do not to begin to take cow's milk until 1 year of age, when they should be given whole milk for its calcium and vitamin content (Department of Health, 1994). Of the formula milks, it is recommended that the newborn should be given a whey-based modified milk. Such formulae consist of cow's milk which has been modified to change the whey-casein ratio, alter the amino acid content, raise the carbohydrate levels, remove butterfat, replacing it with vegetable fat, and change the ratio of saturated to unsaturated fats. The aim is to mimic breast milk as closely as possible, and as new discoveries about the contents of breast milk are made, one can see the baby milk manufacturers competing to be first to include the newly discovered element in their product. Vitamin levels in formula milk need to be higher to allow for less efficient absorption. All infant formulae have to meet European Union Directives.

Most manufacturers market a 'second-stage' milk aimed at hungry babies. These tend to be less modified and to be casein dominant. Taitz and Scholey (1989) doubt that these second-stage milks are necessary, and suggest that they are no more efficient for settling a hungry baby. The introduction of such milks appears to have no effect on the delaying of weaning.

'Follow-on' milks are marketed for infants aged 6 months and older. These are fortified with iron and can be given as a drink. A continuing debate exists as to whether these milks are necessary. There seems to be no reason why children should not continue with their existing formula, but it is suggested that the introduction of a new product delays the transition to cow's milk.

Occasionally, mothers wish to use soya milk or goat's milk. Ideally, soya should be used in the case of proven sensitivity to cow's milk. In the early months an infant formula soya milk should be used. The nutritional balance of goat's milk is unsuitable for infants, and if used for older children it needs to be boiled or pasteurised.

The initial choice of milk comes down to the one most similar to breast milk, which will be a whey-based formula. The writer is reluctant to itemise such milks, agreeing with the Food Manufacturers' Federation (1983) Code of Practice and the World Health Organisation (1981) Code of Practice that they should not be advertised. However, a trip to any supermarket will readily identify the variety of available formulae.

Formula milks can only mimic the nutritional content of breast milk if they are made up according to the manufacturer's instructions. Over-concentration of feed risks over loading the immature kidney, while under-concentration leads to undernourishment of the child. Feeding should be baby led, but an approximate rule of thumb is 150–200 ml per kilogram of baby's body weight per day spread over 5–6 feeds.

With regards to the anti-infective properties of the milk, it has been suggested that all babies should be given colostrum whatever the feeding intention of the mother. High-quality hygiene procedures are vital, and feeding equipment needs to be sterilised by boiling, chemical methods or steam. Clean procedures during feed preparation and the disposal of unused made-up feeds are essential.

Much has been made of the emotional benefits of breast-feeding, but these can be replicated by a calm approach to bottle-feeding with the infant held close. Of course, others can share in this time, and this can be seen as one of the significant benefits of bottle-feeding.

MONITORING OF THE CHILD'S PHYSICAL WELL-BEING

Whether the child is breast or bottle fed, how then does the parent or carer know that he or she is progressing well in terms of physical growth? Observation will show that the child looks well, is alert and interested in his or her surroundings in a way appropriate to his or her stage of development, and the small infant will sleep between some of the feeds. Weight is only one aspect of well-being, but appropriate growth can be monitored on the centile chart (see page 51). The British are said to be obsessed with bowels, but the consistency of the infant stool is another aspect of well-being. The stool of the breast-fed child is soft and bright yellow, with the consistency of scrambled egg! Almost any frequency of passing such stools can be seen as normal. The bottle-fed child has a firmer stool (the consistency of toothpaste) which is yellow/green and more odourous. This type of stool is likely to be passed more regularly. All of these aspects of well-being need to considered together.

Weaning and the weaning diet

WHY AND WHEN TO WEAN

The majority of infants should not be given solid food until they are 4 months old, and should be offered a mixed diet by the age of 6 months (Department of Health, 1994). The growth velocity of children in the first 6 months is high, and they generally double their birth weight by 5 months. Breast milk or its substitute can provide the required nutrients for such growth during the first 4 months, but by 6 months the amounts of protein, energy and vitamins A and D are unlikely to be sufficient (Department of Health, 1994). Prior to 3 months, an infant cannot easily swallow a bolus of solid food. From approximately 5 months infants hold objects and direct them to their mouths, commencing chewing by about 6 months. The development of chewing also seems to be significant in relation to the acquisition of speech. Infants who are not given the opportunity to try solids seem reluctant to accept them if they are introduced at a later stage. Significant to the carer, weaning marks a step towards family food, and is often seen as a developmental milestone in its own right.

The commencement of weaning prior to 3 months is discouraged because of the immature nature of the gut. Enzyme production changes over time, becoming increasingly more efficient at digestion. Prior to 3 months, the gut wall appears to be fairly permeable, allowing the crossing of protein molecules, which seems to increase sensitivity to foreign protein.

Iron deficiency is a recurring theme in pre-school nutrition. By 6 months, the amount of iron contributed by breast milk in insufficient, and other dietary sources are necessary (Department of Health, 1994). The reasons for weaning are therefore social, developmental and physiological.

WEANING FOODS

A variety of foods can be and have been used for weaning, with different cultures having varying traditions. The first food should be smooth, perhaps mixed with the infant's usual milk. Non-wheat cereals, puréed fruit, vegetables and potatoes are regarded as suitable (Department of Health, 1994). Salt should be omitted because of the immaturity of the infant kidney, and added sugars should be avoided in order to prevent the development of a 'sweet tooth'. Egg yolk, once used as a weaning food, is discouraged because of the risk of salmonella. The food should be offered at a time when the child is not voraciously hungry, nor should it be offered when the child is full. The smooth food is placed just inside the child's mouth so that it can be sucked off the spoon. Milk will continue to provide the child's main nutritional needs.

Once the child accepts both the spoon and the new consistency, different tastes can be introduced and the quantities increased. New foods should initially be offered one at a time in order to identify preferences and adverse reactions. Home-prepared food can be used from the beginning, but commercially prepared foods are often used when very small quantities are involved. Carers need to be aware of the contents of such foods, and to read the labels carefully. Home-prepared foods should be offered to give the child a wide variety of tastes and textures, moving the child to the point where he or she shares family foods and meal times. Food hygiene remains important with partly eaten food being discarded and prepared foods covered and refrigerated.

Over a 5- to 6-week period the quantity and frequency of solid food offered can be increased, and this will take place at different speeds for different children Over time, solid foods contribute more nutritional value to the infant's diet, and when the child is having three meals a day milk intake can be reduced. Milk should constitute the majority of the child's drinks, avoiding sugar-laden drinks which contribute to dental caries, particularly if given by bottle.

At around 6 months (although this varies from child to child), soft lumps in the form of mashed bananas or coarsely puréed meats can be managed. Salt and sugar should still be omitted.

By 8 to 9 months the child can chew, coping with finger foods such as toast and fruit. Children can easily choke up to and beyond 2 years of age, and should be supervised by a carer who knows what action to take if this occurs. By the end of the first year, most children are able to cope with the family diet. If this is not suitable for the child, it may be unsuitable for the rest of the family. The social value of mealtimes needs to be borne in mind, as babies and especially toddlers love to imitate, appearing to eat better if in the company of others.

CULTURAL AND ECONOMIC FACTORS INFLUENCING WEANING

Kin groups are a powerful influence on new parents. Families may live in small units, but contact is sustained with mothers and mothers-in-law, and at a time of change, such as the arrival of a new infant, their influence may be significant. By offering practical help and emotional support, they may be providing information on traditional or out-of-date weaning practices.

Professionals in the form of health visitors, chemists and doctors provide information that is valued by many, but the apparent changes in dietary advice over the last few decades have left some parents confused and disillusioned.

Health workers have tried to disassociate themselves from the manufacturers and their sponsorship, with varying degrees of success. The sponsorship of professional conferences and the provision of small gifts leaves professionals open to undue bias and influence. The 'bounty bag and box' distributed via maternity units gives the impression that weaning foods and other baby products are backed by professionals. While infant milks are no longer advertised directly to mothers, it may be that manufacturers can access parents via their professional advisers.

Religious practices and the families' own eating practices are also significant. A vegetarian family will not offer a child meat, and certain foods may be unacceptable for particular groups. It is important to discuss with the family what is significant to them, and to remember that culture changes over time, and some will observe religious practices more than others.

The economic status of the family is important in both weaning and the feeding of pre-school children. Home-produced food may be cheaper if the rest of the family is eating food appropriate for the infant. If the mother feels that family food is unsuitable, buying a jar may be preferable in her eyes, especially if she knows that the infant will eat it and the packaging claims that the contents provide a balanced meal. The time involved in preparation and the lack of confidence that she can produce a baby meal as nutritious as that provided by a manufacturer may all be part of her decision-making process. Blackburn (1991) argues that parents living in poverty largely know what is considered to be good for their children's health in terms of nutrition, but are frustrated that they cannot meet their own goals. They may be more inclined to follow short-term goals, e.g. adding cereals to the bottle in order to quieten a fractious child and so maintain family harmony, rather than following the professionals long-term goals of promoting speech development and a healthy diet.

In many cultures food is caught up with love and nurturing, and the carer feels that she is doing the right thing if the child accepts the food happily. That in itself may influence the types of foods a child is given.

WEANING: WHAT REALLY HAPPENS?

Having outlined government recommendations and factors that may influence weaning, it is worth looking at what really happens. Mills and Taylor (1992) studied 488 infants who were 6 to 12 months old, and found that 16 per cent had commenced solids by 8 weeks and 50 per cent by 12 weeks. The foods given were usually cereals, rusks or commercial foods. Commercial foods were important in the diets of the 6- to 9-month-olds, but less so in the diet of the 9- to 12-month-olds. Commercial foods were a major source of the children's iron intake, and of those that ate no commercial feeds, only 62 per cent had of the recommended nutritional intake. Not surprisingly, those with siblings were more likely to eat family foods.

Cow's milk was consumed by two-thirds of the infants, in contrast to government recommendations. Non-milk sugars were obtained from fruit drinks, raising the question of their necessity, especially as the average vitamin C intake, often given as a reason for consuming fruit drinks, was four times the recommended nutritional intake.

By 9–12 months, 50 per cent of the children had chocolate (albeit in small amounts), and a third had eaten crisps – again in contrast to recommendations to omit salt.

Mills and Taylor (1992) concluded that the diets were, on average, nutritionally adequate, although possibly short of zinc, iron and vitamin D. Clearly parents do not do everything according to Department of Health recommendations!

Feeding the pre-school child

As the child moves on to family food it may seem that recommendations for adult diet become relevant. Certainly the Health of the Nation (Department of Health, 1992) targets to reduce obesity in the adult population and to reduce the food energy derived from fat need to be borne in mind. Recommendations aimed at the adult population need to be modified for the child. High-fibre, low-fat diets are not suitable for toddlers, who have a higher metabolic rate than adults and higher energy requirements per unit body mass. In addition, children's higher body surface area means they lose more body heat. Attention needs to be paid to calorific intake, ensuring that the child has sufficient energy intake. The child who consistently fails to ingest sufficient calories, for whatever reason, will fail to thrive. Fat, particularly from whole milk, is an important source of calories. Although fibre in the form of fruit, vegetables and whole grains needs to be encouraged, care needs to be taken that the diet is not so bulky that the child is unable to obtain sufficient calories.

Iron deficiency is the most commonly reported nutritional disorder in early childhood (Department of Health, 1994). Although widespread among children in the UK, it is particularly common in families with low income, those of Asian origin and vegetarians. Iron deficiency is exacerbated by children's dislike of or reluctance to chew meat. Children so affected are likely to be apathetic, with reduced exercise capacity and possible psychomotor delay. However, some appear happy and healthy and remain undiagnosed (Department of Health, 1994). Iron can be supplied through meat and well-cooked eggs. The iron intake of the vegetarian can be increased by eating green leafy vegetables, grains and legumes, and the uptake of iron can be enhanced by eating foods rich in vitamin C, such as oranges and kiwi fruit.

Vitamin D deficiency leads to rickets, a deficiency disease that affects the bones, with most cases being found in the Asian community. The number of cases has decreased in recent years, although children on a strict vegan diet or from Rastafarian families are also recognised as being at risk (Department of Health, 1994). Vitamin D is synthesised by the skin from sunlight, which may explain why communities from the Indian subcontinent are more at risk in the less sunny UK. Vitamin D can be obtained from commercially manufactured formula and follow-on milks. It is present in fatty fish such as sardines and herrings. These may not be acceptable to some families or palatable to many children. Eggs provide a minor source, and vitamin D is added to many margarines and spreads. Vitamin supplements including vitamin D are recommended from 1 to 5 years of age (Department of Health, 1994) These are not necessary if the child is breast-fed or drinking formula or follow-on milk.

As with the weaning diet, the diet of the pre-school child is subject to many influences. The toddler has a small appetite, but his growth velocity is slowing down so he may need little more than he did as a 1-year-old . The small size of his stomach means that he needs small frequent meals but snacking, particularly on sugar-laden foods, should be avoided. Food refusal and definite food preferences are common, and are often used as a way of asserting personality. Clashes of will with the parent need to be separated from meal times where possible, with a calm approach being taken. Outside influences begin to bear directly on the child, e.g. television advertising is increasingly difficult to withstand, but imitation of sound role models can be encouraged.

The diet of the family remains highly significant, with the child's diet being based on the cultural and religious norms of the family. The desire to do the 'right thing' by young children may be an opportunity to 'upgrade' the nutrition of the whole family, increasing the quantity of fruit, vegetables and whole grains, as well as decreasing the amount of refined carbohydrates and salt in the diet.

Vegetarians may be seen to be at risk of poor nutrition, but well-informed vegetarians are likely to have a well-balanced diet. Early years workers need to establish the type of vegetarian diet that is to be adhered to.

Vegetarians can be classified as follows:

- broad vegetarian – avoids all meat and poultry, but may eat fish, shellfish and dairy products. May or may not eat foods containing animal products such as gelatine and rennet;
- lacto-ovo vegetarian – excludes all meat, fish and poultry, but milk products and eggs are eaten;
- lacto-vegetarian – as lacto-ovo vegetarian, but eggs are excluded.
- vegan – neither eats nor uses anything of animal origin.

Dependent upon the type of vegetarian diet followed, there may be difficulty in obtaining sufficient vitamin B_{12}, which can be given in a supplement, fortified soya milks or spreads. To ensure an adequate supply of amino acids to build protein, a mixture of vegetable proteins, beans, nut and grains needs to be eaten each day. Vegetarian children will not have access to haem iron, but iron can be obtained from peas, beans, lentils and wholemeal grains, with vitamin C improving uptake. Calcium intake can be a problem for those who do not consume milk, but can be found in fortified soya milk, sesame seeds and some nuts.

Poverty is probably a more significant factor in limited pre-school nutrition. Families on low incomes are likely to eat only small amounts of fruit and vegetables, white bread rather than wholemeal bread, cheaper fatty meats rather than lean meats, and food that is fried and has a higher content of sugar and preservatives (National Children's Home, 1991). These foods are eaten because they are usually cheaper and their familiarity means that they are less likely to be wasted. The very familiarity means that the eating habits of one generation form the basis of the eating habits of the next. However, these foods are contrary to virtually all dietary recommendations of recent years.

We do know that parents appreciate what they should be doing (Blackburn, 1991). When parents were asked 'If you had an extra £10 to spend on food for your children, what foods would you like to buy?', the majority of 350 respondents in the National Children's Home (1991) survey said that they would buy fresh meat and poultry (60 per cent), fruit (54 per cent) and vegetables (38 per cent). Only a minority said that they would buy 'unhealthy' luxuries such as cakes, biscuits and ice-cream. Parents in the same survey had often gone hungry in order to feed their children. Exhortations to use cheap markets and budget carefully are thwarted by poor transport, the lack of inclination of those caught up in long-term poverty, a general lack of choice in life, and the knowledge that the children must eat something, even if it is unhealthy.

The preceding discussion has demonstrated that feeding children the 'right' diet can become a complex issue. In summary, children should be offered foods from each of the following four main food groups:

- starch foods, such as potatoes, bread and rice;
- protein foods, such as meat, fish and pulses;
- fatty foods, such as milk, cheese and eggs;
- fruit and vegetables.

Foods with a high sugar content should be taken in small amounts, and hidden fats in fried and commercially prepared foods should be kept to a minimum. Attention also needs to be paid to the possibility of iron deficiency.

Children in the UK are rarely malnourished, but it seems that many are suffering from sub-nutrition. These are likely to be children who are already disadvantaged in other ways. With poorer nutrition than some of their peers, it may be that they are less likely to benefit from care and education programmes to which they have access.

Schoolchildren's diet and beyond

A survey of 300 schoolchildren (Department of Health and Social Security, 1989) who were 10 or 11 year olds and 14 or 15 years old demonstrated that the diet of schoolchildren gives cause for concern and becomes more worrying as the child becomes older. This study considered children beyond the early years, showing that for the 10- to 11-year-olds the main sources of energy in the child's diet were bread, chips, milk, biscuits, meat products, cakes and puddings. More than a 25 per cent of these children were obtaining more than 40 per cent of their energy intake from fat – this at a time when official guidelines are suggesting that fat should constitute a maximum of 35 per cent of the energy intake. While fat intake was higher than recommended, the consumption of fresh fruit and vegetables was less than that recommended.

The parents of children under 8 years of age may retain more control over their children's diet, but their own eating habits may not be ideal. It has been thought for many years that habits started early in life are carried on into adulthood. Epidemiological studies have identified nutritional factors in fetal and infant life that appear to be linked to adult health (Barker, 1992). If this is so, diet becomes all the more significant, affecting not only the early childhood years but the individual's entire life.

CONCLUSION

The monitoring of growth and development is a crucial part of the work of many early years professionals, but it needs to be done sensitively and without rigidity.

Optimum growth and development are dependent upon a variety of components that may be viewed as a hierarchy of need, with the most basic needs requiring to be met before those of a higher order. The meeting of a basic survival need of nutrition, which initially seems simple and concrete, is itself influenced by a variety of social, economic and physiological factors.

References

Alison, L. (1992): Breast Feeding Trends in New Zealand. *Plunket Nursing Newsline,* September issue.

Barker D.J.P. (ed.) (1992): *The Fetal Origins of Ill Health.* London: BMJ Publications.

Bax, M., Hart, H. and Jenkins, S. (1990): *Child Health and Child Development.* Oxford: Blackwell Scientific Publications.

Beeken, S. and Waterston , T. (1992): Health Service Support of Breast Feeding – are we Practising What we Preach? *British Medical Journal* **305**, 285–7.

Bennett, V.R. and Brown L.K. (1993): *Myles Textbook for Midwives,* 12th edn. Edinburgh: Churchill Livingstone.

Blackburn, C. (1991): *Poverty and Health.* Buckingham: Open University Press.

Department of Health (1992): *The Health of the Nation. A Strategy for Health in England.* London. HMSO.

Department of Health (1994): *Weaning and the Weaning Diet.* London: HMSO.

Department of Health and Social Security (1989): *The Diets of British Schoolchildren.* London: HMSO.

Food Manufacturers' Federation (1983): *Code of Practice for Marketing Infant Formula in the UK and Schedule for a Code Monitoring Committee.* London: Food Manufacturers' Federation.

Frankenburg, W.K. and Dodds, J.B. (1967): Denver Developmental Screening Test. *Journal of Paediatrics* **71**, 181–191.

Fry, T. (1993): Charting Growth: Developments in the Assessment and Measurement of Child Growth. *Child Health* **1**, 104–09.

Hall, D.B.M. (1996): *Health for all Children,* 3rd edn. Oxford: Oxford University Press.

Leach, P. (1994): *Children First.* Harmondsworth: Penguin.

Maslow, A.H. (1970): *Motivation and Personality.* 2nd edn. New York: Harper and Row.

Mills, A. and Taylor, H. (1992): *Food and Nutritional Intakes of British Infants 6–12 Months.* London: Ministry of Agriculture, Food and Fisheries.

Minchin. M. (1985): *Breastfeeding Matters.* Victoria, Australia: Alma Publications.

Moreton, J. and Macfarlane, A. (1991): *Child Health and Surveillance,* 2nd edn. Oxford: Blackwell Scientific Publications.

National Children's Home (1991): *Poverty and Nutrition Survey.* London: National Children's Home.

Nettleton, S. and Bunton, R. (1995): Sociological Critiques of Health Promotion in Bunton, R., Nettleton, S. and Burrows, R. (eds), *The Sociology of Health Promotion.* London: Routledge, 41–59.

Palmer, G. (1988): *The Politics of Breast Feeding.* London: Pandora Press.

Royal College of Midwives (1988): *Successful Breastfeeding – a Practical Guide for Midwives.* Oxford: Hollywell Press.

Saarinen, U.M. and Kajosaari, M. (1995): Breast Feeding as a Prophylaxis Against Atopic Disease: Prospective Follow-up Study until 17 Years Old. *Lancet* **346**, 1065–1069.

Sheridan, M. (1975): *Birth to Five: Children's Developmental Progress*. Windsor: NFER-Nelson.

Taitz, L.S. and Scholey, E. (1989): Are Babies more Satisfied by Casein-based Feeds? *Archives of Disease in Childhood* **64**, 619–621.

Thomas, E. (1993): Accidents in Childhood in Glasper, E.A. and Tucker, A. (eds) *Advances in Child Health Nursing*. London: Scutari, 53–64.

UK National Case Control Study Group (1993): Breast Feeding and Risk of Breast Cancer in Young Women. *British Medical Journal* **307**, 17–20.

Verrals, S. (1993): *Anatomy and Physiology Applied to Obstetrics*, 3rd edn. Edinburgh: Churchill Livingstone.

Waterston, T. and Davies, J. (1993): Could Hospitals do more to Encourage Breast-feeding? *British Medical Journal* **307**, 1437–1438.

White, A., Freeth, S. and O'Brien, M. (1992): *Infant Feeding 1990*. London: HMSO.

World Health Organisation (1981): *International Code of Marketing of Breast Milk Substitute*. Geneva: World Health Organisation.

Further Reading

Department of Health and Social Security (1988): *Present Day Practice in Infant Feeding*. London: HMSO.

Department of Health (1994): *Weaning and the Weaning Diet*. London: HMSO.

Fry, T. (1993): Charting Growth: Developments in the Assessment and Measurement of Child Growth. *Child Health* **1**, 104-09.

Hall, D.M.B. (1996): *Health for all Children*, 3rd edn. Oxford: Oxford University Press.

Sheridan, M. (1975): *Birth to Five: Children's Developmental Progress*. Windsor: NFER-Nelson.

Thomas, E. (1993): Accidents in Childhood. In Glasper, E.A. and Tucker A. (eds) *Advances in Child Health Nursing*. London: Scutari. 53–64.

4 Personal, social and affective development

Carolyn Silberfeld and Clare Robinson

> This chapter aims to consider the personal, social and affective development of young children.

Introduction

> *It is the nightly custom of every good mother after her children are asleep to rummage in their minds and put things straight for next morning, repacking into their proper places the many articles that have wandered during the day.*
>
> (Barrie, 1988, p.11)

When Mrs Darling was travelling through her children's minds, she often found things that she could not understand. Her perceptual world, being different from that of her children, meant that she was unable to recognise their interpretations of the day's adventures. Children compartmentalise their explorations, meetings and ponderings into their own 'proper places' which flourish through their experiences. Their perceptual world will alter as they develop personally, socially and affectively – important, if often neglected, aspects of children's holistic development.

In the foreword to *Understanding Children* by Grieve and Hughes (1990), Bruner suggests that as children mature they get to know themselves and others through an accumulation of interactions, responding to the world according to their existing situation. Each child needs to progress through a series of major transitional points which have been described by Schaffer (1989) as all-encompassing or, in contrast, by Fischer (1980) as developing concurrently. These transitional points manifest progressively as the child matures (Schaffer, 1984).

When looking at children's social behaviour, it may be helpful to consider the developmental pattern put forward by Schaffer (1984), who proposed that there are five stages within the first 2 years of life. According to Schaffer (1989, p.7) these are:

- the immediate post-birth period;
- from 2 months onward;
- from 5 months onward;

- from 8 months onward;
- from the middle of the second year.

Schaffer's five categories will serve as a framework to describe these sequential stages of development in more detail.

During the immediate post-birth period a pattern of care is established and several competencies are evident. These include involuntary reflexes, and perceptual, motor and social skills. Involuntary reflexes such as rooting and sucking are essential for feeding. Smelling, tasting and touching are the perceptual skills which help the baby to discriminate his or her immediate environment. Motor skills are mainly restricted to limb and head movements due to undeveloped muscle tone. Although immature, the baby's social skills, even at this very early age, are sufficient for social interaction. A cry will attract attention, and a smile or vocalisation, from about 4–6 weeks, will ensure that attention is maintained (Figure 4.1).

From 2 months onward the baby begins to derive amusement from his or her surroundings, as is indicated by increasing smiles and vocalisation. Feeding becomes a tremendous source of emotional, as well as physical nourishment, and the baby begins to focus on familiar people, especially the mother, and will visually follow the adult. The baby enjoys company and familiar situations, and may smile when realising that bathtime or a feed is imminent.

From 5 months onward, when playing with a familiar adult the baby shows enjoyment by smiling and laughing. Excitement in anticipation of this interaction is often demonstrated. The first signs of shyness in the presence of an unfamiliar adult may be apparent, particularly if the parents are absent. Increasingly, social interaction is centred around the use of objects which the infant may be reluctant to relinquish, often putting them to his or her mouth.

From 8 months onward the child can differentiate between a stranger and a familiar person, and signs of shyness are obvious. Negative emotions can be clearly expressed, such as vocal displeasure if an attempt is made to disrupt play by removal of a toy. During mealtimes, the infant demonstrates a desire to self-feed by trying to hold his or her spoon or cup.

Social relationships may be initiated through play, e.g. passing a toy to a friendly adult. There is a fascination with the reflection of the child in a mirror. However, this is the reciprocal exchange with another friendly face, rather than self-recognition. These social skills continue to develop as the child matures and begins to be more active in his or her own care, e.g. helping to dress and feed him or herself. This is a tremendously inquisitive phase, yet there is little awareness of personal danger. Increasing mobility allows for exploration and discovery of the child's own intentions.

From the middle of the second year the desire for independence becomes apparent. Children become more socially adept and begin to manage increasing amounts of their own care. Needs are expressed through the use of gestures and verbalisation. Play often involves the imitation of everyday activities performed by others, such as household chores and social events

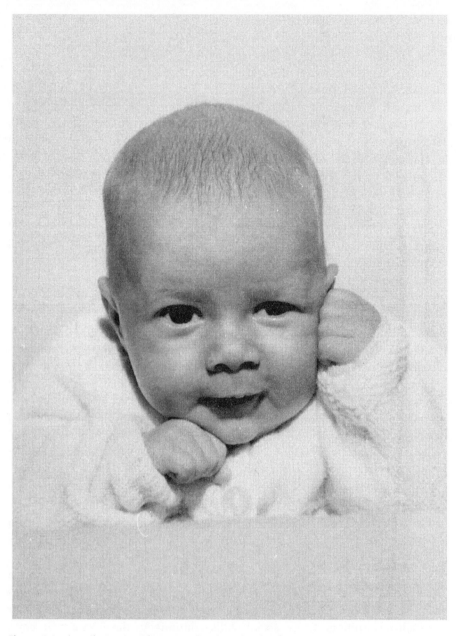

Figure 4.1   A smile ensures that attention is maintained.

(Figure 4.2). A growing self-awareness enables toddlers to reflect more on their own behaviour and that of other people, which in turn helps them to become more socially accomplished.

Chapter 9 discusses how children learn and develop through the process that Piaget termed adaptation (Sutherland, 1992). This involves the assimilation and accommodation of new information through which children consolidate their accomplishments, and from which new understanding and action

Figure 4.2   Play often involves imitation of everyday activities, e.g. household chores and social events.

evolve. The journey through Schaffer's five stages must incorporate personal and affective development, as well as social development.

Personal concepts develop through relationships with self, family and other socialising agents (Dunn, 1988). Self-concept and self-esteem require recognition of the similarities and differences between individuals. This contrast stimulates a deeper and more complex personal understanding.

Social development will depend upon the setting, situation and surroundings that children encounter. They play an active role within these contexts, affecting as well as acquiring meaning. Appropriate displays of emotional behaviour require not only overt acts, such as a smile, but also the associated feelings. Affective development requires emotional and intellectual understanding.

Kipling (1987, p.42) acknowledged that understanding is achieved by asking 'What and why and when and how and where and who?'. Although often infuriating to adults, this common series of interrogatives is used by children to help them make sense of their world. We shall therefore follow the above sequence in order to enable us to explore how children develop personally, socially and affectively.

What affects perceptual development ?

She also said she would give him a kiss if he liked, but Peter did not know what she meant, and he held out his hand expectantly.

'Surely you know what a kiss is?' she said, aghast. 'I shall know when you give it to me,' he replied stiffly, and not to hurt his feelings she gave him a thimble.

'Now, ' said he, 'shall I give you a kiss ?', and she replied with a slight primness, 'if you please.' She made herself rather cheap by inclining her face towards him, but he merely dropped an acorn button into her hand.

(Barrie, 1988, p.29)

Peter was expecting the 'give' to be the transference of an object, whereas Wendy was referring to a symbolic action. For Peter, any object suitable for holding in the hand could be called a 'kiss'. His lack of experience prevented him from understanding Wendy's more mature use of a symbol to represent her feelings of the moment. Peter has a literal interpretation of Wendy's abstract action. Her level of thinking develops through experience, and has been described by Oates' (1994, p.70) as an 'information–acquisition system' – the interpretation of the knowledge to which one is exposed.

This illustrates the complexity of the 'nature versus nurture' debate introduced in Chapter 1; it is also known as nativism versus empiricism, with regard to perceptual development. Nativists, would claim that children are born with certain skills that develop as they get older. This is in contrast to the empiricist view that a baby is a *'tabula rasa'* – a blank slate – on which the child's ability to perceive develops through experience. However, children of the same age are not necessarily at the same developmental stage, and do not necessarily have similar experiences. These are often dependent on the cultural, socio-economic and environmental situations that the child encounters. Therefore it can be seen that perceptual development is affected by a complexity of external factors which are not necessarily dependent upon the way in which the child has acquired certain skills.

When does thinking become more abstract?

Of course the Neverlands vary a good deal. John's, for instance, had a lagoon with flamingoes flying over it at which John was shooting, while Michael, who was very small, had a flamingo with lagoons flying over it. John lived in a boat turned upside down on the sands, Michael in a wigwam, Wendy in a house of leaves deftly sewn together. John had no friends, Michael had friends at night, Wendy had a pet wolf forsaken by its parents; . . . On these magic shores children at play are for ever beaching their coracles. We too have been there; we can still hear the sound of the surf, although we shall land no more.

(Barrie, 1988, p.12)

The children's explanation of the 'Neverlands' may be related to Piaget's (1929) stages of intellectual development. In Chapter 9 these stages are referred to as they relate to children's learning; they are sensori-motor (0–2 years), pre-operational (2–7 years), concrete operational (7–12 years) and formal operational (from 12 years of age). During the sensori-motor period children understand the world in terms of their senses and motor actions. A child's knowledge of an object is interpreted through its taste, feel, smell, sound and look. By the time the child has reached the pre-operational stage, experiences are being internally represented. Once an object has been correctly identified with a particular word, the child may apply this word to similar objects. For example, all animals with four legs may be called dogs. However, physical exploration, is still dominant at this stage.

Sutherland (1992) suggests that as a child's pre-conceptual understanding develops, cognitive activity is demonstrated verbally rather than physically. More reasons are given for their actions. However, because of immaturity, their conceptual understanding of certain adult concepts is flawed. Each of the children offers their own explanation of suitable living accommodation on the island by drawing from their imaginary worlds. Michael is in the pre-operational stage, as he does not consider the reality of obtaining a wigwam – it just exists. John, on the other hand, in the concrete operational stage, would need to have a suitable object that he could use as a house. Wendy, having reached the formal operational stage, can deal with ideas at the same time as events or objects, being able to imagine the construction of a house made from leaves, even though this is not within her own experience. The children's interpretations of friendship reflect their needs at these specific stages of development. John thinks he has no need of friends, Michael needs friends at night because he is afraid of the dark, and Wendy enjoys friendship which enables her to take on a mothering role.

According to Piaget (1929), a child moves through the stages of intellectual development sequentially. The rate at which this occurs depends upon the ability that the individual child has to assimilate and accommodate external stimuli.

Why do children play the games they do?

'O Wendy lady be our mother.'
'Ought I?' Wendy said, all shining. 'Of course it's frightfully fascinating, but you see I am only a little girl. I have no real experience.'
'That doesn't matter,' said Peter, . . . 'What we need is just a nice motherly person.'
'Oh dear!' Wendy said, 'you see that is exactly what I am.'
'It is, it is,' they all cried; 'we saw it at once.'
'Very well,' she said, 'I will do my best. Come inside at once you naughty children; I am sure your feet are damp. And before I put you to bed I have just time to finish the story of Cinderella.'

(Barrie, 1988, pp.66–7)

The process of becoming a person involves taking on cultural values, social rules and traditional practices. One way in which children demonstrate their awareness of accepted cultural behaviour can be seen in their play. Children draw on their observations of the society in which they live. Games such as 'mummies and daddies', 'keeping house' and 'having tea' allow them to prepare for the adult roles they will take on in later life (Figure 4.3). These are intermingled with games that go beyond reality, such as 'knights and dragons' and 'kings and queens'. However, both types of game require imagination and are rule governed. In situations of spontaneous imaginary, play rules may be formulated as the game progresses, but these rules are bound by existing societal rules. This is clearly demonstrated by Wendy's response following her agreement to take on the role of the children's mother.

> *What passes unnoticed by the child in real life becomes a rule of behaviour in play . . . If the child is playing the role of a mother, then she has rules of maternal behaviour.*
>
> (Vygotsky, 1978, p.95)

This view is supported by Barnes (1995), who suggests that play which develops children's creative imagination allows them to act out roles which may enable them to develop interpersonal skills. These may be evident during shared play which is dependent on negotiation and mutual acceptance of one another's contributions. In a study carried out by Dunn (1988), children of 2 and 3 years of age in 33 out of 40 families demonstrated an eager participation in pretend play. These children picked up on the moods of their siblings, taking on compatible roles and sharing the symbolism of the pretence. The

Figure 4.3 Playing games allows children to prepare for adult roles.

children were working towards a mutual goal, whilst exploring social roles and rules.

How do children communicate?

She (the Never Bird) had called out to him (Peter) what she had come for, and he called out to her what was she doing there; but of course neither of them understood the other's language ... Then rather curiously they both snapped out the same remark:
'Shut up!'
'Shut up!'
Then up she flew ... so as to make her meaning clear.

(Barrie, 1988, pp.89–90)

As can be seen from the above quote, a verbal exchange is often insufficient to convey meaning. Non-verbal communication involving eye contact, facial gestures, actions and signals is also necessary to express meaning. Chapter 9 discusses the theoretical basis of language acquisition, but here we shall consider briefly how children learn to communicate, with particular reference to their personal, social and affective development.

Whether innate or learned, very young children require adult assistance to interpret the meaning of both verbal and non-verbal behaviour in different situations. This kind of behaviour has been defined by Feinman (1982, p.445) as 'social referencing'. Children as young as 8 months are able to obtain information from gestures and facial expressions (Bruner, 1983). This is a reciprocal process, as young children also communicate through their own non-verbal exchanges which include smiling, nestling, clinging, frowning, resistive stiffening or pushing away. In addition, different types of vocalization such as gurgling, crying, laughing, squealing and screaming can alert the adult to the needs and desires of the child.

In order to develop speech, the child must learn what effect sound has on others. Initially, crying is an involuntary reflex, and it only becomes purposeful as memory and understanding develop.

Thought is far more developed than language. Even a 1-year-old who is in the process of developing spoken language has been expressing feelings of one kind or another since the earliest weeks of life. The shaping of these early social interactions and the communication that take place between the child and the adult have been described as being dependent upon 'affective expression' (Bloom, 1993, p.160).This is defined by Bloom as being the cognitive understanding of not only the learning and usage of words, but also the emotion underlying the expression. In turn, the response of the adult to the child's display of emotion is paramount to the development of affective expression. As Bruner (1986, p.114) states, 'emotions achieve their qualitative character by being contextualised in the social reality that produces them .'

The feeling of the emotion that is internalised by the child is the key to affective development.

However, emotional intensity may hinder expression. In their longitudinal study, Bloom and Beckwith (1989) found that during heightened emotional intensity the children were less inclined to verbalise. They also discovered that when negative emotions were expressed by the children, this resulted in the need to construct a new strategy in order to achieve their intended communication.

In order for communication to take place between Peter and the Never Bird, there was a mutuality in their exchange. During the incident several non-verbal cues were used (which are not overtly evident in the quotation at the head of this section), such as expressions of impatience which build to the furious climax of their verbal retorts. Emotions were running high, so the Never Bird devised a different strategy in order to demonstrate to Peter her intention to save him. He finally understood when she flew from the nest.

Who is important in the child's development?

'Let us all slip into our beds, and be there when she comes in, just as if we had never been away.'
And so when Mrs Darling went back into the night nursery . . . she saw them, but she did not believe they were there . . . She sat down in the chair . . .
'Mother!' Wendy cried.
'That's Wendy'
'Mother!'
'That's John,' she said.
'Mother!' cried Michael. He knew her now.
'That's Michael, ' she said, and she stretched out her arms . . . they went round Wendy and John and Michael . . . There could not have been a lovelier sight.'
(Barrie, 1988, pp.146–7)

A child's ability to form meaningful, lasting relationships with significant other people is fundamental to his or her holistic development (see also Chapter 7).

The above scene clearly illustrates the intensity of the relationship which can exist between a mother and her children. This process begins in early infancy when the formation of such significant relationships is taking place. Traditionally it is the mother with whom the baby is said to form the strongest attachment (Bowlby, 1969). This may have been the case 50 years ago, but society and family structures have undergone enormous change since then. Either parent may now be the main care-giver, and there may be significant input from other people such as grandparents, siblings, aunts and uncles, and care-givers outside the family structure, which would include friends and neighbours (Rutter, 1981) (Figure 4.4). Rutter suggests that, although there is usually one particularly strong attachment, the majority of children show multiple attachments of varying intensity, the breadth of which is largely determined by their social setting. For example, a child within a nuclear family may not have the same opportunity to form as many attachments as a child living within an extended family.

It is important to be aware that there is also great variation in the quality of relationships, and that the child's own characteristics influence the development of attachment behaviour.

Dunn (1988), in her Cambridgeshire study, examined parent–child and sibling–child relationships. She likened the parent–child relationship to that of David and Goliath, and the sibling–child relationship to that of Cain and Abel, the former signifying a power struggle and the latter indicating jealousy. The conflict that arose through the David and Goliath relationships indicated that children have a growing understanding of the impact of their actions on their mother's feelings and of the accepted family values.

The Cain and Abel relationship revealed that sibling interaction was closely related to the quality of peer friendships, and when friendships were initiated during middle childhood this had a consistently negative impact on their sibling relationships. However, increased support was observed between siblings during periods of major crisis. Wendy, John and Michael demonstrated their need to support each other when they were unsure about the response that they would receive from their parents on their return home.

The significance of family dynamics motivates children to express themselves within these relationships, which in turn leads them to contextualise

Figure 4.4   There may be significant input to child-rearing by individuals other than the parents.

their family within the wider social world. This is in contrast to Piaget's explanation of social understanding, which emphasises that 'the important developmental exchanges are ... those in which they attempt to argue, justify and negotiate' (Dunn, 1988, p.186). This places the emphasis on the child's ability to learn from their own contribution to a social situation rather than from the influence that family relationships have on their social understanding.

Where does the development take place?

You might have seen the three of them going in a row to Miss Fulsom's Kindergarten school, accompanied by their nurse ... This nurse was a prim Newfoundland dog, called Nana ... No nursery could possibly have been conducted more correctly

(Barrie, 1988, p.9–10)

When children, for whatever reason, are not looked after by their parents, the care arrangements can either be formal or informal. Informal care is usually carried out by the extended family – grandparents, aunts, uncles or siblings – or friends (Bee, 1992). This may be for short periods or isolated occasions, or more permanent and long term. The difference between these care arrangements and the formal ones is that no payment is given. Formal day-care arrangements can occur in a variety of situations. The most common of these include childminder, nanny, crèche, playgroup, day nursery, independent nursery, nursery school and after-school care

(Hennessy *et al.*, 1992) (see also Chapter 6)

Many informal care arrangements are made to promote relationships between children and close relatives, especially grandparents, and can occur from an early age. As children grow older, these informal care arrangements are often made to encourage social interaction with others of a similar age. More children are looked after by relatives than receive any other form of day-care, and this includes children who spend all day with their relatives on a regular basis. Parental choice regarding formal day-care is influenced by several factors, including the needs of the parents and their child, the availability of services, the cost of services, and the type of care that parents would prefer.

The needs of both children and parents vary. Although parents theoretically have a wide choice, in reality – due to practical constraints – this can be somewhat limited. According to Hennessy *et al.* (1992), studies of parental preference consistently show that a significant percentage of parents are not able to use their preferred type of day-care.

Hill (1989) suggests that whatever form of child-care provision is chosen, it is the quality of care which remains paramount (this issue is discussed further in Chapter 11). Good care is beneficial, and children are more likely to thrive in this type of environment. Unstimulating, unresponsive, or highly changeable care is likely to be detrimental to the child.

The conclusion that has been drawn from many research studies cited by Hennessy *et al.* (1992) is that attending day-care has no inherent effect on children, and there is no evidence to suggest that any one type of day-care is essentially better or worse for children's development and well-being than any other.

However, it is recognised that day-care settings cannot be considered in isolation from the family network, the local community and wider society (Hill, 1989). They should be examined in the context of how they fit into the larger picture of child-rearing practices, and how they relate to the wider world.

There is evidence to suggest that children who attend day-care are more inclined to participate in group activities (Field *et al.*, 1988). However, this does not always have a beneficial outcome, as there is an increased likelihood of potential conflict between the participants. Nevertheless, this may trigger increased occurrences of pro-social behaviour in which children learn to co-operate and negotiate in order to resolve their differences. It is through such experiences that perspective-taking abilities are developed, although there is no consensus as to when and how long these take to develop (Dunn, 1988). Clearly, Nana provided what Mr Darling considered to be exemplary care in the circumstances. He would have liked to employ a human nurse as his neighbours had done, but he could not afford to because the children drank so much milk! Although humorous, this can be seen as an accurate reflection of what occurs in many families. They have to reach their decisions regarding child care according to their means.

CONCLUSION

Personal, social and affective development is a complex construct which can only be understood by examining a number of different but related social skills and behaviours. What can be concluded is that the ability to adjust to different social situations is important for the development of social understanding. It is difficult to predict the outcome of given situations, as this is dependent upon the individual characteristics of the children and others within their shared environmental and socio-economic contexts. In the same way, children of similar ages are likely to vary greatly in their social abilities as a result of differing individual family circumstances and diverse opportunities for social interaction. An increase in perspective-taking skills is 'closely related to the development of the self and increases in children's social competence' (Barnes, 1995, p.254). Dunn's studies of family interactions during early childhood emphasise the essential role that emotion plays in the development of social understanding (Dunn, 1988). Children utilise language to help them to construct societal rules, which are based on their experience of family rules and can be demonstrated through their play episodes. Along with the emergence of language, children are able to express their feelings, but this ability appears to be linked to social understanding.

This social learning process is not complete even at the outset of adulthood. Although social abilities have been practised, new situations still present themselves, and therefore past experiences are drawn upon when the individual is responding to them. It is an ongoing reciprocal exchange of meanings. Even in adulthood there continues to be a part of everyone that remembers and reflects upon their childhood experiences. It is the sharing of these experiences, as they are passed from generation to generation, that contextualises them in time and place.

> *As you look at Wendy you may see her hair becoming white . . . for all this hap-*
> *pened long ago. Jane is now a common grown-up with a daughter called Mar-*
> *garet: and every spring-cleaning time, except when he forgets, Peter comes for*
> *Margaret and takes her to the Neverland . . . When Margaret grows up she will*
> *have a daughter, who is to be Peter's mother in turn; and thus it will go on, so*
> *long as children are gay and innocent and heartless.*
>
> (Barrie, 1988, p.158)

References

Barnes, P. (ed.) (1995): *Personal, Social and Emotional Development of Children*. Milton Keynes: Open University Press.

Barrie, J.M. (1988): *Peter Pan*. London: William Collins Sons & Co. Ltd.

Bee, H. (1992): *The Developing Child*, 6th edn. New York: Harper Collins.

Bloom, L. (1993): *The Transition from Infancy to Language*. New York: Cambridge University Press.

Bloom, L. and Beckwith, R. (1989): Talking with Feeling: Integrating Affective and Linguistic Expression in Early Language Development. *Cognition and Emotion*, **3**, 313–42.

Bowlby, J. (1969): *Attachment and Loss. 1. Attachment*. London: Hogarth Press.

Bruner, J. (1983): *Talk: Learning to use Language*. New York: Norton.

Bruner, J. (1986): *Actual Minds, Possible Worlds*. Cambridge, MA: Harvard University Press.

Dunn, J. (1988): *The Beginnings of Social Understanding*. Oxford: Basil Blackwell Ltd.

Feinman, S. (1982): Social Referencing in Infancy. *Merrill-Palmer Quarterly* **28**, 445–70.

Field, T., Masi, W., Goldstein, S., Perry, S. and Parl, S. (1988): Infant Daycare Facilitates Pre-school Social Behavior. *Early Childhood Research Quarterly*, **3**, 341–59.

Fischer, K.W. (1980): A Theory of Cognitive Development: The Control and Construction of Hierarchies of Skills. *Psychological Review* **87**, 477–531.

Grieve, R. and Hughes, M. (1990): *Understanding Children*. Oxford: Basil Blackwell Ltd.

Hennessy, E., Martin, S., Moss, P. and Melhuish, E. (1992): *Children and Day Care: Lessons from Research*. London: Paul Chapman Publishing Ltd.

Hill, M. (1989): The Role of Social Networks in the Care of Young Children. In Woodhead, M., Light, P., Carr, R. (eds), *Growing Up in a Changing Society*. Milton Keynes: Open University Press, 97–114.

Kipling, R. (1987): *Just so Stories*. London: Puffin Books.

Oates, J. (ed.) (1994): *The Foundations of Child Development*. Milton Keynes: Open University Press.

Piaget, J. (1929): *The Child's Conception of the World*. New York: Harcourt Brace Jovanovich.

Rutter, M. (1981): *Maternal Deprivation Reassessed*. Harmondsworth: Penguin Books.

Schaffer, H.R. (1984): *The Child's Entry into a Social World*. London: Academic Press.

Schaffer, H.R. (1989): Early Social Development. In Woodhead, M., Carr. R. and Light, P. (eds), *Becoming a Person*. Milton Keynes: Open University Press, 5–29.

Smith, P. K. and Cowie, H. (1991): *Understanding Children's Development*. Oxford: Basil Blackwell Ltd.

Sutherland, P. (1992): *Cognitive Development Today*. London: Paul Chapman Publishing Ltd.

Vygotsky, L.S. (1978): *Mind in Society: the Development of Higher Psychological Processes*. London: Harvard University Press.

Child in society

Val Thurtle

> This chapter aims to:
>
> - consider the difficulty of defining childhood;
> - examine childhood as a social construct;
> - investigate the child within contemporary society.

Just as no man is an island, neither can the child be studied or 'educared' for in isolation. The discussion in Chapter 1 of Bronfenbrenner's ecosystems (1979) has illustrated the point that there is an incredibly diverse range of factors which may have an influence on the individual child.

Early childhood studies students usually have a wealth of experiences and ideas. While these can be used to enrich practice, each individuals' own experience may lead them to see the social world in which children live in a simplistic one-dimensional manner, and to consider their own background as the norm against which others can be compared.

The use of sociological perspectives is one way in which the reader can begin to question beliefs and values that seem common sense or natural, so that consideration can be given to the social influences acting upon an individual and children can be viewed within the context of their social setting. Psychologists have traditionally focused upon the individual child. The sociological concept of the child is rooted in an exploration of the wider social world, which is inevitably an enormous undertaking.

What is a sociological perspective?

Many sociology texts start with the question 'What is sociology ?' For Giddens (1989) 'sociology is the study of human social life, groups and societies' (p. 7). It used to be said that sociology was the 'science of society', but this gives the impression of a discipline that uses the positivistic methods of the natural sciences. Sociology goes further – in a sense it is a way of thinking.

Sociology can be seen as a critical activity, asking questions about the state of society and about the forces that keep institutions going and which preserve social order. In other words, sociology is a discipline which asks awkward questions in a systematic manner. Such an approach will develop the 'sociological imagination' (Mills, 1971), cultivating the ability to think ourselves out of the mundane and familiar, and to take new viewpoints from which we can consider and hopefully to begin to understand our everyday lives.

Sociological perspectives

Any contact with sociological works will soon throw up the terms *functionalism, Marxism, feminism* and *social interactionism*. Theorists from different backgrounds will take different views of the social world, so one cannot say that there is 'a' sociological perspective; rather there exists a variety of different outlooks.

Describing these stances at a purely introductory level, structural functionalists would see society as being composed of various systems that work together. Each part of the social system performs a certain function and thus contributes to the well-being and continuity of society. Beliefs and values are shared, leading to harmonious co-operation. This perspective dates back to Emile Durkheim, and was expounded by Parsons and Merton. The approach was much used in the 1950s and 1960s, particularly with regard to the family but it has less of a following in the 1990s. Such a view may not seem appropriate to the late twentieth century, but is frequently held up as an ideal by politicians discussing the family or education system.

Marxists find their origins in the work of Karl Marx and Friedrich Engels, but these have been re-interpreted and refined. There are therefore many kinds of Marxists. They would see the world in terms of conflict, such conflict being found particularly between those who control the means of production and those who do not. This control influences all sections of a given society – the education system, the media and the health services. While functionalists would see conflict as dysfunctional, the Marxist views conflict as having positive outcomes and indeed as being 'normal'.

Feminists, too, can be seen as viewing the world in terms of conflict, discord between women and men, or discord between women and patriarchal structures. Feminist writing is particularly important to those concerned with the care, health and education of children, as these areas have often been ignored by mainstream sociology and taken up by feminist researchers.

These three views have largely been concerned with the system or infrastructure. Interactionists have been far more interested in the small-scale or micro level, investigating the meanings that actors in any social action give to what is going on. Looking at the work of symbolic interactionists and ethnomethodologists, the reader may find it difficult to decide where sociology ends and psychology begins, demonstrating that traditional subject divides may not always be appropriate when dealing with something as complex as childhood.

Such an overview is incredibly condensed, but it makes the point that a variety of viewpoints exist within sociology. The critical reader needs to ask where any writer is coming from and whether they are they interpreting their findings through their own world view. Given that all of us – teacher, student and researcher – have our own past experiences and dearly held beliefs, we need to reflect on whether sociology or indeed any study can be truly value free.

Anything that happens in wider society can impinge upon the child. For example, a particular political party may come to power and follow a policy which leads to the child's parents becoming redundant, which in turn changes the economic status of the family and consequently of the child. The reporting in the media of the murder of a child and the conviction of another may well influence carers' attitudes and styles of discipline. These two examples highlight the difficulty of knowing where to commence our study.

This chapter further develops two concepts with which you became acquainted in the Introduction. It reflects on how we define a child, looking at the way in which the child has been perceived over a historical period, and considers the family and the place of the child within it. This can only be an introduction to the subject, and further studies are required to examine how children are integrated into wider society. Issues of class, ethnicity, gender and poverty all interrelate, making the study of the child in society a never-ending task.

What is a child?

How should we define a child? A child could be defined in terms of physical growth or developmental maturity. Our own parents may never see us as mature, and always regard us as a child in need of emotional and practical support. Financial independence may mark the end of childhood, but whereas for some that will be at 16 years of age, others will be well into their twenties or beyond. Clearly there is no obvious cut-off point. We may want to define the end of childhood in terms of activities that our particular social world permits us to engage in, e.g. drive a car, vote, buy our own alcohol or get married. Any discussion will soon identify national and social differences in all areas and the variety of definitions of the end of childhood in the twentieth century.

Childhood, then, is not an objective entity, various social groups at different times have defined children in a myriad ways. A brainstorm of current views in western society might come up with some of the following.

Children are innocent and in need of care and protection, whilst others see them as 'devils' needing controls and strict discipline. The James Bulger[5.1] case represented these two views, often in the same news report. The murdered child was presented as the former, while the perpetrators, only a few years older than him, were seen as the latter. For others children are regarded as investments for the future, necessitating the sacrifice of parents. The state is expected to contribute to their health, welfare and education so that they grow up to be effective members of the work force-in the future. Children might be seen as 'products' which require careful monitoring during their production. 'Standard Assessment Tasks and Attainment Targets' in the National Curriculum and surveillance by health visitors could be seen in this light (see Chapter 3 for further discussion). A look at the media might provide the picture of the child as a designer accessory, something the well-turned-out woman (and man) must acquire. In wider society the stigma of infertility indicates the apparent necessity of children for adult fulfilment.

A review of television advertisements in the months leading up to Christmas demonstrates that children represent a potential market in their own right. They are the ones who will buy or demand the current plastic craze (Power Rangers, Sylvanian Families, My Little Pony, etc.) or drag their parents to the 'in' fast-food places.

For most of the time, western society perceives children as being different, and worthy of their childhood, but periodically they are seen as little adults able to watch the same movies and join in almost all adult activities. Lastly, one strong view of children presented by books such as this is that they are of sufficient interest to be worthy of study. Whole curricula can be devised around them, their concerns and experiences.

Would all these views of childhood (and the reader can no doubt think of others) be current in other cultures and in different historical times? Clearly they would not. In a developing country children as young as 5 years old might have defined tasks within and outside the family contributing to the economic stability of the family (see Chapter 13 for further discussion). Our twentieth-century view of childhood is a relatively new phenomenon, and it is socially constructed, as you learned in the Introduction to this book, and as we shall discuss further.

Sociological perspectives on the child

How would the different sociological perspectives view the child ? Functionalists would see children as being socialised into future roles, the family being the primary agent, with institutions such as the school and peer group being involved in secondary socialisation. For functionalists, the firm guidance of vulnerable and volatile children is necessary if society is to survive and prosper (Wagg, 1988).

Marxists would also be concerned with preparation for future life, but would see it as rather more controlled, with those in power ensuring that the majority were equipped for their lives as powerless workers. Hartley (1993) argues that this process is evident in the structure and organisation of the nursery school, where children learn to fit into a regimented timetable – preparation for the factory of the future? According to this mode of thinking children are said to be inculcated with the values of the private property system, and obedience to authority is acquired, as are prejudices, including those of a racial and sexual nature. Indeed it is such value systems and practices which are reputed to keep the oppressed majority divided and therefore not a threat to the ruling classes.

Feminists have been much concerned with the gender roles that children learn or acquire at an early stage. Grabrucker's (1988) reflective diary of her parenting of her young daughter gives a very readable insight into this.

Interactionists would be concerned with the relationships and activities between children. While they would be unlikely to attach this label to themselves, rather being seen as anthropologists, *Children's Games in Street and Playground* (Opie and Opie, 1969) does just this.

Children in history

Medieval period and the Enlightenment

Thinking about children in history we are dependent on the material left behind, and we need to consider its reliability. If children were not very significant in medieval and earlier times, were they worth writing about, and was there a written record? If they were not important to those who had the skills and means to write, does this mean that they were unimportant to others, particularly women? If we draw on 'common knowledge', our information may be distorted by Hollywood movies and television period dramas – in other words, the childhood of the past may have been reconstructed, perhaps with a rosy glow.

Aries (1962) argues that there was no concept of childhood prior to the medieval period – it simply did not exist. Children were viewed as property, but then so were wives. Child mortality in the eighteenth century was high, with two out of three children dying before their fifth birthday. Infanticide has probably been practised in all societies (Trainor, 1988), despite being prohibited as early as Roman times (Shahar, 1990). The level of care was low, with accounts of poor hygiene and wet nursing by dubious mother substitutes. Children lived in the adult world, they were dressed in the same clothing as adults from an early age, shared the same entertainment despite its bawdy nature, and might be apprenticed away from home by the age of 7 years. In contrast to Aries' view, Shahar (1990) argues that childhood did exist in the central and late medieval periods. Children were not idealised as later, but there were traditional child-care practices, as well as emotional and material investment in children. The medical and educational theories might be very different from those of today, but they did exist.

It is often argued that there was little emotional involvement until survival was assured. Montaigne's famous sixteenth-century remark would bear this out: 'I have lost two or three children, not without regret but without great sorrow'. However, Pollack (1983) shows that the loss of young children left some parents distraught with grief. The poverty of the fifteenth and sixteenth centuries meant that many parents could not afford to prolong childhood, sending older children to work while infants were coddled. Parents who lived and worked in servility were used to harsh treatment themselves, and meted this out to their children. Comparison of the methods of child management used by these parents with those of the twentieth-century parent does not mean that their affection and concern for their off spring was any less.

The sixteenth to the eighteenth centuries were times of great change – economic, religious and political. The ideas of the Enlightenment portrayed children as being different from adults and needing care and protection. Rousseau viewed children as individuals to be valued; they were deemed to be working through various stages of development but were essentially romantic innocents. Locke saw them as empty slates ready for learning and education. In the same period, those of a puritan or Calvinistic persuasion, perhaps influenced by a fear of revolution, saw children as inherently sinful and therefore in need of harsh discipline. These ideas were the start of significant trends in educational thinking.

Aries (1962) demonstrates the increasing importance of children in art, reflecting their growing importance in society. Starting with funereal art, he shows how children were initially portrayed as small adult effigies, but over a period of time they were shown as children within the family, and later alone in individual portraits. To commission an expensive portrait of a child indicated that the child had been noticed and valued. Of course only the most affluent would have used resources in this fashion, and the views of the rather less well off might have been quite different.

The coming of the industrial revolution meant that some children found work in the factories and mines, contributing to our picture of the 'dark satanic mills', but children had always been involved in families' work or on their land. Describing New Zealand colonial life in the mid-nineteenth century, Graham (1993) states that children's 'labour was essential to the functioning and economic viability of the family enterprise' (p.67). The same must have been true of farms and smallholdings throughout the western world. There might be gender differences in the work that was expected of girls and boys, but both were expected to work.

The nineteenth century

The nineteenth century saw controls on child labour through the Mines Act of 1842 and the Factory Acts of 1844,1850 and 1853. Humphries *et al.* (1988) point out that children were commencing their working lives while still as young as 12 years in Britain until the 1920s.

Until well into the nineteenth century there was no expectation that any family member would have a separate identity. Macdonald (1990) draws attention to the fact that, in pioneering New Zealand, it was common for the names of a deceased child to be used for a subsequent child. Only later was it seen as morbid and the practice ceased.

Throughout the nineteenth century children were increasingly idealised and seen in a rather sentimental light. Class differences were evident, with the children of the affluent being pampered and educated, while those of the poor might well be working on the land, in factories or as chimney-sweeps. Whilst class differences were evident, child mortality was much reduced ensuring that each child born had a greater chance of reaching adulthood.

Change was under way as a result of stratified diffusion, by which the ideas of the upper classes today because those of the working classes tomorrow. One can speculate about the part played by the Royal Family in this process. Queen Victoria's large and apparently happy family may have increased the prestige of family life and contributed to the status of the child.

Industrialisation went hand in hand with the smaller nuclear family facilitating movement to the industrial centres. Within the smaller family, the focus was increasingly on the child, who became a source of entertainment as well as concern.

Concern for the welfare and control of the child was evident in wider society. Compulsory elementary education was introduced in Britain in 1870, and hospitals for children were opened. Schools, orphanages and reformatories were all devised as 'character factories' turning out obedient and dutiful citizens (Humphries *et al.*, 1988). It has been argued that there was little altruism involved in compulsory education, but rather that it was a way of making the child more civilised and self-disciplined to become suitable factory fodder (Rose, 1991). At the end of the nineteenth century this was done by an authoritarian regime which wielded power in inward-looking institutions. The regimes were not dissimilar, whether they were orphanages for the poor and abandoned, a reformatories for the apparently criminal, or preparatory schools for the children of the rich. Hopkins' (1994) view of universal education is far more optimistic, seeing childhood transformed as it became centred upon schools, which led to improvements in health, nutrition and leisure opportunities.

Ideas of the child as father of the man became widespread in the early twentieth century through the works of Freud and others. At the same time it became obvious that children had a culture of their own, with their own toys and games, manufactured for the rich and devised at home for the poor.

To the present day

Ideas that had their origins in the nineteenth century came to fruition at the beginning of the twentieth century. Families shrank in size, with the small number of children being highly valued and the time and resources of the family becoming increasingly child-centred.

The control and surveillance of children affected just about every child, but in a less repressive way. Services for children were started and developed. The Notification of Births Act in 1907 led to health visiting services being offered to all mothers and their babies. The advent of the School Health Service may have been triggered by the poor health of army recruits and a fear that the empire could not be adequately defended, but it led to health surveillance and treatment being far more freely available to children, and the introduction of school meals made a real difference to the nutritional status of many children.

With the increased influence of psychologists and physicians, all child-orientated services became psycho-medical in nature. Children were increasingly under the clinical gaze of experts, with less of their lives in the private domain. Functionalists might argue that such an approach, and the ensuing interventions, were for the good of the child and his or her wider community, while Marxists would argue that apparent concern, whether expressed in terms of health or education, was merely a means of giving capitalism a human face.

The twentieth century has seen no shortage of experts ready to advise parents on children's upbringing and education. The development of the mass media has meant that their influence has been far-reaching, and the reader may want to reflect upon the effect such experts have had on the confidence of parents in their child-rearing abilities. The work of doctor Truby King reached far beyond New Zealand where he had advocated breast-feeding by a strictly regimented and disciplined regime. In 1917 his first Mothercraft Society was set up in Earls Court, and thousands of infants were reared with the help of his book, *Mothercraft*, raising child rearing to the status of 'scientific motherhood'.

Criticism of the Truby King method followed in the 1950s, with fears that such a rigid approach would harm the child. Liberal theories gained ascendance, with children being encouraged to be creative and to explore their environment. King was replaced by Benjamin Spock's *Common Sense Book of Baby and Child Care* in 1946. This fitted well with the work of the Swiss psychologist Jean Piaget, who argued that children were moving through a variety of stages which could be facilitated by appropriate stimulation by parents and carers (see Chapter 9). The end of the twentieth century sees other authorities, including doctors, psychologists and pop stars (a visit to the child-care section of any high-street bookshop will identify the current guru).

What can we say about the child in history? Clearly there have been a variety of approaches, and our twentieth-century views are undoubtedly derived from them. Both in history and at the present time there is not one view of childhood, but a variety influenced by class, gender, ethnicity, affluence and the very thinking of the time.

The child in the family

We have virtually all lived in a family at some point in our lives, and it is worth reflecting upon your own view of the family. You might picture a nuclear family with Mum and Dad and two, possibly three, children beaming at each other from the cereal packet (Leach, 1986). An Irish student drew me the most detailed family tree, with third, fourth and fifth cousins carefully named. Did she, I asked, consider them all to be 'family' to the extent that she would entertain them if they visited her in England? Of course she did, she replied, as she looked at me pityingly, who only sends a Christmas card to my rarely seen first cousins. If you live away from your aunts and uncles, are they less family? Does family depend on residence? Are you still a family if there is only one parent? Is a lesbian couple rearing a child a family ? Do families have to be based on blood ties, or is a kibbutz an extended family of sorts? Once we start, the variety of permutations is immense. While we consider the variety in family structure, we need to think about the impact that such variations might have on children.

Defining the family

A 'common-sense' starting point for discussions of the family is that of the functionalists, much used in theoretical discussions of the family throughout the 1950s and 1960s. Murdock, writing in 1949 (cited in Haralambos and Holborn, 1995), defined the family as:

> *a social group characterised by common residence, economic co-operation and reproduction. It includes adults of both sexes, at least two of which maintain a socially approved sexual relationship and one or more children, own or adopted of the sexually cohabiting adults.*

Reading this in the late twentieth century we may have doubts about the importance of the common residence, and difficulties in defining a socially approved sexual relationship. Some of the 'families' mentioned in the last section do not fit Murdock's description. For him, the family is universal, with different family forms being variations on the basic family structure.

Clearly functionalist in nature, this definition identifies the functions of the family. A favourite debate of the 1970s centred around the question 'Is the family losing its functions?' The family (in whatever form) is still much concerned with sexual activity and reproduction. While it may no longer be a unit of economic production, it is a significant unit of consumption. For many, its religious functions are not significant but it provides the majority of health care. In some societies, and that of the UK may be one of them, it marks out our niche in society and it gives a place where we can play, experiment or even regress. Parsons (1956) collects some of these ideas together, discussing the functions of the family in terms of the primary socialisation of children and the stabilisation of adult personalities.

Social welfare systems may be the safety net for those who fall on hard times, but kin still provide material help for each other (Finch, 1989), whether in the form of child care or financial loans. Clearly, health care workers do far more than the family ever did in the past, but we know that a high proportion of illness episodes are handled in the home without recourse to health care workers. In the same way, the family is frequently seen as the initial educator of young children. Government comments of 'back to basics' have placed the onus on the family to take responsibility for their own, and far from the family losing its functions, it can be argued that it is having to take on more, including the blame for the 'problems' of society.

If we prefer not to define the family in terms of function, perhaps we should turn to residence. The term 'family' is often confused with household, i.e. those sharing a common housekeeping. If blood ties are important in the definition of the family, a household of students sharing common housekeeping is not a family, but religious sisters may see themselves as such. The concept of household may be useful if we are looking at patterns of consumption or social interaction, but it is not the same as a family. Families may extend beyond a single household, or one household might include more than one family, or indeed none at all.

The definition of family therefore proves difficult and, like childhood, we can argue that it is socially constructed in different places and across time. As a working definition we could use Giddens' (1989) definition: 'A family is a group of people directly linked by kin connections, the adult members of which assume responsibility for the caring of children' (p.384).

We may criticise this definition because it does not allow for interactions of neighbours and friends which might be as significant as kin ties, and it assumes the presence of children. However, it does enable us to focus on families with young children.

Diversity in family structures

Such a definition as cited above allows for a variety of family structures, some of which have already been mentioned. Box 5.1 outlines definitions of types of families and terms used in relation to them.

When reading magazines, watching television and perhaps even watching children's play we may gain the impression that the typical family in the UK and other western societies is the nuclear family. Is the nuclear family statistically typical, or is it an ideal of how families 'should' be?

Abercrombie et al. (1994) cite government statistics demonstrating that in 1990–1991 24 per cent of UK households consisted of one person, reflecting the gradual increase in those of pensionable age who live alone, as well as in other adults who choose to live alone. They draw attention to the fact that between 1961 and 1991 the proportion of households consisting of a married couple with children has declined from 38 per cent to 24 per cent. Clearly we do not all live in the cereal-packet-style family! How then do children live?

Table 5.1 shows the percentage of children living in different types of family, demonstrating changes over a 20-year period. The majority of children do live with an adult couple, but these are not necessarily both their biological parents. Table 5.2 shows the number of children living in some type of step-family.

BOX 5.1   DEFINITIONS OF DIFFERENT FAMILY STRUCTURES

Nuclear family/conjugal family – A unit consisting of sexually related adults and their dependent children

Extended family – a multi-generational family living in the same household

Modified extended families – a group of related nuclear families who have close affective ties and responsibilities to one another based on some extent upon choice, though not necessarily upon geographical proximity.

Lone-parent family – One parent, mother or father, and the dependent children, the other parent being permanently absent

Reconstituted or blended family – family unit in which one or both parents have children from previous relationships

Other terms

Serial monogamy – the practice of having one spouse at any one time; high adult mortality or a high divorce rate may both lead to remarriage

Kinship – the social recognition of biological ties and ties through marriage

Household – all those who reside in one dwelling and share common housekeeping

---

Table 5.1   Percentage of children[a] living in different family types in the UK

	1972	1981	1986	1991	1992
Couple with					
1 child	16	18	18	17	17
2 children	35	41	41	37	38
3 or more children	41	29	28	28	26
Lone mother with					
1 child	2	3	4	5	5
2 children	2	4	5	7	7
3 or more children	2	3	3	6	5
Lone father with					
1 child	–	1	1	–	1
2 or more children	1	1	1	1	1
All dependent children	100	100	100	100	100

[a] Dependent children: children under 16 years or aged 16 to 18 years and in full-time education, in the family unit and living in the household.
Source: *Social Focus on Children 1994*, Office for National Statistics. Crown Copyright 1994. Reproduced by permission of the controller of HMSO and the office for National Statistics.

A minority of children may live in collective or communal settings, but the numbers of these are difficult to estimate, and it seems that few children stay in such settings for all of their childhood (Abercrombie *et al.*, 1994). The rise in the number of children being brought up in lone-parent households has been of much concern to policy-makers, educationalists and church-leaders alike. Table 5.1 demonstrates that in the past 20 years the proportion of children living in a lone-parent family at any one time has increased. Such figures cannot

Table 5.2 Number of dependent children[a] in stepfamilies, also expressed as a percentage of all dependent children, for 1990–1992, in the UK

	Children in stepfamilies (1000s)	Children in stepfamilies as a percentage of all children (%)
Married-couple stepfamiles		
Stepchildren	520	3.9
Natural children	240	1.8
Total dependent children	760	5.7
Cohabiting-couple stepfamilies		
Stepchildren	250	1.9
Natural children	40	0.3
Total dependent children	290	2.2

[a] Children aged under 16 years or aged 16 to 18 years and still in full-time education
Source: *Social Focus on Children 1994*, Office for National Statistics. Crown Copyright 1994. Reproduced by permission of the controller of HMSO and the Office for National Statistics.

describe the way in which each family has reached this point – it may be by death, divorce or separation, breakdown of cohabitation, parents who never married and/or adoption (Hardy and Crow, 1991). We can hardly treat lone parents as an homogenous group, but that may apply to all types of families, nor can such figures show the amount of time that a child spends in a lone-parent household, as for many it may be a transitory period until he or she becomes part of a blended family.

The media frequently presents the child from the lone-parent family as dis-advantaged, but it is difficult to analyse the issues, influenced as we are by media and political hype. Being a lone parent is often linked with socio-eco-nomic disadvantage, particularly as the majority of lone parents are women, who are likely to be in a less advantageous position in the workplace. It can be argued that it is preferable for the child to be in a stable, lone-parent fam-ily than in an emotionally charged two-parent household, but we have noted the transitory nature of many lone-parent families that reform as blended families, which necessitates further readjustments. How should we measure the outcomes of lone-parent families? Perhaps this can be done by reviewing the educational achievements of the child, or by comparing the crime statis-tics of children from one- or two-parent homes. The children's own 'success' in marriage may be relevant, or their mental health in adult life. All of these measures are problematic, involving other confounding variables.

Unfortunately, Table 5.1 does not show what proportion of children in the UK are being reared in an extended family. Some of the 'couple'-style families may be part of larger families living together, but classical extended families such as Arensburg and Kimball's (1968) *Family and Community in Ireland* may now be quite rare. Young and Willmott (1973) have shown that traditional communities as described in their *Family and Kinship in East London* (Young and Willmott, 1957) have moved and changed. It seems likely that extended families all living under one roof are not common, although they may be more the norm within some ethnic groups. We need to beware of viewing our

Figures 5.1–5.3 Families come in a variety of forms.

stereotypes as the way things will remain. Among families from the Indian subcontinent (itself too wide a generalisation), kin networks may be strong, arranged marriages may occur and the kin links may tie in with business, yet increasingly women are working outside the home, kin networks are strained by geographical distance, and smaller domestic units are formed because of the limited size of available housing. For any group the family, whether extended or nuclear, is not a fixed entity.

The typical UK family is no longer a classical extended family, if indeed it ever was (Laslett, 1965), nor is the nuclear family or lone parent raising children generally isolated from the wider kin group. We have already noted that some families will look to the wider kin group for practical help of both a material and a financial nature. This may be most obvious when part of the family is coping with very young children and dependent elderly members. However, there may, be significant differences in the amount of help that can be expected from different cultural groups in society. Kin links are not only about the exchange of services. You might like to consider which members of your family you send Christmas cards to, or whom you would invite to a celebration. Whilst most of us do not live with our kin we have links with them, although the 'rules' about whom we maintain contact with seem to be hap-hazard and ill-defined. Allan (1985) found that the parent–child link was the central bond, whilst siblings were generally less involved in each other's lives. It seems likely that cousins and more distant relatives will, with a few excep-tions, be even less involved. Litwak (1965), describing a modified extended family, believes that there is some degree of obligation in the links that are maintained and the family help that is given. For Allan, with his 'modified elementary family' more choice is involved. This choice will be influenced by geographical proximity as well as by how much individuals enjoy each other's company.

An issue that is still largely unexplored is how these kinship links are main-tained in blended families. How do they work when children have five or six grandparent figures in their lives? Can one look to one's ex-sister-in-law for baby-sitting services, or does it come down even more to questions of choice?

It is clear that children are being brought up within a diversity of family structures, and even if they are apparently self-contained they are likely to have links with other kin members. Whatever is the norm in our own expe-rience may seem very strange to others. The nuclear family is often pre-sented as the ideal and, while numerically most common, it is itself a relatively new form of the family, having become more numerous at the time of industrialisation.

Diversity in the ways in which families work

If there are variations in family structures, there are probably even more dif-ferences in what goes on within families. This is a very private area and not one that most of us feel enthusiastic about exposing to interested researchers.

The aspects which we could discuss are again vast, and the following sec-tion focuses upon the increase in the number of women in the work-force, the division of labour within the family, and the child-centred nature of the family.

Women in the workplace

To say that women who stay at home do not work is to bring down a hail of abuse from feminists and anyone, male or female, who has spent any length of time at home with small children. Women have always worked in the family business, on the land or in the home just as, until the last century, most children did. The twentieth century has seen a marked increase in the number of women working outside the home in paid employment. This has at times been regarded as being detrimental to the child. Since the Second World War women have increasingly taken up paid employment. In 1992, women represented 43 per cent of those in employment, a high proportion compared to most other nations (Abercrombie *et al.*, 1994). While many women are in the workplace, 45 per cent are in part-time employment (Abercrombie *et al.*, 1994). This is particularly true of families who have young children. Table 5.3 shows that 46 per cent of mothers of pre-school children are in paid employment. Who then is caring for the children? Role reversal occurs less than is often supposed (Morris, 1990), but the family is providing much of the care, with fathers working different hours and other family members providing child-care services (Hewison and Dowswell, 1994). This of course reinforces the idea that the nuclear family is not an isolated entity. Other children will be attending pre-school services, as shown in Table 5.4, so that their parents can participate in the workplace, but also to give carers relief and so that the children themselves can benefit. These motives are of course not mutually exclusive, but they do illustrate the point that, for some children, from a very early age the nuclear family will not be the primary agent of socialisation.

Do women and their families benefit according to whether they are in the home or in the workplace? Emotions run high on this issue, and good arguments can be put forward on both sides, although most of them start with the notion that it has been or should be the mother who has primary responsibility for the care of the young child. For some families the discussion is purely academic, as the mother's income is a vital part of the family budget, providing necessities. The argument is influenced by the quality of care available for the child. For the very young child, it is seen as critical that close relationships can be formed with one or two main care-givers. In the longer term, it may be significant that girls have had a strong role model of an achieving and confident mother, and for women the mental health of those who combine part time work with child care may be better than those working full time who suffer role overload and those who remain out of the workplace (Payne, 1991). For the individual child we might want to reflect on the anonymous quote 'better a working mother than a boring one'!

Table 5.3 Mother's economic activity status: by age of youngest dependent child, autumn 1993, in the UK, expressed as percentage values

	0–4	5–9	10–15	All aged under 16 years
Working full-time	16	21	32	22
Working part-time	30	44	42	37
Unemployed	6	6	4	8
Inactive	48	29	21	36
All mothers (=100%) (millions)	3.2	1.7	1.7	6.7

Source: *Social Focus on Children 1994*, Office for National Statistics. Crown Copyright 1994. Reproduced by permission of the controller of HMSO and the Office for National Statistics

Table 5.4   Percentage of pre-school children using day-care services by age, for 1990, in England

	Age (years)					All pre-school children
	< 1	1	2	3	4[a]	
Location of service						
Care on domestic premises only	38	28	25	6	1	20
Day-care facility only	7	21	25	43	47	28
Combination of domestic and non-domestic services	6	21	31	46	49	30
Main providers of services[b]						
Regular day-care on domestic premises[c]						
Father	19	18	24	24	24	21
Grandparent	22	24	25	22	18	23
Day-care facility						
Parent and toddler group	12	36	31	13	7	21
Day nursery	2	6	8	13	9	8
Playgroup	–	1	18	50	42	21
Nursery class or school	–	–	4	30	54	15
Any regular day-care service	52	70	80	95	97	78

[a] In addition 51 per cent of children aged 4 years in the sample attended school full-time.
[b] Children may receive regular day-care from more than one source.
[c] Regular day-care on domestic premises was also provided by friends or neighbours ((7 per cent), registered child-minders (6 per cent), nanny, mother's help or au-pair (3 per cent), siblings (3 per cent) or other relatives (4 per cent).
Source: *Social Focus on Children 1994*, Office for National Statistics. Crown Copyright 1994. Reproduced by permission of the controller of HMSO and the Office for National Statistics

Division of labour within the family

Marxists have traditionally seen the family, or at least the wife, as being there to service the worker, to allow him to go off to work each day knowing that his domestic needs will be met and that he will be greeted at the end of the day by the knowledge that in his home, if not in the workplace, he is valued and loved. In the traditional view the father goes to work and the mother stays at home. Such a view lingers in our stereotype of the nuclear family. Oakley (1974) found that women saw housework as monotonous, fragmented, lonely and not regarded as real work. Feminists have frequently claimed that the family oppresses women, forcing them into a powerless position where they continue to work longer hours than their spouses (Oakley, 1974). Hochschild (1989) asks whether, with the increase in the number of women in the work-force, particularly those with young children, domestic labour has been more equally shared, or whether the working mum is now working the 'second shift'.

Young and Wilmott (1973), describing the symmetrical family, suggested that the family was becoming more centred on the home, wider kin were of less significance, and the roles of men and women were less segregated. They might not contribute the same domestic labour, but the roles were more flexible, and both would contribute a similar amount to the home. Thinking of a family you know well, you might like to compile a list of tasks that get done and decide which are gendered and which are truly inter-changeable. If you compare your findings with, for example, your family of origin, are there significant differences? Many students when asked to do this can identify differences over time and at different points in the life cycle. For example, the arrival of a first baby may lead to more traditional roles being adopted, whereas retirement or unemployment may facilitate more shared roles. We may like to think that the division of labour has become more equitable, with an exchange system in operation – while mum cooks all of the meals dad does all of the home maintenance.

Reviewing evidence from both the UK and the USA, Morris (1990) suggests that there has been little significant change in established roles, although there are some signs of flexibility in domestic tasks. In the UK, husbands do engage in child care while their wives work, and men do increase their domestic input if there are young children and the wife is working, but if the wife is not working outside the home the spouse is likely to decrease his domestic input and spend more time at his paid work. Unemployed men were found to be unlikely to take over a housewifely role, and married women's employment did not prompt a significant rise in domestic involvement by their spouses. Overall, Morris concludes that the traditional female responsibility for household work has not been eroded, and while male input may have increased, it is insufficient to compensate for an increased number of female hours in the workplace.

What impact does this have on the child in the family? There may be increased flexibility in the area of child care, with fathers being more inclined to play with their offspring than they were 30 years ago, but they are only involved to a limited extent in the monotonous aspects of housework. If the family is a powerful agent of socialisation, as most sociological perspectives maintain, the picture can be regarded as rather depressing. Stereotyped roles are being passed on by a process of imitation, identification, role learning and conditioning. This apparent maintenance of the status quo needs to be balanced by the fact that change has occurred, and ultimately children are socialised not programmed. Choice is therefore possible.

The child-centred family

The family is regarded as having become far more child-centred in its approach in recent years, reflecting a growing interest in children in western society as a whole. As noted previously, the symmetrical family was centred on the home, especially when children were small, the inward focus puts the child centre-stage, and he or she is perhaps the *raison d'être* of the family. Families tend to be smaller than those of the nineteenth century, with much higher expectations that each child will reach maturity. Children are healthier and spend far longer in formal education, making then financially dependent upon their families for an extended period. Increased affluence for some has meant that there are more resources to spend on the child, while in general terms the number of working hours has decreased, allowing more time to be spent with children and families, although one can quickly see that this does not apply to every western child at the end of the twentieth century.

Returning to the loss-of-functions argument, Fletcher (1988) argues that the family is centrally concerned with the upbringing of children. This has become its prime function, demonstrated by an increased recognition by governments and other agencies of the importance and responsibility of families in the life of individuals in general, and young children and adolescents in particular.

Alongside this we need to consider very briefly those couples who are childless, whether by accident or design. The right not to have children has grown as fast as the right to have them, and childlessness is seen as a valid choice – not every couple wants to be child-centred. Of those with children, there is an expectation that they will provide, care for and educate them , but there is variation in the resources, inclination and ability which families have at their disposal. The majority may seek to be child-centred, but the standards set and those achieved tell another story (see, for example, Chapter 10).

CONCLUSION

Diversity and variety are the watchwords in terms of sociological perspectives, views of childhood, and structures of families and how they operate. The student of the child in society needs to observe critically, look beyond common sense, and take nothing at face value!

Endnote

[5.1] James Bulger was a 2-year-old who in 1993 while shopping with his mother was led from the shopping mall by older children and subsequently found murdered.

References

Abercrombie, N., Warde, A., Soothill, K., Urry, J. and Walby, S. (1994): *Contemporary British Society*. 2nd edn. Cambridge: Polity Press.

Allan, G. (1985): *Family Life*. Oxford: Basil Blackwell.

Arensburg, C.M. and Kimball, S.T. (1968): *Family and Community in Ireland*. 2nd edn. Cambridge, MA: Harvard University Press.

Aries, P. (1962): *The Centuries of Childhood*. London: Cape.

Bronfenbrenner, U. (1979): *The Ecology of Human Development.* Cambridge, MA: Harvard University Press.

Finch, J. (1989): *Family Obligations and Social Change.* Cambridge: Polity Press.

Fletcher, R. (1988): *The Shaking of the Foundations: Family and Society.* London: Routledge and Kegan Paul.

Giddens, A. (1989): *Sociology.* 2nd edn. Cambridge: Polity Press.

Grabrucker, M. (1988) *There's a Good Girl. Gender Stereotyping in the First Three Years of Life. A Diary.* London: The Women's Press.

Graham, J. (1993): The Pioneers. In Sinclair, K. *The Oxford Illustrated History of New Zealand.* Auckland: Oxford University Press, pp. 49–74.

Haralambos, M. and Holborn M. (1995): *Sociology Themes and Perspectives.* 4th edn. London: Collins Educational.

Hardy and Crow G. (eds) (1991): *Lone Parenthood: Coping with Constraints and Making Opportunities.* Hemel Hempstead. Harvester.

Hartley, D. (1993): *Understanding the Nursery School.* London: Cassell.

Hewison, J. and Dowswell, T. (1994): *Child Health Care and the Working Mother: The Juggling Act.* London: Chapman and Hall.

Hochschild, A. (1989): *The Second Shift. Working Parents and the Revolution at Home.* New York: Viking Penguin.

Hopkins, E. (1994): *Childhood Transformed: Working Class Children in 19th Century England.* Manchester: Manchester University Press.

Humphries, S., Mack, J. and Perks, R. (1988): *A Century of Childhood.* London: Sidgwick and Jackson.

Laslett, P. (1965): *The World We Have Lost.* London: Methuen.

Leach, E. (1986): The Cereal Packet Norm. *The Guardian,* **29 January**.

Litwak, E. (1965): Extended Kin Relations in an Industrial Democratic Society. In Shanes, E and Streib, G. F. (eds), *Social Structure and the Family: Generational Relations.* Englewood Cliffs. Prentice Hall, 290–323.

Macdonald, C. (1990): *A Woman of Good Character.* Wellington: Allen and Unwin.

Mills, C.W. (1971): *The Sociological Imagination.* Harmondsworth Penguin.

Morris, L. (1990): *The Workings of the Household.* Cambridge: Polity Press.

Oakley, A. (1974): *The Sociology of Housework.* Oxford: Martin Robertson.

Opie, I. and Opie P. (1969): *Children's Games in Street and Playground.* Oxford: Oxford University Press.

Parsons, T. (1956): The American Family: its Relation to Personality and the Social Structure. In Parsons T. and Bales, R. F. (eds), *Family Socialization and Interaction Process.* New York: Free Press

Payne, S. (1991): *Women, Health and Poverty: an Introduction.* Hemel Hempstead. Harvester.

Pollack, L (1983): *Forgotten Children.* Cambridge. Cambridge University Press.

Rose, L. (1991): *The Erosion of Childhood: Child Oppression in Britain 1860–1918.* London. Routledge.

Shahar S. (1990): *Childhood in the Middle Ages.* Routledge. London.

Spock, B. (1946): *Common Sense Book of Baby and Child Care.* New York: Duell Sloan.

Trainor B. (1988): Having and Not Having Babies. What Power do Women Have? *Women's Studies Journal* **3**, 44–72.

Wagg, S. (1988): Perishing Kids? The Sociology of Childhood. *Social Studies Review.* March, p. 126–31.

Young M. and Willmott, P. (1957): *Family and Kinship in East London.* London: Routledge and Kegan Paul.

Young, M. and Willmott, P. (1973): *The Symmetrical Family.* London: Routledge and Kegan Paul.

Further Reading

Abercrombie, N., Warde, A. Soothill, K, Urry, J. and Walby, S. (1994): *Contemporary British Society*. 2nd edn. Cambridge, MA: Polity Press.

Grabrucker, M. (1988): There's a Good Girl. Gender Stereotyping in the First Three years of Life. A Diary. Belfast: Women's Press.

Haralambos, M. and Holborn M. (1995): *Sociology Themes and Perspectives*. 4th edn. London: Collins Educational.

Hardy and Crow G. (eds) (1991): *Lone Parenthood: Coping with Constraints and Making Opportunities*. Hemel Hempstead : Harvester.

Social policy: the state, the family and young children

6

Erica Joslyn, Christine Such and Cath Dixon

This chapter aims to:

- explore developments in policy and provision relating to young children and their families;
- examine the impact of these policies on children, families and various sectors of society.

Introduction

The post-war political consensus on the provision of welfare in the UK was guided by the dominant view that the government had both the resources and the responsibility to provide a range of services to ensure a basic and rising standard of living for all of its citizens (Sullivan, 1996). However, by the 1970s this view was being strongly challenged by those who believed that the state had intruded too far into the private life of individuals (Joseph, 1976). This challenge was given greater legitimacy by the economic arguments about the UK's economy. The UK was in the position of having, on the one hand, one of the highest rates of public expenditure and direct taxation and, on the other, one of the lowest rates of economic growth among developed countries (Cripps, 1981) .

These economic arguments provided the impetus to shift welfare policy into an arena dominated more by financial considerations and less by social ideals. Economic concerns over the extent of state responsibility have been heightened more recently by demographic trends which indicate the potential for increased public expenditure on high-dependency groups such as pensioners and lone parents (George and Miller, 1993). As a consequence, policy-making over the last two decades has been guided by three principle objectives:

- to reduce the level of dependency on benefits and state provision;
- to create a more efficient welfare system by targeting benefits at those most in need;
- to move away from the state as the main provider of services.

The welfare of children has always attracted a great deal of both social and political support. However, despite continuing rhetoric about concern for the welfare of children, polices which impact on the lives of young children and their families have not been either exempt or protected from the influence of these principles. The needs of young children and their families are addressed in a range of general policies, including health, education, housing and social security, as well specially formulated policies such as the Children Act 1989 and the Child Support Act 1991. This chapter will examine the main changes in policy and provision for young children and their families. It will address the ways in which both general and specific policies have sought to redress dependency on the state and to redirect the focus for help and assistance back on to the family and the private and voluntary sectors.

As society has developed, so have our perceptions of what constitutes and contributes to the welfare of children and their families. Modern child-care law has inherited much from the Poor Law legislation and amendments of the mid-nineteenth century, and this chapter will analyse the contribution of the past to the present. It will also examine the trends and developments of current policies in relation to care and provision, and will explore the political rationale for change.

Foundations of child-care policy

Provision under the New Poor Law legislation of 1834 included the care of the growing number of children – orphaned, deserted, or abandoned to the work-houses. This legislation introduced an enforceable legal duty upon parents to provide for children who would otherwise be left destitute. It also empowered civil parish authorities to set to work or compulsorily apprentice those children whose parents could not help them. The emphasis of care services was on making productive use of children as cheap labour and ensuring their contribution to the improvement of the economy.

The Poor Law is considered to be responsible for introducing the concept of 'less eligibility' into legislation in general. The concept of less eligibility was influential in designing a system in which the poor would receive assistance only if they entered a workhouse, where conditions would be harder for them than for those who remained out of the workhouse and on low wages. The rationale that those in work should always be better off than those on state benefits was, and remains, an important factor in the fashioning of policy. In the nineteenth century the concept was not only applied to adults, but also to the care of children. As a consequence, improvement in conditions for children in workhouses was severely restrained in order to ensure that work-house children would not have better conditions than the children of the employed poor (Eekelaar and Dingwall, 1990).

Concern for children and their environment was a primary issue for the philanthropists of the time, who sought to establish alternatives to the workhouse. The philanthropists promoted a number of different schemes, including boarding out, care in a scattered home or voluntary home, or emigration. The influence of these philanthropic ideas is reflected in the Poor Law Amendment Act 1889, which provided the first framework for the legal adoption of children and for taking children into the care of the authorities. The 1889 Amendment gave local authorities the power to transfer all parental rights for a child from their natural parent, or parents, to a guardian. In 1899, this power was extended to include orphans and the children of those who were considered 'unfit' to be parents. Such intervention into family life by the state was not particularly popular, and Eekelaar and Dingwall (1990) suggest that it was probably only tolerated because these were the families of the 'disreputable' poor. Much headway was made in developing new approaches to child care, and by the beginning of the twentieth century, of the 69 030 children in Poor Law care in 1908, less than a third were in workhouses or infirmaries (Heywood, 1978).

As a result of emerging concerns about mortality rates and the physical degradation of the working class, efforts were made to improve basic conditions for poor families through separate legislation. The Education Act of 1870 had created local education authorities which had the responsibility for providing primary school education for all children. The Public Health Act of 1847 facilitated the development of community health services aimed almost exclusively at improving environmental conditions. Responsibility for these new services was given to local authorities who also continued to hold responsibility for the provision of child care under the Poor Law and its amendments. Consequently, provision under the Poor Law legislation shifted to focus on home conditions for children, while the new legislation was used to guide education and public health developments. At the turn of the century, subsequent legislation was passed to support the development of both health and education provision. One of the most important of these developments was the establishment of the Ministry of Health in 1919, which instructed Local Authority Boards of Education with regard to the inspection and treatment of schoolchildren.

Early twentieth-century legislation has not only laid the foundation for many of the features which can be found in current legislation, but demonstrates the progress of social values and their impact on policy. In particular, the Poor Law can be seen as the stem from which many principles of modern child-care policy have evolved. Provision of child-care under the Poor Law remained essentially unchanged until 1948, and responsibility for children in care and powers to organise the legal adoption of children were maintained under local authority children's departments when they were created in 1948.

Local authorities

Local authorities hold responsibility for a wide range of services, including housing, social services and, to a considerable extent, education. The theme that a local authority should no longer perform the role of a direct provider of services has been a driving force for change over the last decade. Policies have been directed at developing more pluralistic systems, with a variety of public, private and voluntary agencies working alongside local authorities. Although local authorities are no longer seen as the main providers, they are to continue to have a key role in ensuring that there is adequate provision to meet needs (Ridley, 1988). Growth in new provision is encouraged in both the private and the voluntary sectors, with the local authorities acting as an 'enabler' for the development of services.

Providing for the child

The principle of protecting the rights and interests of the child was included in Acts such as the Children Act of 1948 and the Children and Young Persons Act of 1969. Both promoted the view that children should only be taken into the care of a local authority as a last resort. The most recent Children Act of 1989 not only provides a framework which maintains this principle, but also extends the responsibilities of both parents and local authorities in a way which seeks to operationalise this principle.

The 1989 Act protects the rights of the child by stipulating that (1) authorities must pay particular attention to the wishes and feelings of the child and (2) in making alternative care arrangements, authorities must take into consideration the different racial groups in the area to which the child belongs. The Children Act (1989) emphasises avoiding taking children into care wherever possible and, where a child is seen to be in need of care, efforts must be made to provide this care without actually removing the child from his or her natural home. Concern for the prevention of the breakup of families and the rights of the child has greatly increased, and local authorities have a statutory duty to develop preventive work such as the setting up of family centres. This policy, which seeks to maintain family values and to uphold the rights of the child, has resulted in the abandonment of the large institutional type of children's home in favour of a policy supporting the fostering of children in ordinary homes.

These arrangements are further supported by the replacement of the concept of parental rights with the less divisive concept of parental responsibility (Fox Harding, 1991). The 1989 Act stipulates, for the first time, that parents should continue to have some responsibility for their child, who may be living away from home under the care of authorities. These arrangements can be seen to support not only preservation of family values but also a revival of family responsibilities in relation to children in care. It is an important principle of the 1989 Act that parents do not lose complete parental responsibility just because a guardian has been appointed. Parents may therefore find themselves sharing the responsibility for their child with others, such as foster parents. Given the number of adults, including the authorities, who may hold some measure of responsibility for a child, there is concern that, in practice, upholding the rights of the child would not necessarily be either easy or possible (Brown and Payne, 1995). Eekelaar and Dingwall suggest that recognition of the child's interest is in fact limited as, if there is a disagreement, decision-makers' views will normally take priority over those of the child.

> *This emphasis on foster care can be seen to uphold the values of family life and also be judged to be part of the movement towards encouraging private and family responsibility for the care of children. This strategy maintains the push on reducing the role of the state and has had serious implications for the level of provision available to assist children deemed to be at risk. The* 1994 Audit Commission, *on examining the identification and provision of services provided evidence that the focus for service provision has been narrow and limiting. The Commission warned that children at risk of abuse had become a priority group and that insufficient attention had been given to the broader concept of 'children in need' as contained within the spirit of the 1989 Children Act.*
>
> (Eekelaar and Dingwall, 1990)

Education

Post-war education policy has continued to promote the interest of the child and to provide legislation which seeks to enable pupils to develop their full potential to a standard which is likely to serve the interests of the nation. While primary education was made compulsory in 1870, it was the Education Act 1944, often referred to as the Butler Act, which provided secondary education for all. The focus of this legislation was on providing equal educational opportunities for all children. Through this legislation, primary and secondary education was provided free of charge and education was made compulsory between the ages of 5 and 15 years. The school-leaving age was not raised to 16 years until 1974.

While the education system can be seen to have improved opportunities for children in general, the system does not necessarily service the needs of all children equally. Two examples are nursery education and education for children with special needs. With regard to nursery education the government is reticent about extending state responsibility, and although policy does offer some leadership in relation to the provision of education for children with special education needs, education provision for this group remains fragmented.

Provision of nursery education was not considered for inclusion as part of the education system until the Plowden Report (1968) and the 1972 White

Paper, *Education: A Framework for Expansion* (Department of Education and Science, 1972). This document outlined proposals which, over a 10-year period, would have made nursery school provision available to all children aged 3 and 4 years. However, the comparative neglect of this area of provision by education authorities has led instead to considerable developments of private and voluntary services outside the school system (Brown and Payne, 1994). A preference for parental responsibility continues to influence government policy with regard to nursery education, and the debate on nursery education is conducted as an issue outside state provision for education.

The *Rumbold Report* (Department of Education and Science, 1990) reinforced the principle that care and education for the under-fives are complementary and ought to be inseparable (Figure 6.1). Over the past year, the Department of Education has been experimenting with the use of vouchers for children. In pilot areas vouchers have been provided for parents of 4-year-olds, and these can be exchanged at accredited education settings, including playgroups. This strategy is designed to facilitate parental choice and equity

Figure 6.1 Care and education for the under-fives should be complementary and inseparable.

of access, and voucher-holders are able to seek nursery provision from both private and state sectors. The use of vouchers also raised concerns about quality and standards for accreditation of nurseries and about equality of access to services (Milne, 1994). In addition to these concerns, vouchers did not enjoy political concensus, and were discontinued by the incoming Labour government of 1997.

The 1981 Education Act reaffirmed the 1944 principle that, wherever possible, children with special education needs should be educated in mainstream education. According to the Education Act 1981, a child has special education needs if he or she has a learning disability which requires education provision that is additional to, or otherwise different from, the educational provision made generally for children in that school, or if he or she has a physical disability. The categories of handicap specified in the 1944 Education Act were abolished and replaced by the concept of 'special education needs', and this principle is maintained within the Education Act 1993.

The change of categorisation was designed to move away from the notion that children with the same diagnosis (e.g. Down's syndrome) had the same educational needs and required the same educational provision (Jones, 1995). In the past, when the type of problem was used to determine the provision, a number of separate special schools designated for particular handicaps were set up. However, now that needs are not regarded as being solely derived from the type of problem, some of these separate schools have been closed, or pupils have been moved into mainstream schools so that many children with special needs are not isolated from children of their own age and communities. However, despite a great deal of support for this policy, the integration of children into mainstream education remains slow. The Audit Commission (1992) estimated that in 1990 there was a total of 1.2 million pupils in England and Wales with special educational needs, with 63 per cent still attending special schools.

One reason commonly identified for the low level of integration has been insufficient funding for the implementation of this policy. Recent changes in the financial management of schools are unlikely to improve the pace of change. The Education Reform Act of 1988 requires schools to be accountable for their own finances, and the Act enables schools to opt out of the control of local education authorities. Constraints on school budgets, for schools both in and out of local authority control, continue to limit the adaptation of building and levels of support which schools would require to be able to provide for pupils with disabilities.

Many of the changes introduced by the Education Acts of 1981, 1988 and 1993 emphasise the role of parents as consumers (David, 1993). In recent years a number of significant changes have been initiated, including standard attainment tasks (SATs), which have been accepted with varying degrees of enthusiasm, league tables of schools in relation to performance, and the requirement for schools to ballot parents about issues such as opting out.

These changes sought to reinforce the role of parents in making informed choices about the schools, and to encourage parents to play a more active part in the development of schools.

Day care

Day-care provision is primarily regarded as the parents' responsibility. Day-care is officially viewed as a private matter for the parents and, to some extent, for the employer, and not as a matter of public concern or for public funds. Such a philosophy is reflected in the government stance – viewing children and child care as, in general, private issues except in cases of extreme need (e.g. dire poverty or abuse) (Brannen and Moss, 1991).

Despite the attempt at selectivity in providing day-care to those in need, low-income families and in particular, lone parents' needs for day-care have been poorly addressed (Oldfield and Yu, 1993). Policies and provision for nursery education have consistently failed to recognise the interconnecting issues of employment hours, income (Hardy and Glover, 1991), cost of day-care and accessibility of day-care facilities. Until such issues are adequately addressed, the dichotomy of the 'dependency' culture is likely to persist – parents must either remain on benefit or battle with the conflicting difficulties of earning an adequate income and caring for children.

The range of day-care in the UK is a variety of home-based and institutional care (see Moss, 1991, for an in-depth review of the provision). Care at home by relatives, particularly by maternal grandmothers, provides the most commonly used form of care. The next most common form is the childminder service which, under the Children Act 1989, is subject to registration and inspection by social services. Day nurseries for under-threes are provided mainly via the private sector and at a cost which is often prohibitive for low-income families (Holterman, 1993). The state had previously provided more day nurseries but, since the 1980s, many have become family centres aimed at addressing inadequate parenting and child-protection concerns. The influence of the private sector was significant in the 1980s, with some employers, such as the Midland Bank, attempting to provide some day-care for their employees.

There is minimal state interference in care which is undertaken in the home, in contrast to care undertaken outside the home, which is subject to registration and inspection. Local authority social service departments are required to hold a register and regularly to inspect facilities, such as childminders and nurseries, regularly in order to monitor them and ensure that standards are being met (Elfer and Wedge, 1992).

Housing

The changing role of local authorities is most obvious in social housing. Recent government policy has shifted the responsibility for providing, maintaining and managing housing provision from local authorities to housing associations. In addition, because of restrictions on local government, the number of new homes being built to meet social housing needs is dependent upon developments by housing associations and not local authorities. These changes in effect curtail the role of local government as a provider of accommodation and as a landlord.

The stock of social housing available for people in need has significantly decreased in recent years. The Conservative government preference for home ownership was given its fullest expression in 1980, when tenants were given the right to buy their council house. Many families who were encouraged to buy during the economic boom of the 1980s unfortunately suffered in the subsequent recession of the 1990s, and many became trapped in homes that they could ill afford (Atkinson and Durden, 1994). As a result of this legislation, a large number of homes have been lost to the private sector – while, ironically, the government is committed to providing financial help to cover mortgage costs for unemployed home-owners.

An actual shortage of dwellings has given rise to a number of social issues. Rent values tend to become exorbitant, especially in areas of highest demand. This means that the poorest families suffer, especially families with several dependent children, as they cannot afford the accommodation that they require (Blackburn, 1991). Consequently multi-occupancy of property occurs, with subsequent lowering of standards of privacy and amenities. Overcrowding of small dwellings results in a variety of difficulties, such as young children lacking space for play and older ones lacking a quiet place to study (Kumar, 1993). Sharing houses with relatives or living in one- and two-roomed flats also imposes intolerable strains on marital relationships.

Where poor-quality housing is amassed together, the whole area becomes unfit. Houses in deprived areas are frequently damp, insanitary and structurally unsafe, and there is a clear risk to the health of the occupants (Blackburn, 1991). There is a constant battle against disease, high mortality rates and general child neglect. Deprivation is seen to be equally bad for the morale of the occupants of such housing. If individual houses are cramped and unattractive, their occupants will spend more time outside, and young children will play on dangerous streets and in unsafe areas. There is evidence that children from deprived areas fail to take advantage of educational opportunities and are generally restricted in their development as a consequence of their environment (Kumar, 1993). Holterman (1996) links the notion of well-being with investment in the child – it is seen as important to their growth and as essential to achieving their potential. She argues that children living in adverse conditions will not be able to achieve their potential and that, as a society if we fail to invest in this generation then the economic potential of the UK may well be damaged.

In the past, as now, housing policies have given priority to provision for families with children. The statutory duty of local authorities to provide accommodation is based on criteria of need. The Housing (Homeless Persons) Act 1977 identified vulnerable families with dependent children, including single-parent families, as having high priority, and childless couples and single homeless people as having low priority. The concept of priority groups was revisited in the Housing Act 1985, which restated the local authority duty to secure permanent accommodation for those in 'priority need'. Priority need is defined as families with dependent children, pregnant women, people who are vulnerable because of old age, physical disability, mental illness or handicap, and special reasons include children at risk and victims of domestic violence (Burrows and Walentowicz, 1992).

However, even with prioritising of those families in need, the limited amount of social housing available cannot at present meet the needs of this group. Unfortunately, the number of families with children in need far outstrips the amount of housing available. Therefore many families considered to be in priority need are being accommodated in temporary facilities – mostly bed and breakfast and sub-standard accommodation in the private sector. With regard to the rented sector of the housing market, lone parents are more likely to occupy accommodation of inferior quality. Lone parents are prominent among those groups of disadvantaged people who 'tend to get very worse council housing; older rather than newer; flats rather than houses; higher floors rather than lower' (Harrison, 1983). The rising number of families with children requiring accommodation and the restrictions on building new properties for social housing have served to fuel the growth and use of the private sector for temporary housing provision.

In the absence of available social housing, the cost of accommodating families with dependent children in the private sector is met by the local authority. In this way the state is seen to maintain one of its primary objectives – to pay for housing provision for those considered most in need, but not actually to provide the necessary accommodation. Since its inception, housing benefit has proved to be costly, mainly because of the large proportion of local authority tenants who are entitled to Housing Benefit and because of the higher rents in the private and voluntary sectors (Hill, 1984).

These developments accentuate the trend towards the residualisation of the council sector. This means that the limited amount of public housing is being used for those most in need, but unfortunately it tends to do so by allocating poorer people to poorer housing. Thus current housing policy continues to contribute to the differentiation of life chances between the families of the poor and those who are able to invest in their own housing.

Health care

The National Health Service Act 1948 remains the guiding legislation for comprehensive health care provision, free of charge, to all children under 16 years of age. The legislation provides for a system of primary, community and hospital services for all children. A major theme within the National Health Service is addressing the balance between curing ill health and the promotion of good health (Department of Health, 1992). While advances in technology continue to improve diagnosis and treatment, there has been a revival of interest in encouraging families and health professionals to devote more effort to the prevention of illness and to health promotion (Audit Commission, 1994).

The importance of prevention is not new in relation to children and a number of services have traditionally been provided to ensure the early identification of problems in children. The health centre is the main vehicle through which a wide range of primary health care is provided by a multidisciplinary team. A number of professionals are involved in primary care services specifically – general practitioners with a focus on early diagnosis and referral, and midwives and health visitors who have a statutory duty to care for neonates and young children in the community. Health centres are usually run by general practitioners, and provide a range of services which would normally include general practitioner surgeries, child health clinics including developmental surveillance, immunisations and well-woman clinics. The range of services being offered at health centres has been on the increase and some health centres may also provide services for children with chronic illness who are being nursed in their own homes, in conjunction with community paediatric nursing services.

Community health services are run by health authorities and provide a school health service which is one of the oldest public services to be set up by the state. It pre-dates the NHS when, for some children, the school health service supplied the only access to health care. This service continues to be available despite the fact that today all children should be registered with a general practitioner and have access to free health care. Its value is seen to lie in the important part that it can play in preventive care. However, there are questions about the justification for this additional health surveillance, given that similar services are provided by health centres. The school health service also has an important part to play, together with teachers, in seeking to identify and protect children who may be suffering some form of abuse. The school health service is well placed to provide the opportunity for professionals from health, social services and education to work together in the interest of and fot the protection of children (Nutbrown, 1994).

The issue of funding health care has been a persistent one, and the most recent attempt at a solution was published in the NHS and Community Care Act 1990. This legislation has reformed the structure of the health service by displacing the traditional modes of public service administration and professionalism by a form of private sector managerialism. This can be characterised by five interlinked factors:

- the emergence of NHS trusts as the dominant form of provider;
- the development of the purchaser role;
- the growth of GP fundholding;
- greater involvement of the private sector in health care;
- introduction of an accountable financial management system.

This new structure continues to provide services free at the point of delivery, although the introduction of an accountable system of finance has imposed a measure of rationing and an emphasis on value for money which affects everyone, including children.

The NHS Act and Community Care Act 1990 also emphasised the role of parents and families as users of the health services. The role of the consumer has been further reinforced by target setting as a means of encouraging greater collaboration between health professionals and the consumer. Targets may be designed to promote healthy behaviours, such as increasing the proportion of infants who are breast-fed to 75 per cent at birth and 50 per cent at 6 weeks of age (Department of Health, 1991). The Patients' Charter (1991) prompts users of the health service to seek detailed information on local health services. The aim of this target is to enable users to participate more fully in decisions about service provision.

However, George and Miller (1994) are critical of this target-setting approach, which they describe as focusing solely on outcomes of health care. They argue that it fails to identify the means, particularly in relation to resources, for the achievements of these targets. While target-setting identifies important objectives to be achieved in health care, the failure to address more fundamental problems such as family resources, which could improve nutrition and access to local services, will exclude poorer families from the benefits to be gained.

Poverty and children

The plan for social security proposed by Beveridge in 1942 was based on social insurance for the majority, backed up by means-tested social assistance for the residual few. Beveridge argued that, to be successful, his social security programme needed to be underpinned by three measures: the maintenance of full employment, the provision of an allowance for each child, and the provision of free health care. The social security system is a complex one and Box 6.1 provides a simplified outline of the different kinds of benefits available.

In the 1990s it has been shown that children are more vulnerable and more at risk of experiencing poverty than others in society (Kumar, 1993; Holtermann, 1996). However, this coincides with the search for greater efficiency in

Contributory benefit

These benefits are financed through a form of taxation from earnings paid into the National Insurance fund. When families want to make a claim, they have to show that they paid into the fund which is held by the government. Only those who have paid in will be able to claim. Unemployment benefit (UB) is a contributory benefit. Widowed mother's allowance (WMA) is paid to widows who have children or are pregnant.

Means-tested benefit

These are safety-net benefits paid out if a family's income and capital is sufficiently low that they cannot meet their everyday needs. When making a claim, families have to show that they have little or no income. Income Support (IS) is paid out if income falls below the level set by parliament. Family Credit (FC) is paid to low-paid workers with children. Housing Benefit (HB) is paid to low-income families who pay rent.

Non-contributory benefit

These are benefits that are not dependent upon families paying into the NI fund. In order to claim, individuals have to show that they need help because of their condition or disabilities. Families do not have to be on a low income to receive help. Examples include benefits for disabled people, such as the Disability Living Allowance.

Universal benefit

These are benefits which are paid to everyone who falls within the category. Child Benefit (CB) is paid for all children to their parents or carers. Every child will receive benefit, no matter how rich or poor their parents are.

Discretionary benefit

These benefits are paid out to families in special circumstances at the discretion of the benefits agency. The Social Fund created in 1988 is paid out in the form of either a grant to those in need and living in the community, or through a loan which must be repaid to the family.

Box 6.1 Benefits for families and children, shown according to type of benefit

the benefits system and a focus on the principle of means-testing for assessing eligibility for benefits. An increasing number of benefits that can be claimed by families in financial need are means-tested using levels set by Parliament – for example, family credit, free school meals, housing benefit, and grants from the social fund.

Child Benefit was introduced in 1977/8 to replace both Family Allowance and income tax relief for children. The most significant change was that Child Benefit was to be paid to all mothers (fathers or carers) on behalf of their children. It had previously been paid to fathers, but it was argued that the best way to ensure that children did gain as a result of the benefit was to make the benefit payable to the mother and not to the father. Child Benefit is a universal benefit payable to all children aged 16 years and under, continues up to the age of 18 years for those in full-time education, and is as such costly to provide.

More recently, its progress has been less than smooth. It is not seen as a payment which covers the entire cost of keeping a child, so families with low incomes can still find themselves in poverty (Piachaud, 1987). To combat this, a means-tested benefit known as Family Credit (previously called Family Income Supplement) is available to working families whose normal gross weekly income is less than the amounts prescribed by Parliament. Thus the debate of the 1990s is centred around the effectiveness of Child Benefit in helping children, given that poor families must still rely on additional assistance. However, the utility of Child Benefit for families in need is not in question, and a survey conducted by the Child Poverty Action Group in 1987 showed that mothers felt that child benefit was crucial in helping to make ends meet (Henwood *et al.*, 1987).

Given these concerns about its efficiency as a universal benefit, the level of Child Benefit is at present retained at a low value while the debate about its future continues. It has been suggested that the best way to ensure benefits are received by those in most need is to replace the universal benefit with a means-tested benefit targeted at low-income families with children. However, the main difficulty with means testing is that not everyone who is entitled to claim will do so, and therefore children who are entitled to this benefit may not necessarily receive it. If it were to become a means-tested benefit, this would continue the current trend in policy towards more specific targeting of benefits.

While Child Benefit is paid to all families, Family Credit and Income Support are targeted according to the work status of families, and the concept of less eligibility is important in setting the limits of these benefits. Family Credit targets help to low-paid workers with children, while for those who are out of work the main source of income will be Income Support.

Family Credit was introduced by the Social Security Act 1988, and is an additional payment to low-paid families. Anyone, including lone parents, with at least one dependent child can claim Family Credit if he or she is in paid employment. Those who are entitled to Family Credit are automatically entitled to free NHS dental and prescription charges, but not to free school meals, as Family Credit already includes a contribution towards the cost of school meals.

In keeping with the concept of less eligibility, the amount of Family Credit is normally set so as to ensure that low-wage families on family credit would be no worse off than out-of-work families on Income Support. Families earning more than the applicable amount up to a ceiling receive proportionately less Family Credit.

Income Support is paid as of right, and is therefore a non-contributory benefit for people whose income, whether obtained from other benefits or private resources, is below a level laid down by Parliament. It is a means-tested benefit that broadly represents the amount which the state is prepared to make available to people who are not in work in order to bring their incomes up to a basic level. The rates are different for people treated as couples, and there are additions for dependent children. People on Income Support are also entitled to exemption from certain charges, e.g. NHS charges and school meals.

The Social Fund provides payments and interest-free loans to help people on low incomes to cope with exceptional expenses. The Social Fund provides most of its help (70 per cent) through loans reclaimable from weekly benefits – reducing weekly incomes for successful claimants. These payments are means-tested and only payable to people who are on Income Support and on very low incomes. The criteria for obtaining a grant from the Social Fund are both complex and dependent upon locally set guidelines. The Social Fund is cash limited, and the process of application and appeal is sufficiently complex to warrant the involvement of a social worker to provide support for a particular case.

Hill (1994) argues that in recent years government has set in place policies which address what they see as a problem – that benefit policies and housing policies actively encourage single parenthood and family breakdown. He warns that, while an elaborate system of means-tested benefit will not affect the very poor, it will however disadvantage those just a little above the state-determined 'poverty line'. More specifically, he suggests that provision for lone-parent families has been weakened in ways designed to force parents to consider low-paid part-time work.

The Child Support Act 1991

A further move to reduce the role of the state in income maintenance was introduced with the Child Support Act 1991. The White Paper entitled *Children Come First* (Department of Social Security, 1990) identified a number of problems with the existing system of maintenance through the courts, including low levels of awards being granted, no systematic review or updating of awards, no parity between families with similar means, and non-compliance with court orders. It also noted the need to provide state support for lone-parent families because of the increasing numbers of lone parents who were reliant on state benefits in the absence of effective maintenance from absent partners. The number of one-parent families as a proportion of all families with dependent children rose from 8 per cent in 1971 to 19 per cent in 1990 (Central Statistical Office, 1992, p.39).

The White Paper proposed to minimise state support for female lone parents by pursuing errant fathers to persuade them to accept financial responsibility for their children. This approach was not only favoured by the New Right, but also overlapped with demands by some sections of the feminist movement to encourage greater involvement of men in child-care responsibilities. The Child Support Act 1991 is based on the principle that both natural parents have a duty to contribute to the maintenance of their child or children.

The Child Support Agency (CSA) began operations on 5 April 1993, and established for the first time a standard formula for calculating child-support payments. The CSA took over the responsibility for maintenance, and all previous orders made by the courts were to be overridden by the CSA. The CSA replaced the previous administration of maintenance through the courts, although the courts continue to decide on matters of contact and residence. The first 3 years in the life of the CSA have been particularly stormy, and a number of charges have been made, including the following:

- an unacceptable focus on families claiming benefits;
- property settlements were not taken into account, nor is informal support in cash or in kind recognised by the agency;
- the emphasis has been on formal maintenance settlements for the child;
- an imbalance of interest in favour of the first family.

Research by Clarke *et al.* (1995) into the circumstances of lone mothers on means-tested benefits suggests that the focus on formal maintenance has left out and marginalised the informal involvement and cash support by absent fathers. This study showed that lone mothers and children placed great value on this informal help, as it enabled fathers to maintain control and to have some involvement in the lives of their children. The study also shows that, following the involvement of the CSA, some fathers were no longer able or willing to provide informal support either in cash or in kind. For some children the result was that the frequency and quality of contact with their absent father declined, and for some mothers it meant an actual reduction in support in general. For children of second families the effect of CSA involvement has been a reduction in already limited resources. These negative consequences which may result from the involvement of the CSA mean that neither family gains, and both families may well end up with inadequate financial support. The CSA does not appear to work within the same philosophy of concern for the welfare of the child as the Children Act 1989. It fails to take account of issues concerning contact and residence which influence family relationships following breakdown. The consequences of prioritising financial matters may be that the child may have less contact with the absent father, and fuel is added to the potential for a clash of interests between parents who are no longer living together.

Critics suggest that the focus on claimant families by the CSA and on formal financial arrangements indicates that the government has been rather more keen to collect finance to reduce welfare costs than to assist lone parents. The CSA is seen as a vehicle whereby government has sought to change the balance of financial support away from the state and on to families, with a greater proportion of child income support coming from parents.

The voluntary sector – the changing contribution

Charitable organisations no longer dominate the field of child welfare, but they continue to fulfil an important function in relation to statutory services. Large organisations have coped with change by adapting from being universal providers to a new and more selective role. For example, since 1969 Dr Barnados has changed its emphasis from residential homes to care within the family, and has increasingly concentrated upon the needs of socially disadvantaged children in the most deprived areas.

However modified, in form or function, these organisations have had to fit in alongside the new wave of providers of services, either through new ventures such as the provision of playgroup facilities, or as adjuncts to official machinery such as advice centres or family service units. Voluntary services are needed to seal the gaps left by the financial and legislative restrictions upon statutory services. It is recognised by professionals and experts that there are insufficient funds to meet all needs and that statutory care can be both insensitive and inflexible. Hence formal voluntary care continues to flourish, particularly for the specialist needs of minority groups – most notably blind and deaf people continue to be largely catered for by charities. However, the continued presence of charitable organisations in welfare services has attracted some criticism, as they are seen as potential obstacles to the provision of universal and comprehensive services by the state (Lowe, 1993).

Charitable organisations also often play an important role in identifying and highlighting social problems, as has been demonstrated in the contribution of the National Society for the Prevention of Cruelty to Children (NSPCC) in relation to the neglect and abuse of children. The work of pressure groups such as the Child Poverty Action Group plays an essential part in disseminating information about the welfare of children, and in ensuring that the welfare of children remains on the political agenda.

CONCLUSION

Policies which affect young children and their families have, like all other areas of policy, been subjected to the pursuit of ideological restructuring. Over the last two decades policies have been used to redraw the boundary lines between the responsibilities of the family and the responsibilities of the state.

Although policies continue to provide the framework for the continued support for families, at the same time they have been used to minimise and limit the capacity of that support. Changes in the provision of housing are designed to encourage families to look primarily towards the private and voluntary sectors to meet their housing needs, with the state providing limited financial support in the form of housing benefit. The affirmation in law of parental responsibility in relation to both children in care and maintenance of children facilitates the gradual withdrawal of state involvement and reaffirms family responsibilities in these areas.

Changes in social security, designed as they are around the concept of 'less eligibility' and based on means-testing, result in individuals and families being maintained at a level of subsistence. Despite the targeting of benefits, many individuals and families are unlikely to be able to lift themselves above this level of subsistence. This is particularly true for lone parents who are unable to enter the employment market due to an inability to cover the costs of both child-care arrangements and household bills. The impact of subsistence living on young children will therefore continue to be a cause of concern for our society because of, and not necessarily despite current welfare policies.

References

Atkinson, R. and Durden, P. (1994): Housing Policy Since 1979: Development and Prospects. In Savage, S.P., Atkinson, R. and Robins, L. *Public Policy in Britain*. London: Macmillan, 182–202.

Audit Commission (1992): *Getting the Act Together: Provision for Pupils with Special Needs*. London: HMSO.

Audit Commission (1994): *Seen but not Heard: Co-ordinating Community Child Health and Social Services for Children in Need*. London: HMSO

Beveridge, W. (1942): *Social Insurance and Allied Services*. London: HMSO.

Blackburn, C. (1991): *Poverty and Health Working with Family*. Milton Keynes: Open University Press.

Brannen, J. and Moss, P. (1991): *Managing Mothers: Dual Earner Households after Maternity Leave*. London: Unwin Hyman.

Brown, M. and Payne, S. (1995): *Introduction to Social Administration*. London: Routledge.

Burrows, L. and Walentowicz, L. (1992): *Homes Cost Less than Homelessness*. London: Shelter.

Central Statistical Office (1992): *Social Trends. No. 22*. London: HMSO.

Clarke, K. Craig, G. and Glendinning, C. (1995): Money isn't Everything. Fiscal Policy and Family Policy in the Child Support Act, *Social Policy and Administration* **29**, 26–39.

Cripps, F. (1981): The British Crisis: Can The Left Win? *New Left Review* **128**, 93–7.

David, M. (1993): *Parent, Gender and Education Reform*. Oxford: Polity Press.

Department of Education and Science (1972): *Education: a Framework for Expansion*. London: HMSO.

Department of Education and Science (1990): *Starting with Quality: Report of the Committee of Inquiry into Educational Experiences Offered to Three-and-Four-Year-Olds* (Rumbold Report). London: HMSO.

Department of Health (1991): *The Patients' Charter*. London: HMSO.

Department of Health (1992): *The Health of the Nation: A Strategy for Health for England and Wales*. London: HMSO.

Department of Social Security (1990): *Children Come First*. London: HMSO.

Eekelaar, J. and Dingwall, R. (1990): *The Reform of Child Care Law: a Practical Guide to the Children Act 1989*. London: Routledge.

Elfer, P. & Wedge, D. (1992): Defining, Measuring and Supporting Quality. In Pugh, G. *Contemporary Issues in the Early Years*, London: National Children's Bureau, 49–67.

Fox Harding, L. (1991): *Perspectives in Child Care Policy*. Harlow: Longman.

George, V. and Miller, S. (1994): *Social Policy Towards 2000; Squaring the Circle*. London: Routledge.

Hardy, M. and Glover, J. (1991): Income, Employment, Day-care and Lone Parenthood. In Hardy, M. and Crow, G. (eds), *Lone Parenthood*. Hemel Hampstead: Harvester Wheatsheaf, 88–109.

Harrison, P. (1983): *Inside the Inner City: Life Under the Cutting Edge*. Harmondsworth: Penguin.

Henwood, M., Rimmer, L. and Wicks, M. (1987): *Inside the Family*. London: Family Policy Centre.

Heywood, J. (1978): *Children in Care*. London: Routledge & Kegan Paul.

Hill, M. (1984): The Implementation of Housing Benefit. *Journal of Social Policy* **3**, 297–320.

Hill, M. (1994): Social Security Policy under the Conservatives. In Savage, S., Atkinson, R. and Robins, L. (eds), *Public Policy in Britain*. Basingstoke: Macmillan, 241–58.

Holterman, S. (1993): *Becoming a Breadwinner*. London: Day Care Trust.

Holterman, S. (1996): The Impact of Public Expenditure and Fiscal Policies on Britain's Children and Young Children. *Children and Society* **10**, 3–13.

Jones, G. (1995): Education and Assessment Services. In Malin, N. (ed.) *Services for People with Learning Disabilities*. London: Routledge, 125–54.

Joseph, K. (1976): *Stranded on the Middle Ground*. London: Centre for Policy Studies.

Kumar, V. (1993): *Poverty and Inequality in the UK: The Effects on Children*. London: National Children's Bureau.

Lowe, R. (1993): *The Welfare State in Britain since 1945*. Basingstoke: Macmillan.

Milne, K. (1994): Schools of Thought. *New Society & New Statesman* **4 November**, 18–19.

Moss, P. (1991): Day Care for Young Children in the UK. In Melhuish, E. and Moss, P. *Day Care for Young Children*. International Perspectives. London: Routledge, 121–41.

Nutbrown, C. (1994): Teachers and Young Children in Education Establishments in David, T. *Working Together for Young Children*. London: Routledge, 35–46.

Oldfield, N. and Yu, A. (1993): The Cost of a Child: Living Standards for the 1990s. London: Child Poverty Action Group.

Piachaud, D. (1987): *Poor Children: A Tale of Two Decades*. London: Child Poverty Action Group.

Plowden Report (1968): *Children and their Primary Schools*. London: HMSO.

Ridley, N. (1988): *The Local Right: Enabling not Providing*. London: Centre for Policy Studies.

Sullivan, M. (1996): The *Development of the British Welfare State*. Hemel Hampstead: Harvester Wheatsheaf.

7 Children's relationships

David Rutherford

This chapter aims to: study the development, nature and impact of the more significant relationships in the lives of young children.

Introduction

When I recently asked our 5-year-old son, Nathaniel, who his important relationships were with, he immediately listed his parents, sister, brothers, grandmothers, cousins, aunts and uncles, friends, friends' parents and the cats (but not the goldfish!). Most psychologists would agree that these individuals are likely to play a significant part in the emotional, social and cognitive development of children in western societies. In all cultures the survival, health, behaviour and development of skills of children are dependent upon the nurturance, training and control offered by the people with whom they have close relationships (Whiting and Edwards, 1988). The process of socialisation, whereby children are shaped to fit their own particular culture, has traditionally portrayed children as passive recipients of adult influence but, as any parent knows, it is not as simple as that, and children are clearly and determinedly active participants in their own socialisation, constantly modifying and challenging intended influences in pursuit of their own goals and personalities.

The study of relationships is central to social psychology, but until recently children's relationships have been largely ignored by social psychologists. Currently, theorists from social psychology, ethology, social anthropology and sociology, as well as from developmental psychology and psychiatry, are making significant contributions to our understanding of children's relationships. From the early work of Sigmund Freud and John Bowlby (1953), where the emphasis was almost entirely on the mother–child relationship, there have been some important developments in recent years. First, the whole area has become much more complex, and the multiple interactive nature of children's relationships is being explored. Secondly, pivotal concepts such as attachment, the family and temperament have been refined and elaborated to reflect the subtlety of relationships. Thirdly, a multicultural perspective has evolved which enables us to examine possible universals of relationships, as well as cultural diversity. Fourthly, the significance of a child's relationships with father, siblings, grandparents, other care-givers and, most recently, friends and peers is increasingly recognised as being important for that child's future development. Fifthly, it is recognised that children's relationships always occur within a social context of already existing relationships which may exert a powerful influence upon the child. Finally, our understanding of the impact upon a child of relationship disturbance, such as parental discord or sexual abuse, encourages intervention strategies and ways of improving relationships.

Family relationships

Most children are born into a family. Although there are many problems about defining precisely what comprises a family, ranging from the relatively straightforward conjugal nuclear family to the non-conjugal/reconstituted/extended family, members of families are likely to have persistent relationships involving emotional bonds – that is to say, they belong to a group of interconnected and interdependent people who have psychologically meaningful social interactions (Richards, 1995). In the 1990s, blood ties, common residence or legal connections are not considered necessary for the recognition of a family unit. What is important is that there is *mutual recognition* of family membership. This allows for the diversity of family units which have developed over the past 50 years. Although the traditional nuclear family with both parents and two children still exists, the majority of children today are being brought up in families with variable and often changing members. Some children have step-parents and siblings, half-brothers and half-sisters and numerous grandparents, whereas others live in lone-parent families with no siblings and little contact with relatives.

Whatever a child's family type, psychologists and lay people all acknowledge the significance of family relationships as sources of socialisation, nurturance, happiness and comfort (as well as irritation, anxiety and frustration). Life-events studies, from the initial work of Holmes and Rahe (1967) onwards, demonstrate that many significant aspects of a person's well-being are related to changes in family relationships. Both major changes (such as the birth of a child into an existing set of family relationships) and minor changes (uplifts and hassles such as birthdays or tonsillitis) have direct and indirect influences on family members. There is currently a large body of research showing that, in general, our physical and mental health, recovery from illness, and even the number of accidents we have are related to the quality of our close relationships. However, although relationships often provide a buffer against adversity, they can also be sources of severe injury, distress and life-long psychological damage. For example, details of the complex destructive family relationships which emerged during the trial of Rosemary West will undoubtedly provide research material for generations of students of family relationships.

Parenting styles

Early research into the ways in which families affect children identified two main dimensions of parental behaviour that were thought to affect a child's subsequent development:

- the dimension *warmth – coldness* referred to the amount of affection and playfulness shown towards children;
- the dimension *permissiveness – restrictiveness* referred to parental toleration of aggressiveness and control of a child's behaviour.

Few associations between parenting styles and children's development were found, but this research paved the way for the influential work of Baumrind (1971), who examined the ways in which different types of relationships between parents and children affect a child's behaviour. Following a research tradition in the study of leadership, she identified three parental styles related to three patterns of children's behaviour (Figure 7.1).

Permissive parents have very relaxed relationships with their children and, because they do not believe in restricting their child's independence, they exercise less control and accept lower levels of performance, both cognitively and behaviourally. Often their discipline is inconsistent and a child's freedom of expression is valued highly.

The children of permissive parents are often found to be aggressive in their relationships with parents, other adults and other children, unable to control their own feelings of anger, impulsive in their actions and to have low levels of goal-directed achievement orientation.

Authoritarian parents have very controlling relationships with their children. They tend to restrict a child's activities, set strict rules for the child and use harsh, punitive discipline for transgressions. They show low levels of affection and are uninvolved in family and cultural events.

The children of authoritarian parents are often very vulnerable to stress, fearful and anxious about their relationships and appear moody and unhappy. They react irritably, are rather deceitful, and tend to alternate between sulky, passive withdrawal and overt aggression.

Authoritative parents achieve a workable balance between setting high and clear standards for a child's behaviour and encouraging independence. Discipline is firm but fair, with the child's viewpoint being taken into consider-

Parental style	Child's behaviour
Permissive	Impulsive – aggressive
Authoritarian	Conflicted – irritable
Authoritative	Energetic – friendly

Figure 7.1 Parental styles and children's behaviour

ation and control achieved by reasoning and explaining from an early age. Such parents are warm and committed to the child's cognitive, social and moral development.

The children of these (ideal!) parents were found to be energetic and cheerful, to have good relationships with peers and other adults, and purposefully to pursue high levels of achievement.

Several independent studies have confirmed Baumrind's findings, and recent work shows that the association between parental styles and children's behaviour persists over the longer term.

It is important to note that this research is mostly *correlational*, and that we cannot conclude that parental style *causes* patterns of children's behaviour. As any parent knows, it is easy to be warmly involved with a child who cheerfully co-operates with parental wishes. The child's characteristics influence the parenting styles as much as the parent affects the child.

Critiques of Baumrind's classification of parental styles suggest that identifying only three styles greatly oversimplifies the real situation. Not only do most parents use a mixture of styles, rather than just one, but styles may change over time as children develop. Parents know how impossible it is to achieve absolute consistency with different children at different ages in different situations.

Family structures

Research over the last 25 years has identified two main dimensions on which families can be differentiated (Olson and McCubbin, 1983). The first of these, namely *adaptability*, refers to the ability of a family to change in response to external or internal demands. The second dimension, *cohesion*, refers to the strength of emotional bonding between family members. On each of the dimensions a family can be classified into one of 4 different types, and therefore located on a space on a four-by-four grid (see Figure 7.2).

Families located at the extremes of either dimension are postulated to function less well than those that fall in the mid-range or balanced cate-

		Cohesion			
		Disengaged	Separated	Connected	Enmeshed
Adaptability	**Rigid**	Extreme	Mid-range	Mid-range	Extreme
	Structured	Mid-range	Balanced	Balanced	Mid-range
	Flexible	Mid-range	Balanced	Balanced	Mid-range
	Chaotic	Extreme	Mid-range	Mid-range	Extreme

Figure. 7.2 Cohesion in family structures

gories. A *chaotic* family has few clear rules or roles, the children receive little guidance and inconsistent discipline, and they consequently are uncertain about appropriate behaviour and difficult to control. On the other hand, a *rigid* family has rules and roles strictly defined with power exercised by inflexible authoritarian control. In *structured* and *flexible* families rules and roles are negotiated by parents and children democratically, and discipline is firm but fair.

Extremely cohesive families are described as *enmeshed*. Here family members are so strongly identified and bonded with each other that the outside world is of little significance. *Disengaged* families have little sense of family identity, and each member functions separately with little reference to the others. Between the two extremes the members of *connected* and *separated* families are bound together by emotional ties at the same time as maintaining their own individual identity and activity.

Empirical evidence in relation to this model offers clear support for the hypothesis that balanced families function better than other types. They cope with the changing needs of developing children more effectively, with fewer disruptions and less unhappiness than either the mid-range or extreme families.

Balanced, optimal, healthy, energised, well-functioning families

Despite concern expressed by political parties and the tabloid press about the 'breakdown of the family', many families continue to function very well, the members caring for each other with little conflict, and producing responsible, well-adjusted, contributing members of society.

The following characteristics have been identified by a number of different researchers, and although the list is not exhaustive, it indicates the range of desirable attributes:

* relationships – close and warm;
* communication – clear, supportive and empathic;
* power – shared but with parental control;
* roles – clearly defined but not rigid;
* rules – negotiated and modifiable;
* conflict – regulated and resolved by discussion;
* world view – collectively agreed and continually reviewed;
* autonomy – encouraged and accepted.

As anybody who lives within a family knows, these counsels of perfection are easier to state than they are to achieve. Nevertheless, many families do strive to reach the ideals with relatively good success. Some families, however, seem to fail more often than they succeed, and these are identified as dysfunctional families.

Dysfunctional families

Leo Tolstoy wrote in *Anna Karenina*, 'All happy families resemble each other; each unhappy family is unhappy in its own way.' Although the foregoing discussion suggests that he was probably right about happy families, he was clearly mistaken about unhappy families in that they, too, share common characteristics. Whether they are rigid or chaotic, enmeshed or disengaged, they are incapable of consistently dealing successfully with ordinary everyday life, and are very likely to do significant harm to the psychological wellbeing of their members. As can be seen from the Olson model, dysfunctional families are characterised by their extremity. They are extremely rigid or extremely chaotic, extremely disengaged or extremely enmeshed. In terms of the desirable attributes of healthy families, dysfunctional families seem to operate differently, and the following characteristics have been identified:

- relationships – either distant and cold or engulfing, may be abusive;
- communication – inadequate, unclear, ambiguous, double-binding;
- power – rigid hierarchy, cross-generation alliances;
- roles – either inflexibly or poorly defined;
- rules – rigidly enforced or very inconsistent;
- conflict – frequent destructive clashes without resolution;
- world view – idiosyncratic and distorted;
- autonomy – either strongly inhibited or irrelevant.

Any family with many of these characteristics is unlikely to provide an adequate environment for its members, particularly for children, and it is likely that at times of stress in particular, one or more of the family members will come to a community's attention as being in need of help in coping with adversity.

Mothers

More has probably been written about a child's first relationship, usually with his or her mother, than all of the child's other relationships put together. Following the work of John Bowlby in the first edition of his popular classic *Child Care and the Growth of Love* in 1953, there has been a massive development of theory and research evidence in the area, much of it within the framework of two major theoretical positions. *Ethology* adopts an evolutionary, biological perspective and takes the view that the survival of an infant depends upon the inborn behaviour and characteristics of infants (crying, smiling, chuckling, large eyes, round faces) which elicit care-giving behaviour from the mother such as feeding and comforting. Although it is presumed that these care-giving behaviours of mothers have a biological basis in humans, they are, very significantly modified by cultural learning. The *social learning* approach takes the view that the interaction between biological bases and social environment is best accounted for by principles of reward, punishment, imitation and observation in the relationship between a child and his or her primary care-giver. Mutually rewarding encounters between mother and child begin the process by which an enduring emotional bond is formed, the quality of which is thought by many theorists to be the foundation for all other relationships that the child will develop.

The concept of *attachment* is central to an understanding of the mother–child relationship. Originally the term was used to denote an emotional bond of affection for one individual, not interchangeable – an intense driving force towards seeking closeness with another person. This view sees attachment as residing in the individual, whereas more recent researchers have taken the position that attachment refers to a dynamic set of behaviours in the relationship between two people, a transaction in which both child and mother play crucial parts.

Although the newborn baby shows no evidence of attachment, it soon shows preferences – for other people to be nearby, for human faces, for social stimuli, and for human voices – which permit the development of attachments. By 6 weeks the infant is using its limited repertoire of behaviour to attract attention (smiling or crying), and by 3 months infants are reacting more positively to their usual caretakers than to strangers. At between 6 months and 8 months the infant begins to show clear evidence of primary attachment, usually – but not always – to the mother. Several factors seem to be important at this stage. First, *object permanence* emerges as part of the child's cognitive development, and the infant realises that someone out of sight still exists. The mother's absence is noticed and *separation protest* occurs. *Fear* begins to emerge as a strong emotion and wariness of strangers often causes crying and searching behaviour in the child. Mobility also increases at this stage, and the infant now begins to be able to crawl towards the primary care-giver when anxious. After about 9 months attachments begin to be formed with others in the child's environment, such as siblings, the father and grandparents.

Maternal bonding, which is the mother's emotional attachment to the child, begins before the baby is born and continues through the first hours and days of the baby's life. Early contact with the baby, with skin-to-skin touching, is thought by some researchers to be important but not necessary for good bonding to occur (Rode *et al.*, 1981).

Ainsworth *et al.* (1978), using the *Strange Situation Procedure*, have identified three main categories of attachment.

Type B – Secure attachment

This was found in 50 to 70 per cent of children studied. The child:

- shows a clear preference for the mother;
- is outgoing with strangers while the mother is present;
- uses the mother as a base for active exploration of the environment;
- maintains periodic eye contact with the mother;

- shows distress on separation from the mother;
- is comforted and warmly greets the mother's return.

The mother

- is sensitive and responsive to the baby's needs;
- encourages exploration and communication;
- is warm and emotionally expressive.

Type A – Anxious – avoidant attachment

This was found in 20 to 25 per cent of children studied. The child:

- ignores the mother;
- is not especially wary of strangers, and ignores them;
- shows little exploration when with the mother;
- is not distressed upon separation;
- avoids the mother upon her return;

The mother

- is rigid and self-centred;
- is cold and uninvolved with the baby;
- avoids physical contact;
- tends to be intolerant and irritable;
- is unresponsive to the baby's needs;

Type C – Insecure – ambivalent attachment

This was found in 10 per cent of children studied. The child:

- is sometimes clinging and sometimes rejecting;
- is reluctant to explore;
- is very wary of strangers;
- becomes very distressed at the mother leaving;
- both seeks and rejects comfort upon reunion.

The mother

- is inconsistent in her care-giving;
- has difficulty in interpreting the child's needs;
- attempts close physical contact;
- has difficulty synchronising with the baby.

More recent studies have found a fourth pattern, namely *disorganised* attachment, which occurs in high-risk families and where the child appears confused and apprehensive about his or her relationship with the mother (Main and Solomon, 1986).

There is some clear evidence that the quality of the primary attachment has significance for a child's subsequent relationships in childhood, and even later. Securely attached infants are likely to become more confident, skilful, socially orientated, co-operative and outgoing, and to be more popular and to have more friends (La Freniere and Sroufe, 1985). There is also evidence that poor-quality attachment between mother and child is linked to the mother's own insecure attachment as a child. Both security and insecurity may be transmitted from one generation to the next.

Fathers

As a sensitive, 'New-Age' father of five children, maximally involved in responsibility for the care of the children from birth onwards ('I wish', says my wife!), I have long been frustrated by the lack of knowledge about the nature of the father–child relationship and the impact of the father on the development of the child. Although most writers assert the father's importance, the mother–child relationship has been predominant in research until recently. Now, however, with growing numbers of women bringing up children on their own, with increasing numbers of women in the work-force and with high levels of male unemployment, both the presence of fathers and their absence have been studied.

According to Lamb (1987), the three main dimensions of parental involvement are:

- engagement – the time spent interacting with a child on a one-to-one basis, e.g. while reading a story;
- accessibility – the parent is occupied but available to respond to the child if necessary, e.g. while reading the paper;
- responsibility – the parent is accountable for the everyday care and welfare of the child, e.g. feeding, clothing.

Fathers appear to spend about 20 per cent of the time mothers do *engaged* with their children, 30 per cent of the time mothers are *accessible* to their children, and take only 10 per cent of the *responsibility* for child care. Thus, although there is undoubtedly a culture advocating the significance of the father's role, the reality has probably not changed greatly in recent years. Mothers still do the majority of the work associated with children.

Research by Parke and his co-workers (Parke, 1981) has shown that, with newborn infants fathers were just as involved as mothers in interaction with their babies, and nurtured, touched, looked at, kissed, talked to and held them equally. In only one behaviour – smiling – did mothers surpass the fathers. However, in the earliest days, even with bottle-fed babies, fathers spent less time than mothers in feeding and related caretaking activities, which suggests that parental role allocation operates from the beginning of a child's life (see also Chapter 5).

Beyond the newborn period fathers spend less time feeding and caretaking than mothers, and spend more time in play activities. Whereas mothers pick children up for caretaking activities such as nappy-changing, fathers pick them up to play with them. Not only do fathers play more with their children, but they also play differently to mothers. From as early as 8 months fathers engage in physical play, lifting, pushing and rough and tumble activities, whilst mothers engage in toy-stimulated play and reading to their children. These differences seem to be consistent throughout the early years, and lead to a preference for fathers as playmates, with more than two-thirds of children choosing to play with their father rather than their mother (Figure 7.3). Research shows that the quality of the father's social, physical play is significantly related to the cognitive development of boys, whilst the quality of the father's verbal interactions with girls is important in female cognitive development.

The absence of a father is likely to be significant in a child's life. Apart from the poverty frequently found in families headed by a single-mother, there is some evidence that IQ scores are lower, that achievement at school is poorer, and that 75 per cent of the children whose parents divorce feel rejected by their fathers even when the fathers visit frequently (Wallerstein and Kelly, 1980). There is also some evidence that a father's absence is associated with psychiatric problems, lack of self-control and violent behaviour, particularly in boys. Girls seem to be less affected in this way.

One of the areas thought to be very important in relation to fathers is that of sex-role development. First, fathers appear to prefer boys, and from birth onwards actually treat boys and girls differently. They encourage boys to be more 'masculine' and consistently pay more attention and give more stimulation to boys than to their daughters (although they cuddle their daughters

Figure 7.3 Children show a preference for playing with their fathers.

more than their sons). They also appear to discriminate more than mothers in the treatment of male and female children, and seem to have somewhat rigid views about what constitutes appropriate sex-role behaviour, which they communicate to boys by providing masculine role models. Interestingly, boys who live in households without fathers generally show fewer sex-typed behaviours and attitudes than boys who live in intact families. The role of fathers is clearly important in a number of areas, yet there is also a pronounced discrepancy between popular cultural beliefs and actuality. To bring the two closer together, cultural support systems designed to encourage fathers' involvement, clearer role allocation and expectations, and better early socialisation of males in nurturance and responsibility-taking, are all needed for the benefits to be realised.

Sibling relationships

The birth of a second child into a family is of significance not only to the parents but also to the first-born child. Until the early 1980s there were few systematic studies of sibling relationships (except for birth-order effects and sibling rivalry), but since then there have been major developments in our understanding of the impact of a second child on the family, how sibling relationships develop and change, the links between parent–child relationships, and the effects of early relationships upon a child's later friendships and adjustment. The leading instigator of these developments was Judy Dunn (Dunn and Kendrick, 1982), and she continues, with her co-workers, to make important advances in this area (Dunn, 1995).

The commonly held view that a first-born child's reaction to a new baby will create behavioural problems, jealousy and rivalry seems to be borne out. Increased disturbance of bodily functions, anxiety, withdrawal and dependency are among the immediate consequences to have been noted. Although hostility may occur, first-born children show a range of reactions, ranging from interest, concern and empathy, through ambivalence to outright aggressiveness. In general, however, first-borns are keen to help to care for the new baby and to cuddle and play with him or her. One of the factors that influences the beginning of a sibling relationship is the way in which the mother talks to the first-born about the new baby before it is born. When mothers make reference to the expected baby, relationships between the siblings are subsequently much more friendly than when the newcomer has not been introduced in discussion.

The birth of a second child changes the existing relationships within a family. Mothers may reduce the amount of time spent with the older child while they concentrate on the baby, and fathers often spend more time with the older sibling, whilst both parents have less time for each other. Same-sex siblings seem to develop friendly relationships with each other, particularly in families with first-born boys. Older children seem to become particularly vigilant about the mother's interactions with a new baby, and often demand absolute equality of maternal attention. The second-born child is also very vigilant in monitoring the mother's relationships with her older children, and it is out of this interest that a child's social understanding develops.

In the early years siblings serve a number of functions for each other. They provide affection and security, companionship and intimacy. They give support and help to each other, provide models for imitation and the learning of both skills and language, and through conflict and co-operation develop their own internal working model of relationships, and an understanding of the feelings of others (Figure 7.4).

There is some evidence that the quality of sibling relationships is associated with the *security of attachment* each child has to its mother. That is, securely attached older and younger siblings are likely to have friendly relationships with each other, whereas insecurely attached children are more likely to have antagonistic relationships with one another. Although it is plausible that maternal attachment provides a template for subsequent relationships, we must note that the evidence is correlational and as yet does not indicate a causal effect between attachment and the quality of sibling relationships.

One of the areas of sibling research that has received considerable attention in recent years is concerned with differential parental treatment of children,

Figure 7.4 Siblings provide support for one another.

especially the notion of favouritism towards one of the siblings. Many adults who report a poor sibling relationship in childhood often attribute this to their parents either positively favouring one of the children, or scapegoating one of them. An early study found that mothers were less affectionate and had less social interaction with second children than with first-born children (Jacobs and Moss, 1976), but in an even earlier study Lasko (1954) found that parents were less warm and more coercive towards their first-born children. Recent studies show a high level of consistency of treatment by mothers at 12 and 24 months, although in one study there was a sizeable group of mothers (34.5 per cent of the sample) who appeared to treat their children differently (Ward *et al.*, 1988). This, of course, may be because their children's temperaments need differential treatment. At a given point in time with, say, a 12-month-old boy and a 24-month-old girl, maternal treatment may be quite different because of the age-determined or temperamental needs of the children.

What seems to be important in the different treatment of children by their parents is the *discrepancy* between one child and another. Bryant and Crockenberg (1980) found that, even when a child's own needs were being well met, if there was a discrepancy of treatment by the mother, that child would show more hostility and negative behaviour towards his or her sibling. Hetherington's (1988) study showed that it is the *relative* treatment of children that is significant, rather than the absolute parental behaviour that affects children most deeply. A sibling treated less warmly, less affectionately, more irritably or more punitively is likely to behave more aggressively and with less affection towards the other sibling. The favoured child is also more aggressive and unaffectionate towards the sibling. The *favouritism* → *hostility* hypothesis would seem to be supported. Recent research suggests that some children are particularly susceptible to differential treatment by parents. This seems to be related to the child's perception of having less responsive parents. The child attributes a negative meaning to parental actions, and may create a situation in which it is almost impossible for the parents to be perceived as fair. There is a growing research interest in this aspect of a child's interpretations of reality, and there are many questions yet to be answered about the effects of perceptions upon the child's future development.

Friends

In adults, friendships are based on the reciprocal exchange of benefits between equals, in which there is a sense of commitment and affection. Friendships are special in a way that simple peer interactions are not. Young children are clearly primarily attached to their parents in the first year or so of their lives, but they show increasing interest in other children, and by the age of 4 or 5 years most children have formed a special relationship with at least one other child. At school they develop relationships with about five children, a figure which continues into adolescence.

Children's conceptions of friendship begin somewhat simply, and become more elaborate and differentiated as the child grows older. Infants' conceptions are likely to focus on concrete aspects ('he lets me play with his toys'), whereas older children will use more complex and abstract ideas. Many psychologists argue that these differences are related to the general cognitive and language development of the child.

Identification of a child's friendships has been attempted by several different methods:

- asking children to indicate their best friends;
- asking children who they 'like especially';
- observing the proximity between children.

In general the level of agreement between these methods, although not perfect, has been very high. In general, a friend identified by a child will also be identified by a parent or a teacher, and the two children will clearly prefer to play together.

Children's friendships, like those of adults, move through a series of 'stages' (Levinger, 1983). A necessary condition for a child to begin a friendship is *proximity* – that is, being in the same place at the same time. However, this is not sufficient for the establishment of a friendship, because if the initial encounter is not rewarding at a superficial level, the relationship is unlikely to develop. At the second stage, the *build up* of the relationship is characterised by repeated encounters which are mutually rewarding, in which the children communicate with each other and establish common interests by exchanging information and beginning the process of reciprocal self-disclosure. The *consolidation* of a friendship is marked by the development of a 'we feeling', where the two children develop a commitment to one another, and stable patterns of conflict resolution and successful management of the relationship occur. Sometimes the *deterioration* of a friendship happens when clear disagreements or conflicts are not successfully resolved. However, children's friendships often end without any clear argument and seem simply to fade away because the children stop interacting with one another, presumably because the interaction is no longer mutually satisfying. The *ending* of a child's friendship usually results in the children avoiding one another, reduced interaction and dependence, and usually little recrimination or conflict.

According to Hill (1987), the need for affiliation and relationships with friends serves four main functions. *Social comparison* allows children to establish their own position in relation to others ('My friend Tommy's got lots of guns, why can't I have some?'). *Emotional support* is provided by friends when a child is distressed ('Emily comforted me when I fell over at nursery today'). *Positive stimulation* is provided by conversation, ideas and suggestions for play activities. *Attention* is paid by friends to a child's own being, and praise is offered for successes, raising the level of a child's self-esteem.

The functions of friendship in children probably vary with the age of the child, but a number of areas have been identified as important in child development. First, friendships are significant in the development of social competence. Howes (1983) found that in children aged 44–9 months, social behaviour with friends (as opposed to non-friends) was more elaborate, play was more co-operative, emotional exchanges were more positive and vocalising was increased. Friends are both cognitive and emotional resources for each other. They provide information about the world (not always accurately, e.g. 'My dad's a millionaire') and the opportunity for co-operative learning where, because of the nature of the relationship, the quality of the learning is likely to be better and problem-solving capacities are maximised. There is some evidence that friends increase the amount of laughing, talking, smiling and looking, i.e. positive emotional feelings, and that they also increase a child's sense of security in a strange situation. Studies of adult relationships strongly suggest that friendships provide a buffer against the adverse effects of stressful life events such as divorce or a death in the family. Those with good-quality close relationships seem to suffer fewer physical illnesses or psychological disturbances than more isolated individuals. It would seem likely that this is true for children as well, but as yet the evidence to confirm this has not been gathered.

Studies of adult friendship indicate that one of the major factors in the formation and continuation of relationships is *similarity*. Not only do we develop relationships with and eventually marry people similar to ourselves, but children, too, base their choices of friends upon similarity. Although choices are sometimes made on the basis of dissimilarity, e.g. higher status or more attractive or more popular children may be sought as friends, there is strong evidence of similarity between friends on a number of dimensions. From early childhood to adolescence children have friends of similar *age*. To some extent this is determined by the age structure of nurseries and schools and imposed by adults, but when given a free choice, most children usually form friendships with those of the same age. This is probably because of the egalitarian, horizontal power distribution between friends.

From pre-school years onwards *same-sex* friendships predominate, and opposite-sex friendships are rare until adolescence, although even then only 5 per cent of friendships are with the opposite sex. Studies indicate that race, educational aspirations, attitudes towards achievement, and children's culture (e.g. music and sport) are all found to be similar between friends. Not only do children choose friends similar to themselves, but they actually become more similar to one another over time. Finding someone who is very like oneself is obviously highly rewarding, and the potential risks of conflict created by dissimilarity are significantly reduced.

The overall outcome of children's friendships is that they are important, if not absolutely necessary, for optimal development in a number of areas. Hartup and Rubin (1986) argue that most of the benefits of friendship may be achieved by other relationships – with parents, siblings or other family members. However, there is a developmental advantage for a child with friends. Perspective-taking, co-operation, altruism, social competence and adjustment and conflict management are all best learned within friendships.

Abusive relationships

Although child protection issues are fully discussed in Chapter 10, this chapter would not be complete without a discussion of the implications of abusive relationships. In the last 20 years an ever-increasing body of evidence has shown that, although a child's relationships with mother, father, siblings, grandparents and friends provide care and nurturance, they may also be the main sources of profound damage. It is usually someone to whom the child is closely connected by family or emotional ties who carries out acts of psychological, physical or sexual abuse.

Emotional neglect, in which a child is not given adequate emotional support and essential stimulation, probably results from a failure in the primary attachment relationship, usually with the mother. It is likely to have severe cognitive and social consequences for the young child, with disturbances continuing into adolescence and probably into adulthood.

Psychological abuse has only recently been identified as one of the most frequent types of child maltreatment, and is characterised by the following caretaker behaviours:

- rejecting – the child is made to feel unwanted and is avoided;
- degrading – the child is frequently criticised and humiliated;
- terrorizing – the child is threatened, frightened and verbally assaulted;
- isolating – the child is not permitted social contact or interaction;
- corrupting – the child is taught to behave antisocially and unacceptably;
- exploiting – the child is used to meet the caretaker's needs;
- depriving – the child is denied loving attention and stimulation.

The results of this pattern of mistreatment are thought to be severely injurious to the child's development of self-esteem, his or her perception of other people, and his or her future social relationships (Briere, 1992).

Physical abuse is often difficult to define clearly in a society where physical punishment has traditionally been used to control or modify a child's behaviour. However, although low-level violence towards children seems to be socially acceptable in our culture at present, many children are physically injured by caretakers beyond levels that are tolerable. Approximately 100 children in the UK are killed by their parents each year, and thousands in the USA. Severe injury, such as brain damage, skull and limb fractures, internal injuries and serious burns caused by parental violence, including kicking, biting, punching and hitting with objects are not uncommon, with rates of parental violence of between 10 and 20 per cent being reported. The long-term effects of physical abuse, especially when combined with neglect or psychological abuse as is often the case, are likely to include post-traumatic stress reactions, cognitive distortions, altered emotionality and depression, identity confusion, and poor self-image and difficulties in relating to important others.

Sexual abuse occurs when developmentally immature children are involved in sexual activities, ranging from fondling to intercourse, which they do not truly understand and to which they are unable to give informed consent. The prevalence of child sexual abuse is dependent on complex definitional issues (for example, is contact necessary? is a 5-year age difference necessary?), but seems to be quite high. Ray Wyre, an expert on the treatment of child abusers, recently estimated that there were around a million sexually abusive events occurring every year in the UK. In 13 of 26 dioceses in Ireland investigations are being carried out into sexual abuse by priests and in the USA it is estimated that one in 5 females and one in 10 males have been sexually abused.

A number of studies have identified the main risk factors associated with sexual abuse. First, although both boys and girls may be sexually abused, girls are at higher risk than boys. Secondly, pre-adolescents (aged 10–12 years) are at particularly high risk, although abuse can begin at any age. Abused children are also more likely to have lived in a home without their natural fathers, with stepfathers present, with mothers employed, disabled or ill, and to have witnessed conflict between their parents. A poor relationship with one or both parents also increases the risk of sexual abuse. Race and social class do not appear to increase the risk for abuse (Finkelhor, 1986).

The effects of sexual abuse have been recently researched more fully than other forms of abuse. Survivors show a wide range of psychosocial symptoms, in both the short and long term. Sexual abuse occurring within a relationship of warmth and affection, with bribery and special privileges as well as secrecy and threats, is as likely to produce traumatic results as abuse that is based on violence and coercion. Anxiety, difficulty in giving and receiving affection, sexualising of all relationships, depression, confusion, anger, aggression, psychosomatic illnesses, suicide attempts, self-mutilation, learned helplessness, sleep disturbance, moodiness and social isolation from peers, have all been noted in children who have been victims of sexual abuse.

In adult survivors of sexual abuse, post-traumatic stress disorders sometimes occur, but major depression is the symptom most frequently recorded in child-abused adults. Anxiety is also common, with hypervigilance with regard to danger in the social environment, and a preoccupation with controlling threats or perceived dangers is often present. Major difficulties are encountered in relationships with significant others, and problems with intimacy and trust, as well as sexual dysfunction (either promiscuity or sexual coldness), aggression, alcohol and drug abuse and also frequent suicide attempts by sexually abused survivors range from 51 per cent to 79 per cent (Briere, 1992). These are *failed* attempts, and the extent of successful suicides in sexually abused victims is not known.

Adults who have been sexually abused often become abusers of their own or other children. In the highly publicised case of Frederick and Rosemary West, who appear to have physically and sexually abused and indeed murdered at least 10 young females, both of the abusers were physically and sexually abused themselves as children, and appear to have continued and elaborated the abuses perpetrated upon them. However, not all abused children, are destined to become child-abusing adults. Therapeutic help, support from family and friends, and sympathetic and understanding partners in adulthood may all diminish the adverse effects of sexual abuse and prevent the repeated pattern of abusive behaviour.

CONCLUSION

In reviewing the ideas, theories and evidence discussed in this chapter, the importance of a child's relationships becomes apparent. Relationships of high quality, whether they are with mother, father, siblings or friends, have a profound and long-lasting effect on the emotional, cognitive and social development of children. Although all children have their own unique characteristics, they are very responsive to the influences of their culture, their family and all of those with whom they interact. Widening our understanding of the reciprocal nature of these interactions and revealing the complex subtleties of a child's relationships are the tasks for the future.

References

Ainsworth, M.D. (1978): *Patterns of Attachment: a Psychological Study of the Strange Situation*. Hillsdale, N.J., Erlbaum.

Baumrind, D. (1971): Current Patterns of Parental Authority. *Developmental Psychology Monographs* **4**, 1–103.

Bowlby, J. (1953): *Child Care and the Growth of Love*. Harmondsworth: Penguin.

Briere, J.N. (1992): *Child Abuse Trauma*. London: Sage.

Bryant, B and Crockenberg, S. (1980): Correlates and Dimensions of Prosocial Behaviour. *Child Development* **51**, 529–44.

Dunn, J. (1995): Studying Relationships. In Barnes, P. (ed.) *Personal, Social and Emotional Development of Children*. Oxford: Blackwell.

Dunn, J. and Kendrick, C. (1982): *Siblings: Love, Envy and Understanding*. London: Grant McIntyre.

Finkelhor, D. (1986): *A Sourcebook on Child Sexual Abuse*. London: Sage.

Hartup, W.W. and Rubin, Z. (eds) (1986): *Relationships and Development*. Hillsdale, N.J., Erlbaum.

Hetherington, E.M. (1988): Parents, Children and Siblings. In Hinde, R.A. and Stevenson-Hinde, J. (eds), *Relationships within Families*. Oxford, Open University Press.

Hill, A.C. (1987): Affiliation: People Who Need People. *Journal of Personality and Social Psychology*. **52**, 1008–18.

Holmes, T.H. and Rahe, R.H. (1967): The Social Readjustment Rating Scale. *Journal of Psychosomatic Research* **11**, 213–8.

Howes, C. (1983): Pattern of Friendship, *Child Development*, **54**, 1041–53

Jacobs, B.S. and Moss, H.A. (1976): Birth Order and Sex of Siblings. *Child Development* **47**, 315–22.

La Freniere, P. and Sroufe, L.A. (1985): Profiles of Peer Competence in the Preschool: Interrelations Between Measures, Influence of Social Ecology, and Relation to Attachment History. *Developmental Psychology* **21**, 56–9.

Lamb, M.E. (1987): *The Father's Role: Cross-cultural Perspectives*. Hillsdale, N.J., Erlbaum.

Lasko, J.K. (1954): Parent Behaviour Toward First and Second Born Children. *Genetic Psychology Monographs* **49**, 97–137.

Levinger, G. (1983): Development and Change. In Kelley, H. *et al.* (eds) *Close Relationships*. New York: Freemans.

Main, M and Solomon, J. (1986): Discovery of a Disorganized/Disorientated Attachment Pattern. In Brazelton, T.B. and Yogman, M.W. (eds), *Affective Development in Infancy*. Norwood, N.J: Ablex.

Olson, D.H. and McCubbin, H.I. (1983): *Families: What makes them Work*. Beverley Hills, California: Sage.

Parke, R.D. (1981): *Fathering*. London: Fontana.

Richards, M. (1995): Family Relations. *The Psychologist*, **8**, 70–72.

Rode, S, Chang, P., Fisch, R. and Sroufe, L.A. (1981): Attachment Patterns of Children Separated at Birth. *Developmental Psychology* **17**, 188–91.

Wallerstein, J.S. and Kelly, J.B. (1980): *Surviving the Breakup*. New York: Basic Books.

Ward, M.J., Vaugh, B.E. and Robb, M.D. (1988): Social-emotional Adaptation and Infant-Mother Interaction in Siblings. *Child Development* **59**, 643–51.

Whiting, B.B. and Edwards, C.P. (1988): *Children of Different Worlds*. Cambridge, MA: Harvard University Press.

Further Reading

Barnes, P. (1995): *Personal, Social and Emotional Development in Children*. Oxford, Blackwell.

Boer, F. and Dunn, J. (1992): *Children's Sibling Relationships*. Hillsdale, NJ: Erlbaum.

Corby, B. (1994): *Child Abuse*. Buckingham: Open University Press.

Erwin, P. (1993): *Friendships and Peer Relations in Children*. Chichester: John Wiley & Sons.

Frude, N. (1990): *Understanding Family Problems*. Chichester, John Wiley & Sons.

Child health

Jayne Taylor

This chapter aims to:

- explore the origins of child health practice from an historical perspective;
- discuss the current situation within an holistic framework;
- examine personal and professional partnerships in relation to child health matters.

Introduction

Health is a very emotive subject. As we read in Chapter 2, one of the very first questions new parents ask after the birth of a baby relates to the *health* of the newborn infant. This concern with health continues throughout childhood and into adulthood. As a nation, we commonly greet each other with the question 'hello – How are you'?, we write phrases such as 'hoping you are keeping well' in Christmas and birthday cards, and we lift our glasses to each other and say 'good health'.

The answers we give to questions such as 'how are you?' also frequently demonstrate our health-mindedness – 'I'm very well thank you', 'not too bad, although I've got a sore throat . . . ', or 'I've had a terrible time of it recently with my back. I'm on four sorts of tablets, the doctor says . . . '. One sometimes wonders if we would ever successfully start a conversation if we did not have health to talk about!

This concern extends beyond our own health to that of our children. Adults in general, and parents in particular, become very concerned when the health of a child or a group of children is threatened. The media frequently focuses upon such issues – the case of 'child B' who was denied treatment for leukaemia, the links between nuclear power and childhood cancers, the potential causes of congenital anomalies among the children of Gulf War veterans, the ritual abuse of children in Rochdale and the Orkneys, the birth of Siamese twins, and so on. Stories relating to child health appear on an almost daily basis in our newspapers and on our television screens.

This chapter begins by looking at the origins of the current child health focus within our society, before moving on to look specifically at the health of children today and its importance within our holistic philosophy. It then concludes by exploring professional and personal partnerships in relation to health promotion, health maintenance and health intervention.

Child health – a national concern?

An historical concern?

Our nation's concern with child health is an interesting phenomenon, and it is useful to reflect for a moment upon the origin of this concern, so that we may be able to understand it more clearly and perhaps utilise it in a positive way. But is this concern new? Certainly in the pre-Victorian era, and to some extent during the Victorian age, the value placed on the lives of children by the nation appeared to be less significant than it is today. That is not to say that parents did not love their children as much as we do now, but rather it reflects the treatment of children by society – particularly the children of the poor, and the orphaned. According to Cox (1983), many of these children grew up in the workhouses or, worse ended up on the streets of the major cities (this is discussed in more detail in Chapter 6). Kosky (1992), in an account of the founding of the Queen Elizabeth Hospital in Hackney Road, cites an account in the *Daily News* from 1870, which vividly describes the plight of such children:

> *In this district of Bethnal Green, in the centre of which the new child's hospital stands, we know of hundreds of tiny breadwinners of two and a half years upwards. It is here that the trade of Lucifer boxes absorbs the energies of infants long before they can speak, and where street after street can be shown full of little workers who pass from infancy to childhood and from childhood to maturity without ever seeing a toy or gazing upon a green field.*

Surprisingly, many attempts to help the plight of children met with marked opposition, mainly due to their ability to provide cheap labour for the powerful industrialists and at least some income (albeit meagre) for the family (Kosky, 1992). Whilst various Education acts (e.g. those passed in 1887 and 1906) had introduced social reforms which made education both compulsory and free, and the Coal Mines Act (1845) and various pieces of legislation relating to factories, including the Ten Hours Act of 1847 and the Factory Act of 1901, had limited the legal number of working hours and improved the social conditions of children working in the factories, mines and mills, many children still worked long hours in appalling conditions, and had little or no schooling.

However, even during these seemingly 'dark ages' for children there were glimmers of the concerns which we are familiar with today. The public health movement of the mid-nineteenth century, for example, which developed following two cholera outbreaks in England, was a prime example of middle-class concern for the children of the poor (and marked the beginning of the health visiting service). Voluntary organisations such as Barnardos and the National Children's Home helped many, many homeless and orphaned children, and philanthropists such as Thomas Coram and Charles West campaigned tirelessly to open the Foundling Hospital in Coram Fields and the Hospital for Sick Children in London (more commonly known as Great Ormond Street Hospital), respectively.

Another development which influenced the nation's view of child health at the beginning of this century resulted from the 1904 Interdepartmental Committee on Physical Deterioration. The knowledge that over half of the young men who had volunteered for the Boer War were unfit for service had prompted the instigation of the committee which recommended, among other reforms, the setting up of a school health service (Meredith Davies, 1975).

At this time there was also a growing interest in the infant welfare movement, which led to the setting up of the first milk depots, improved medical and nursing care, developments in pharmaceutics and better sanitation. These measures undoubtedly made a contribution to the fall in the infant mortality rate, which decreased from 163 per 1000 live births in 1899 to less than 100 per 1000 live births in 1915 (Clark, 1973).

Advances were also being made in our knowledge of epidemiology, and 'killer' diseases such as cholera and typhoid became more rare, although scarlet fever, tuberculosis, diphtheria and poliomyelitis were still prevalent (Department of Health and Social Security, 1976). In 1947, for example 7984 cases of poliomyelitis were recorded, and almost 10 per cent of sufferers died. A second major epidemic between 1952 and 1954 saw 845 deaths in the UK (Department of Health and Social Security, 1976).

The number of cases of tuberculosis gradually decreased with improved social conditions and diet, and with the introduction of mass screening and improved drugs, as well as the introduction of the BCG vaccination in the early 1950s. Diphtheria continued to kill 3000 children a year until the early 1940s, when mass immunisation became available and both morbidity and mortality rates declined dramatically (Kosky and Lunnon, 1991).

Following the Second World War, and the decline of infectious and nutritional disorders, attention moved away from these childhood problems and tended to focus on children with chronic illness and disability (Hall, 1992). It was recognised that most childhood disability could be traced back to the perinatal period and that 'early intervention might lead to cure or at least substantial improvement' (Hall, 1992, p. 649). The conviction that if intervention occurred quickly enough disability would be minimised was a popular notion, and led to one of the most dramatic changes in the child health services during the last century. No longer were health professionals to wait for parents to notice anomalies in their child's development and then to seek health. Instead, health professionals needed to go out and assess development in a proactive way so that intervention could be instigated as soon as possible. Nor, according to Hall (1992), was it sufficient only to focus upon those children who were thought to be at risk. All children should be brought into the assessment process, and routine developmental screening should be a universal activity.

This view has, to a large extent, remained consistently to the present day, although the value or routine screening in a world where technological advancement can identify disability during the prenatal or early postnatal period has been questioned (Deparment of Health, 1996), and in some areas of the country the practice has virtually ceased.

A second change which has occurred since the Second World War, and which has had an impact upon child health and the management of ill health, is the move away from hospital services towards a primary care-led National Health Service (see also Chapter 6).

A third change which is gradually occurring at all levels within the health services relates to the relationship between professionals, children and their parents. 'Empowerment' of patients/clients is a popular 'buzz word', and involves enabling better decision-making through the acquisition of knowledge (Kendall, 1993). The Patient's Charter and the Children's Charter have both made it very clear what can be expected of contact with the health services, and what to do if expectations are not met.

Empowerment, it can be argued, has also been facilitated by the media and technological advancement in communication structures. As we mentioned at the beginning of this chapter, newspapers, the television and radio news liberally allocate their columns and time-slots to issues about child health and well-being. Usually such news reports adversity, but it nevertheless serves an educative function and helps to empower through the acquisition of knowledge. Take a look also along the shelves in any large newsagent and you will find a vast array of magazines devoted solely (or largely) to health. Many of these relate specifically to child health matters. Such magazines play an important role with regard to child health in that they are able to inform parents about current practices and child care issues, including prevention of ill health as well as health promotion.

The situation today

The situation today is therefore a complex one in terms of child health. We have hospital services for children which are generally for acute, short-term care, after which care tends to be transferred to community-based services. This means that there are increasing numbers of children within the community who are in some way 'ill', and who would traditionally have spent a longer period of time in hospital, or in some cases would have been permanently institutionalised (Hall, 1992). These childen attend playgroups, nurseries and schools, and their care is shared by parents, educationalists and health professionals within communities. We shall discuss those later on in this chapter.

Secondly, we have a nation-wide comprehensive developmental screening service which is changing, evolving and, in some parts of the country, disappearing in its current form. The Department of Health (1996) suggest a general move away from the traditional 'blanket screening', preferring to target resources towards families with complex needs. According to Hall (1992), most disability should be detected in the prenatal period or in the early neonatal period. However, some professionals have expressed concern that a reduction in routine screening may lead to greater numbers of children at risk being 'missed', and anomalies will not be detected at an early stage. We must also recognise that not all illness and disability by any means, is, congenital and will not therefore be present during the perinatal period. The health of a child can be affected at any stage of development. Early years professionals may be among the first to recognise changes in behaviour, physical or psychological symptoms, or other sometimes subtle changes which are indicative of health problems.

Thirdly, we have a nation of parents who, on the whole, more than at any other time in history, are informed and knowledgeable about child health and their rights in relation to child health – not least because of the attention paid to the subject by the media. However, it is important that we do not become complacent. Patterns of childhood morbidity and mortality indicate that there are both geographical and socio-economic variations, indicating that there is still room for improvement. For example, there are still a significant number of deaths attributed to *signs and symptoms and ill-defined conditions*, which include sudden infant death syndrome as well as preventable deaths from other causes, particularly accidents (Office of Population Censuses and Surveys, 1996).

The holistic perspective

Our holisitic philosophy advocates that all early years professionals have a responsibility towards the prevention of childhood mortality and, as we discussed in the introduction to this book, whilst specialism (e.g. education or health) is feasible within an holistic framework, intra-agency collaboration and co-operation is vital for success. Each professional has a role to play, which may be quite specific, in terms of improving the health of the nation's children, health promotion, parental support and holistic assessment (Department of Health, 1996). However, professionals must recognise that there are many factors which influence a child's development and it is important that the roles of other professionals are understood.

However, we cannot assume that this will happen just because we all have the best interest of young children at heart. The Department of Health (1995) publication entitled *The Health of the Young Nation* recognises that there are barriers, such as funding mechanisms, which can prevent effective inter-agency working. Each professional group requires understanding of the others, which can best be achieved through shared learning, and the facilitation of skills such as advocacy, negotiation and communication, and ultimately through integrated early years services (see also the Introduction).

Partnerships in child health

We have mentioned above that, in line with our holistic philosophy, each early years professional working with young children has a responsibility towards enabling each child to reach and maintain optimum health. A useful model for exploring this concept is the preventive approach described by Caplan (1969), which was originally proposed as an approach for promoting mental health in the community, but which has wider applications. The model identifies three levels of prevention:

- *primary prevention* – which involves preventing the occurrence of disease or disability in healthy individuals;
- *secondary prevention* – which involves activities that identify actual or potential disease or disability through early detection;
- *tertiary prevention* – which involves the prevention of deterioration of existing disease or disability.

Primary prevention

There are many activities which can be classified as primary prevention which involve young children directly or which impact upon the health of young children. In many of these activities the responsibility for primary prevention falls on the early years professional working in partnership with the parents.

EXAMPLE 1

The immunisation of young children against communicable disease fits comfortably within this category. Immunisations may be discussed during the antenatal period by the midwife. The health visitor will discuss immunisations further after the birth of the baby, and will ensure that the baby's carer is able to give *informed consent* to the immunisation programme, and that the baby's details are entered in a database which will generate appointments at the appropriate times for the baby to receive the immunisation. The practice nurse and, in later childhood, the school nurse will give the immunisation. On entry of the child to nursery or school, the education service may confirm that he or she is fully immunised and work in collaboration with the school health services where they find deficits. Furthermore, in some cases there are identified risks, such as in 1994 with a predicted measles epidemic, when the health and education services undertook a mass immunisation programme in schools, providing an excellent example of inter-agency collaboration.

EXAMPLE 2

The prevention of coronary heart disease in later life through the promotion of a healthy life-style in childhood, e.g. regular exercise, healthy eating and avoidance of precipitating factors such as smoking, is another example which fits the primary prvention category. Schools play an important role in primary prevention (Campbell, 1994) by supporting physical education, teaching about nutrition and extending what is taught in the classroom to the wider school environment (there is little point in teaching about healthy eating if children are served 'unhealthy' foods at lunchtime), and teaching about the dangers of smoking, which again should be extended to the wider school environment (the teacher who is seen smoking after teaching about the dangers of tobacco will cause confusion and conflict in the minds of the children for whom he or she is responsible). School has a very powerful impact upon children, and it is important that health education is not seen as an isolated activity. The notion of the 'health-promoting school' (Taylor and Forster, 1996) is one which we fully support.

EXAMPLE 3

The prevention of accidents is one of the key areas identified in the White Paper entitled *Health of the Nation* (Department of Health, 1992), and provides a further exemplar of primary prevention. One of the identified targets is 'to reduce the death rate for accidents among children aged under 15 by at least 33% by 2005' (Department of Health, 1992).

Again there is a great deal of scope here for inter-agency collaboration in terms of helping children to develop safe pedestrian skills, encouraging cycling proficiency and the wearing of safety helmets, the provision of safe play areas and the use of safety restraints in cars, as well as a variety of activities which can promote safety within the home.

Secondary prevention

Child surveillance and developmental screening are discussed in depth in Chapter 3, and provide an excellent example of secondary prevention. The purpose of screening is to detect at an early stage any problems which may affect the health of the child, and to make referrals to appropriate agencies so that intervention can be organised which aims to minimise detrimental consequences.

However, secondary prevention is not only about formal screening procedures. For example, the early detection of behavioural changes by a teacher may be indicative of problems at home, or of substance abuse in an older child. The principles remain the same in that early referral to an appropriate agency may prevent long-term harm to the child.

EXAMPLE 1

Screening for hearing impairment is routinely carried out by trained health visitors when the child is around 7 months of age, so that intervention can be organised before the hearing difficulty results in speech and other learning dysfunction. However, prior to the 7-month stage, and indeed at any time thereafter, early years professionals working, for example, in nurseries or schools may detect that a child has difficulties which may be attributable to hearing impairment. Prompt discussion with the parents and referral to the health visitor is essential so that further investigation can be instigated.

EXAMPLE 2

The early detecion of sexual abuse by a teacher is a further example of secondary prevention. Peake (1995) suggests that 'teachers are the only professionals who are in regular contact with school-aged children, and they are in a unique position to monitor situations where there are concerns about a particular child' (p. 243). Peake suggest that the child's body language and behaviour, play, drawing and writing, attendance, mood swings and language may all give rise to suspicion. Where such signs are evident, working closely with other agencies such as social services, the educational psychology department, the National Society for the Prevention of Cruelty to Children (NSPCC) or the police will enable clarification and allow appropriate action to be taken.

Tertiary prevention

Tertiary prevention during the early years, where the aim is to minimise the deleterious effects of identified disease or disability, will also involve early years professionals in different ways through active treatment, rehabilitation or palliative care (Taylor and Forster, 1996). As with primary and secondary prevention, collaboration and co-operation by early years professionals is of the utmost importance.

EXAMPLE 1

Campbell (1994) discusses the growing incidence of asthma, which affects about 15 per cent of children. The management of asthma in early childhood involves a partnership between parents, health professionals and early years professionals who may be responsible for the child at school, playgroup, nursery, etc. In cases where a child is prescribed bronchodilators, it is important that he or she has access to medication at all times, and that the medication is used appropriately. This involves efficient communication and education of professionals with regard to inhaler techniques and asthma management.

EXAMPLE 2

Capewell (1996) discusses the role of professionals working with children experiencing grief and loss, which is a further example of tertiary prevention. In these situations, Capewell suggest that where the loss is anticipated, 'multi-agencies strategies' are required to plan effective intervention for the child and support for the professionals involved. The impact of major loss upon individual children and their peers can clearly be enormous, and is an ideal area for inter-agency training. Capewell suggests that where organisations do not have strategies in place, they should rectify this rather than waiting for a situation to arise: 'Begin preparing for loss and grief *now* – it can strike *now*' (p. 94).

EXAMPLE 3

At some time during their working life most early years professionals will know or care for a child who is seriously ill, and who may ultimately die. For such children, who are often suddenly catapulted into the strange and some-times frightening world of aggressive medical intervention, it is important that as many aspects of their life remain as stable as possible. They need the normality of familiar experiences, such as their regular school or nursery, to help them to cope with the unfamiliar experiences. Lavelle (1994) writes:

> *continuing formal education is important for two main reasons. First, it is the right of all children to have the opportunity to develop their potential abilities to the full and enjoy the enrichment which education brings to life, however long or short that life may be. Secondly, going back to school re-establishes the normal pattern of life for a child and reaffirms membership of the peer group. Being with your contemporaries locks you into life. Family life and relation-ships are easier to handle when the daily routine is a comfortable and familiar one. (p. 87)*

Clearly these children present one of the greatest challenges for early years professionals, and sensitive and effective communication between parents and other agencies involved in the care of the child is of the utmost impor-tance. When a child has been absent for a period of time because of serious illness peers should be encouraged to make cards and pictures, etc., for their ill friend. Open and frank discussion with peers can smooth the way for the return of the child, who may be physically scarred or altered in some way. The return can be a daunting experience for the ill child, the healthy peers and the professional responsible for the group. We recommend an excellent text edited by Hill (1994) which gives sensible advice to professionals involved in the care of dying children and their families.

The examples above represent a selection of activities which involve part-nerhships in caring for children's health, and clearly there are many more examples which could be used. The importance of looking at this area is that, if holism is more than an ideal, and if we are to value the whole child, then this involves working together and breaking down barriers which may pre-vent the attainment of our goals.

CONCLUSION

The health of children is an issue of national concern, and in this chapter we have discussed how the value placed upon children's health has developed over time. It is now relatively easy to access information about child health, and we have a much more educated population of parents than ever before. We cannot be com-placent, however, and the health of children has to be the responsibility of all early years professionals who must take, and seek out, opportunities to promote the health of children and to prevent ill health. This can only be achieved through training and a greater understanding of inter-professional roles and responsibilities. Professional barriers must *never* be allowed to overshadow the need to provide excellent educare.

References

Campbell, S. (1994): The Well and Sick Child. In Webb, P. (ed.), *Health Pro-motion and Patient Education*. London: Chapman and Hall, 80–97.

Capewell, E. (1996): Planning an Organisational Response. In Lindsay, B. and Elsegood, J. (eds), *Working with Children in Grief and Loss*. London: Ballière Tindall, 73–96.

Caplan, G. (1969): *An Approach to Community Mental Health*. London: Tavi-stock Publications.

Clark J. (1973): *A Family Visitor*. London: Royal College of Nursing.

Cox, C. (1983): *Sociology: an Introduction for Nurses, Midwives and Health Vis-itors. London: Butterworths.*

Department of Health (1992): *Health of the Nation*. London: HMSO.

Department of Health (1995): *Health of the Young Nation*. London: HMSO.

Deparment of Health (1996): *Health for all Children*, 3rd edn. London: HMSO.

Department of Health and Social Security (1976): *Prevention and Health: Everybody's Business*. London: HMSO.

Hall D.M.B. (1992): Child Health Promotion, Screening and Surveillance *Journal of Child Psychology and Psychiatry* **34**, 649–58.

Hill L. (ed.) (1994): *Caring for Dying Children and their Families*. London: Chapman and Hall.

Kendall S. (1993): Promoting Health. In Hinchliff, S.M., Norman, S.E. and Schober, J.E. (eds), *Nursing Practice and Health Care*, 2nd edn. London: Edward Arnold, 51–76.

Kosky, J. (ed.) (1992): *Queen Elizabeth Hospital for Sick Children: 125 Years of Achievement*. London: Queen Elizabeth Hospital.

Kosky, J. and Lunnon, R. (1991): *Great Ormond Street Hospital and the Story of Medicine*. London: Great Ormond Street Publications.

Lavelle J. (1994): Education and Sick Child. In Hill, L. (ed.) *Caring for Dying Children and their Families*. London: Chapman and Hall, 87–105.

Meredith Davies, J.B. (1975): *Preventive Medicine, Community Health and Social Services*, 3rd edn. London: Ballière Tindall.

Office of Population Censuses and Surveys (1996): *Mortality Statistics 1994*. London: HMSO.

Peake, A. (1995): Dealing with the Suspicion of Child Sexual Abuse: the Role of the Teacher. In Wilson, K. and James, A. (eds), *The Child Protection Handbook*. London: Ballière Tindall, 242–65.

Taylor, J. and Forster, D. (1996): Promoting Health. In Mcquaid, L., Parker, E. and Huband, S. (eds), *Children's Nursing*. Edinburgh: Churchill Livingstone, 23–45.

Play, language and learning

Anne Greig

This chapter aims to:

- explore the nature of, and interrelationship between, play, language and learning.

Introduction

Consider the following scene from a Wendy-House, involving Simon and Rebecca, both aged 4 years, who are not friends.

S: Oh, it's half-past one! Cor, I think it's time we've to go to bed!

R: (Ignores him).

S: Goodnight! I'm going to bed.

R: (Ignores him).

S: I'm going to bed!

R: But mummies and daddies stay up for late . . . take a book to bed . . . let's take our babies to bed!

S: I'm going to sleep, I won't bother (mutters).

R: (Follows him). It's time to go to sleep now.

S: Come on, shut the curtains shall we? I'm going to have some water and then I put some aspirin in a cup. I got a poorly head.

According to Garvey (1991), we may regard this play-scene as charming, silly or disturbingly perceptive in its portrayal of adult behaviour. However, for the serious student of the child, there is much more to discern and discover. It can tell us, for instance, about relationships on many levels – between the children themselves, with adults at home, and in the little cultural rituals of going to bed. It tells us about their communicative and social competencies, and also how they think, learn and feel. Researchers examine hundreds of such encounters between children in order to detect the patterns and rules which govern their interaction and communication.

In this chapter we shall explore the nature of this play with its associated language and learning, and examine their role in early childhood. We shall also focus on the complex and special relationship between these three aspects of early childhood.

Our approach to early childhood has been expressed as an holistic one, and the nature of the relationship between play, language and learning is an example, *par excellence*, of the holistic nature of the child. Children play, learn, talk, build relationships – and more besides – all at once, making the child observer's task a difficult one. In addition, specifying the exact nature of interacting elements is often contentious. For instance, does the child develop language after, before or in parallel to the development of cognition? The relationship between play, language and learning is of this highly complex and contentious nature. An apt analogy to introduce the nature of the relationship comes from Bjørkvold (1987), who describes the Swahili concept of *ngoma*. This is a special word meaning 'dance-ritual-song', actvities which in the Swahili culture are inseparably moulded together – no song without dance, no dance without words and song. It is a nice idea, and in considering the play of Simon and Rebecca, it is apparent that their play, language and learning are inextricably linked, but would we go so far as to say 'no play, no language, no learning' or 'no language, no play, no learning'? Clearly there are links, but to what extent and in what way? Finding the answers to these questions is the ongoing and daunting task of both theoreticians and practitioners.

The study of language is a very large, well-defined research area in itself, including specialised research on acquisition, including literacy, oracy, reading, bilingualism, linguistics, psycholinguistics, sociolinguistics, applied linguistics, grammars, phonology, syntax and semantics, language and mind, semiotics and signs, non-verbal communication and paralinguistics (see Whitehead, 1990, for an overview). Learning theory has a variety of perspectives, and it has been claimed that, although research on play has produced some valuable results, the overall pattern is disconnected, much of it not following a clearly thought out or promising agenda (Nicolopoulou, 1993). Our agenda is to introduce the available theoretical approaches to play, language and learning. The field will also be delimited in that we are focusing on early childhood, and the relevant theorists (mainly Piaget and Vygotsky), in addition to being learning theorists, subscribe to theories on play and the role played by language. Consequently, the chapter will have a theoretical flavour, with less attention being given to more applied, practical specialisms.

Special issues and influential theories on play, language and learning

As we do not have to whip children into playing and learning how to say 'mama', most people would be happy to agree that play, language and learning are all spontaneous activities. None the less, they need examination with regard to the influences of genes, environment, or both. For example, are cognition and language both natural and equally spontaneous activities? That is, to what extent is each innate or acquired? Consequently, the nature-nurture controversy will be a recurring theme in this chapter (see also Chapter 1). In addition, the special relationship between language and learning promotes a debate as to which one has supremacy. Does language determine thought, or is it a by-product of the learning process? Both language and learning are relatively easy to define, and research on language usually refers either directly or indirectly to research on learning, and vice versa. Having a special relationship, they go together, like lips and kisses. However, they need not refer to play. 'Play' seems to be one of those words, like 'beautiful' or 'pornographic', that you know when you see it, but that is difficult to define (Goodman, 1994).

In this section we shall focus on play, language and learning, together with their special issues. Furthermore, because play is usually viewed as the context for the display or improvement of learning and language, the sequence of discussion will be learning, followed by language, and finally play.

Special issues in learning

The question of *how* children learn has been much studied. The first few years of a child's life are a period during which the child will learn more than in the rest of his or her lifetime. The early years, including the time in the womb, are regarded as critical in terms of vulnerability to infection, damage and environmental modification (see Chapter 2 for a more detailed discussion of this aspect). Consequently, it is important to understand this early learning process so that we are in a position to enhance it, intervene and develop new theories. In essence, learning theories occupy various positions in the nature-nurture controversy. As you will already be aware, these positions are known as nativist, empiricist, and constructivist views.

You will recall from Chapter 1 that nativists argue that we are born with the knowledge we have. As such, they are biologists who argue that the child is genetically pre-programmed to unfold in certain ways, and that attainment of knowledge takes place only gradually and via inherent maturational mechanisms. For a modern nativist approach to the genetic pre-wiring of cognitive processes, see Karmiloff-Smith (1995). Empiricists argue that the child is not born with genetic blueprints, but is instead a *tabula rasa* or blank slate which is filled in only as a consequence of environmental experience. This is the approach of behaviourists such as Pavlov and Skinner, who believed that learning is the process of forming associations between external stimuli and internal responses. This type of learning is mainly passive, with the child responding to the environment, although operant conditioning sees the child or organism as operating on the environment. Constructivists represent a combination of both genetic pre-programming and environmental adaptation or experience. The child actively constructs a version of reality from his or her unique experiences. It is this approach which has been most influential in educational research, and has greater holistic relevance.

Influential learning theories

The constructivists Piaget, Vygotsky and Bruner all share an interest in the relationship between the inner, biological, individual child and the outer, environmental, social child – that is, the extent to which a child's knowledge is determined biologically and culturally, compared with the child's freedom to act independently and creatively. All three theorists agree that the child is both determined and a determiner of knowledge and understanding. Where they differ is in the emphasis that they each place on the direction of the relationship.

In the process of learning, Piaget's child is an isolated individual who attempts to adapt to the world around him or her. This process of adaptation takes place via four important processes: schemas, assimilation, accommodation and equilibration. Schemas are present from the start, and are initially purely physical or sensory actions. The infant does not plan, intend or internally represent objects by means of mental pictures, but instead responds only to stimuli that are immediately available. For instance, the infant will have a looking scheme, a holding scheme and a grasping scheme. As the child develops, he or she acquires more obviously mental schemas, such as categorisation and comparison of objects. After further maturation, more complex schemas are added, such as deductive analysis. However, it is the three basic processes of assimilation, accommodation and equilibration which enable the development from the simple action schemas of infancy to the increasingly complex mental schemas of later childhood. Assimilation involves taking in and absorbing experiences into existing schemas. Thus when a child already knows how to pick up one object, new objects and situations can be acted out and understood within the existing schema. There is also room for subjectivity in the process, because a child may assimilate a roundish object into a round schema and remember it as being more round than it actually is.

Accommodation occurs when the child changes an existing schema as a result of new information taken in by assimilation. For instance, a child will have a sucking schema for the breast which will have to be adapted to a new form of action in order to cope with a bottle and subsequently to drink from a cup. Subtle sensorimotor changes will be necessary in order to cope with the less familiar objects. In this way, accommodation is crucial for the developmental progress. As the child adapts existing schemas to new ones presented in the environment, Piaget believed the child to be seeking a balance in his or her understanding of the world, and this he termed equilibration. The child strives to create a coherent and internally consistent understanding and knowledge. According to Piaget, there are four crucial stages when the child is faced with challenges resulting in disequilibrium, after which, through adaptation, the balance is restored and the child achieves a significant shift on to a higher level of understanding. In essence, then, the child is inner, biological and individual – many adults and educators have believed that they must wait for the child to reach the appropriate level of development before they can enhance his or her emerging capabilities. While such a strict interpretation of the theory has not been advocated recently in practice, the Piagetian approach does to a considerable extent place the responsibility for learning on the child who develops in isolation, making and testing theories as he or she constructs understanding by operating or acting on his or her environment. Piaget's child therefore becomes social only gradually as his or her cognitive capacity to do so matures.

Vygotsky's child, by contrast, is the child in society. The social nature of the child is present right from the beginning when the infant arrives into a complex world of social relationships and culture – a culture which itself has an historical development. Vygotsky proposed two lines of development for the child: the natural line of organic growth and maturation, and the line of cultural improvement of the psychological functions. At a certain point, they meet up, mediated by speech (Vygotsky writes about speech rather than language) and external, cultural knowledge becomes internal. Whilst Vygotsky viewed individual forces and cultural forces of development as being equally important, his general emphasis is often regarded as being on the impact of culture on the child. Vygotsky does not accept that a child is in the position of creating a conceptual world 'from scratch', but believes that they need instead to appropriate the conceptual resources of the pre-existing cultural world which are transmitted to them by parents, adults and peers. He argued that psychological functions originate in interaction with other people and therefore such knowledge appears initially in interaction with others or interpersonally, and only later becomes intrapersonal (within the child). The example of this cited in *Mind in Society* (Vygotsky, 1978) is the development of pointing, highlighting the importance of gesture and communication in cognitive development.

> *Initially, this gesture is nothing more than an unsuccessful attempt to grasp something ... At this initial stage, pointing is represented by the child's movement ... that and nothing more .. . When the mother comes to the child's aid and realises his movement indicates something, the situation changes fundamentally ... Pointing becomes a gesture for others ... conse-*

quently, the primary meaning of that unsuccessful grasping movement is established by others.

(Vygotsky, 1978, p.56)

The facilitative role for the more competent other is further developed by Vygotsky in his theory of the zone of proximal (next) development. He complained about the generally accepted method of assessing a child's level of development using standardised tests, because these do not differentiate between the child's actual developmental level and what he or she might reasonably achieve with some assistance (see also Chapter 3). In this situation, individual children will demonstrate greater interpersonal variation in terms of potential development. According to Vygotsky, then, the zone of proximal development (ZPD) is '... the distance between the actual developmental level as determined by independent problem solving and the level of potential development as determined through problem solving under adult guidance or in collaboration with more capable peers.' (Vygotsky, 1978, p.86).

Vygotsky's child is therefore a social, outer, culturally determined child. None the less, through the ZPD any child is capable of making a unique contribution to his or her learning, knowledge and understanding.

Bruner's approach to learning was influenced by both Piaget and Vygotsky, but ultimately owes more to Vygotsky. Bruner's child assimilates and accommodates, but the nature of mental representation is crucially influenced by the child's social interactions and environment. Children learn to think in actions (enactively), in pictures (iconically) and in words (symbolically), because actions, pictures and words are used by people around them. That is, learning and knowledge are social in origin and, although the developmental sequence is enactive, then iconic and finally symbolic, Bruner believes that all three remain available to adults. Although he has not presented a unified theory of learning, his work has formalised many of Vygotsky's ideas into educational strategies such as 'scaffolding' (a culturally imposed framework for learning) and the 'spiral curriculum' (the notion that any subject can be taught effectively in some intellectually honest form to any child at any stage of development) (Bruner, 1972) (see Newman and Holzman, 1993, for a critical review).

Later in this chapter we shall examine in more detail the play and language theories of Piaget, Vygotsky and Bruner, amongst others, and finally we shall consider the interrelationships between them.

Special issues in language

In defining language, in order to be consistent with our holistic views elsewhere, it is necessary to make our definition in the broadest sense of both verbal and non-verbal communication. Smith and Cowie (1991) discuss how communication systems exist within almost all species, yet what sets humans apart is the creative flexibility of generating new meaningful utterances, communication of ideas, shared thoughts and consideration of themes that are remote in time and place. As such, communication is an excellent example of complex human behaviour, recruiting information processing to the full. The fact that children have already quickly mastered the complexities of communication by the tender pre-school years is an ongoing research concern. Are children born pre-programmed to learn language? What is the effect of the environment? How does language develop? These questions are directly relevant to learning and the nature versus nurture issue already mentioned.

The recognition that there is a fundamental connection between language and thinking has existed since the time of Aristotle. However, the general claim that thought and language are intrinsically related raises a number of questions. Can there be thought without language? Do different languages reflect different ways of thinking? Do different languages cause differences in the ways in which people think? The view that language determines thought and mentality is traditionally known as *linguistic determinism*, and consistent with this is *linguistic relativity*, which means that differences in languages cause differences in thinking. From a developmental point of view, there has always been some debate about which develops first – thought or language – and the exact nature of the interdependence between them. The contention that it is language which dictates thought has serious implications for children and their free will – children will be socialised into a restricted world view, habitual patterns of language use in some subcultures will disadvantage children educationally, thought will not exist without language, thought will not develop before language, and communication across cultures will at best be limited. Such views have been attacked as being narrow and pessimistic, and a number of alternatives have been in circulation for some time (Mead, 1934; Piaget, 1959; Vygotsky, 1962).

Other theorists have examined cognitive development empirically and have differing notions of the role played by language, culture and social relationships. The two main approaches could be described as Western (Piaget, 1959) and Eastern (Vygotsky, 1962). Piaget and Vygotsky agree that thought does not originate in language. However, Piaget virtually ignored language except in relation to the unsocial nature of egocentric speech – a view he later revised – and how the child's stage of cognitive development is manifested in the language of the child. This egocentric speech reflects the child's cognitive developmental level as being unable to take the 'social' point of view of others. Whilst acknowledging the importance of peers over parents for cognitive development, owing to the opportunity they present for interaction on an equal footing, Piaget none the less gave the child's inherent creativity and individuality precedence over social factors in cognitive development. Vygotsky, on the other hand, considered both language and adults to be crucial for the development of cognitive processes. Language and thought, which are initially separate functions, join forces at about 2 years of age to transform the inner mental life of the child. A child initially uses overt speech (egocentric) to organise the inner mind, and the overt speech then becomes covert or inner thought. Speech is a powerful source of signs, and empowers the child to restructure his or her environment. In addition, language is an important feature for internal cognitive restructuring – as the child plays, he or she will often maintain a monologue on what he or she is doing. The outer speech is not unlike the commentary that adults provide for very young children, e.g., counting out loud as the child climbs the stairs ' . . . one . . . two . . . two . . . oops . . . two . . . three'. Such monologues represent over-socialised speech, which eventually become internal or silent inner speech, thus enabling verbal thought (for a modern account of egocentric speech see Bråten, 1991; Diaz and Berk, 1992).

Interactionists who take account of both individual and social influences on language and thought are well represented in modern developmental research (Donaldson, 1978; Youniss, 1980; Trevarthen, 1987).

Influential language theories

The main theoretical approaches to language acquisition are learning, nativist, cognitive, and social interactionist. The learning theory or behaviourist approach to language explains acquisition as a matter of imitation and reinforcement. As an infant says 'goo goo', babbles, etc., the sounds are shaped by adults until they become words. It is also argued that when a child imitates an adult, the adult rewards the child, and these words will then be learned and used again under similar stimulus conditions. Whilst one can readily find examples of imitation, reinforcement and shaping in language, they do not necessarily occur in all utterances. It is too simplistic to account for the child's spontaneous, original speech efforts and their sensitivity to the regularities of speech that is evident from their systematic errors as they try to generate meaningful utterances. The nativist view of Chomsky is one in which infants are pre-programmed to learn a language and are highly sensitive to the linguistic features of their environment. As Chomsky is concerned with the mental structures within the mind, he spoke of an internal Language Acquisition Device (LAD), namely the mental apparatus that supposedly innately programmes human beings to a universal grammar, thus making it possible for us to speak and comprehend language. Examples of the evidence which suggests that children do generate their own language around rules might include their tendency to over-generalise a rule such as plurals (e.g. 'mans') and tenses (e.g. 'goed'). The traditional cognitive (Piagetian) view of language acquisition is that it is seen as part of general cognitive development. In effect, language acquisition must wait for sensorimotor thinking to develop first. However, the importance of the role played by adult and child relationships in learning has been applied to the study of language acquisition. As a social interactionist, Bruner proposed, in addition to the LAD, a 'sister' known as a Language Acquisition Support System (LASS). *'If there is a Language Acquisition Device, the input to it is not a shower of spoken language but a highly interactive affair shaped . . . by some sort of an adult Language Acquisition Support System'* (Bruner, 1983, p.39).

This approach is pragmatic in that it emphasises language use and its social functions. According to Bruner, the LASS is not exclusively linguistic, but forms part of an overall system for passing on the culture of which language is both instrument and creator, and is passed on through a complex system of rules (for a critical analysis see Newman and Holzman, 1993).

Aitchison (1983) proposed that something specific to language is innate, even though we are not entirely sure what that 'something' consists of. Neither can language be explained as a general offshoot of general intelligence, although we undoubtedly use it when we speak in an as yet undefined way. Aitchison considers learning theories such as those of Skinner to have failed dismally as an explanation of how children acquire language.

There have been many studies of the relationship between language and learning (Wells, 1987). More will be said about the relationship between play, language and learning at the end of this chapter.

Special issues in play

Play and childhood usually go together. Indeed, much of what children do is regarded as play. However, much of what children do is also clearly not play (Garvey, 1991). Different cultures may view play and childhood differently (see Chapters 5 and 13 for further discussion of this aspect). For example, in the Greek language, the word for play comes from the word for child, and a separate word is used for organised games or contests, mostly associated with adult life. The English 'play' comes from the Anglo-Saxon *'plega'*, which referred to play or rapid bodily movement, and was also used to mean performing with musical instruments. However, Roman languages do not distinguish between play and games, and use one word for both (e.g. French and Italian).

Although play has been passionately and widely studied, authors have repeatedly noted that the most troublesome aspect of studying play arises from the fuzziness of the concept and the lack of a precise behavioural definition (e.g. Fein, 1981). There are many ways of approaching play, and there are also many different kinds of play (see Smith and Cowie, 1991), so it is perhaps unsurprising that a firm working definition eludes us. Consider a baby babbling in his or her cot or shaking a rattle, or two boys chasing each other and wrestling on the floor, or the elaborate role play of 4-year-old doctors and nurses. Play may be viewed differently depending on personal characteristics such as age, gender, culture, social class, features of the environment, e.g. space, weather and equipment, and cultural factors, e.g. behavioural conventions and fashions. These are some of the factors which are known to influence play and the difficulty in defining it. Consequently, whilst authors agree that it is best not to define play, most of them have attempted to identify the general characteristics of play. It is generally agreed that play is *non-literal*, that is, a non-serious attitude to reality (Garvey, 1974), and that play is *pleasurable*, enjoyable and indexed by laughter. Other more contentious characteristics include *freedom from extrinsic motivation*, that is, play is unconstrained by external rules or social demands, but is engaged in for its own sake (Bruner, 1976); the *flexibility* of play in utilising alternatives for action, which means variation in the form and content of the play, and play as having a *means* rather than *ends* orientation (e.g. Hutt, 1979; see also Smith and Cowie, 1991, for a discussion of this criterion approach to play). Sutton-Smith and Kelly-Byrne (1984) accuse researchers and practitioners alike of over-emphasising the importance and positive aspects of play. Instead, they remind us that play can be non-egalitarian (e.g., dominance and conflict), may not be voluntary, spontaneous or intrinsically motivated (obligation to and the power of friends and restricted environments), often manifests negative affect (fighting, brutal teasing), and finally, can be dysfunctional. Smith (1993) urges theoreticians, practitioners and students of play to proceed with caution and to take a balanced view of play and its value and relationship to children. None the less, most practitioners are convinced of the empowering potential of play for developing language and learning (Moyles, 1994), and this view has been reflected in the burgeoning interest in play in the fields of psychology, education, anthropology and sociology, and also in the recommendations of policy-makers and practitioners.

Mellou (1994), in a contemporary review of play theories, prefers to view them as either classical (early) theories (e.g. *surplus energy theory, recreation/ relaxation theory, practice theory, recapitulation theory*) or modern theories (e.g., *psychoanalytical theory, metacommunicative theory, cognitive theory*). More will be said about these theories later, but Mellou is keen to point out that the much-criticised early theories actually provide a basis for the modern theories. In all theories, she claims, there is a duality in the process of play in terms of personal expression vs. social adaptation.

Influential play theories

The forum for the discussion of the nature and purpose of play was opened by Schiller in the eighteenth century with his letters on the *Aesthetic of Man*. He was responsible for formulating the evolutionary-type theory, notably what became known as the *surplus energy theory of play*, according to which the young of both animals and humans have large quantities of superfluous energy that are invested in the aimless activity of play. Spencer's (1873) elaboration of this notion (cited in Smith and Cowie, 1991) included classification of types (e.g. sensorimotor, artistic-aesthetic, memetic, games) of play. Other evolutionary/biological theories include those of recreation and relaxation (Lazarus, 1883, cited in Smith and Cowie, 1991) and Patrick (1916, cited in Smith and Cowie, 1991) who argued that play was needed by adults and children as a natural consequence of experiencing fatigue. Thus the function of play was to renew the organism by way of its alternative and more primitive source of energy. An extreme evolutionary theory is Hall's *recapitulation theory*, in which the development of the individual mimics the development of the species. In this way, children's play was seen to represent the evolutionary history of our species, e.g. climbing was related to the early animal stage of mankind, whilst playing with dolls was linked to a later agricultural/patriarchal stage. One particularly influential evolutionary theory was that of Groos (1901, cited in Smith and Cowie, 1991). Under a Darwinian influence, he proposed *practice theory*, according to which, the young of various species went through more or less extensive periods of immaturity during which they had the chance to practise skills that would prove indispensable to them in adult life. These included the practice of physical, mental and social skills. The *results* of such playful activities were regarded as being of secondary importance, as what mattered most was the behaviours involved in the process (see Smith and Cowie, 1991, for a critical appraisal).

The more recent and widely accepted theories of play are of a more psychological nature, dealing with the emotional, social and cognitive functions. First, play is presented as being important in the emotional life of individuals – it helps to overcome problems of reality and it satisfies basic emotional needs. Secondly, the social functions of play, normally studied by sociologists or social anthropologists, are what could be described as affiliative in that play is akin to ritual in social groups and contributes to a temporary inversion of reality and of given social structures, offering a sense of 'togetherness'. This approach is still only represented by a few studies in developmental research (e.g. Corsaro, 1979). The social function of play is perhaps more commonly studied in conjunction with cognition (socio-cognitive) as, for example, in the work of Leslie (1987), Bateson (1955), Bruner (1976) and Vygotsky (1967), or in conjunction with emotion (socio-emotional), as in the work of Freud (1920). Thirdly, the purely cognitive function of play is the domain of Piaget, who differs from the socio-cognitivists noted above, not only with regard to their interest in the social context, but also in the role that language plays in the development of the cognitive function. We shall now consider each of these approaches to play in slightly more detail.

For the psychoanalysts, play has an important role in resolving the emotional conflicts that arise as a consequence of the child's relationships with others. Children and adults alike are subject to anxiety and neuroses, the foundations of which begin in childhood and persist into later life. Psychoanalysts therefore view childhood as critical and the role of play as therapy as particularly important. It is this psychoanalytical approach to play which has established the play therapy system currently used for highly disturbed children, although there are now many different therapeutic approaches (e.g. Erikson, 1963). Erikson argued that children are partners with their futures in play because their 'as if' play seemed to serve as a metaphor for their lives. When children grow up, their adult life-style will have been implicit in their childhood free-play. It is through play that they learn to deal with disappointment and failure, and learn to approach life with a sense of increasingly focused purpose.

Piaget considered play to be characterised by the primacy of assimilation over accommodation – the child incorporates events and objects into existing mental structures. As the child evolves through cognitive developmental stages, there is an equivalent manifestation in play behaviours. First, sensori-motor play is practice play involving repetitious actions which gradually become purposive. When language and representation emerge, the child is able to play symbolically. However, this is a solitary affair, directed initially towards self, and is a simple ability, for instance, to pretend to go to sleep out of the context of reality. Soon, the child will move from this self-reference to other-reference, e.g. he or she will put teddy to sleep (Figure 9.1). This is followed by the ability to use objects symbolically, e.g. a peg serves as a substitute for a doll. Finally, the child is able to make sequential combinations i.e. a whole play-scene. Socio-dramatic play is evident between 4 and 7 years, when the child engages in pretend play with others. Between 7 and 11 years the child moves into the realm of collective symbols, rules and games with rules, and it is this play which marks the transition to a socialised individual. Play thus moves from purely individual, idiosyncratic, private processes and symbols to social play and collective symbols. As play is about assimilation, pretend play serves to enable the child to relive past experiences, rather than to create possible future ones.

The other play theorists who have been concerned with cognition have, without exception, also addressed how language and the social environment

Figure 9.1 Putting teddy to sleep: children move from self-reference to other-reference.

interact with the child's learning or developing cognitive abilities. Vygotsky discussed play as arising from social pressures, i.e. social and emotional needs. For Vygotsky (1967), play is always a social symbolic activity. Even when a child plays alone, there will be implicit socio-cultural themes, e.g. toys are cultural inventions and role play entails socially constructed rules for behaviour and interaction. Vygotsky believed that solitary play was a later development than social play, and that genuine play emerged at about 3 years of age. Genuine play has two main characteristics, namely the imaginary situation and the rules implicit in that imaginary situation. For example, a child playing as a 'mother' can freely select her behaviour, but must also follow the rules of maternal behaviour as she understands them, and this entails cognitive effort. Later on, pretend play with games and rules, such as chess, involves explicit rules but an imaginary situation (Figure 9.2). The function of play is socio-emotional – the child desires to act in the ways of an adult, but is not yet able to do so. This need can be satisfied through fantasy. Furthermore, in submission to implicit and explicit rules, children are empowered with self-control over their impulsive desires. Importantly, play also contributes to cognitive development rather than simply reflecting it. It is through early play that the child first creates the zone of proximal development: *'In play a child is always above his average age, above his daily behaviour; in play it is as though he were a head taller than himself'* (Vygotsky, 1967, p.6).

Consider also a pretend world in which a piece of wood can be used as a substitute for a doll or a horse or a car. This is the creation of a world dominated by meanings – one in which action arises from ideas rather than from

Figure 9.2 Chess: children later play games with explicit rules but an imaginary situation.

objects – and this paves the way for abstract internalised thought (see Nicolopoulou, 1993, for a critical review of Piaget and Vygotsky).

Bruner (1976), clearly influenced by Groos and Vygotsky, noted that the increased dominance of play during immaturity among higher primates, serves as practice for the technical social life that constitutes human culture. He also realised the practical educational implications of his theory and the role played by others (especially adults), in particular, referring to interactional routines such as 'peek-a-boo' as 'scaffolding'. It is such conventional routines and formats of games which prepare children to take their place in society and culture.

The remaining socio-cognitive theorists have developed further the importance of communication and language in play or, more precisely, pretend play for the development of knowledge and understanding. There is more consideration given to the nature of mental representation and the child's ability to comprehend his or her own understanding and that of other people. Bateson (1955) was interested in the 'not really serious' aspect of play which presupposes that children are well able to distinguish between what is play and what is not. This ability to stand back from their activities and represent it as 'not serious' is a particular type of higher understanding between players which Bateson termed *metacommunication*. Play behaviour signals convey the message 'what I am about to say is not to be taken exactly as I say it'. Thus it is in play that a child learns about the different ways in which social rules can be 'framed' and 'reframed'. According to Bateson, then, what a child actually learns in play is about learning itself.

In a similar vein, Leslie (1987) focused on pretend play as a means whereby a child develops knowledge about his or her own and other peoples' thinking or *metacognition*. When children engage in imaginary role play, some statements may be true (e.g. 'this cup is empty') and others false (e.g. the imaginary tea 'is cold') (where both statements are used with reference to a child's empty play cup). Children know that whilst it is true that the cup is empty, any tea in the cup will be imaginary. Thus pretend play is about the overall understanding of the situation, and not the truth value of statements within the situation. Consequently, the emergence of pretend play between 18 and 24 months can be seen as the development of the faculty of *metarepresentation*.

The most influential of these theorists for educational policy and reform have been Piaget, Vygotsky and Bruner (1972). However, these theorists are essentially psychologists. There is another species of theorist for whom the philosophy of education is the direct and principal concern, including Froebel (1782–1852), McMillan (1860–1931), Dewey (1859–1952) and Isaacs (1885–1948). Another way in which these theorists differ from those already mentioned is in their eclectic approach to the holistic well-being of the whole child – physical, mental, emotional, social and spiritual (for a detailed overview see Bruce, 1991). Froebel believed play to be a unifying mechanism which integrated the child's learning, and as the highest phase in the child's functioning, viewed play as a spiritual activity. McMillan developed the free-play side of the curriculum, seeing greater cohesion between Froebe-lian ideas and practical application. In the twentieth century, Dewey helped teachers to take play seriously in the classroom, whilst Isaacs was more spe-cific about the emotional nature of the child and how play helps to meet their emotional needs. It is interesting to note that, despite clear indications by leading thinkers and practitioners of the importance of emotional and spiri-tual development in education, there remains a glaring gap in relevant research and practice.

Summary and interplay of the theories

A discussion of the interplay between play, language and learning presents a considerable challenge. The task is a thesis in itself, and specific research on this complex three-way relationship is scant. However, if we turn to devel-opmental psychology, we find many exciting and relevant developments. In a recent review of theory and research, Dunn (1996) describes the links between emotion, cognition and interpersonal relationships. This work illus-trates what is currently missing from many traditional, early education-based programmes which feature play, language and learning as a single unit. We now also know much more about the social (see also Chapter 4) and emo-tional lives and abilities of young children to go on ignoring their obvious impact on children's play, language and learning. Indeed, an holistic approach to child development and behaviour *demands* that we paint on a much broader canvas.

In summarising this chapter, some of the common ground shared by clas-sical and modern theories of play includes the folllowing: the categorisation of types of play (e.g. functional, sensorimotor, artistic-aesthetic, memetic, games), all of which appear in the work of Spencer and Piaget in various forms; the non-literal ('as if') nature of play is crucially important for all mod-ern cognitive theorists, such as Bateson and Leslie, as well as for the classical theorists. The importance of the lengthy period of childhood for the purpose of practising skills through play features in the work of Groos, Piaget and Bruner. Interestingly, a diversity of authors agree on the emotional functions of play. Piaget (1962) describes play as 'pleasure in mastery . . . illusion of omnipotence', Vygotsky (1962) describes play as 'wish-fulfilment' after hav-ing experienced early disappointment, and for psychoanalysts play is des-cribed as the only remedy that children (and sometimes adults) have at their disposal after confronting the real side of living with others. The views of Piaget, Vygotsky and Freud have been seized upon by the holistic education theorists.

Those features of play which relate closely to learning include play as pressure-free – in that the consequences of success or failure are very different in play and in reality, play as symbolic and play as interactive. Such theories include ideas from cognitive science, such as script theory – knowledge acquisition through social interaction (Nelson, 1981) – and schema theory (Athey, cited in Nutbrown, 1993), which is based on Piagetian concepts. From sociology comes the frame analysis of Goffman, which has a dramaturgical approach, sharing much with script theories, and from studies on communication come theories of metacommunication and metarepresentation. Those aspects of language which relate particularly to play include play with words (see Smith and Cowie, 1991, for an overview of Weir's account of language play; Nelson, 1989) humour and teasing, and play theories on metacommunication and metarepresentation.

CONCLUSIONS

Simon and Rebecca could be anywhere one might expect to find children playing – in your own home, at preschool, in a hospital, in a care facility or with a child-minder. What do all of these theories and special issues on play, language and learning mean for them and the adults who are caring for or studying them? At once it is clear that children are both fascinating and complex individuals and, given the holistic nature of the child, it is important to concede that no single special issue or theory is absolutely correct and able to account for the total complexity of behaviour involved in play, language and learning.

REFERENCES

Aitchison, J. (1983): *The Articulate Mammal: an Introduction to Psycholinguistics*, 2nd edn. London: Hutchison.

Bateson, G.A. (1955): A Theory of Play and Fantasy. *Psychiatric Research* Reports **2**, 39–51.

Bjørkvold, J.R. (1987): Our Musical Mother Tongue – World-wide. In Soderbergh, R. (ed.), *Children's Creative Communication*. Lund: Lund University Press.

Bråten, I. (1991): Vygotsky as Precursor to Metacognitive Theory. II. Vygotsky as Metacognitivitist. *Scandinavian Journal of Educational Research* **35**, 305–20.

Bruce, T. (1991): *Time to Play*. London: Hodder & Stoughton.

Bruner, J.S. (1972): *The Relevance of Education*. London: Allen & Unwin.

Bruner, J.S. (1976): Functions of Play in Immaturity. In Bruner, J.S., Jolly, A. and Sylva, K. (eds), *Play: its Role in Evolution and Development*. New York: Basic Books, 28–64.

Bruner, J.S. (1983): *Child's Talk: Learning to use Language*. New York: W.W. Norton & Co.

Corsaro, W.A. (1979): We're Friends, Right? Children's use of Access Rituals in a Nursery School. *Language in Society* **8**, 315–36.

Diaz, R.M. and Berk, L.E. (1992): *Private Speech: from Social Interaction to Self-regulation*. Hillsdale, NJ: Lawrence Erlbaum Associates.

Donaldson, M. (1978): *Children's Minds*. London: Fontana.

Dunn, J. (1996): The Emanuel Miller Memorial Lecture 1995. Children's Relationships: Bridging the Divide Between Cognitive and Social Development. *Journal of Child Psychology and Psychiatry* **37**, 507–18.

Erikson, E. (1963): *Childhood and Society*. London: Routledge and Kegan Paul.

Fein, G. (1981): Pretend Play in Childhood: an Integrative Review. *Child Development* **52**, 1095–118.

Freud, S. (1920): *Three Contributions to the Theory of Sex. Nervous and Mental Disease Monographs No. 7.* New York: Nervous and Mental Disease Publishers.

Garvey, C. (1974): Some Properties of Social Play. *Merrill-Palmer Quarterly* **20**, 163–80.

Garvey, C. (1991): *Play,* 2nd edn. London: Fontana.

Goodman, J.F. (1994): 'Work' Versus 'Play' and Early Childhood Care. *Child and Youth Care Forum* **23**, 177–196.

Hutt, C. (1979): Play in the Under-fives: Form, Development and Function. In Howells, J.G. (ed.), *Modern Perspectives on the Psychiatry of Infancy.* New York: Brunner/Marcell.

Karmiloff-Smith, A. (1995): *Beyond Modularity: a Developmental Perspective on Cognitive Science.* Cambridge, MA: MIT Press.

Leslie, A. (1987): Pretence and Representation: the Origins of 'Theory of Mind' *Psychological Review* **94**, 412–26.

Mead, G.H. (1934): *Mind, Self and Society.* Chicago: University of Chicago Press.

Mellou, E. (1994): Play Theories: a Contemporary Review. *Early Child Development and Care* **102**, 91–100.

Moyles, J.R. (ed.) (1994): *The Excellence of Play.* Buckingham: Open University Press.

Nelson, K. (1981): Social Cognition in a Script Framework. In Flavell, J. and Ross, L. (eds), *Social Cognitive Development.* New York: Cambridge University Press, 97–118.

Nelson, K. (ed.) (1989): Monologues in the Crib. In Nelson, K. (ed.), *Narratives from the Crib.* Cambridge, MA: Harvard University Press.

Newman, F. and Holzman, L. (1993): *Lev Vygotsky: Revolutionary Scientist.* London: Routledge.

Nicolopoulou, A. (1993): Play, Cognitive Development and the Social World: Piaget, Vygotsky and Beyond. *Human Development* **36**, 1–23.

Nutbrown, C. (1993): *Threads of Thinking.* London: Paul Chapman Publishing.

Piaget, J. (1959): *The Language and Thought of the Child.* London: Routledge and Kegan Paul.

Piaget, J. (1962): *Play, Dreams and Imitation in Childhood.* London: Routledge and Kegan Paul.

Reiber, R.W. and Garton, A.S. (1987): *The Collected Works of L.S. Vygotsky. Vol.1. Problems of General Philosophy.* New York: Plenum Press.

Smith, P.K. (1993): Play and the Uses of Play. In Moyles, J.R. (ed.), *The Excellence of Play.* Buckingham: Open University Press, 15–26.

Smith, P.K. and Cowie, H. (1991): *Understanding Children's Development.* Oxford: Basil Blackwell.

Sutton-Smith, B. and Kelly-Byrne, D. (1984): The Idealisation of Play. In Smith, P.K. (ed.), *Play in Animals and Humans.* Oxford: Basil Blackwell, 305–21.

Trevarthen, C. (1987): Infants Trying to Talk: How a Child Invites Communication from the Human World. In Soderbergh, R. (ed.), *Children's Creative Communication.* Fourth International Congress for the Study of Child Language. Lund: Lund University Press, 9–31.

Vygotsky, L.S. (1962): *Thought and Language.* Cambridge, MA: MIT Press.

Vygotsky, L.S. (1967): Play and its Role in the Mental Development of the Child. *Soviet Psychology* **3**.

Vygotsky, L.S. (1978): *Mind and Society.* Cambridge, MA: Harvard University Press.

Wells, G. (1987): *The Meaning-makers: Children's Learning, Language and Using Language to Learn.* London: Hodder & Stoughton.

Whitehead, M. (1990): *Language and Literacy in the Early Years.* London: Paul Chapman Publishing.

Youniss, J. (1980): *Parents and Peers in Social Development. A Sullivan-Piaget Perspective.* Chicago: Chicago University Press.

Further reading

Kane, S.R. and Furth, H.G. (1993): Children Constructing Social Reality: a Frame Analysis of Social Pretend Play. *Human Development* **36**, 199–214.

Lee, V. and Das Gupta, P. (1995): *Children's Cognitive and Language Development.* Oxford: Basil Blackwell in association with the Open University.

Mead, G.H. (1932): *The Philosophy of the Present.* La Salle, Il: Open Court Publishing Company.

Meadows, S. (1993): *The Child as Thinker: The Development and Acquisition of Cognition in Childhood.* London: Routledge.

Moll, L.C. (ed.) (1992): *Vygotsky and Education: Instructional Implications and Applications of socio-historical Psychology.* Cambridge: Cambridge University Press.

Moyles, J.R. (1989): *Just Playing.* Milton Keynes: Open University Press.

Nelson, K. and Seidman, S. (1984): Playing with Scripts. In Bretherton, I. (ed.), *Symbolic Play.* London: Academic Press Inc., 45–71.

10 Child protection, welfare and the law

Kevin Pettican

This chapter aims to:

- consider key issues in relation to the physical, sexual and emotional abuse of children and to child neglect in the context of multidisciplinary child protection work;
- discuss some of the professional challenges presented by operating the child protection system;
- suggest a child protection curriculum for professionals who have early years responsibilities.

Introduction

Child protection is integral to child care policy and to good child care practice, and therefore forms an essential element of early childhood studies. The professional task of protecting children from abuse and helping those who may have already been abused, or significantly harmed, is both complex and emotionally demanding, and presents an enormous challenge to all those who have child care and child protection interests and responsibilities.

The professional challenge exists for several related reasons. It arises through the very nature of responding to painful situations in which children, who are dependent upon adults for their care and protection, may suffer significant harm or exploitation. A professional worker may emotionally absorb, in a very small measure, something of what the victim might be feeling, even though they consciously guard against over-identification with the victim and strive to manage the powerful feelings that can colour perceptions and influence thinking and judgement-making. The professional challenge is evidenced by the need to protect the child, sensitively but realistically, without destroying the *positive* aspects of the child's family life. The task is to remain child-focused and supportive while responding to the legitimate therapeutic interests of the child in a manner that does not undermine any legal and evidential processes that arise from an investigation.

These challenges are located within a context in which public, professional and organisational expectations of what child protection workers *should do* in any given situation are often ambiguous, or appear to be at odds with each other. For instance, it is often a very difficult task to strike the correct balance between respecting a family's right to privacy and non-interference by the state, with regard to the way in which they bring up their children, with the state's legitimate responsibility to intervene and protect children against abuse and exploitation. Professionals often feel that they are damned when they do intervene, but also damned if they do not.

Seden *et al.* (1996) have provided some encouraging evidence to support the contention that the complex process of reconciling state intervention in child protection situations with the need to preserve family autonomy *can* be achieved by child protection workers in a manner that is empowering both to the child and to the family, and which shows how well professionals can co-operate and work effectively together. However, the requirement of the Children Act 1989 that child protection workers must work in partnership with parents and fully involve them in the child protection processes can be quite a challenging and daunting task, as the research of Thoburn *et al.* (1995) has so clearly revealed.

The task, then, for the early childhood studies student is also a substantial one in trying to understand something of the nature of the challenges of child protection and the way in which professionals and others respond to it on a day-to-day basis, and how they set about explaining, justifying and accounting for their actions.

This chapter will provide some signposts for the early childhood studies student in terms of the content and direction of their learning pathway in studying the complexities of child abuse and child protection. It will suggest the content of a child protection curriculum and raise issues of social policy and social values before discussing, in turn, emotional abuse, neglect, sexual abuse and physical abuse. Finally, the importance of the multidisciplinary child protection system will be considered in relation to responding to serious concerns about the welfare of children.

Learning about child protection

Students are likely to appreciate quite early on that there is much more to studying child abuse and child protection than might at first appear to be the case. The child abuse and child protection curriculum is substantial, and tends to be continually growing, expanding and reconstructing. One of the consequences of this has been an explosion of information to feed the perceived needs of professionals and others, but the rate has been so fast that proper evaluation, dissemination and assimilation of the material is often much slower than its rapid and continuous production.

One of the paradoxical results for many professionals has been a feeling that, far from being helpful and empowering, the appearance of too much complex information, at too fast a pace, can result in a sense of anxiety, confusion and powerlessness, rather than leading to a sense of enlightenment, stability and feelings of empowerment. Professionals, managers and organisations need to devise appropriate strategies to enable staff to keep up to date with changes and developments in thinking and practice, but in such a way that this does not become perceived as another pressure – another burden to carry. In this respect there is enormous scope for the creative use of information technology, including software packages designed for the caring professions, as well as on-line information and interpersonal communications.

A child protection curriculum

A curriculum that is designed to address the subject of child abuse and child protection would be one that is firmly located within a child care framework to enable it to build upon the wealth of knowledge, experience and research material that is widely available about child care. However, unlike a purely academic course of study, learning which is practice-based would be fundamentally concerned not just with theory and research, but also with developing skills in making conceptual and operational linkages to day-to-day child care and child protection practice, in context.

It would also be concerned with broadening and extending the professional's repertoire of practice skills in accordance with his or her own particular professional role and responsibilities. Bearing these points in mind, the following guide is provided as a suggested learning pathway to give students an indication of what a comprehensive curriculum for child abuse and child protection might cover, although the selection and focus of any individual student's studies is likely to reflect his or her own interests, responsibilities and career pathway:

- an understanding of the nature and extent of child abuse in its social and cultural context, including perspectives drawn from Europe and other countries (Birks, 1995);
- an appreciation of the notion of child abuse as a social construct, and the relevance of social, cultural, political and legal frameworks for child protection work;
- a consideration of the short- and long-term effects of abuse upon the child, and of the impact of professional intervention upon the child and his or her family;
- an awareness of how the multidisciplinary child protection system works to identify, recognise and investigate child abuse and protect children;
- an understanding of the roles and responsibilities of all relevant professionals and agencies with child protection responsibilities;

- an appreciation of the issues of race, gender and disability, including abuse of children who have a physical, sensory and/or learning disability;
- theories which address causation of child abuse and which provide explanatory frameworks for the persistence of abuse in all its forms;
- assessment of children's needs and family circumstances, and of the risks faced by children, as a basis for decision-making and action;
- an understanding of differential treatment and therapeutic approaches for victims and survivors of abuse, for non-abusing carers, and for those who have perpetrated the abuse;
- an evaluation of the outcomes and effectiveness of different treatment and therapeutic programmes in the UK and elsewhere;
- an appreciation of some of the significant findings from various research studies, and lessons to be learned from child abuse inquiry reports.

Central to this child-focused curriculum is a clear recognition of the feelings, perceptions and interests of the child and the crucial role that he or she plays in any subsequent child protection processes. A good starting point for students to acquire a general understanding of many of the aspects and issues identified above would be an up-to-date general text on child abuse or child protection, such as those provided by Corby (1993) or Wilson and James (1995). Other relevant texts are mentioned later in this chapter.

Child abuse – private act, public issue

Child abuse is an intensely private act which usually occurs without witnesses, as is commonly the case with sexual abuse and with serious physical abuse. Similarly, a child may be neglected and emotionally abused in the privacy of his or her own family home, often over a lengthy period of time, even though many other people may have had access to the home and may have witnessed for themselves signs of a child's unhappy situation.

The *private* act of abusing a vulnerable and dependent child is also a matter of *public* interest and concern (Parton, 1985). Child abuse presents a direct and unwelcome public challenge to society's most cherished values, beliefs and ideologies about the care of its children, about the tasks and responsibilities of parenthood, and about family life. The frequently reported occurrences of serious injury or the death of a child, or the sexual abuse of children *in our very midst*, produces a sense of moral outrage, public anguish, frustration and helplessness. It can also serve to generate a general feeling of unease and concern about the welfare and safety of *all* children in society.

In such a climate, support for the dominant ideology of family life and family values – so beloved by the advertising media – is challenged. The cumulative effect of media reportage of child abuse and the evidence from research and the professional literature raise questions about the notion of the family as a safe and secure environment in which to bring up children. The counter-ideology, that families can be dangerous places for children, opens up a far more challenging and controversial discourse and political debate (Dale, 1986).

However, the *culture of blame* that follows media reporting of child abuse tragedies serves to deflect public debate away from an informed analysis of the different causes of child abuse (other than an individual aberration) and the way that it persists as a serious social problem in our society. By blaming individual families and individual professionals, an important debate is avoided about the way, as a society, we care for our children, and the reasons for not developing effective strategies for resourcing and supporting vulnerable children and families in order to improve the quality of their life and help prevent abuse from occurring. Similarly, in those situations where abuse has already occurred, what level of resourcing are we as a society prepared to provide to create effective systems of family support – including treatment and therapeutic services – for children who have been abused, for their brothers and sisters, for non-abusing parents/carers and, importantly, for those people who, for whatever reason, are the abusers?

What is child abuse?

A narrow definition of child abuse has been provided by the Department of Health (1991b), which is used to assist multidisciplinary Child Protection Conferences in deciding whether or not to enter a child's name upon the Child Protection Register. This set of definitions, subdivided into *emotional abuse*, *neglect*, *physical abuse* and *sexual abuse*, is now so widely adopted that it seems to have acquired a kind of self-validation as the acceptance and usage of these definitions has become embedded in official documentation, professional language and practice, and media-speak.

The notion of child abuse, child maltreatment (Department of Health, 1995) or *significant harm*, to use the term adopted by the Children Act 1989, usually refers to individual acts, events or processes that are judged to be significantly harmful and which occur *within* the family or some other caring or social setting (see Adcock *et al.*, 1991, for a full discussion of how this term is applied to child protection practice).

However, child abuse also occurs *outside* the family, with people who are known or unknown to the child. It may involve two or more people, who may or may not be related to the child, or it may involve an organised group, network or 'ring.' Some instances of organised or network abuse have revealed how a very large number of family members and friends have become covertly involved in sexually abusing many children drawn from several families living in different locations, and have shown that this may continue for a period of months or even years (Department of Health, 1995). In such circumstances the victims may be teenagers as well as younger children, and indeed the abusers themselves may also be teenagers and not exclusively adults.

The true extent of child abuse in its different forms in the UK remains debatable. However, research information is beginning to emerge from several sources (see, for example, Department of Health, 1995) to improve our understanding of child abuse and professional intervention as part of the child protection processes. Over many years the National Society for the Prevention of Cruelty to Children (NSPCC) has collected and made available statistical information relating to such factors as the age, occupation and background of abusers, and the family background and circumstances of the victim and other family members (Creighton, 1995). An interesting attempt to begin the process of assessing the prevalence of child sexual abuse in the UK has been made by Ghate and Spencer (1995), who have argued the case for undertaking a full-scale national survey based upon the model that they employed in their pilot research.

The term 'child abuse' is a socially constructed concept that is rooted in a particular social, cultural, legal and historical context, and hence has been subject to considerable changes, developments and reconstructions. For instance, the definition of child sexual abuse has been changed from that provided in *Working Together* (Department of Health and Social Security and the Welsh Office, 1988) to the re-definition currently used in the post-Children Act edition of *Working Together* (Department of Health, 1991b). Similarly, the category known as *grave concern*, commonly used before the Children Act, was abolished and all cases previously registered under this heading were reviewed and either re-registered under another category or de-registered.

Each of the four categories of child abuse, namely *neglect, physical abuse, sexual abuse* and *emotional abuse*, will now be discussed, beginning with the category that often receives little attention in its own right – *emotional abuse*.

Emotional abuse

Emotional abuse has been defined as:

> an *'actual or likely severe adverse effect upon the emotional and behavioural development of a child caused by persistent or severe emotional ill-treatment or rejection'* (Department of Health, 1991a, p.49).

EXAMPLES OF EMOTIONAL ABUSE

A *child's* observed behaviour, mood, deportment, language and development (physically, socially, cognitively, educationally and emotionally) may reveal delays and disturbances under one or more of the following features: a general sense of hypersensitivity, over-reaction, acute fearfulness, low self-esteem, solitary or destructive behaviour or emotionally detached and vacant behaviour.

The *parental/carer's* behaviour might reveal serious rejection, an inability to consider or persistent denial of the child's own feelings, emotions and value, emotional distancing from the child, constant belittling, ridiculing, scapegoating or blaming, or it might reveal detachment and indifference. Behaviour may be consistently *low on warmth and high on criticism* (Department of Health, 1995) (see Chapter 7 for further discussion of parenting styles).

The definition of emotional abuse taken from *Working Together* (Department of Health, 1991a) is poorly framed in many ways in that it is not really a definition at all, but a kind of re-statement of the problem itself. Emotional abuse is not a single or fixed condition or state. It is as likely to be an ongoing process for the child, lasting for a period of weeks, months or years, as it is to be a series of significant events in a child's life. Like all other categories of child abuse, it can also be conceptualised as a *continuum* ranging in nature and degree from very mild emotional abuse at one end to very severe and persistent emotional abuse at the other, with corresponding implications for the impact upon the child, in both the short and long term.

Children who experience other forms of abuse, e.g. neglect, sexual abuse or physical abuse, are likely to suffer from emotional abuse as well – an important factor that needs to be addressed equally as part of the child's treatment programme. However, this category tends to reflect *individual* acts of abuse, and it fails to recognise other collective forms of emotional harm, such as the damaging effects upon children of bullying, sexism, racism, disablism, poverty, homelessness and 'bed-and-breakfast' living.

Professionals engaged in child care and child protection work frequently refer to the notion of emotional abuse as being a vague term, which renders attempts to define, detect and deal with it exceedingly difficult. This, it is argued, accounts for the small numbers of children who appear on the Child Protection Register under this category. This seems rather curious, since the same professionals are just as likely to acknowledge that emotional abuse will be present in *all* forms of child abuse to a greater or lesser extent, as well as being manifested in its own right.

A glimpse is thus provided of some of the difficulties encountered in achieving consensus about determining emotional abuse in a particular cases. Hence professionals tend to register children on the Child Protection Register under *other* categories, rather than under emotional abuse alone. Taking these two factors together, it is easy to see just how much under-reporting of emotional abuse is likely to occur in the UK.

O'Hagan (1993) has challenged the proposition that emotional abuse is difficult to recognise by arguing that, while the term itself is very imprecise, the harm caused by such abuse *is* recognisable if one only knows what to look for, where to look, and what questions to ask. He subdivides emotional abuse into emotional abuse and psychological abuse, both of which he defines as parental or carer behaviour that is sustained, repetitive and inappropriate (1) to the child's expression of feelings, emotions and expressive behaviour (*emotional abuse*) and/or (2) to the child's creative and developmental potential of crucially important mental faculties and mental processes, including intelligence, language, perception, recognition, memory, attention and moral development (*psychological abuse*).

When the early years child is at playgroup, placed with a daily child-minder, in a nursery or at school, O'Hagan would argue that careful monitoring and observation with accurate recording can often reveal tell-tale signs and indicators of possible abuse which can be placed alongside other information provided by professionals.

Another helpful conceptual and operational approach to the problem of emotional abuse has been provided by Iwaniec (1995), who distinguishes between *emotional abuse* (an *active* process) and the notion of *emotional neglect* (a *passive* process). Whilst there are echoes here of O'Hagan's work in relation to psychological abuse, the definition is distinct: '*the hostile or indifferent parental behaviour which damages the child's self-esteem, degrades a sense of achievement, diminishes a sense of belonging, prevents healthy and vigorous development, and takes away a child's well-being*' (Iwaniec, 1995, p.35).

Iwaniec defines emotional neglect in terms of the parent's or carer's inability to meet a child's emotional needs, providing little attention, stimulation or engagement, and failing to care, supervise, guide, teach and protect. She argues that parents who emotionally neglect often do so because of ignorance, poor general awareness, depressive moods, mental illness, chaotic life-styles, poverty, lack of support and lack of good child-rearing modelling. Parents who are just unable to give themselves emotionally to their own demanding and needy children, because they themselves are so emotionally needy and demanding, are not an unfamiliar problem to child care and child protection workers (see also Chapter 5).

One such parent, who could not bring herself to touch, cuddle or express any emotional warmth in any way towards her own daughter, aged 7 years, told the author sadly about the way her own mother had emotionally retreated from her when she was a child, and the legacy that had been left as a result of her experiences:

> the only times my mother ever touched me in the whole of her life were when I was born and when she used to hit me! She just couldn't bring herself to touch me in any way. I just feel nothing at all for my own children now. I have nothing to give them.

The young girl was subsequently registered under the category of emotional abuse on the Child Protection Register. Interestingly, the same mother felt able to touch, play with and emotionally engage with her neighbour's children and those of her sister, but not with her *own* children.

The connection made by Iwaniec between neglect and emotional abuse seems especially helpful here in that it provides a conceptual bridge between two currently distinct categories, namely *emotional abuse* and *neglect*, as well as recognising that child abuse can be active or passive, or a combination of both. Further significance of the operational use of the term emotional neglect has been highlighted by Parton (1996). Quoting from *Messages from Research* (Department of Health, 1995), he draws attention to the finding that:

> *if (we) put to one side the most severe case, the most deleterious situations in terms of longer-term outcomes for children are those of emotional neglect where the primary concern is the parenting style which fails to compensate for the inevitable deficiencies that become manifest in the course of the 20 years or so it takes to bring up a child.*

(Parton, 1996, pp.3–11)

What is clear is that emotional abuse is often present in the background of many children's lives, although its status and impact are frequently down-played because it seems to lack the drama, suddenness, seriousness and sense of unpredictable riskiness of other event-driven forms of abuse, such as sexual and physical abuse. Emotional abuse may also be so commonplace, so enduring and so apparently intractable that professionals and others may become immune and blunted to its insidious effects upon the life and development of the child. As with all other forms of abuse, busy and hard-pressed professionals often feel that if they only had more time and clearer resources, they would be better placed to undertake the much-needed therapeutic work with emotionally abused and emotionally needy children and parents.

However, many individual and collective therapeutic approaches have been developed for working with such children and their families within the community, in family and resource centres, and in other therapeutic settings (see the examples discussed in Wilson and James, 1995).

Child neglect

Child neglect has been defined as:

> *the persistent or severe neglect of a child, or the failure to protect a child from exposure to any kind of danger, including cold or starvation, or extreme failure to carry out important aspects of care, resulting in the significant impairment of the child's health or development, including non-organic failure to thrive.*

(Department of Health, 1991a, p.48)

EXAMPLES OF CHILD NEGLECT

The *child* may appear to be constantly hungry, fatigued, emaciated, inadequately and inappropriately clothed for the prevailing weather, have the appearance of being unkempt, uncared for and unclean, be frequently late or absent from nursery, playschool or school, have untreated medical conditions or be prone to regular accidents, and may appear to be left unsupervised and unattended, given his or her age and circumstances. Such, children appear to be failing to thrive and not developing appropriately for their age and stage of development.

The *parental/carer's* behaviour may reveal a preoccupation with their own unmet emotional needs and their own problems and interests, to the extent that they have little left over for their children – emotionally, socially and practically. Parental behaviour towards the child(ren) may also resemble that discussed under the heading of emotional abuse.

Child neglect is often confused with poverty. It may also be dismissed as referring to *dirty children who are poor but happy*. Whereas neglectful parents may indeed live in poverty, middle-class and upper-class (including wealthy) parents may also be neglectful of their children emotionally as much as they may be neglected materially. This category of abuse clearly overlaps with that of emotional abuse, and especially with the notion of emotional neglect (Iwaniec, 1995).

Although the problem of child neglect has itself often been neglected (see Moore, 1992), there is some evidence that a much greater degree of interest is now being shown in addressing the problem than has sometimes previously been the case. Work has been undertaken by several organisations – such as the NSPCC, for example – to develop assessment protocols which provide a framework for understanding the nature and form of neglect in a particular family, and which also serve to pin-point the tasks that need to be undertaken, the outcomes to be achieved and the time scale; all of these may be written into a contract or agreement with the parents (Minty and Pattinson, 1994).

Stevenson (1996) lends support to the therapeutic efforts of social workers, health visitors, education social workers and others with regard to the need to provide a clear framework for organising their collective interventions in neglectful situations, in order to avoid a sense of drift and vagueness in their general approach.

She advocates long-term work that is purposeful, focused in its sought-after outcomes and especially clear about determining the point beyond which standards of care and parenting are judged to have fallen to an unacceptably low level, at which the child is clearly not developing appropriately and must be removed.

Although some specific attention has been paid to a consideration of the long-term effects of child neglect (Rose, 1985), unlike other categories of abuse, neglect tends to be subsumed under the general heading of 'the effects of child abuse', (Corby, 1993). Part of the reason for this seems to be due to a tendency to confound the effects of neglect with those of poverty. Moreover, discussions and judgements about the effects of neglect can become deflected *away* from the children themselves, towards a value-laden and inconclusive debate about what is or is not *good enough parenting*, what is or is not an acceptable parenting style, and towards questions of standards, measurement, and cultural diversity and relativity.

Another reason may lie in the false belief that child neglect is not significantly harmful to children since, it is argued, many children in the UK, and
even more so elsewhere in the world, are often brought up in appallingly
neglectful circumstances without any apparent undue ill effects. Such a dubious and unsustainable proposition is not supported by the evidence, which
tends to provide counter-claims such as that strongly argued by Moore (1994),
who writes that: *'neglect is a serious form of child abuse (which) can have alarming
consequences. Research shows that neglected children, living in poverty, have a higher
death rate than children of other poor families'* (Moore, 1994).

Stevenson (1996) has tried to steer a pathway through the neglect debate in
order to identify and separate out some of the important questions, issues and
implications for the neglected child, for their parents and for child protection
workers. She acknowledges the need to be realistic about what change and
progress might be possible in a particular family, and recognises that there are
limitations placed upon professional achievement in especially complex and
intractable cases which may lead to the need to make difficult decisions about
the child's future.

In many situations, however, change, movement and progress are clearly
possible and highly desirable both for the child and for the whole family.
Many family centres and resource units provide specialist assistance for families in which there are concerns and child protection issues relating to neglect,
and in which change can be clearly demonstrated and evidenced. Social workers, family aides/home carers and health visitors are also heavily involved in
undertaking structured work with neglectful parents in order to achieve
specifically agreed goals and to monitor the child's overall health, welfare and
development, as well as the ongoing risks.

Sexual abuse

Sexual abuse has been defined as:

> *'actual or likely sexual exploitation of a child or adolescent. The child may be depen-
> dent and/or developmentally immature'* (Department of Health, 1991a, p.49).

EXAMPLES OF SEXUAL ABUSE

A *child* may provide physical, social, psychological, behavioural and/or linguistic clues about inappropriate sexual encounters and experiences. For
example, they may complain of soreness, bleeding or a rash around their gen-
ital area for non-medical reasons, their behaviour and language with other
children and/or with adults may be overtly sexual, they may be preoccupied
with their own thoughts or experience occasional flashbacks, and they may be
fearful about undressing, being touched or being left alone with particular
adults. Their attitude, mood or behaviour at playgroup, with their daily child-

minder or at school may deteriorate and their performance may be adversely affected, and they may also develop sleep disturbances, have nightmares or begin to wet their bed. Taken together, there may thus be some outward clues of their internal disturbance and unhappiness.

The *parent/carer's* behaviour may provide few if any direct clues or indications that their child is being sexually abused. Such abuse tends to be characterised by secrecy, and even when there are strong suspicions but little direct evidence of abuse, it may not be immediately obvious exactly who the perpetrator is or what actually took place.

In the case of child sexual abuse, as with other forms of abuse, a baseline is sought to help determine what is and what is not *normal* sexual behaviour within a family. As Smith and Grocke (1995) have pointed out, much of the UK literature has concentrated upon behaviour that is regarded as being sexually *abnormal* and deviant, rather than delineating that which falls within the broad range of socially tolerated sexual experience and sexual development in UK society. The size of the problem is difficult to quantify, although attempts have been made to tackle this challenging research task (Ghate and Spencer, 1995).

In making professional judgements about child sexual abuse, child care and child protection workers often find it difficult (as do parents and carers) to avoid making references to their own moral values, standards and beliefs. The evidence they are presented with may itself be unclear and expressed in emotional and value-laden language. It may be difficult to unravel fact from opinion in order to arrive at a sound judgement about actual *significant harm* to a child, despite references to the law and to departmental policies and procedures. This is an important point, because the harm done to the child may *not* equate with the degree of physical harm, nor can the professionals rely solely upon their *own* values, assumptions and experiences to determine the true extent of psychological harm done to the child.

As with physical abuse, a continuum may be adopted as a way of conceptualising and distinguishing between different forms of sexual experiences and processes, rather than lumping together all forms of sexual abuse as if they all amounted to the same thing. A distinction can be made between sexual encounters and behaviour that may or may not be construed as abuse, and that which is clearly and directly harmful, unlawful and may involve violent physical contact with a child, including rape and murder.

Another distinction can be made between sexual experiences of which the 'victim' is unaware and those of which they only gradually become aware. The left-hand side of the continuum (see Figure 10.1) refers to sexual behaviour by an adult or adolescent which involves no personal contact with a child, nor any awareness by them, e.g. when an adult or adolescent fantasises sexually about children from magazines, video or television, or by watching children at school, at play or as they are engaged in youth activities.

Moving along the continuum, intentional sexual contact may occur with a child, with or without their awareness that anything untoward has taken

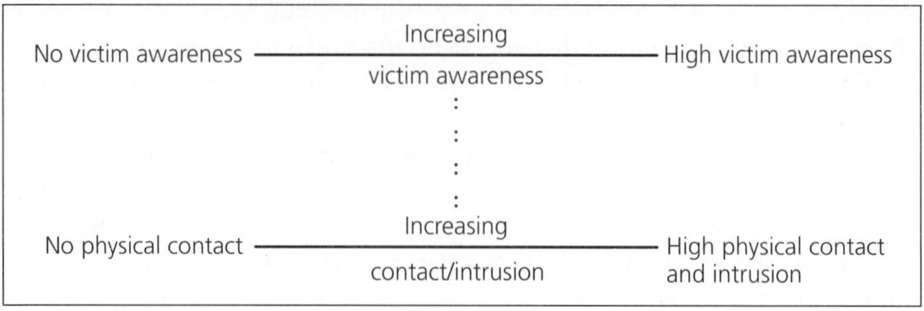

```
No victim awareness ──────Increasing────── High victim awareness
                          victim awareness
                                :
                                :
                                :
                                :
No physical contact ──────Increasing────── High physical contact
                          contact/intrusion             and intrusion
```

Figure 10.1   Degrees of victim awareness and abuser contact.

place, e.g. through what appears to be 'appropriate' adult touching with their hands, or through other bodily contact. Further along the continuum is a recognition that the child's awareness may increase as the degree of unwelcome sexual contact and intrusiveness increases, particularly in cases where an adult or adolescent applies pressure, e.g. through threats, guilt, emotional manipulation or promised reward. The right-hand side of the continuum refers to sexual exploitation and physical and sexual violence that has become very severe and, in extreme cases, may lead to the murder of the child following a sexual attack.

Sexual abuse is a form of abuse that affects children in different ways, both in the short term and over the longer term, and the effects are far from always being predictable and uniform. Children vary in their capacity to cope with inappropriate sexual experiences, and often find ways to accommodate and incorporate in their mind their external experiences in order to reduce the discomfort, conflict and dilemmas, and thus decrease the cognitive dissonance that has been created (Summit, 1983).

One of the pitfalls that professionals and others need to avoid is responding to the label *sexual abuse*, rather than responding directly to the individual child as a person in his or her own right. This label is so powerful that it sometimes persists in the mind of the professional workers long after the child concerned may have moved on. Secondly, there can be a tendency to attribute all subsequent problems and difficulties to the sexual abuse rather than to other *normal* life events and problems. Some professionals even appear to be put off working with children who have been sexually abused because the label seems to intimidate them in such a way that they feel they have no skills or expertise at all to offer a child who has the *sexually abused* label, whereas in practice interpersonal skills are highly transferable, as are a great many therapeutic skills.

One of the most common references to the effects upon children of sexual abuse is through the notion of post-traumatic stress disorder (PTSD), which Salter (1995) describes as follows:

a recurrent cycle of intrusive thoughts, images and feelings followed by periods of emotional denial or numbness. The intrusive phase may be marked by night-

mares (which) sometimes shade into hypnogogic imagery or flashbacks and survivors may waken from a nightmare only to see the perpetrator in the room.

(Salter, 1995, p.189)

While many victims of sexual abuse confirm the presence of such symptoms, they also report additional effects not covered by PTSD. It has been argued by Salter (1995) that PTSD is not the most apt or comprehensive way to describe the full range of responses to child sexual abuse, partly because it was developed from study of the traumatic consequences for victims of sudden, dramatic events such as road accidents, explosions, earthquakes and plane crashes.

Finkelhor (1988) has also suggested that, given the nature of sexual abuse, most child victims show few signs of PTSD because it does not occur under conditions of danger, threat and violence. More often it is a matter of manipulation, with an adult abusing their powerful position to achieve their own purpose. According to West (1991), the very idea of many paedophiles using force or threats to overcome a child's resistance to their advances would be seen as being counter-productive and unsatisfying, and would risk denunciation, with all the dire consequences that would follow.

Salter (1995) has provided many evidence-based descriptors of the short- and long-term effects of sexual abuse on children, building upon the work of Finkelhor (1986) and others in this area. In particular she refers to *anxiety* and *depression* as the two key consequences that most often occur as a result of child sexual abuse over the longer term. She suggests that the anxiety and depression which adult survivors experience may be:

- derived directly from affective flashbacks;
- secondary to cognitive distortions; or
- secondary to current realities.

The flashbacks may be triggered by such things as the sudden memory of the smell of the abuser's aftershave, or similarities of clothing, hair or beard style, linguistic expressions or mannerisms of other people (Salter, 1995).

Other effects of child sexual abuse can include *cognitive distortion* of the victim's thinking, i.e. the victim reconstructs the events in such a way that blame and responsibility are shifted onto their own shoulders rather than upon those of the more powerful abuser. The victim may adopt a *denial strategy*, claiming that nothing sexual happened at all, or that if something happened it was not abuse, or if it was abuse it must have been their fault. Other long-term effects may include *dissociation*, i.e. constructing a separation between what happened to the mind and what happened, against one's will, to the body.

Another long-term effect frequently reported by victims and survivors is either to live in fear of, and to avoid, any social and/or sexual intimacy, or quite the reverse, to experience an overwhelming desire for excessive social or sexual intimacy. Contact with the perpetrator before the victim has had time properly to work through his or her cognitive distortions and painful feelings can also produce flashbacks and other negative consequences which may have a devastating effect (Salter, 1995).

It may take weeks, months or even years for the child or young person to begin to express his or her deeper thoughts and feelings of pain, embarrassment, guilt, shame, anger, resentment and frustration. It is often a slow process for a skilled counsellor/play therapist to begin to access and use therapeutically some of the feelings, thoughts, images and perceptions that the child or young person now holds about him- or herself and about his or her everyday life, about his or her family and about the abuser, who – despite the abuse – may be a person whom they still love very much (Ryan, 1995).

Physical abuse

Physical abuse has been defined as:

> *'actual or likely physical injury to a child, or failure to prevent physical injury (or suffering) to a child, including deliberate poisoning, suffocation and Munchausen syndrome by proxy'* (Department of Health, 1991a, p.48).

EXAMPLES OF PHYSICAL ABUSE

The *child* may appear with unexplained bruises, burns, bite marks or scald marks, or other physical injuries such as a black eye, cut lip or torn frenulum. A young child may have been severely shaken or attacked in such a way that there are *no* clear signs of external damage, but which may have led to severe internal injuries. The child may hesitate to undress for fear of revealing their injuries, or they may have chunks of hair pulled out of their head. They may be afraid of returning home for fear of being physically hurt by their parents, or their behaviour may have changed for the worse and their performance at school may have seriously deteriorated. The child may be physically bullied at home or indeed at school.

The *parent/carer* may admit to hitting, punching, shaking or using a hard object or instrument upon their child. Conversely, they may deny all knowledge of the way in which the injuries occurred when the circumstances indicate that it would be unrealistic *not* to know what had happened. They may also provide several explanations which conflict with each other, that lack plausibility, or which are at odds with the evidence. They may have failed to have the child's injuries medically examined and treated, for no valid reason. Sometimes the parent or carer may have a severe mental health problem, e.g. depression, anxiety or panic attacks, or they may have a serious personality disorder, which is not immediately obvious, but which entangles their child in a web of false concerns and false worries that adversely affect the child's health and development, as is the case with Munchausen syndrome by proxy (Horworth and Lawson, 1996).

Public recognition that parents, who have a social and moral responsibility to care for and protect their children, might also physically abuse those children, has had a long and chequered history, which is described in many standard texts on child abuse (see, for example, Parton, 1985). One interesting example of post-war social policy developments is to trace the changes in nomenclature and conceptualisations of child abuse. Henry Kempe's concept of the *battered baby syndrome,* which was first developed in the USA in 1962, was adopted by the British Paediatric Association in 1966, just as Kempe had decided on the term *battered child syndrome.* In the UK this was later followed by the concept of *non-accidental injury to children* (Department of Health and Social Security), and then *child abuse, child protection* and *significant harm* (Children Act 1989). More recently the American and European concept of *child maltreatment* (Department of Health, 1995) has gained more widespread currency in the UK.

As with other forms of child abuse, there is no watertight baseline in the UK for determining what constitutes *normal* and *lawful* chastisement and, conversely, what constitutes *unlawful* physical abuse can often be imprecise and value-laden. By comparison, in other European countries corporal punishment has been unlawful for many years in Finland, Denmark, Sweden, Norway and Austria, although that is not to suggest that child protection workers in those countries are not faced with instances of serious physical abuse. However, what is noticeable about the experiences of the Nordic countries is the difference in public policy and social attitudes, which tend to be overtly anti-corporal punishment (anti-smacking and anti-hitting), regardless of the parents' own backgrounds or the stressful nature of their lives or social circumstances.

Much of child abuse relates to the misuse of adult power and control, as is clearly the case with physical abuse. Some awareness of the way in which parental control, authority and power are exercised in families has been provided by Smith *et al.* (1995), who undertook an interesting study designed to examine control strategies in families. They found that variables such as poor marital relationships, family violence and serious aggression between siblings tend to correlate with high levels of physical punishment of the children, which was especially compounded in families that scored high on criticism and low on emotional warmth.

With regard to some of the adverse consequences of physical abuse for the child, Corby (1993) has provided a summary of several research studies and reported experiences based on an examination of the short- and long-term effects, from the point of view of the child's health and his or her social, emotional and educational development. In a similar manner, Moore (1992) has written of the damaging long-term social and emotional effects that physical abuse can have upon children in terms of their social, emotional and cognitive development through such negative experiences as witnessing violence towards their parents and experiencing it themselves on a regular basis. Furthermore, little attention has often been paid to the child victim who is caught up in his or her parent's violent relationship, although the research evidence of the damaging consequences has been available for some time (see, for example, Moore *et al.*, 1981).

Some of the key theories that seek to explain physical abuse of children have also been provided by Corby (1993). However, some of the studies in this area, particularly those that relate to *cycles of abuse,* have been put to another use (Gelles and Loseke, 1993). They have been used to support the contention that child abuse, i.e. physical abuse, is inter-generational, and that it takes place as a result of the way in which parents create a violent environment for their children which will socialise them and demonstrate to them that violence is a common, legitimate and preferred channel of communication, punishment and control for adults. Egeland (1993) has supported this view, arguing that a history of physical and emotional abuse is a major factor contributing towards the next generation having the potential to abuse their children.

On the other hand, Gibbons *et al.* (1995) have obtained some very interesting research data on the long-term effects of physical abuse upon children, drawing their follow-up sample from the Child Protection Register, some 9 to 10 years after the children were first abused. They concluded that:

> *on the whole, the data pointed away from the conclusion that physical abuse in early life had a direct effect upon children's development. It seemed rather that physical abuse was in some cases an important sign of a number of other generally damaging circumstances, in particular of a harshly punitive, less reliable and less warmly involved style of parenting. The findings suggested that whenever physical abuse was uncovered in a family, attention needed to be paid to the way the parents generally dealt with their children and to the temperature of family life.*

> (Gibbons *et al.*, 1995, pp.68–70)

Kaufman and Zigler (1993) have argued that the intergenerational transmission of violence thesis is seriously flawed and overstated, and that most adults do *not* go on to abuse their children, although this is not easily verifiable because they escape the usual research selection and sampling processes. In other words, researchers tend to interview those parents who *have* subsequently abused their children, rather than learning from those who did not abuse, despite having had a very violent background.

One of the criticisms frequently made of child protection workers in Child Abuse Enquiry Reports, both by employing organisations and by the media, is that physical abuse should have been recognised by the professionals by accurately interpreting all of the signs and symptoms and by working together effectively, a tragedy could have been predicted and prevented. The argument is beguilingly simple but naive and, for the most part (but not invariably) unsupported by practice experience, since it is based upon the perfect wisdom of hindsight which believes that physical abuse is both a predictable and a preventable phenomenon.

The argument avoids reference to the substantive and contextual issues raised in this chapter, as well as to the way in which child protection workers, i.e. primarily social workers and health visitors, agonise daily about their work with families with their line managers and professional colleagues and also with parents and children themselves over issues of judging risk, uncertainty and danger, balancing parents' rights with the interests of their children, assessing identifiable parental strengths and limitations, managing dilemmas of principle and value, and understanding the significance and impact of social class, culture, race, gender and religion upon their judgements, as they operate within the frameworks of the law, departmental procedures, policy and over-stretched resources.

None the less, there are always lessons to be learned from Child Abuse Enquiry Reports, research studies and practice experiences. In this respect the study of Child Abuse Enquiry Reports provides a great deal of helpful information about patterns of parental and family behaviour that correlate strongly with the occurrence of subsequent physical abuse (Department of Health, 1991b).

Professionals have also found this research to be helpful in another respect. It provides a rough check-list of risk indicators, predisposing factors and general information about patterns of warning signs that can often be missed or incorrectly interpreted in complex child protection cases. This study, with other research material, can also be helpful when constructing theoretical models that identify the relevant risk factors which, combined negatively together, can produce acute stress and conflict, and which substantially increase the likelihood of the child being physically abused.

Multidisciplinary child protection work

The multidisciplinary approach to child protection is based upon the premise that, whilst each professional has his or her own specific duties and responsibilities to perform, in relation to child protection the welfare of the child is served best when professionals combine their individual skills, knowledge and expertise and work together for the benefit of the child (see Hallett and Birchall, 1992).

Each professional therefore needs not only a clear understanding of his or her own role and responsibilities in child protection work, and an understanding of the boundaries and limits to that role, but also an informed appreciation of the role and responsibilities of the *other* relevant professionals. The document that most clearly indicates why such co-operation and communication are fundamentally important in child protection is aptly entitled *Working Together* (Department of Health, 1991a). It has generally been considered that *Working Together* is much more than the title of a book – rather it reflects an attitude of mind and a philosophy of co-operation and shared working.

The child protection system consists of a number of distinct elements (people, processes, policies, procedures and resources) which, when combined together, should create synergy that maximises the collective professional efforts to protect children from significant harm and generally to help them

and their families. It is also the mechanism that determines many of the subsequent child protection decisions and processes. The different elements of
the child protection system are represented by the following:

- the core professionals who have statutory child protection responsibilities;
- other key professionals who have child care and some child protection
  interests and responsibilities;
- the application to practice of child protection procedures and policies;
- the application to practice of relevant legislation, e.g. the Children Act 1989,
  the Criminal Justice Act 1991, police and criminal evidence legislation, etc.;
- the practice culture of child protection work, i.e. shared working and decision-making, providing mutual support, sharing feelings and risks, achieving joint understanding about threshold criteria for determining abuse,
  agreeing the form and direction of intervention, pooling and monitoring
  information, etc.;
- the professional and organisational structures for resourcing, supporting
  and managing the child protection processes.

The work of Hallett and Birchall (1995) has confirmed much of the above,
especially in relation to their identification of the *four* levels of multidisciplinary involvement which provide a professional network for child protection
workers. The first level involves the core professionals – social workers, police
and paediatricians. The second level refers to other front-line workers, such as
health visitors and schools, and to general practitioners. The third-level contacts include professionals such as school nurses and education social workers,
and the fourth level contacts refer to psychiatrists, psychologists and lawyers.

Hallett and Birchall also reported that profession was *the* key determinant
that affected an individual's point of view most of all. They observed that levels of complete consensus were rare, and that in most cases agreement had as
much to do with professional posture as with the merits of the particular case
(Hallett and Birchall, 1995).

Reder *et al.* (1993) studied 35 cases in which a child had died and in which
failure by the professionals to work together effectively was regarded as having being significant to the outcome of the case. Such perceived failure was
attributed, *inter alia*, to organisational changes which left staff feeling very
vulnerable, to professional networks which operated as 'closed' professional
systems, to professional relationships that were strained and polarised, and to
confusion of role, task and status.

It is clear, then, that while professionals attach great importance to working
together, they also recognise that its success is never guaranteed and that it
needs continuous investment of effort and good will to succeed. Often the reasons why professionals and organisations fail to work more closely together
are poorly articulated and understood. If one considers all of the structural
differences that separate the professional groups, i.e. different training and
backgrounds, different professional language and value systems, different
employment and organisational conditions, and different priorities, responsi-

bilities and goals, it is surprising just how much communication, co-operation and working together is effectively achieved, and how we have come to expect near-perfection in multidisciplinary work. Ironically, professionals sometimes experience poor communication *within their own* organisation, while their line managers expect communication to be effective and efficient *across* complex organisational and professional boundaries.

One of the approaches that the professionals adopt for reconciling these structural differences is to develop an effective *practice culture* for child protection work – at a *local* level. The practice culture provides an opportunity for the professionals to develop shared ways of thinking and working, to reconcile differences in values, perception and approach, to acquire a sense of mutual trust and respect, and to enable them to achieve a negotiated agreement or accommodation with one another's idiosyncrasies and preferred style of working.

It should be remembered that *working together* in child abuse situations also means working effectively together with parents, children and young people. Apart from the statutory duty imposed upon child protection workers to do so, there is also a considerable literature available which indicates that it is usually the most realistic and effective way to operate in order to help children and their parents at a vulnerable point in their lives (Thoburn *et al.*, 1995). Partnership with parents is also supported by a general shift in policy and practice direction away from the preoccupation with simply undertaking child abuse investigations (Section 47, Children Act 1989) to consideration of tangible ways of directly assisting children and their families by providing *family support* and assisting all *children-in-need* work (Section 17, Children Act 1989).

Responding to child abuse

Concerns about the welfare of a child, or suspicions that a child may be being abused, can arise for many reasons, but are often brought to the attention of either the social services department or the police, and sometimes to other professionals, e.g. the health visitor, the doctor or the school nurse. Concerns may also occur in other circumstances, but for the most part they will arise via one or more of the following:

- when a child discloses or reveals information about his or her own abusive experiences or those of another child;
- by direct personal observations of a child in which the concerns may centre around such aspects as the appearance of injuries, burns, or bruises, of highly sexualised play, language or behaviour, or of behaviour which suggests that a child may be seriously rejected, constantly belittled or clearly unwanted, or that he or she is not receiving an adequate standard of care or parenting;
- by receiving information – or by piecing together and accumulating discrete pieces of information acquired from different sources – which taken together, may lead to serious concerns and worries about a child's health,

welfare or safety, e.g. concerns that a child is not being adequately fed or clothed, or that he or she is not being properly cared for or supervised.

The professional and organisational response to such concerns has to be provided in such a way that it reflects good professional practice and is applied within the context of local Area Child Protection Committee (ACPC) policies and procedures. It must also be in keeping with the requirements and principles of the Children Act 1989 and, where appropriate, the Criminal Justice Act 1991.

It should be remembered that the appearance of any *one* of the indicators discussed earlier does *not* constitute, *ipso facto*, proof of child abuse. Each single indicator may be accounted for by other reasonable explanations that are accurate and valid, and which are satisfactory in the circumstances. Caution is therefore needed to avoid stamping a label upon a child or parent – and causing more suffering – before an accurate and comprehensive picture has been compiled by the various professionals involved in the case. This principle applies equally to all forms of child abuse. However, to avoid labelling is not to avoid responding to legitimate concerns and worries about a child.

Part of the difficulty of child protection work is that recognition and identification of child abuse, whether at the initial referral stage or later on, is not a precise science. Rather it relies upon multidisciplinary assessments and judgements, made either individually or collectively, to inform the decision-making process. Such judgements draw upon the information collected by the *core* professionals involved with the child and family, and from other sources.

Farmer and Owen (1995) have studied the investigatory processes in cases of physical abuse, a process that is normally hidden and conducted in private. Examples of good practice were revealed alongside many examples of bad professional practice, both of which provide indicators for improving overall practice and intervention strategies.

Although professional practice may vary somewhat from county to county and from borough to borough, there tends to be an agreed sequence to be followed by social services departments and by the police for receiving and responding to serious concerns about children, which is summarised in Figure 10.2.

When the professionals require a detailed picture of the child, their family and their home circumstances, it may be agreed at a child protection conference that the core professionals should undertake a formal assessment, using an assessment model adapted from the so-called *Orange Book* (Department of Health, 1988). Adcock (1995) has provided an interesting account of an alternate assessment model explaining how the different processes, components and outcomes can positively help to inform professional judgements, decision-making and planning. She also points out many of the risks and dangers that arise from poor or incompetent assessments, or from relying upon assessments a delaying tactic or as a substitute for clear action.

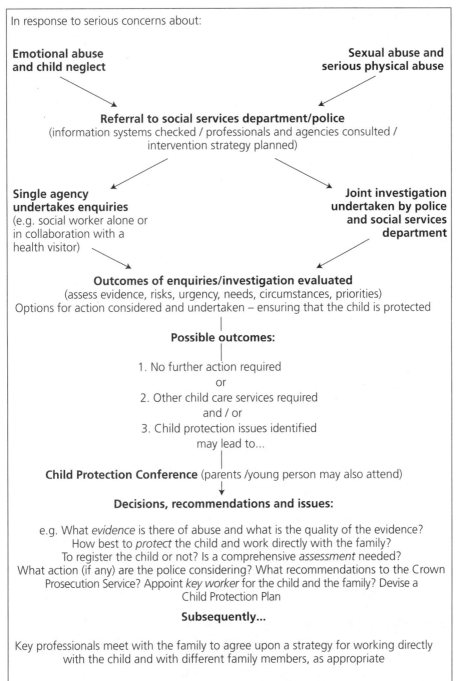

In response to serious concerns about:

**Emotional abuse
and child neglect**

**Sexual abuse and
serious physical abuse**

Referral to social services department/police
(information systems checked / professionals and agencies consulted /
intervention strategy planned)

**Single agency
undertakes enquiries**
(e.g. social worker alone or
in collaboration with a
health visitor)

**Joint investigation
undertaken by police
and social services
department**

Outcomes of enquiries/investigation evaluated
(assess evidence, risks, urgency, needs, circumstances, priorities)
Options for action considered and undertaken – ensuring that the child is protected

Possible outcomes:

1. No further action required
or
2. Other child care services required
and / or
3. Child protection issues identified
may lead to...

Child Protection Conference (parents /young person may also attend)

Decisions, recommendations and issues:

e.g. What *evidence* is there of abuse and what is the quality of the evidence?
How best to *protect* the child and work directly with the family?
To register the child or not? Is a comprehensive *assessment* needed?
What action (if any) are the police considering? What recommendations to the Crown
Prosecution Service? Appoint *key worker* for the child and the family? Devise a
Child Protection Plan

Subsequently...

Key professionals meet with the family to agree upon a strategy for working directly
with the child and with different family members, as appropriate

Review and evaluate work, progress and developments

Figure 10.2 Responding to serious concerns about children.

Professional judgements call for considerable reflective and decision-making skills and a strong knowledge-base appropriate to one's professional contribution to the multidisciplinary decision-making process. They go far beyond a *technical* assessment of the various observations, evidence, inferences, opinions, options and choices, risk calculations and information gathered. They call into play feelings, personal and professional values and beliefs, expectations and assumptions, and analytical, interpretative and reflective skills, as well as decision-making skills.

The influence of past Child Abuse Inquiry Reports upon all professionals and their organisations should be considerable. Important lessons can also be learned from research and from qualitative studies such as that undertaken by Reder *et al.* (1993), who adopted a systematic framework to analyse and evaluate practice issues that arose from published Inquiry Reports. Their own findings reveal how situations such as collusion over care and control can arise when working with vulnerable families, how easy it is to over-identify with a vulnerable parent at the expense of a vulnerable child, and how professionals may unwittingly collude with unjustifiable optimism, or indeed pessimism, in a case, or allow it to drift.

Howitt's research (1992) has complemented that of Reder *et al.* (1993) in drawing attention to the way in which, once started, the child protection process can acquire such a powerful momentum of its own that it can sometimes operate against the child's best interests. Howitt argues that the investigation can become so procedurally driven and logistically complex to manage that it loses its focus upon the child and concentrates upon the needs of the professionals, the organisations and the justice system. He has also identified some of the errors in professional thinking and practice, in making incorrect assumptions and in creating adversarial processes and practices that can cause quite unnecessary and counter-productive distress and suffering to parents, who may be left with a sense of burning injustice, disempowerment and alienation from future professional assistance.

However, it is apparent from many of the studies commissioned by the Department of Health and reported in *Messages from Research* (Department of Health, 1995) that examples of good child protection practice are commonplace. They suggest that effective practice builds upon sensitive and informed professional–client relationships, an appropriate balance of power between the key parties; a broad perspective on child abuse, effective supervision and training of key professionals and a determination to enhance the quality of children's lives.

Areas for improvement were also clearly identified, such as keeping parents better informed about what was happening, increasing their general level of participation, recognising and building upon the family's strengths, and using their help and support networks. There were also important training issues. Finally, there was clear recognition of the need for investment in high-quality child care service with effective family support systems and therapeutic and other treatment services, which should be community-based, properly resourced, well publicised and to which vulnerable parents and vulnerable children would have ready access.

CONCLUSION

This chapter set out to provide an introductory overview for early childhood studies students, and for other students new to child abuse and child protection studies. It might also provoke some interesting questions and identify issues for more experienced students, practitioners and managers as ongoing learners. A child protection curriculum was suggested as a possible line of study that students might follow, or from which selections might be made, as appropriate, depending upon one's role, responsibilities and interests. Other headings come to mind which could be included on such a programme of study – the list tends to grow longer rather than to shrink. Each of the four aspects of child abuse, emotional abuse, neglect, sexual abuse and physical abuse, were briefly considered and specific issues and questions raised. Suggestions for further reading have also been made.

Child protection was located within the framework of the multidisciplinary child protection system, which is facilitated by the development of a positive and productive practice culture at a local level. It is within this dynamic context that inquiries into, and investigations of, possible child abuse take place, and which constitutes one of the key mechanisms for effectively protecting and helping vulnerable children and families. It is also against this background that the different treatment and therapeutic services operate.

References

Adcock, M., (1995): Assessment, In Wilson, K. and James, A. (eds), *The Child Protection Handbook*. London: Baillière Tindall, 188–210.

Adcock, M., White, R. and Hollows, A., (eds) (1991): *Significant Harm*. Croydon: Significant Publications.

Birks, C. (ed) (1995): *Child Abuse in Europe*. Glasgow: Glasgow Caledonian University.

Corby, B. (1993): *Child Abuse – Towards a Knowledge Base*. Buckingham: Open University Press.

Creighton, S. (1995): Patterns and Outcomes, In Wilson, K. and James, A. (eds), *The Child Protection Handbook*. London: Baillière Tindall, 5–26.

Dale, P. (1986): *Dangerous Families: Assessment and Treatment of Families*. London: Tavistock Publications.

Department of Health (1988): *Protecting Children – a Guide to Undertaking Comprehensive Assessments in Child Protection*. London: HMSO.

Department of Health (1991a): *Working Together – Under the Children Act 1989*. London: HMSO

Department of Health (1991b): *Child Abuse: a Study of Inquiry Reports 1980–1989*. London: HMSO.

DepartmentofHealth (1995):*ChildProtection–MessagesfromResearch*.London:HMSO.

Department of Health and Social Security and the Welsh Office (1988): *Working Together*. London: HMSO.

Egeland, B. (1993): A History of Abuse is a Major Risk Factor for Abusing the Next Generation. In Gelles, R.J. and Loseke, D.R. (eds), *Current Controversies on Family Violence*. London: Sage, 197–207.

Farmer, E. and Owen, M. (1995): *Child Protection Practice: Private Risks and Public Remedies – Decision-making, Intervention and Outcomes in Child Protection Work*. London: HMSO

Finkelhor, D. (1986): *A Sourcebook on Child Sexual Abuse*. London: Sage.

Finkelhor, D. (1988): The Trauma of Child Sexual Abuse, In Wyatt, G.E., and Powell, G.L., (eds), *Lasting Effects of Child Sexual Abuse*. Newbury Park, CA.: Sage, 61–82.

Gelles, R.J. and Loseke, D.R. (eds) (1993): *Current Controversies on Family Violence*. London: Sage.

Ghate, D. and Spencer, L. (1995): *The Prevalence of Child Sexual Abuse in Britain: a Feasibility Study for a Large Scale National Survey of the General Population*. London: HMSO.

Gibbons, J., Gallagher, B., Bell, C. and Gordon, D. (1995): *Development after Physical Abuse in Early Childhood: a Follow-up Study of Children on Child Protection Registers*. London: HMSO.

Hallett, C. and Birchall, E. (1992): *Co-ordination and Child Protection: a Review of the Literature*. London: HMSO.

Hallett, C. and Birchall, E. (1995): *Inter-agency Co-ordination in Child Protection: Working Together in Child Protection*. London: HMSO.

Horworth, J. and Lawson, B. (1996): *Trust Betrayed – Munchausen Syndrome by Proxy*. London: National Children's Bureau.

Howitt, D. (1992): *Child Abuse Errors – When Good Intentions go Wrong*. Hemel Hempstead: Harvester Wheatsheaf.

Iwaniec, D. (1995): *The Emotionally Abused and Neglected Child*. Chichester: Wiley.

Kaufman, J. and Zigler E. (1993): The Intergenerational Transmission of Abuse is Overstated, In Gelles, R.J. and Loseke, D.R. (eds), *Current Controversies on Family Violence*. London: Sage, 209–21.

Minty, B. and Pattinson, G. (1994): The Nature of Child Neglect. *British Journal of Social Work* **24**, 733–47.

Moore, J. (1992): The Neglect of Neglect – Child Neglect. In *The ABC of Child Protection*. Aldershot: Ashgate Publishing, 80–94.

Moore, J. (1994): Lethal Weapon – Neglect of Children is a Killer, *Community Care* **1011**, 20.

Moore, J. Galcius, A. and Pettican, K. (1981): Emotional Risk to Children Caught in Violent Matrimonial Conflict. The Basildon Treatment Project. *International Journal of Child Abuse and Neglect* **9**, 225–35.

O'Hagan, K. (1993): *Emotional and Psychological Abuse of Children*. Milton Keynes: Open University Press.

Parton, N. (1985): *The Politics of Child Abuse*. Basingstoke: Macmillan.

Parton, N. (1996): Child Protection, Family Support and Social Work, *Child and Family Social Work* **1**, 3–11.

Reder, P., Duncan, S. and Gray, M. (1993): Beyond Blame – Child Abuse Tragedies Revisited. London: Routledge.

Rose, S.J. (1985): *Recognition of Child Abuse and Neglect*. London: Gower Medical Publications.

Ryan, V. (1995): Non-directive Play Therapy with Abused Children and Adolescents. In Wilson, K. and James, A. (eds), *The Child Protection Handbook*. London: Baillière Tindall 354–71.

Salter, A. (1995): *Transforming Trauma*. London: Sage Publications.

Seden, J., Hardiker, P. and Barker, M. (1996): Child Protection Revisited: Balancing State Intervention and Family Autonomy Through Social Work Processes. *Child and Family Social Work* **1**, 57.

Smith, M. and Grocke, M. (1995): *Normal Family Sexuality and Sexual Knowledge in Children*. London: Royal College of Psychiatrists/Gorkill Press.

Smith. M., Bee. P., Herverin, A. and Nobes, G. (1995): *Parental Control within the Family: the Nature and Extent of Parental Violence to Children*. Messages from Research. London: Department of Health and HMSO.

Stevenson, O. (1996): Emotional Abuse and Neglect: a Time for Reappraisal. *Child and Family Social Work* **1**, 13–18.

Summit, R. (1983): The Child Sexual Abuse Accommodation Syndrome. *Child Abuse and Neglect* **7**, 177–93.

Thoburn, J., Lewis, A. and Shemmings, D. (1995): *Paternalism or Partnership? Family Involvement in the Child Protection Process.* London: Department of Health and HMSO.

West, D. J. (1991): The Effects of Sex Offences. In Hollin, C. and Howells, K. (eds), *Clinical Approaches to Sex Offenders and the Victims.* Chichester: Wiley, 55–73.

Wilson, K. and James, A. (eds) (1995): *The Child Protection Handbook.* London: Baillière Tindall.

Further reading

Emotional abuse

Iwaniec, D. (1995): *The Emotionally Abused and Neglected Child.* Chichester: Wiley.

O'Hagan, K. (1993): *Emotional and Psychological Abuse of Children.* Milton Keynes: Open University Press.

Wolfe, D.A. (1991): *Preventing Physical and Emotional Abuse of Children.* New York: Guildford Press.

Child neglect

Iwaniec, D. (1995): *The Emotionally Abused and Neglected Child.* Chichester: Wiley.

Moore, J. (1992): The Neglect of Neglect – Child Neglect. In *The ABC of Child Protection.* Aldershot: Ashgate Publishing, 80–94.

Stevenson, O. (1996): Emotional Abuse and Neglect: a Time for Reappraisal. *Child and Family Social Work* **1**, 13–18.

Sexual abuse

Hollin, C. and Howells, K. (1991): *Clinical Approaches to Sex Offenders and their Victims.* Chichester: Wiley.

Salter, A. (1995): *Transforming Trauma.* London: Sage Publications.

Saradjian, J. (1996): *Women who Sexually Abuse Children.* Chichester: Wiley.

Physical abuse

Buchanan, A. (1996): *Cycles of Child Maltreatment.* Chichester: Wiley.

Frude, N. (1993): *Understanding Family Problems.* Chichester: Wiley.

Gelles, R.J. and Loseke, D.R. (eds), (1993): *Current Controversies on Family Violence.* London: Sage.

Gibbons, J., Gallagher, B., Bell, C. and Gordon, D. (1995): *Development after Physical Abuse in Early Childhood: a Follow-up Study of Children on Child Protection Registers.* London: HMSO.

Multidisciplinary child protection work

Cloke and Nash (eds) (1993): *Key Issues in Child Protection for Health Visitors and Nurses*. London: Longman.

David, T. (1993): *Child Protection and Early Years Teachers*. Buckingham: Open University Press.

Department of Health (1991): *Working Together*. London: HMSO.

Department of Health (1995): *Paternalism or Partnership? Family Involvement in Child Protection Conferences*. London: HMSO.

Hallett, C. (1995): *Inter-agency Co-ordination in Child Protection: Working Together in Child Protection*. London: HMSO.

Child protection intervention

Department of Health (1995): *Messages from Research*. London: HMSO.

Department of Health/Home Office (1994): *Memorandum of Good Practice*. London: HMSO.

Gough, D. (1993): *Child Abuse Interventions: a Review of the Literature*. London: HMSO.

Howitt, D. (1992): *Child Abuse Errors: When Good Intentions go Wrong*. Hemel Hempstead: Harvester Wheatsheaf.

Parton, N. (ed), (1997): *Child Protection and Family Support*. London: Routledge.

Reder, P. (1993): *Beyond Blame: Child Abuse Tragedies Revisited*. London: Routledge.

Reder, P. and Lucey, C. (1995): *Asessment of Parenting: Psychiatric and Psychological Contributions*. London: Routledge.

Wilson, K. and James, A. (eds), (1995): *The Child Protection Handbook*. London: Ballière Tindall.

Law

Allen, N. (1992): Making Sense of the Children Act, 2nd edn. Harlow: Longman.

Herbert, W. (1993): *Working with Children and the Children Act*. Leicester: British Psychological Society.

Early childhood education in pre-school settings

Margaret Woods

This chapter aims to:

- consider concepts and functions of education;
- explore why we should have good quality early years provision;
- examine the nature of quality in early childhood education.

Introduction

Look in any contemporary dictionary and you will surely find somewhat simplistic definitions of education, which tend to equate it with the processes of nourishing, rearing, schooling, training and instruction. But how do those who are more intimately acquainted with the nature of young children define the concept and functions of education?

Vygotsky, currently one of our most favoured educational theorists, viewed education as a 'quintessential socio-cultural activity' very much 'central to (children's) cognitive development' (Moll, 1990, p.1). For Vygotsky, education was the means of developing every child's potential and also of transmitting the culture within a particular society. We have here a dual notion of the constructivism mentioned in Chapters 1 and 9. The individual develops cognitively by building on his or her previous learning and experience, and society develops as some of these individuals use their new-found competences to extend the frontiers of human knowledge.

Another view of education, which often seems to appeal to early childhood students, is that of Mellor (1970), who considers it to be the process whereby 'man gives direction to each successive generation starting out on the road of life' (p.1). She portrays education, albeit in somewhat old-fashioned terminology, as being concerned with the whole child and all of his or her experiences – whether these take place in nursery, family or the wider society. For her, education should foster the child's natural growth and development to their full potential and support each child in becoming an effective member of society. Mellor claims it also involves reaching (and for some presumably extending) the threshold of the culture's accumulated knowledge and wisdom. Within her vision there is again the notion of individual and societal constructivism and, implicitly, the idea of reciprocity between the individual and his or her culture through the medium of education.

Much like Vygotsky, Gammage (1994) regards education as 'a cornerstone of a developed society', necessary to 'keep society functioning' (p.5) and for the preservation and regeneration of the culture(s) and very much about 'human development, personal creativity, about happiness and beauty, about art and aspiration' (p.5).

Blenkin and Kelly (1996) envisage education as supportive of children's development and as a means of equipping them with the skills and enthusiasm to learn whatever becomes necessary during their lifetimes. They deem education to be very much a process concerned with 'learning *through* subject-knowledge, rather than merely with the learning *of* subject-knowledge' (p.13). They do not deny the existence of essential knowledge, skills and understanding which educationalists must promote with children.

In a similar vein, the Northern Group of Advisors (1992) presents education as a range of opportunities, experiences and encounters with people which occur in all of a child's environments, and not only within the nursery or school setting. Also through education, children's learning and development are maximised and their 'knowledge, skills and attitudes become personalised tools for ongoing learning' (Northern Group of Advisors, 1992, pp. 2–3).

This recommendation that educators should create practices which will prepare children to cope effectively with the changing demands of society is extended by Dahlberg and Asen (1994). They view education very much as a 'pedagogical challenge' with the fundamental intent to achieve 'the integration of the next generation into society' (Dahlberg and Asen, 1994, p.164-5); this integration is for them essential if society is to thrive.

We can create from these selected but not atypical declarations a consensus concept of early childhood education. It can be considered to be a sociocultural activity that is essential for the survival, enrichment and advancement of society and indicative of society's responsibility to each individual. Perhaps more importantly for us as practitioners, education should be an enjoyable time in children's lives and have the potential to maximise their all-round development and creativity; it should also support them in working towards being able to function effectively within their daily lives and in becoming competent learners. All of a child's environments and experiences should be regarded as influential, and ideally these should be utilised in making (nursery) education as meaningful as possible for each child. Implicitly understood is the sense of mutuality whereby individuals and society benefit each other through the educative process.

In articulating such a concept of education, we have in fact embodied a set of universal aims which many early years educationists would probably regard as worthwhile, if perhaps a trifle idealistic and ambitious. Nevertheless, these give our chapter educational direction and hopefully they may inform and underpin our current study of education and, for some readers now or in the future, their curriculum planning and day-to-day practice as early years professionals.

With such a concept of education interwoven within our holistic philosophy and incorporating this textbook's definition of early years, early childhood education might be considered to embrace all of a child's experiences from birth until 8 years. In the rest of this chapter, however, we shall largely confine our discussion to the education which occurs in various pre-school settings, for the most part concerned with children aged 3–5 years. We must consequently be sure to remember that the learning in these early years groups would be complementary to the opportunities and interactions occurring within children's families and other socio-cultural environments.

Our discussion should be equally relevant and applicable to the main forms of early years provision found in the UK today. These are local education authority (LEA)/grant-maintained/private nursery schools or classes and reception classes, private/social services day nurseries and family centres, community nursery centres and voluntary/private-play groups. Chapter 6 has already provided a helpful discussion on some of these.

Why we should have good-quality early childhood education in our early years provision

Froebel (1782–1852), perhaps the most famous early childhood education pioneer, was in no doubt about the reason: 'The earliest age is the most important one for education, because the beginning decides the manner of progress and the end' (Froebel, 1877, p.143). You will recall in our introductory chapter a similar sentiment from Plato (fourth century BC).

Also explained in the introduction was the principle that we should always understand and be able to justify our actions with sound and reasoned evidence. Let us, therefore, summarise briefly many of the established benefits to children and their families of high-calibre educare. We should note that all of these emanate from valid research and experience.

The Consultative Group on Early Childhood Care and Development (1994) takes a global perspective and presents eight arguments which explain why there should be investment in early childhood development. These are set out in Box 11.1 (note that our summary concept of education renders it entirely valid to interchange the terms 'early childhood education' and 'early childhood development').

In addition, it is also widely recognised that good-quality early childhood education:

- has positive developmental effects (Department of Health, 1991);
- establishes attitudes and behaviour patterns which are 'central to further educational and social development' (Department of Education and Science, 1990, p.36; Blenkin and Kelly, 1996);

Box 11.1   Why invest in early childhood development: eight arguments (reprinted from Newsletter No. 74 of the Bernard van Leer Foundation, April 1994, p.2 with kind permission of the Bernard van Leer Foundation).

A scientific argument Scientific research demonstrates repeatedly that the early years are critical in the development of intelligence, personality and social behaviour. There are long-term effects associated with a variety of early intervention programmes.

A human rights argument Children have a right to live and to develop to their full potential.

A moral and social values argument Through children humanity transmits its values. That transmission begins with infants. To preserve moral and social values or to change them for 'the better' – one must begin with children. Values such as living together harmoniously or appreciating and protecting the environment begin to take hold in the pre-school years and can be promoted through child care and development programmes.

An economic argument Society benefits economically from investing in child care and development through increased productivity of children, by freeing caregivers to earn and learn, and by saving social costs in such areas as school repetition, juvenile deliquency and the use of drugs.

A social equity argument By providing a 'fair start' it is possible to modify distressing socio-economic and gender-related inequities. The girl child can be a particularly important beneficiary.

A social mobilisation argument Children provide a rallying point for social and political actions that can help to build consensus and organisation for the common good.

A programme efficacy argument The success of other programmes (for example, survival programmes, emphasising health and nutrition, or primary school education, or women-in-development programmes) can be improved by incorporating an element of early childhood care and development focusing on healthy mental and social development. This is because sound psycho-social development increases the chances of survival, makes educational programmes more efficient by reducing repetition, and supports programmes focused on the productive role of women.

Changing social and demographic circumstances The increasing survival of vulnerable children (14 of 15 children born world-wide now survive to age 1 year vs. 5 out of 6 in 1960), changing family structures and migration, and growing participation by women in the paid labour force are increasing the need and demand for more and better and different ways to care for and ensure the well-being of young children.

Source: Meeting Basic Learning Needs. Prepared for *The Education for All Forum*, New Delhi, September 1993, by the Consultative Group on Early Childhood Care and Development.

- can improve the quality of life for children (European Commission Childcare Network, 1990, p.14);
- has long-term beneficial outcomes of a social, educational and personal nature (Berrueta Clement, 1984; Myers, 1990; Anderson 1992; Schweinhart *et al.*, 1993; Pascal and Bertram, 1994);

- can reduce the gap between the academic performance of advantaged and disadvantaged pupils including higher scores in SAT and Teacher Assessments (Athey, 1990; Shorrocks *et al.*, 1993);
- is critical because the early years are apparently when the brain is most susceptible to environmental modification and education can provide 'food for thought' (Athey, 1990, p.205; Meadows, 1993; Brierley, 1994);
- can 'help parents reconcile the demands of responsible parenting and work outside the home' (National Commission on Education, 1993, p.120);
- is cost-effective for society. With the High/Scope project 2 years of pre-school returned 7.16 dollars for every dollar spent (Schweinhart *et al.*, 1993, p.168);

'And finally, of course, there are the children themselves, whose bright-eyed enthusiasm and positive engagement in pre-school activities are all too rarely paralleled later in their school careers' (Woodhead, 1989, p.128).

With such strong evidence one is compelled to agree with Gammage (1994, p.4) that 'we neglect early childhood education at our peril.' Relevant to this conviction an extremely significant issue is, however, highlighted by Professor Kathy Sylva. After surveying much of the literature on the effects of pre-school experiences, she concluded that 'quality early education and care lead to enhanced child development, while lower quality care is associated with poor outcomes' (Sylva, 1992, p.687). Similar cautions are echoed by many, e.g. Melhuish (1993) and Pascal and Bertram (1994). If we wish to ensure the outcomes that are most advantageous for children, their families and society, there seems little doubt that early childhood education must not merely exist, but also be of the highest quality attainable.

Quality in early childhood education

If we are logically to strive towards this desirable high-quality educare, we must naturally endeavour to investigate the concept of quality in early childhood education and consider the ensuing implications for practice.

Quality certainly seems to have become a national buzz word and a universal business and educational aim; in my experience many organisations are awash with quality terminology and processes, e.g. quality assurance, quality enhancement, quality control. Yet a concise and specific definition remains elusive because quality is a value-laden and dynamic term, often meaning quite different things to different people even within the same organisation.

Moss (1994) captures this difficulty by classifying quality as 'a relative concept, not an objective reality'(p.1). We must bear this in mind as we examine the issue of quality in early years settings.

Because of its subjective nature, Pascal and Bertram (1994) advise us to seek 'a broad range of experiences and interpretations of educational quality' (p.104). Only thus, they claim, can we begin to understand its essential characteristics.

A useful starting point is The Children Act (1989), which encourages early years practitioners to strive towards quality educare in any pre-school setting for children from birth upwards. A total of 13 factors likely to influence the level of quality are identified, all of which are claimed to be backed by valid research. These are:

- 'the nature of the adult–child interaction;
- the nature of the interaction between children and peers;
- size of group and numbers of staff;
- continuity, training and experience of staff;
- recognition of children's developmental needs;
- type of contract/involvement between parent and provider;
- ability to structure and support children's learning;
- elements in programmes of activities;
- equality of opportunity policy in employment and service delivery;
- children's involvement in planning and choosing activities and projects;
- organisation, display and accessibility of equipment, toys and materials;
- attention to health, safety and type of physical environment.

(Department of Health, 1991, p.37)

The much-respected *Rumbold Report* (Department of Education and Science, 1990) was primarily concerned with a more limited age range (3- and 4-year-olds) and admitted to a stronger educational bias. Nevertheless, this report explores the principles of greatest significance to quality educare and several, especially the paramountcy of responding to children's needs and development, were not dissimilar to the factors identified in the Children Act. However, greater emphasis was given to young children as learners noting, for example, the special value of play, talk and first-hand experience. The process of learning was considered to be as important as the content, which should consist of a broad, balanced and meaningful curriculum. A user-friendly, secure, comfortable and stimulating context was seen to be an additional powerful source of learning. Quality was also considered to emanate from the adults, who should be particularly sensitive and responsive to the holistic needs of children, thus ensuring that the children are happy, secure and learn effectively. A clear management structure, a policy specifying the setting's aims and objectives, and regular monitoring and evaluation of all aspects were also strongly recommended (Department of Education and Science, 1990, pp.35–47).

The document produced in January 1996 by the School Curriculum and Assessment Authority (SCAA) outlines the 'desirable learning outcomes' for under-fives in pre-compulsory school provision. The Conservative government of the time proposed that early years settings wishing to access the nursery voucher scheme would have to demonstrate that they were working towards these 'desirable outcomes' and heed the brief advice on common features of good practice that were also outlined (pp.6–7). These quality characteristics show some similarities to those of The Children Act (1989) and the *Rumbold Report* (Department of Education and Science, 1990). However, it is disappointing that adult–child interaction and relationships are only implied, and child–child interaction, equality of opportunity and anti-discriminatory practice seem to go unheeded.

A powerful argument concerning the elements of quality in early childhood education is provided by Gammage (1994). His strong contention is that the early years curriculum should be child-centred and holistic, rather than a watered-down version of the National Curriculum. For him it should be developmentally appropriate or 'internally consistent' with a 'particular child's needs and levels of cognition' (p.6), and should build upon what each child can do. Here we have a marked constructivist ethos. Of course such an individualised approach requires careful 'diagnosis' of children's stages of learning and development – educators must possess great skill, adaptability and creativity as the quality curriculum becomes a 'constant vehicle of negotiation' (p.8). As with the *Rumbold Report*, Gammage deems the process of learning to be as significant as any body of knowledge which, he advises, should be rich and meaningful. Like Blenkin and Kelly (1996) with their developmental curriculum, Gammage recommends that knowledge should be the transmitter of learning rather than the prime objective. Gammage's (1994) ultimate educational aim is to develop in its participants the facility and will to 'question the answers not answer the questions' (p.10). Gammage defends his concept of quality on the grounds that it is the only one which fits with his examination and interpretation of the research evidence.

A further definition of quality in early education, with the additional intention to use the criteria simultaneously to evaluate standards and improve quality, can be found in the work of Laevers (1994). This specifies three categories of quality criteria. The first, and apparently the most common, consists of the treatment variables such as the classroom environment, programme content, teacher style, methods, opinions and level of training, and the teacher/child ratios. Laevers expresses some concern about their use, claiming it is not clear precisely what aspect of those criteria constitutes quality, or how exactly they impact on individual children's learning.

Laevers' second category of quality criteria is ascertained via the measurement of the effects or outcomes of early education programmes and evidence of the determinants of these. This strategy was used in the well-known longitudinal research on the HighScope pre-school programme of the early 1960s. Early phases of the study found that the HighScope students, upon leaving school, were more functionally and socially competent, with higher levels of school achievement, motivation, employment, income and educational and occupational aspirations. The incidence of criminal convictions was lower, and there were fewer teenage pregnancies (Berrueta-Clement *et al.*, 1984). The latest report on the longer-term benefits of the programme indicate, for the HighScope graduates, significantly higher levels of social adjustment (including marital stability and employment), higher achievement at 27 years, as well as the considerable cost-effectiveness we noted earlier (Schweinhart *et al.*, 1993). The aspects of the original HighScope programme that are deemed to have determined its high quality are as follows:

- a developmentally appropriate curriculum;
- effective systems of in-service training and curriculum supervision;
- workable parent-involvement strategies;
- good administration;
- sound and developmentally appropriate assessment procedures;
- effective evaluation of provision;
- an appropriate adult/child ratio.

(Adapted from Schweinhart *et al.*, 1993, p.231)

While such methodology has been and will no doubt continue to be most useful, for Laevers the main problem with this approach to specifying quality is its long-term nature – it does not help to improve the quality of experience for children at any given moment in time.

Laevers (1994) consequently focuses on the third category as the most interesting and fruitful, namely the process variables. These are considered to assess and improve quality simultaneously by focusing on the extent of children's emotional well-being and their level of involvement in activities within their educare setting. Involvement is characterised in children by their concentration, persistence, motivation, fascination and intensity of experience – according to Laevers, deep learning and development are occurring. The provision of stimulating, developmentally appropriate but challenging activities becomes imperative, as do positive relationships and ensuring that children are happy and secure in a stable and caring environment.

In any discussion of quality we cannot omit perhaps the richest and most dynamic, democratic and ambitious research into the concept – the Effective Early Learning Research Project of Pascal and Bertram (1994). Indeed, Williams (1995) esteems it for being close to what is termed a *total quality* approach. Through involvement of all of the participants from different types of early years provision, Pascal and Bertram have improved quality by enhancing the experiences of children, parents/carers and staff, by generating new standards and developing new understanding and new techniques. Ideas and energy have come from children, parents, staff, managers, experts and regulators, and apparently there has been much talking, feedback, training and learning (Williams, 1995, pp. 42–3).

Using the *Rumbold Report* as a theoretical framework, and consulting with many early years practitioners from a variety of early years settings, Pascal and Bertram (1994) identified, via consensus, the following 10 dimensions of quality on which to base their data collection:

1. aims and objectives;
2. curriculum;
3. learning and teaching styles;
4. planning, assessment and record-keeping;
5. staffing;
6. physical environment;
7. relationships and interaction;
8. equal opportunities;
9. parental partnership, liaison and co-ordination;
10. monitoring and evaluation.

(Adapted from Pascal and Bertram, 1994)

Next they formulated a set of research questions for each dimension in order to collect their rich and detailed qualitative descriptions of quality educare. The results, according to Williams (1995), provided the means to identify, evaluate and enhance quality.

By now I am sure you will have realised that a consensus on the concept of quality has emerged from our survey, and certainly would from careful reading of these few but significant source reports. This consensus identifies the aspects of early years provision on which we should concentrate our study of early childhood education and in which, as practitioners, we must develop our understanding and expertise in order that the children in our educare may experience the highest quality of educare available.

Do remember that these criteria do not constitute a check-list, but rather provide a framework for a rich qualitative account of quality educare. It is also worth noting that, while confining a discussion of early childhood education to one chapter has restricted the number of perspectives on quality that we could examine, an earlier study of a much wider range of international reports (Woods, 1994) evoked a not dissimilar result.

The emerging consensus concept of quality early years education/educare

Quality educare probably would:

- adopt an holistic and child-centred approach to the educare of young children, with practitioners having close liaison with other relevant professionals;
- ensure that children are happy, secure and confident and find their educare experiences satisfying and rewarding;
- make certain that educators have the appropriate knowledge, understanding, skills and attitudes to work with young children and their families;
- provide a broad, balanced curriculum with developmentally appropriate yet challenging activities;
- maintain a rich, stimulating and appealing learning context;

- undertake thorough and regular observation and assessment of individual children and keep careful records; the outcomes of these processes should inform the long-, medium- and short-term curriculum planning;
- promote equality of opportunity for all children, with strong anti-discriminatory principles underpinning practice;
- work towards effective home–nursery collaboration;
- undertake regular monitoring and evaluation of the provision;
- develop a public policy outlining the aims and objectives and based on the agreed philosophy of educators, managers and parents, and taking into account the principles of good practice validated by rigorous research;
- have a high (and certainly the legal) ratio of educators to children; parents and students should be supernumerary rather than essential to any setting;
- ensure effective management of appropriately and highly trained adults with regular and ongoing in-service training in response to identified staff development needs.

Having arrived at a democratic and therefore also, according to Pascal and Bertram (1994), valid concept of quality educare, we shall now consider some of the characteristics in a little more detail in order that readers' current or future practice might be more informed. The aspects that are not mentioned elsewhere in this book and those deemed to be of most immediate and direct relevance to practitioners have been selected.

Public policy outlining aims, objectives and processes that will produce quality experiences for the children

At the beginning of this chapter, we noted that the emerging concept of education could in fact also provide a set of general aims. We might use our consensus concept of quality in a similar manner. It could become a further and most commendable aim – to strive to attain the highest quality educare possible within our setting. With some minor adaptations for different types of early years provision we could, from each of these aims, formulate a set of practical objectives or learning outcomes that could constitute the basis of the public policy towards which we might work within our particular early years setting.

This process would necessitate considered analysis of the individual aims. We should endeavour to develop from each of them specific goals towards which we might work and on which we might base the actual experiences that we offer children. Of course, as the Schools Curriculum and Assessment Authority (1996) *Desirable Outcomes* document is now a legal requirement, we must ensure compatibility between these and our own outcomes.

The *Rumbold Report* (Department of Education and Science, 1990), Pugh (1992), Pascal and Bertram (1994), the Schools Curriculum and Assessment

Authority (1996) and many other research reports recommend involving all practitioners, managers, headteachers and parents in developing such policies. We should, therefore, adopt a democratic procedure for consultation amongst all of the relevant parties in order to formulate the outcomes and processes for realising each of the agreed aims.

An holistic and child-centred approach to the educare of young children with close liaison with other relevant professionals

Readers should return to the introductory chapter of this book for a more detailed account of our holistic philosophy, which considers the whole child and avoids any artificial segregation of care and education. Incidentally, this holistic philosophy is my justification for interchanging the terms 'education' and 'educare'. However, we should mention the child-centred aspect, which certainly need not be synonymous with an over-liberal or excessively permissive and unstructured regime. Child-centred means putting the child's needs at the heart of the education process and starting 'where the child is at' (our constructivist standpoint) in curriculum planning and teaching and learning approaches. Of course, Singer (1996) thoughtfully cautions us about too extreme an interpretation of the child-centred approach which, she contends, can exclude children from the real and very exciting tasks undertaken by adults in everyday life. Such exclusion, she argues, may provide a limiting environment of 'child-only' play which could actually impede children's learning.

Within a multidisciplinary approach, the other professionals with whom early years educators might liaise, for the benefit of the child and his or her family, could include reception-class teachers, headteachers, practitioners from other early years settings, early years/special needs advisers, health visitors, social workers, family doctors, speech therapists, school nurses, educational psychologists, physiotherapists, college tutors, researchers and police. Obviously the co-ordination of such a wide range of expertise could, with strong commitment and adequate resources, take us much closer to providing the ideal of truly holistic educare and total responsiveness to children's needs.

Ensuring that children are happy, secure and confident and find their educare experiences satisfying and rewarding

The Guidance on the Children Act (Department of Health, 1991), the *Rumbold Report* (Department of Education and Science, 1990) and Laevers (1994) strongly emphasise the importance of this achievement, which has been shown to enhance many aspects of children's development and learning. How can early childhood educators begin to create such an ethos?

Being sensitive and responsive to children's needs, interests, motivation and circumstances is naturally helpful. Laevers (1994) highlights in particular the significance of children's emotional well-being and their need for attention, affection, social recognition and support in feeling competent. The provision of appropriately challenging activities to match children's potential levels of development as well as their interest can be useful here, and we shall consider this in a little more depth later in the chapter.

Warm secure relationships will also contribute significantly to this end – naturally, it is to be hoped that early years professionals will be chosen for their warmth, empathy with and liking for children. The importance of stable early relationships within the family and within a gradually widening circle of significant others has long been recognised (e.g. Rogers, 1961; Kellmer-Pringle, 1975). Recent research also supports the notion of development taking place within a context of relationships, and indeed of 'aspects of social and cognitive development depend(ing) on early relationships' (Hinde, 1992, p.17). Sensitive interaction with children, and being mindful of their interests and background, would be essential. Tizard and Hughes (1984) would advise relaxed one-adult-to-one-child conversations whenever possible.

Marsh (1994) commends nurseries where there is a general climate of respect in the interactions among children, among adults and between children and adults, and where all individuals treat others and are themselves treated with respect and courtesy (Figure 11.1). She has observed that the resulting positive relationships are 'reflected in a calm, happy and productive working atmosphere' (p.141). Marsh concludes her chapter by providing a

Figure 11.1 Nurseries should foster a climate of respect and courtesy in the interactions among staff and children.

most useful (and validated) framework which could aid practitioners in assessing and improving many of the relationships within their early years settings (1994, pp.146–51).

Elfer (1996) tells us that most early years professionals would agree whole-heartedly that 'warm and responsive relationships are of great importance in supporting children's learning and development' (p.30). Sadly, however, he reports that in practice such relationships do not appear to exist. For him, therefore, there remains the challenge for practitioner researchers to develop 'this aspect of early years practice, and its theoretical underpinning' which 'needs to be as rigorous and detailed as the early years literature on support-ing and extending children's cognitive development'.

Of course, in seeking to ensure that children are happy, secure and confi-dent, we must also consider their self-esteem. This is defined by Lawrence (1987) as the 'evaluation of the discrepancy between *self-image* and *ideal self* (p.4). The *self-image* is the child's awareness of his or her characteristics and abilities, whereas the *ideal self* is his or her view of the ideal characteristics, skills, behaviours, etc., that he or she has come to value and would like to possess. Murray White (UK representative of the International Council for Self-Esteem) has a slightly different but not incompatible view of self-esteem. For him it consists of '*self-efficacy* – confidence in our ability to think, choose and make wise decisions – and *self respect* – confidence in our right to be happy, and a belief that success, friendship, respect, love and fulfilment can be ours' (White, 1996, p.2).

Lawrence describes the child with high self-esteem as likely 'to be confi-dent in social situations and in tackling scholastic work' and to have a 'natural curiosity for learning' (p.6). White's experience strongly confirms this link between self-esteem and personal competence.

A child's concept of self develops as he or she internalises the social values, preferences and expectations of significant others. Parents, extended family and early years educators are exceedingly influential in this process (Rogers, 1961; Lawrence, 1987; Harter, 1990). It is therefore important that early years professionals value each child's personal characteristics. In addition, White (1996) advises us that 'sound approaches to self-esteem are based on realism, not inflated self-images'. At a practical level this might include avoiding the use of superlatives until they are fully deserved, and in general giving honest and specific praise for a task well done, for effort and for different talents and abilities (our holistic approach). Adult behaviour such as exclaiming in an artificial voice '*Super*' or showing intense pleasure in response to every mini-mal achievement, e.g. a quick drawing or getting ready on time, is unlikely to be helpful to any child's self-esteem and may hinder his or her desire to reach higher levels of attainment. Faber and Mazlish (1980) tell us that if you always give the same praise whatever the behaviour, children may be unsure of your true feelings and whether you genuinely do value something that they have done; acknowledgement is more often what children seek or need. Cole (1991) also warns us against constantly labelling children e.g. as a 'naughty boy'.

Instead, the recommendation is to praise or criticise the deed rather than the child.

Lawrence (1987) further advises us to promote healthy levels of self-esteem in children by ensuring that our body language is positive (e.g. establishing eye contact, smiling, talking to them at their height level), listening carefully to what they have to say, being genuinely empathetic, and demonstrating our liking towards them. He also advocates treating children with respect and having high but realistic expectations.

Knowledge, understanding, skills and attitudes needed by educators to enable them to work successfully with young children and their families

In the *Rumbold Report* (Department of Education and Science, 1990) there is a useful set of summary statements outlining the attributes that a group of educators in any particular early years setting should jointly possess (p.47). Being sensitive and responsive to the needs, characteristics, development and socio-cultural background of children, and having a sound knowledge of quality provision and an appropriate curriculum for pre-school children, as well as a genuine fondness and respect for children, probably captures in essence the vital qualities and expertise that each and every educator needs to possess in order be effective.

While maintaining our underpinning holistic philosophy, within all types of early years provision and also in a chapter on early childhood education it would be particularly important for practitioners to understand how young children learn. I refer naturally to an holistic view of learning which encompasses concepts, skills and attitudes relating to all aspects of a child's development, e.g. intellectual, linguistic, emotional, social, cultural, gender-related, moral and spiritual development.

As you read in Chapter 9, the theories of Piaget and Vygosky tell us that children construct knowledge by constantly organising and reorganising their experiences within their environments (people, objects and materials) in the process of refining and extending their learning. 'We know children construct knowledge because they possess so many ideas that adults do not teach them' (National Association for the Education of Young Children, 1991, p.25). We must therefore constantly provide interesting opportunities and experiences to allow children to experiment, ask questions and discover answers. Vygotsky (1978) advocated encouraging children's learning via social interaction and apprenticeship-type relationships with a more cognitively skilled adult or child. Learning would be promoted through talk, play, instruction, first-hand experience and observation and imitation of the other. The child then needs to practise and reflect upon his or her newly acquired behaviour or knowledge before that can become internalised as an integral and usable part of his or her repertoire.

There is in fact strong agreement about Vygotsky's advice among most of the research papers and reports mentioned in this chapter, especially with regard to the tremendous value of play, talk and first-hand experience in facilitating children's learning.

The position statement of the American National Association for the Education of Young Children (1991) succinctly summarises the benefits of play. It is seen as providing opportunities for children to:

- explore, experiment and manipulate;
- learn to deal with feelings, to interact with others, to resolve conflicts and to gain a sense of competence;
- practise spontaneously in a variety of situations;
- examine and refine their learning in the light of feedback that they receive from the environment;
- strengthen their skills and deepen their understanding of concepts;
- develop representational thought, imagination and creativity.

> (based on National Association for the Education of
> Young Children, 1991, p.26).

While these are widely held views about play, Smith and Cowie (1991) caution us that attempts to establish empirical proof of the value of play have not been entirely successful. Moreover, Tizard and Hughes (1984), in their famous comparative study of the learning benefits of the home and nursery environments, and much like Singer (1996), claim that there may be disadvantages to the totally child-centred play-oriented nursery where children miss the interest and challenge of imitating adults engaged in the typical chores and activities of daily life. I doubt, however, that there are many early years educators who feel the need for, or indeed the lack of, evidence to ratify their use of play. Vygotsky (1978) in fact believed that young children's development benefited so much from play that it was 'the highest form of pre-school development' (p.102).

The beneficial outcomes of play for children's learning and development do not happen by chance, of course. Moreover, 'we cannot assume that when children are playing they are automatically learning' (Wood and Attfield, 1996, p.153). Once again the *Rumbold Report* (Department of Education and Science, 1990) carefully provides a set of conditions to ensure that the potential of play can be realised. These are as follows:

- sensitive, knowledgeable and informed adult involvement and intervention;
- careful planning and organisation of play settings in order to provide for and extend learning;
- enough time for children to develop their play;
- careful observation of children's activities to facilitate assessment and planning for progression and continuity.

> (Department of Education and Science, 1990, p.11)

Wood and Attfield (1996) also provide much invaluable discussion and guidance on play and learning as they relate to the early years curriculum. Do be aware, however, that planning and organising for holistic and educative play is an exciting but never easy aspect of the role of early years educators – even though it may appear quite effortless in the hands of a skilled practitioner!

As we have already seen, much research also confirms the importance of 'talk' in children's learning, with the quality and quantity of interaction between adults and children being crucial.

Unfortunately there is also a body of research (see McAuley and Jackson, 1992) which indicates that much of the talk which takes place in nursery settings is not particularly advantageous to the development of children's learning, and is in fact mostly used for organisational purposes, with sustained conversations between one adult and one child being rare. McAuley and Jackson provide rather humorous evidence from the USA of teachers confining their talk with children to questions which merely elicit known information, e.g. 'What shape is that?' 'What colour is that?' We certainly do need to assess children's levels of knowledge periodically in order to plan for their future learning, but we must not confuse this type of talk with meaningful conversation which extends their knowledge and understanding of the world and contributes to the development of relationships. The National Oracy Project (1990) in fact urges us to be mindful of the three main functions of talking and, of course, listening – these are the social, communicative and cognitive functions. The National Oracy Project suggests that there is a definite need to raise the status of talk in the eyes of children and their parents, because it is often perceived as being of less significance than reading and writing.

Wells' (1986) recommendations based on 15 years of longitudinal research on children's language would encourage meaningful conversations with young children and would therefore be as relevant in developing relationships as in developing linguistic competence. Wells advocated that we:

• treat what children have to say as worthy of careful attention;
• do our best to understand what they mean if we are uncertain what they have said to us;
• take children's utterances as the basis for what we say next to them
  (*and these last two points of advice mean careful listening*);
• take account of children's ability to understand (*this would mean knowing each child well*).

(Adapted from Wells, 1986, p.218)

In addition, Wells (1986) recommended that educators should engage in equal and sustained conversations with children – sometimes they will initiate the talk, and at other times the adults will initiate it. It is interesting that Tizard and Hughes (1984) actually found that the most 'intellectually challenging conversations at (a child's own) home took place at times of relative leisure for mother and child' (p.261). This would suggest that we should be placing considerable emphasis on the social aspects, such as milk/juice time, within the nursery routine. Asking children open-ended questions encourages thinking and discussion, as does providing many rich and interesting experiences which act as stimuli for conversations. Remember also to value languages other than English, and strongly support children's acquisition of English as their second language. Such skills are exceedingly important for educators to develop, but beyond the scope of this single chapter.

A broad, balanced curriculum with developmentally appropriate yet challenging activities

The word 'curriculum' stems from the Latin noun meaning 'a course to run'. There are many definitions of the early years curriculum. For example, Bruce (1991) envisages it as consisting of three Cs – the child, the content and the context. The content is developed around what the child already knows, what the child needs to know, and what the child wants to know. If we assume that 'what the child needs to know' can be equated partly with what society advises or the Government decrees, this model might conceivably be viewed as an acceptable compromise amalgamating the constructivist child-centred approach with the externally determined curriculum. Of course any curriculum needs to be made personally meaningful (Department of Education and Science, 1990; Gammage and Meighan, 1995). Skilled educators apply children's own experiences, natural interests and enthusiasms to the forms of learning with which they must or could usefully become familiar – here we can incorporate Bruce's 'what the child wants to know'. By inspiring and motivating children in this manner, we can take them on to the highest level of learning possible for them, or cover a compulsory curriculum in an enjoyable and meaningful way.

The National Association for the Education of Young Children (1991) chooses to describe the curriculum as 'an organised framework that delineates the content children are to learn, the processes through which children achieve the identified curricular goals, what teachers do to help children achieve these goals and the context in which teaching and learning occur' (p.21). Hazareesingh et al. (1989) present a more holistic account: 'the sum total of experiences that the child discovers within the learning environment' (p.35). This consists of the planned elements and the unplanned or incidental aspects – the latter are often termed the 'hidden curriculum'. This might include educator attitudes, styles, values and expectations, the way in which adults talk with children and parents, the varying levels of interest that the practitioners show in the different toys which children may bring from home into the nursery, and the value that they place on social and affective learning and play.

Whatever definition we choose, it is important to realise that the early years curriculum is not haphazard, aimless and based on the whims of individual educators, but rather a carefully structured programme designed to be 'broad and balanced' and 'appropriate to the social, emotional, spiritual and intellectual development of individual children' (Department of Education and Science, 1990, p.35). Detailed and careful forward planning (long-, medium- and short-term) for the individual child and for groups of children is necessary to ensure that there is appropriate content and logical sequence in children's learning.

The broad, balanced curriculum content of the *Rumbold Report* (Department of Education and Science, 1990) has been widely accepted for several years. It originated from the HMI discussion document entitled '*The Curriculum from 5 to 16*' (Her Majesty's Inspectorate, 1985) and included nine areas of experience and learning. These are set out in Table 11.1. The *Rumbold Report*, like most early years curriculum documents, recommends curriculum integration, since young children do not naturally compartmentalise their learning into discrete areas. Of course, as Edwards and Knight (1994) wisely propose, there is a definite need for educarers to ensure mastery of the concepts, terminology and ways of working within each of the different learning areas. Interestingly, their recommendation for a broad curriculum framework was one composed of the nine National Curriculum subjects and religious education – 'an uncomfortable prospect to many early years practitioners'(p.52). However, they did acknowledge that subjects will overlap, and they consequently advocated subject integration whenever this was possible and natural.

Table 11.1   Nine areas of experience and learning from the Rumbold Report (adapted from Department of Education and Science, 1990)

Linguistic	Speaking, listening, reading and writing
Aesthetic and creative	Art, craft, design, music, dance and drama. Promoting children's imagination and appreciation of beauty and fitness for purpose
Human and social	Concerned with people, now and in the past; how and where they live
Mathematical	Basic mathematical processes, concepts and terminology
Moral	Developing an understanding of right and wrong
Physical	Developing fine and gross motor skills, knowledge of how the body works and positive attitudes to a healthy and active way of life
Scientific	Developing children's interest in biological and physical phenomena and introducing scientific processes and thinking
Technological	Stimulating children's interest in, and mastery of, technology
Spiritual	Developing an understanding of the significance and quality of human life

The most recent basis for formulating the content of an early years curriculum is the Schools Curriculum and Assessment Authority (SCAA) document (1996) which we discussed earlier in the chapter. Desirable outcomes for six areas of learning are presented as learning goals to be achieved by children by the time they enter compulsory schooling (see Table 11.2). These objectives are intended to constitute a foundation for Key Stage 1 of the National Curriculum. Much concern has been voiced by educators in the educational press about this emphasis on outcomes at the expense of the process of learning. As readers will realise, this is not necessarily compatible with the principles of

Table 11.2   Schools Curriculum and Assessment Authority (1996) desirable outcomes for six areas of children's learning (summary) (adapted from Department of Education and Employment, 1996, p.13)

a	**Personal and social development** – focuses on children learning now to work, play, co-operate with others and function in a group beyond the family
b	**Language and literacy** – focuses on children's developing competence in talking and listening, and in becoming readers and writers
c	**Mathematics** – covers aspects of mathematical understanding and provides the foundation for numeracy
d	**Knowledge and understanding of the world** – focuses on children's developing knowledge and understanding of their environment, other people and features of the natural and manmade world
e	**Physical development** – focuses on children's developing physical control, mobility, awareness of space and manipulative skills in indoor and outdoor environments
f	**Creative development** – focuses on the development of children's imagination and their ability to communicate and to express ideas and feelings in creative ways

the developmental curriculum and some of the concepts of education and quality educare we discussed earlier in the chapter.

Equality of opportunity/anti-discriminatory practice

Article 2 of the United Nations Convention on the Rights of the Child states that children should be treated 'without discrimination of any kind, irrespective of the child's or his or her parents or legal guardian's race, colour, sex, language, religion, political or other opinion, national, ethnic or social origin, property, disability, birth or other status' (Newell, 1991). The Children Act (1989) and the *Rumbold Report* (Department of Education and Science, 1990) make similar demands.

To be effective as early years educarers, we must be fully cognisant of such a fundamental right and make certain that it underpins and permeates our practice. It must certainly not be tokenistic or added as an afterthought.

Unfortunately research such as that undertaken in Scottish multi-ethnic nurseries by Ogilvy *et al.* (1990) demonstrated that discrimination is often unwittingly directed towards non-indigenous children by otherwise caring, thoughtful and well-intentioned staff. In this particular study, children from ethnic groups received less attention from staff and were engaged in fewer interactions. Verhallen *et al.* (1989) reported similar cultural bias in Holland, and Derman-Sparkes (1993) and David (1990) also discuss many instances of bias relating to gender, race and disability within a wide range of early years settings. It is also well recognised that young children make discriminatory and stereotypic statements after absorbing the attitudes of those whom they observe and with whom they interact (David, 1990; Derman-Sparkes, 1993).

It is easier to understand the negative impact of oppressive practices on the children who are subjected to these practices. Derman-Sparkes and the ABC Task Force (1989) explain, for example, how discrimination may:

- reduce children's opportunities and possibly limit development of their potential;
- adversely affect children's self-esteem, behaviour, aspirations, confidence and well-being;
- make children unable to act as effectively as they might do;
- cause uneven cognitive development if there is self-limiting of learning experiences, perhaps because of gender stereotyping.

Often less obvious is the potential damage caused by prejudice to the children who are not targets, but who absorb or perhaps activate discriminatory attitudes. Again, Derman-Sparkes and the ABC Task Force (1989) consider that we have reason to believe such children may:

- develop negative and inaccurate images of other groups;
- develop a false sense of superiority;
- become fearful of some groups of people who are different to themselves, e.g. black or with a disability;
- be less well prepared to deal with the realities and demands of everyday life.

It is important to remember that equality of opportunity is not about treating all children in exactly the same way, but rather it reflects our holistic approach of sensitive and responsive educare. All children must feel that they are being treated fairly, and indeed this must be seen to be the case by all parties within a setting. They must also receive as near equivalent attention as you can manage, but each according to his or her needs. Equality of opportunity then becomes much more of a probability.

Naturally it is also essential that early years educators understand fully their own attitudes towards racism, sexism and disability, and are able to confront instances of discrimination firmly but tactfully. We need to support children in developing bias-free attitudes, and often we may have the difficult task of discussing such sensitive issues with parents and acknowledging their views, which may be quite irreconcilable with anti-bias principles and practice.

The texts by Derman-Sparkes and the ABC Task Force (1989) and Siraj-Blatchford (1994) will be exceedingly helpful to early childhood students in both increasing their self-knowledge and in developing sound anti-discriminatory practice within any early years setting. Such practice aims to help children realise the similarities, understand, accept and behave comfortably with differences, and deal effectively and decisively with biased attitudes and behaviours.

Effective home–nursery collaboration

A crucial aspect of our holistic philosophy was to consider and work with each child within the context of his or her family and socio-cultural context. The *Rumbold Report* (Department of Education and Science, 1990) reflects dominant current thinking by urging us to acknowledge parents as children's prime educators and to develop with them 'shared understanding, and mutual respect and dialogue' (p.35). The term 'parents' implies those persons who have major responsibility for the care and upbringing of a child. This might include, for example, legal guardians, grandparents and step-parents.

The benefits to children and their families of close collaboration with a child's family are now well known. Bastiani (1995), who for many years has researched this topic, confirms that 'there is clear argument, supported by extensive and convincing evidence, that the most effective education occurs when families and schools work together, as part of a shared enterprise' (p.7). An 'efficient, workable method of parent inclusion and involvement' was also deemed to be one of the major significant aspects of quality within the famous HighScope programme (Schweinhart *et al.*, 1993, p.231). The National Commission on Education (1993) also tells us that early childhood practices are more successful where there is 'effective parental involvement' (p.120), and that nursery is the optimum stage of schooling to establish the whole concept and practice of parent-professional collaboration.

Of course such links may also present some problems. Not all parents want to be involved, and parent participation must not become a ruse to employ fewer professionals by having parents work alongside teachers in the classroom. Bastiani (1995) also acknowledges that 'conflicts and tensions are inevitable and normal' (p.120), and that the relationship may advantage the children and families who least need it. Educators therefore need to be sensitive to different family contexts and circumstances. The National Commission on Education (1993) report that the Adult Literacy and Basic Skills Unit have, for example, identified the need for and value of schools making strenuous efforts to involve in their children's education those parents who have poor literacy and numeracy skills. The National Commission on Education (1993) particularly welcomes family literacy programmes, but this type of involvement can pose quite a daunting challenge for early years educators.

There is general agreement (e.g. Stacey, 1991; Wolfendale, 1992; Bastiani, 1995; Schools Curriculum and Assessment Authority, 1996) that effective home–nursery links would involve:

- an integrated and planned approach to the home–nursery relationship;
- joint professional–parent involvement in decision-making and daily activities to help with children's learning;
- parents being considered to possess important expertise and skills which they are invited to offer (not simply mixing paints and sharpening pencils);
- joint sharing of responsibility and accountability;
- parents feeling welcome and at ease within the early years setting;
- effective and friendly communication with parents, who are made fully aware of the aims, ongoing practices and changes within the nursery group;
- home-visiting schemes where possible.

Such processes serve to acknowledge and reinforce the crucial role of parents in their children's education, as well as maximising the learning potential of the nursery environment.

Regular monitoring and evaluation of early years provision

In constantly striving to work towards ensuring that our early years provision is of the highest standard attainable, such provision must be subject to regular and rigorous monitoring and evaluation.

Katz (1993) argues that the quality of any early childhood programme must be considered from five perspectives – those of the children, parents, practitioners, visiting adults (e.g. other professionals, colleagues, governors, researchers) and society's representatives (e.g. inspectors, advisers, managers, headteachers).

The Office for Standards in Education (1995) and the Department for Education and Employment (1996) have established formal criteria and processes for inspection of pre-school provision. These documents are publicly available, and early years professionals are obliged, in the current climate, to pay careful attention to the specified requirements.

Using the list of criteria from our consensus concept of quality cited earlier in the chapter can, however, provide an additional valuable framework for evaluation from the perspectives of children, parents and practitioners. Readers will recall that Williams (1995) was highly complimentary about Pascal and Bertram's Effective Early Learning Research Project because it achieved its 'twin objectives of evaluation and improvement' (p.21). The intentions of Laevers (1994), Gammage (1994), Katz (1995), The Northern Group of Advisers (1992) and the National Association for the Education of Young Children (1991) are similar.

We would, therefore, be well advised to evaluate (with a view to improving) all aspects of quality by utilising the strategies of these acclaimed researchers. For example, we could:

- formally and informally observe what goes on in our setting and note the effects;
- ask questions of all participants in order to ascertain their views;
- listen carefully to what children, parents, colleagues, inspectors, advisors, managers and headteachers say;
- compare our provision and practice with that of others (which we visit or read about);
- share views, and discuss educational ideas and practice with others;
- ask a critical friend to observe and assess our practice;
- occasionally use formal and standardised procedures for assessing children's experiences and learning outcomes, e.g. Laevers' (1994) Leuven Involvement Scale for Young Children;

- ask and answer questions of ourselves.

The Northern Group of Advisors (1992, chapter 6) provides three ostensibly simple questions for evaluating our educare.

- What are the children doing?
- What are the adults doing?
- What does the learning environment look like?

Several subsidiary questions accompany each of these questions and, because these are fairly searching, they could be extremely useful in helping us to execute an exacting evaluation of our own practice.

As part of the overall strategy of evaluation of quality within our setting, we would also evaluate the day-to-day activities. There are two main types of evaluation – evaluation of the *process* and evaluation of the *product*.

Process evaluation actually takes place as practitioners interact with children, or while children are involved in an activity. Observation would, for example, include:

- verbal and non-verbal cues and feedback;
- the extent of children's involvement and enthusiasm;
- the quality of their responses and reactions;
- the aspects which the educator felt went well;
- the aspects with which the educator was less happy.

Product evaluation involves evaluating the outcome of activities. Practitioners would be looking for changes in children's awareness, attitudes, interests, understanding, knowledge, learning, behaviour, skills and competences. These changes could be ascertained by:

- observing children's play, conversations, contributions to discussions, explanations, reactions, behaviours, application of knowledge, decisions, questions;
- asking questions and considering the children's answers;
- setting up specific activities to assess whether the desired changes have occurred;
- listening to relevant feedback from parents, colleagues, helpers and other children.

Most crucially, just as with our observations in Chapter 1, we must act on the results of these evaluative procedures, especially when we have identified an aspect of practice that is in need of improvement. Indeed monitoring and evaluation must be viewed as an integral aspect of our regular planning cycle when we engage in the more complex form of that observation cycle, namely reflective practice.

Through such a process, evaluation emerges as an important strategy for the regular review and enhancement of our educare provision. It is of course an enormously difficult task for early years professionals to attain the high standard of provision that most of us seek. By studying in depth, by publicly articulating the agreed concept of quality in our early years setting, by proclaiming our aim to work towards that particular vision of early childhood educare, and by implementing the necessary actions, we may hopefully come just a little closer to realising these high ideals.

CONCLUSION

We commenced this chapter by considering the concept and aims of education. We then developed a sound rationale for the pursuit of quality early years provision by investigating its benefits for children, families and society. Finally we established a consensus concept of quality educare and examined several of its emerging characteristics, thus providing readers with a meaningful strategy for working towards more effective early childhood education.

References

Anderson, B.E. (1992): Effects of Daycare on Cognitive and Socio-emotional Competence of Thirteen-year-old Swedish School Children. *Child Development* **63**, 20–36.

Athey, C. (1990): *Extending Thought in Young Children: a Parent-teacher Partnership.* London: Paul Chapman Publishing.

Bastiani, J. (1995): *Taking a Few Risks.* London: Royal Society for the Encouragement of Arts, Manufacture and Commerce.

Beruetta-Clement, J., Schweinhart, L.J., Barnett, W.S., Epstein, A.S. and Weikart, D.P. (1984): Changed Lives: the Effects of the Perry Pre-school Programme on Youths Through Age 19. *Monographs of the HighScope Educational Research Foundation* **8**, 16–28.

Blenkin, G.M. and Kelly, A.V. (eds) (1996): *Early Childhood Education*, 2nd edn. London: Paul Chapman Publishing.

Brierley, J. (1994); *Give me a Child until he is Seven.* London: Falmer Press.

Bruce, T. (1991): *Time to Play in Early Childhood Education.* London: Hodder & Stoughton.

Cole, D.A. (1991): Change in Self-perceived Competence as a Function of Peer and Teacher Evaluation. *Developmental Psychology* **27**, 682–8.

Consultative Group on Early Childhood Care and Development (1994) Why Invest in Early Childhood Development: Eight Arguments. *Bernard van Leer Foundation Newsletter* **74**, 2.

Dahlberg, G. and Asen, G. (1994): Evaluation and Regulation: a Question of Empowerment. In Moss, P. and Pence, A. (eds), *Valuing Quality in Early Childhood Services*, London: Paul Chapman Publishing, 157–71.

David, T. (1992): *Under Five – Under-educated?* Milton Keynes: Open University Press.

Department for Education and Employment (1996): *Nursery Education Scheme: the Next Steps.* London: Department for Education and Employment.

Department of Education and Science (1990): *Starting with Quality: Report of the Committee of Inquiry into the Educational Experiences offered to Three and Four-Year Olds (Rumbold Report).* London: HMSO.

Department of Health (1991): *The Children Act (1989) Guidance and Regulations. Vol. 2. Family Support, Day Care and Educational Provision for Young Children.* London: HMSO.

Derman-Sparkes, L. (1993): Challenging Bias in Child Care. *Coordinate* **33**, 8–13.

Derman-Sparkes, L. and the ABC Task Force (1989): *Anti-bias Curriculum.* Washington, DC: National Association for the Education of Young Children.

Edwards, A. and Knight, P. (1994): *Effective Early Years Education*. Buckingham: Open University Press.

Elfer, P. (1966): Building Intimacy in Relationships with Young Children in Nurseries. *Early Years* **16**, 30–34.

European Commission Childcare Network (1990): *Quality in Childcare Services*. Brussels: European Commission.

Faber, A. and Mazlish, E. (1980): *How to Talk so Kids Listen and Listen so Kids will Talk*. New York: Avon Books.

Froebel, F. (1877): *Reminiscences* (translated by H. Mann). London: Cambridge Press.

Gammage, P. (1994): In Defence of Children. In Laevers, F. (ed.) *Defining and Assessing Quality in Early Childhood Education*. Leuven: University Press, 3–12.

Gammage, P. and Meighan, J. (eds), (1995): Introduction. In *Early Childhood Education: the Way Forward*. Derby: Education Now Publishing Cooperative, i–iii.

Harter, S. (1990): Processes Underlying Adolescent Self-concept Formation. In Montemayor, R. Adams, G.R. and Gullota, T.P. (eds), *From Childhood to Adolescence: a Transitional Period?*, Newbury Park, CA: Sage, 205–39.

Her Majesty's Inspectorate (1985): *The Curriculum from 5 to 16. Curriculum Matters 2*. London: HMSO.

Hinde, R.A. (1992): Human Social Development: an Ethological/Relationship Perspective. In McGurk, H. (ed.), *Childhood Social Development*. Hove: Erlbaum Associates, 13–29.

Katz, L.G. (1993): Multiple Perspectives on the Quality of Early Childhood Programmes. *European Early Childhood Education Research Journal* **1**, 5–9.

Kellmer-Pringle, M. (1975): *The Needs of Children*. London: Hutchinson & Co.

Laevers, F. (1994): The Innovative Project Experiential Education and the Definition of Quality in Education. In Laevers, F. (ed.), *Defining and Assessing Quality in Early Childhood Education*. Leuven: Leuven University Press, 159–72.

Lawrence, D. (1987): *Enhancing Self-esteem in the Classroom*. London: Paul Chapman Publishing.

McAuley, H. and Jackson, P. (1992): *Educating Young Children*. London: David Fulton Publishers/Roehampton Institute.

Marsh, C. (1994): People Matter: the Role of Adults in Providing a Quality Learning Environment for the Early Years. In Abbott, L. and Rodger, R. (eds), *Quality Education in the Early Years*. Buckingham: Open University Press, 132–51..

Meadows, S. (1993): *The Child as Thinker*. London: Routledge.

Melhuish, E.C. (1993): Pre-school Care and Education: Lessons from the 20th for the 21st century. *International Journal of Early Years Education* **1**, 19–32.

Mellor, E. (1970): *Education through Experience in the Infant Years*. Oxford: Basil Blackwell.

Moll, L.C. (1990): *Vygotsky and Education*. Cambridge: Cambridge University Press.

Moss, P. (1994): Defining Quality: Values, Stakeholders and Processes. In Moss, P. and Pence, A. (eds), *Valuing Quality in Early Childhood Services*. London: Paul Chapman Publishing, 1–9.

Myers, R.G. (1990): *Towards a Fair Start for Children*. Paris: United Nations Educational, Scientific and Cultural Organization.

National Association for the Education of Young Children (1991): Guidelines for Appropriate Curriculum Content and Assessment in Programs Serving Children Ages 3 through 8. *Young Children* **46**, 21–38.

National Commission on Education (1993): *Learning to Succeed*. London: Heinemann.

National Oracy Project (1990): *Teaching Talking and Learning in Key Stage One*. York: National Curriculum Council.

Newell, P. (1991): *The UN Convention and Children's Rights in the UK.* London: National Children's Bureau.

Northern Group of Advisers (1992): *Right from the Beginning: Assuring Quality in Early Education.* Gateshead: Metropolitan Borough Council Education Department.

Office for Standards in Education (1995): *Guidance on the Inspection of Nursery and Primary Schools.* London: HMSO.

Ogilvy, C.M., Boath, T.H., Cheyne, W.M., Jahoda, G. and Schaffer, H.R. (1990): Staff Attitudes and Perceptions in Multicultural Nursery Schools. *Early Childhood Development and Care* **64**, 1–13.

Pascal, C. and Bertram, A. (1994): Exploring Definitions of Quality for Children Aged 3–5 in Practice. In Laevers, F. (ed.), *Defining and Assessing Quality in Early Childhood Education.* Leuven: Leuven University Press, 103–9.

Pugh, G. (1992): *An Equal Start for all our Children.* (Times Educational Supplement/ Greenwich Lecture 1992). London: Times Educational Supplement/Greenwich.

Rogers, C.R. (1961): *On Becoming a Person: a Therapist's View of Psychotherapy.* London: Constable.

Schools Curriculum and Assessment Authority (1996): *Nursery Education: Desirable Outcomes for Children's Learning.* London: Department for Education and Employment/Schools Curriculum and Assessment Authority.

Schweinhart, L.J., Barnes, H.V. and Weikart, D.P. (1993): *Significant Benefits.* Yipsilanti, MI: The HighScope Press.

Shorrocks, D., Daniels, S., Stainton, R. and Ring, K. (1993): *Testing and Assessing 6 and 7 Year Olds: the Evaluation of the 1992 Key Start 1 National Curriculum Assessment Final Report.* London: NUT/School of Education, University of Leeds.

Singer, E. (1996): Prisoners of the Method. *International Journal of Early Years Education* **4**, 28–40.

Siraj-Blatchford, I. (1994): *The Early Years: Laying the Foundations for Racial Equality.* Stoke-on-Trent: Trentham Books.

Smith, P.K. and Cowie, H. (1991): *Understanding Children's Development*, 2nd edn. Oxford: Basil Blackwell.

Stacey, M. (1991): *Parents and Teachers Together.* Buckingham: Open University Press.

Sylva, K. (1992): Quality Care for the Under-fives: is it Worth it? *Royal Society for the Encouragement of Arts, Manufacture and Commerce Journal* **140**, 683–90.

Tizard, B. and Hughes, M. (1984): *Young Children Learning.* London: Fontana.

Verhallen, M., Appel, R. and Schoonen, R. (1989): Language Functions in Early Childhood Education: the Cognitive Linguistic Experiences of Bilingual and Monolingual Children,' *Language and Education* **3**, 109–30.

Vygotsky, L.S. (1978): *Mind in Society: the Development of Higher Psychological Processes.* Cambridge, MA: Harvard University Press.

Wells, G. (1986): *The Meaning Makers: Children Learning Language and Using Language to Learn.* London: Hodder & Stoughton.

White, M. (1996): What's so Silly about Self-esteem? *Times Educational Supplement* **2, (26 April)**, 2.

Williams, P. (1995): *Making Sense of Quality.* London: National Children's Bureau.

Wolfendale, S. (1992): *Empowering Parents and Teachers.* London: Cassell.

Woodhead, M. (1987): Is Early Education Effective? In Desforges, C.W. (ed.), *Early Childhood Education.* Monograph Series of the British Journal of Educational Psychology No. 4. Edinburgh: Scottish Academic Press, 128–43.

Wood, E. and Attfield, J. (1996): *Play, Learning and the Early Childhood Curriculum.* London: Paul Chapman Publishing.

Woods, M. (1994): *The Training of Early Years Tutors in Suffolk.* Ipswich: Social Services Department/Local Education Authority.

Multidisciplinary care of the sick child in the community

Val Thurtle

This chapter aims to:

- consider the development of paediatric health care for young children;
- investigate and evaluate the community health care currently available for sick children and their families.

Introduction

The last 40 years have seen a gradual shift away from the hospital-based care of sick children towards a community care-based approach. This chapter examines this shift, considering everyday self-limiting illness, long-term conditions and life-threatening diseases. In doing this it discusses the work of early years practitioners with such children and their families, encouraging the reader to reflect on the work of multidisciplinary care in practice.

Types of sickness

Almost any one who regularly cares for a child has been in the position of wondering if the child is up to par or whether he or she is sick. Studies of adults demonstrate that there is a huge symptom iceberg (Hannay, 1979) that sometimes is defined as sickness and at other times is played down or even ignored. It seems likely that this is also the case with children. The definition of the child as sick is mediated through parents, carers and relatives as well as through health workers. It seems well accepted that the definition of an individual as sick involves a biological state with accepted pathology, but that it also involves the subjective state of being unwell. This is agreed by others and changes the status of the individual, so that they can be excused from their normal social duties. In the case of a child this may give him or her a day off school and lead to the parent being more lenient about the child's behaviour. When the carer and particularly the doctor labels or diagnoses the child as ill, he or she can be regarded as entering the 'sick role' (Parsons, 1951).

A variety of strategies are involved in the definition of illness. The parent or carer may adopt a 'wait and see' approach , use over-the-counter medication and check with significant others in what is often termed the *lay referral system* (Freidson, 1970). The approach may be similar whether the condition is self-limiting or life threatening. Simple illness (and what appears simple to one may cause inordinate anxiety to another) may involve contact with a variety of individuals, e.g. mother-in-law, pharmacist, health visitor and the playgroup supervisor. Serious, long-term and terminal illness widen the number of disciplines involved, with families reporting that they are in contact with more than 30 different agencies and disciplines including, for example, physiotherapists, self-help groups, special needs advisers, social workers, paediatricians and voluntary organisations. Whether these disciplines work together, effectively sharing similar aims and objectives, is a question that deserves to be addressed. If you know a child with a long-term illness you might like to spend a few minutes listing all of the disciplines with which they and their family come into contact, and reflecting upon whether they ever meet together and asking who co-ordinates their activities.

In the community

Health professionals do not have a monopoly in caring for sick children. A recurring theme both of this chapter and of the literature on sick children in the late twentieth century, is that the parents are the most significant role players, and they must be included in all decision-making. When we consider self-limiting illness, they may be the only health carers involved.

That said, the belief continues that health care takes place in hospitals or, at best, in general practice surgeries and health centres (Figure 12.1). Historically the hospitals were late in appearing on the health care scene. Separate development of hospital and dispensary medicine led to a hospital–community divide, but this artificial division has been slowly breaking down since the 1950s. Parents of sick children and other visitors have been welcomed and encouraged into the hospital, and outreach nurses may have their base in a hospital but work with families in their homes (Bignold *et al.*, 1994). There has been a growth in different styles of care, including day-care, hospices and hospital at home. Professional preparation for nurses and medical students has included some community experience from early in the programmes. Community care has become a part of policy, not only for children but also for a variety of other groups. It has, of course, been criticised for being a strategy which seeks to cut back on expenditure.

With barriers breaking down we need to move away from the hospital–community divide and see the hospital as a functional part of the community. Extrapolating from Bronfenbrenner's (1979) model (see Chapters 1 and 5), for some children the hospital will be one of the microsystems within the exosystems of health care. For effective care of a child the various systems and

Figure 12.1   Much health care takes place outside the hospital.

disciplines need to interact and collaborate. The community for any individual child may include the geographical area in which they live as well as the social network within which they and their parents operate. This will include school, health care agencies, nursery, church, friends and families. For some it will include an even wider perspective, perhaps a national self-help group or a supra-regional centre for health care.

Historical perspectives

Changes in mortality and morbidity

Life in earlier centuries has been seen as 'nasty, brutish and short' for the majority of the population, and particularly for children. Stacey (1988, p.35) cites John Graunt's estimate for 1662 that for every 100 children born live in London, 36 children died during their first 6 years and a further 24 children died during the following 10 years. Epidemics of bubonic plague, smallpox and influenza caused deaths of both adult and child, but the limited earning power of young children may have made them apppear dispensable.

Patterns of mortality have changed over time. Between 1840 and 1990 the life expectancy for women has risen from 43 years to 77 years and for men from 40 years to 72 years (Fitzpatrick, 1991). Much of this can be attributed to the dramatic improvement in infant mortality rates. This remained at 150 per 1000 live births throughout the nineteenth century (Leathard, 1991), but was recorded as 6.9 per 1000 live births for males and 5.4 per 1000 live births in

1994 (Central Statistical Office, 1996). The reasons for this improvement have been much debated, but it seems that smaller family size, improved nutrition, improved housing and public health measures, including a clean water supply and an effective sewerage system, have been as instrumental as developments in medical technology.

Patterns of morbidity have also changed. Infectious diseases such as diphtheria and polio are now uncommon and not as feared as they would have been in the 1930s, but accidents constitute a significant proportion of health encounters. Virtually all accidents occur in the community, and result in one in six of all children attending an Accident and Emergency Department each year (Child Accident Prevention Trust, 1991). This of course excludes all accidents that are managed by carers and parents in the home. Conditions that would have led to death have become causes of long-term morbidity. Children who would previously have died of congenital abnormalities frequently survive, and life-shortening diseases such as leukaemia can now be seen as serious but long-term illnesses. Conditions that only a few years ago were life-threatening have become chronic illnesses necessitating frequent contact with health workers over a period of years (see also Chapter 8 for further discussion).

A glossary of important terms can be found in Box 12.1.

Box 12.1   Glossary of important terms

lay referral system	the friends, families and acquaintances with whom health problems are discussed prior to seeking professional help
self-limiting illness	a condition that is likely to resolve with little or no health care intervention
sick role	the social role of being sick, as conceptualised by Parsons (1951). The sick individual has the right to be exempt from normal obligations and to be looked after. He or she in turn has the duty to want to recover and to comply with prescribed treatments
chronic illness	a long-lasting but not necessarily life-threatening condition, often associated with some degree of disability
life-limiting illness	a condition that is likely to reduce the child's life expectancy and possibly reduce the quality of his or her life
morbidity	the state of being ill or diseased; morbidity rates relate to the incidence of disease in a population
mortality rate	the incidence of death in a population
oncology	the sum of knowledge related to neoplasms or tumours, and the care of such conditions

otitis media	inflammation of the middle ear (with effusion involves the presence of fluid)
terminal illness	the last stages of a life-ending illness
primary health care team	the group of health care professionals working outside the hospitals who provide preventive services and are likely to be involved with and manage illness episodes in the first instance. The team is often seen to consist of the district nurse, general practitioner, health visitor and midwife, although many others may be involved in primary care
serious illness	a term used in this chapter to encompass chronic and acute illness that is likely to be life-shortening

The move in to hospitals

Health care – in whatever form – has always been delivered primarily in the home, mostly by members of the household, with input from traditional healers and possibly physicians. The availability and desirability of hospital care for children was late in coming.

The early nineteenth century saw a growth in hospitals for some adults. The voluntary hospitals, which treated the deserving poor, provided doctors with a ready supply of clinical material for teaching and research. The medical men were selective in their interest, focusing on areas in which expertise might lead to financial gain in their private practice. Children did not warrant much attention, and were excluded from many of the voluntary hospitals. Individuals who were not considered interesting clinical material, especially if a successful outcome was unlikely, and who could not be cared for at home, might end up in the workhouse infirmary, where standards of care were low. In general, hospitals were not places to be visited by choice, and until the twentieth century those who could afford it would receive all their medical care, including surgery, in their own homes.

Early hospitals for children, such as the Foundling Hospital in Coram Fields, established in 1756, were probably more akin to orphanages. Early voluntary hospitals may have been reluctant to admit children (and other types of cases) but lack of room in the hospitals was a disappointment for ambitious young doctors who wanted to pursue specialist interests, and led to the founding of specialist hospitals in the mid-nineteenth century. This, together with an increasing concern about children in the Victorian period, led to the setting up of children's hospitals in Liverpool, Norwich and, of course, the famous Great Ormond Street Hospital for Sick Children in London .

The growth of hospitals was linked to the development of the speciality of paediatrics, with a focus on individual cases. At the same time, linked with the Poor Law, dispensary medicine was evolving, which included child welfare clinics, school health and milk depots (Armstrong, 1983). The separate development of two systems, with the dispensaries being seen as the poor relation, was an inheritance that divided hospital and community care well into the twentieth century, and perhaps influences thinking even now.

The association of hospitals with military-style discipline and a genuine fear of infection made them places which were, when considered in the light of twentieth century views on child care, hard and unfeeling.

Children in the nineteenth and first half of the twentieth century spent long periods in hospitals with little or no contact with their parents. Munro Davies (1949, cited in Robertson and Robertson, 1989) quotes hospital visiting hours in 1949. The West London Hospital had no visiting of children, at St Thomas's Hospital there was no visiting of children during the first month of admission, but parents could see their children asleep between 7 and 8 p.m., and Guy's Hospital had visiting on Sunday afternoon between 2 and 4 p.m. Despite the prolonged separation of children from their parents, the nursing staff were discouraged from becoming emotionally involved with their patients.

Out of the hospital

Bowlby's work on attachment theory and, more directly, Robertson's writing and campaigning (Robertson and Robertson, 1989) did much to change attitudes and practices. Robertson filmed 'Laura', a 2-year-old being admitted to hospital. He demonstrated that it was her separation from her mother and familiar routine which caused distress – perhaps more than any pain or medical intervention. He argued that children on admission demonstrated protest by clinging and crying; they then sank into despair, initially with sobs, but eventually became quiet and uncomplaining. After a time, particularly if they were long-stay patients, they became detached in that they denied any wish for a relationship. They might appear superficially friendly with strangers, but they were indifferent to their parents, craving the sweets they brought but being destructive in their behaviour. Robertson comments that the young nurses were initially distressed on seeing the protest shown by the children. They later became controlled by the system and conformed to the usual practice of the ward, but were frustrated that they could not build up a sustaining relationship. The staff, he felt, were not unkind, but merely conditioned by the system within which they worked.

The diligence and enthusiasm with which Robertson campaigned, taking his film to any group that would watch it, did much to alter practice. The developing changes in professional thinking and policy views were demonstrated in a series of official reports. The *Welfare of Children in Hospital* (Department of Health and Social Security, 1959), known as the *Platt Report*, is regarded as the turning point in the new approach to children. It recommended that children should not be nursed with adults, mothers should be admitted with the under-fives, preparation for admission should be encouraged, unrestricted visiting should be allowed, doctors and nurses should have training in the emotional development of children, and there should be liaison with local authority staff on discharge. Prominent in the report are the alternatives to in-patient treatment, propagating the idea that the child should stay at home, with care by his or her mother supported by special nursing services. Out-patient and day facilities should be utilised, and there should be an increased use of day surgery. Perhaps most critical of all in the context of this chapter, the report suggested that children should not be admitted if this could possibly be avoided.

As the 1950s gave way to the 1960s there was a growing public interest in hospital child care. Child mortality rates had fallen, the majority of children were better nourished than ever before and, with the advent of the National Health Service, health care was available to all. Bowlby's ideas held wide credence and there was increased emphasis on the emotional needs of the child. Robertson's film was shown on television and the National Association for the Welfare of Children in Hospital (now Action for Sick Children) was formed. This organisation was campaigning in its approach, producing a succession of well-respected reports. Change was not instant and was certainly patchy, but lobbying paid off, with open visiting of children in hospital becoming the norm.

Various reports

Points first raised by the *Platt Report* have been reiterated in subsequent reports with depressing regularity. The *Court Report* (Department of Health and Social Services, 1976) emphasised the need for family and child-centred services, with the child being seen as a 'whole and developing person.' This report stressed the involvement of community services, with specialisation in paediatrics by general practitioners and health visitors, and an integration of child health services.

The *Welfare of Children and Young People in Hospital* (Department of Health, 1991) talked of a quality service as providing for the whole child. The service would be child- and family-centred so that they experienced a 'seamless web' of care treatment and support in the various parts of the National Health Service. Five years later, looking at health promotion for all children, Hall (1996) emphasised the same theme, stressing that 'a clear pathway of referral must be agreed' (p.3) so that those who are identified through screening as having a potential difficulty follow a 'seamless pathway to secondary and, if necessary, tertiary specialists.' (p.4). One is left wondering why, with a seamless web of care, hospital and non-hospital services are repeatedly discussed in separate reports.

Both *The Welfare of Children and Young People in Hospital* (Department of Health, 1991) and *Children First* (Audit Commission, 1993) stressed the need for specially skilled paediatric staff. Both reports were commenting on hospital care, but the same needs apply to care outside such institutions. It is worth reflecting upon why there was such tardiness in implementing this recommendation, which first appeared in the 1959 *Platt Report*. The horror of the Allitt[12.1] case caused such questions to be re-addressed, with the Secretary of State for Health commenting that between 1989–1990 and 1993–1994 there had been a 47 per cent increase in the number of Registered Sick Children's Nurses or Project 2000 child branch nurses (Department of Health, 1994a). The recommendations of the Allitt Inquiry (Department of Health, 1994b) led to a greater commitment to having paediatric trained nurses on the wards at all times.

Children First (Audit Commission, 1993) pointed out that separate outpatient and accident and emergency services for children have been difficult to achieve. These areas are particularly relevant to this chapter, as they mark the interface between hospital and community. However the breakdown of the hospital–community divide is commented upon, with the Audit Commission noting that . . . 'the place in which a service is delivered is becoming less relevant as a basis for service organisation' (p.23).

The sister report from the Audit Commission (1994), entitled *Seen But Not Heard*, which looked at community health and social services for children in need, again stressed the need to develop joint partnerships and working together of health and social services. The recommendations of all of these reports can essentially be distilled into two strategies, both of which have been employed – first, strive to make hospitals better, and secondly move care into the community.

In terms of care of the sick child in the community, the recurring themes have been the need for specialised paediatric staff and the call for more effective multidisciplinary working.

Community children's nurses

Outside the hospital, the development of specially trained paediatric nurses has been focused on the community children's nurse. Health visitors and school nurses would rightly claim that they have had specialist preparation to work with children, but their expertise is likely to be in the fields of health promotion, screening, education and counselling skills. Many would argue that they are as interested in communities or populations of children as in the individual case. They may have good relationships with families and children who later become sick, but are unlikely to have up-to-date skills in or be contracted to provide sophisticated 'hands-on' nursing care.

Community children's nursing is not new, with the first scheme commencing in Rotherham in 1948 in response to a high infant mortality rate (Lessing and Tatman, 1991). There was little development during the 1960s, but after that other schemes were initiated, some of which provided general home care while other specialist services were caring for neonates or children with a particular condition. The rationale for such schemes varies. Southampton's scheme, which started in 1969, was set up to look after children who had undergone day surgery, but expanded to include the nursing of patients who were discharged home early and the care of those with malignant disease. It also took referrals from general practitioners and liaised between the hospital and the primary health care team (Atwell and Gow, 1985).

Among those seeking to set up such a service, cost is likely to be at least a consideration, with the aim of reducing the expense of in-patient services. For the family, the specialist paediatric service may allow the child to remain in his or her own home environment. Although hospital care has become far more relaxed in its approach to parents during the last 40 years, it still involves a separation from friends, pets, some family members and the neighbourhood. Staying at home may improve the family's economic position by not incurring transport costs, and it allows family members to sustain their normal employment. Siblings are not excluded from the experience of the child's illness, which aids their adjustment to the situation, whether it involves long-term illness, death or full recovery. As we consider working together, it is important that the parents and the child become full members of the multi-disciplinary team – being in their own home they are more likely to have the confidence to feel in control and to be able to voice their concerns, hopes and fears.

Care at home will not be suitable for all families. The physical environment may not be considered adequate by care workers or the family. Some families will miss the security of the hospital ward and prefer the professionals to take complete control. Some will neither have nor want to develop the coping strategies needed to manage home care. For others, the pre-existing stresses and strains in the family could be such that caring for a seriously sick child at home would be disastrous. It follows, therefore, that the decision to care for the child at home supported by a community children's nursing service is, like others, a decision that needs to be taken in partnership with the parents and the child.

Collaborative care

When a child is cared for outside the hospital, all of the disciplines are likely to work from different bases with a variety of different managers. Having all of the relevant professionals involved with a sick child and the family working together effectively seems an ideal on which all will agree and to which we all aspire. However, there is a history of different care workers from a variety of disciplines finding this goal difficult to achieve. Emphasis on the distinctiveness of particular groups and the specialised skills that they bring to the family has led to tribalism and often to defensive practice. The development of market-driven services with purchasers and providers is unlikely to have helped the situation. Whether we are talking of social workers, community nurses, teachers or therapists, each brings resources that can be shared with the family. When an attitude of sharing skills with the family and each other – rather than of professional empire-building – dominates, holistic care of the sick child is more likely to be achieved. Such collaborative care needs careful planning with honest sharing of the pressures under which each discipline is working. Shared educational activities, both at pre-qualification and in-service levels, will do much to identify underlying principles that are held in common. Such educational and practice-based collaboration will lead to a developing respect for and recognition of differences and similarities between the various workers (Cowley, 1993). Collaboration does not have to start on a grand scale. Those at the grass roots often feel powerless to commence interdisciplinary working, but Phillips (1994) suggests that critical dialogue is a powerful mechanism for changing practice. This can start in small groups at a local level, based on the conversations that different professionals have in the course of their usual contact. It will give rise to questions of 'why?' and 'what if?', leading to new ways of working together.

Family-centred care, partnership, empowerment and just surviving

Parents may be the key (indeed only) workers when illness is self-limiting. As has been noted earlier, when illness is long-term and life-threatening, the number of members of the multidisciplinary team that is involved increases.

Partnership between the various disciplines has been mentioned, and there is much discussion of partnership with clients. The literature is full of references to *family-centred care* and *empowerment of the family*. Campbell and Summersgill (1993), commenting on family-centred care, note that it is often unexplained, and that there have been few attempts to define exactly what it means. If care workers have this difficulty, it is hard to see how parents coping with a sick child can evaluate exactly what is on offer.

Campbell and Summersgill (1993) cite the framework of Shelton *et al.* as a rare attempt to identify the elements of family-centred care. This model recognises that the family is a constant in the child's life and that there should be parent–professional collaboration at all levels of health care. Unbiased and complete information should be shared with the parents, and programmes should be implemented that meet the family's needs, both emotionally and financially. The strengths of the family should be recognised and their individual methods of coping should be respected. The developmental and emotional needs of children should be incorporated into the health care delivery systems and parent-to-child support should be encouraged and facilitated. Finally, the health care delivery system should be flexible and responsive to family needs. Taking on board all of these aspects will not provide a package of care that is the same for all children, but rather one that will be tailored to the family in question.

Empowerment fits well within this philosophy, involving the giving of information to families, and the child if he or she is of sufficient maturity, so that they can ascertain what care they would like, making their own choices supported by the professionals. Such approaches sound wonderful, but one should ask whether they are happening in practice, or if they are of a quality to which we should aspire, but which has not yet been attained.

In a study of Canadian families with children with persistent otitis media with effusion, Wuest and Stern (1990) suggest that families become empowered to manage their health despite, rather than because of, the interventions of health care professionals. The families in their study made great efforts to obtain the knowledge and skills that would allow them to participate in the management of the problem. Wuest and Stern describe parents first of all entrusting themselves to health professionals, then becoming disillusioned, learning the rules, and finally using a process of negotiation. The parents in this study apparently became disenchanted with the health care system because they believed that their feelings and opinions were not being heeded. In order to compensate, the parents became experts in the child's condition and in the rules of the system, so that they could experiment in order to influence the course of events. The family which has become expert can manage effectively, rearranging roles and responsibilities and minimising the effects both on the child and, presumably, on the rest of the family.

There is much talk of empowerment of families, but Wuest and Stern (1990) suggest that there is a need for nurses (and other health professionals) to work with families as equal partners in their quest for health. One is left wondering whether their experience of children with a non-life-threatening condition is typical. *Partnership in care* is a popular phrase, but the reality may not yet have arrived. Again, it is worth taking a moment to think of a case of a child you know where there are at least two disciplines involved, e.g. the health visitor and pre-school or teacher and therapist, and consider how effectively the professional/family team works. Could it be made improved?

The seriously ill child and their family

In a similar chapter written 20 years ago, this final section would be on the terminally ill child. Sadly, children do still die in childhood, often of malignant conditions, but there has been a dramatic decrease in the number of deaths from childhood cancers due to the introduction of combination chemotherapies (Waterworth, 1992). While for many a cure is achieved, the effects of the cancer and its therapy may have physical, psychological and social effects months, if not years, later. As malignant diseases may be terminal or may have a protracted treatment phase with long-term effects, it seems unreasonable to 'sort' conditions into life-threatening and chronic illness. A child with a chronic condition such as cardiac disease or even cystic fibrosis may eventually become terminally ill, and therefore it seems preferable to use the term *seriously ill*.

The realisation that their child is seriously ill and may die is inevitably a great shock to parents and carers. It may come at the end of many contacts with health workers as various investigations have been pursued, or it may be very sudden and come 'out of the blue'. Heggarty (1994), drawing on his experience as a paediatrician, describes a variety of parental reactions to the breaking of bad news. Biological responses, he suggests, might occur in the form of a desperate wish by the parents to protect the child, or in some cases a revulsion at the abnormal. Parents who are told of their child's illness or defect at or around the time of birth may feel a great sense of inadequacy that they were unable to produce a healthy child. Others may have an enormous sense of guilt about something which they should or should not have done (see also Chapter 2). Many will work through a bereavement process, feeling anger, disbelief, numbness and grief as they mourn for the child and the future that might have been. Heggarty (1994) describes the family that hopes for the 'magical solution', seeking out new therapies in different parts of the world, while others reject the news, the help offered and even the child. He summarises parental reactions as being emotionally shattered, drawing on a variety of defence mechanisms, and for some, arriving at a mature adaptation.

Care of the seriously ill child is a complex and skilled activity. The closing sections of this chapter can only focus on a few aspects; texts mentioned in the Further Reading section will provide more information for the interested reader.

Children's understanding of illness and death

Children's ideas about illness can be seen as sick role behaviour that they have learned from others, or in terms of a cognitive approach, working through a series of stages akin to those proposed by Piaget, with a move from concrete to abstract reasoning. Magical thinking in various forms is common at around 5–7 years of age, with children making unusual connections between events in order to explain the situation in which they or their siblings find themselves. Unusual or terrifying perceptions of what is happening need to be explored and simple, developmentally appropriate explanations given, perhaps repeatedly.

The late-twentieth-century child has little contact with death other than in violent television programmes. The young child does not regard death and life as mutually exclusive, and cannot appreciate the finality of death – an idea that is supported by many such television programmes. For the pre-school child the significant concern will be that of separation.

The primary-school-aged child shows an increasing awareness that plants, animals and people die, noting their immobility and later the irrevocability of death. Death may be associated with violence, or pictured as a frightening form, although this may depend on the culture of the child. The need to know the cause of death may be very important to the child. This age group may well be fascinated by the details of death, funerals and cremation, which parents under stress may find difficult to handle. The older child is able to appreciate that death is final and that parents are not all-powerful beings who can prevent death. The universality of death becomes evident and the reactions and concerns of the older child or young adolescent are likely to be similar to those of an adult. Their reactions to their own possible death or to the death of a sibling or friend are likely to be of shock, anger, denial and bargaining. The fears of the older child are likely to be focused on the process of dying, rather than on death itself.

Children who are facing the possibility of their own death or that of a family member need to be given the opportunity to explore their ideas at an appropriate level, with plenty of time to both talk and to be listened to. Quality books give an opening to such a discussion, and a list of titles (which is by no means exhaustive) is given in Box 12.2. Death can be seen as our last great taboo, and it might be argued that such issues should be explored with children generally. Whether these books are to be used with sick or well children, they need careful choosing, so that the ideas that are offered fit in with the belief system of the family.

Where should the seriously ill child receive their care?

The above discussion will have highlighted the fact that home, with appropriate support, is likely to be the aim for the majority of children, so that they can maintain their links with family, school and neighbourhood. Such decisions particularly in the case of seriously ill children, need to be taken in full partnership with both parents and child. Many will value the opportunity to care for their child during the last days, but will miss the security of constantly being with staff who have coped with such situations before. Parents of a child with a long-term illness may desperately want to care for their child,

---

Box 12.2 Books about death and loss suitable for use with children

Althea 1988: *When Uncle Bob Died.* London: Dinosaur.
Curtis Stilz, C. 1988: *Kirsty's Kite.* Tring: Lion Publishing.
Johnson, J.M. 1982: *Where's Jess?* Nebraska: Centring Corps.
Green, W. 1989: *Gran's Grave.* Oxford: Little Lion.
Limb, S. 1993: *Come Back Grandma.* Red Fox.
Perkins, J. and Morris, L. 1991: *Remembering Mum.* London: A.C. Black.
Ross, K. and Ross, A. 1995: *Cemetery Quilt.* Boston, MA: Houghton Mifflin Co.
Sims, A. 1986: *Am I Still a Sister?* Louisiana: Big A.
Varley, S. 1984: *Badger's Parting Gifts.* London: Collins.
White, E.B. 1952: *Charlotte's Web.* Harmondsworth: Puffin Books.
Wilhelm, H. 1986: *I'll Always Love You.* Sevenoaks: Picture Knight.

but need the physical and emotional respite provided by a hospice or other care setting.

Children's wards are busy places with a high turnover of patients, and it was in response to the feeling that they were not the best places for children with life-limiting or terminal illnesses that children's hospices developed. Such hospices seek to provide total care for children and their families. A multidisciplinary team aims to create a supportive atmosphere in a non-institutional setting. Helen House was the first such hospice, opening in 1982, and a further four children's hospices have been established since then (Goldman and Baum, 1994).

Stein and Wooley (1990) comment that the hospices have been helpful to individuals, have increased the awareness of the special needs of the terminally ill, and have focused on the educational needs of those working within them.

With only five children's hospices in the country, distances become significant and some parents, having built up relationships with staff at a local or regional hospital, may be reluctant to build up relationships with new staff at a late stage of their child's illness. With the distances involved, intermittent respite care or terminal care takes the child and his or her family away from their own community. This inevitably reduces normality for the child and his or her siblings, and disrupts existing support networks.

These disadvantages must be set against the findings of Stein and Wooley's study (1990). Parents who had used hospice services valued the constant availability of the hospice, feeling that they could telephone whenever they needed help and support. The availability of emergency beds reduced their sense of isolation, and they valued the home-like atmosphere, complete with every day activities. The flexibility of the hospice meant that siblings could accompany the child and parents, making it feel like a 'holiday' for the whole family. By seeing others 'come through', fear of death was reduced and reassurance ensued. At the time of the child's death, parents appreciated the attendance and support of staff. They also valued the continued contact with cards at anniversaries and at Christmas.

The aspects which parents appreciated are clearly based on quality care provided by skilled medical and nursing staff in an informal setting. For many, hospice care will involve planned respite care over time, some will have one admission for the terminal phase of the child's life, while others will continue to care for their child at home, knowing that hospice care is available if they so wish.

Sister Francis Dominica (1990), the founder of Helen House, comments that 'hospice (is) a philosophy rather than a facility, a whole approach rather than an in-patient facility' (p.4). Hospice care will include hospitality and caring, a break from the everyday stresses of caring for a seriously ill child, the knowledge that others are prepared to share in the stress by listening, and the provision of practical and emotional support. A separate building certainly helps, but aspects of this care can and are often provided on hospital wards and in the homes of ill children.

Children's outreach oncology nurses contribute to such a service in many parts of the country, bridging the gap between the specialist oncology centres and the local hospitals and primary health care teams. Bignold *et al.* (1994) found that these nurses, who were all trained in the care of children and most of whom had a background in paediatric oncology, were able to teach parents skills, thus increasing their confidence. They were able to facilitate a local nurse as the key worker, but were only a telephone call away from parents and the local health care staff. They would go into schools and playgroups, with the parents' permission, if explanations were needed, and in general they could provide the expertise that the local primary health care team might not possess. The study concluded that paediatric oncology nurses were valued by families and professionals, and that this service would be needed in the future. The authors reason that expansion of these services needs to be seen in relation to existing community services, particularly community children's nursing services.

Siblings, friends and the wider community

When a child is seriously or terminally ill, the focus is likely to be on him or her. Mikkelson (1993) outlines the need for sibling care. Siblings of a child with a life-threatening condition might exhibit abnormal behaviours, do less well at school, and experience guilt and jealousy, feeling that their own importance is devalued. Mikkelson describes the 'Auckland experience' in which a 4-hour programme is offered to the siblings of children with cancer or leukaemia. During that time they are given age-appropriate information and visit various laboratories and relevant areas of the hospital. Older children have an opportunity to discuss their feelings, while younger children have a session with a play therapist. Such support and information aims to reduce the risk of the siblings developing psychological problems. Mikkelson recognises the need for long-term evaluative research, but such projects are likely to do much to help these seemingly forgotten children.

Education for the seriously ill child is important in that it maintains the normal routine, allowing the child to develop his or her potential abilities, and it provides a focus of interest, which may well offset boredom and frustration. Long periods of time away from school may mean that friendships have been disrupted and the child returning to their own school may find that, as well as having to cope with physical difficulties and what they have missed academically, relationships between peers have changed and their interests no longer correspond to those of the peer group.

Teachers can reduce the difficulties by liaising with the hospital or home tutor and encouraging classmates to maintain contact with the child. The child needs to be referred to as a member of the class even when he or she is not present – it can be helpful for educators to comment on what part he or she might have played in any particular school project. His or her peers need to be kept informed of his or her situation in an age-appropriate fashion, so that features such as hair loss do not come as a shock on the child's return to school.

Unfortunately, some classes will need to cope with the death of one of their number. As children are likely to have little previous experience of death, the teacher provides a model for his or her class. Time will be needed to talk through what has happened, share class memories and cry together, thus acknowledging that the death is important. Siblings and close friends may need someone who provides the role of a counsellor or confidant, and a minority of such children may need specialist help. The books mentioned previously (see Box 12.2) are likely to provide a starting point for discussions. Staff, too, are likely to be upset and in need of support. Working out how to handle the situation when in the midst of it may be difficult, and schools may even need a protocol for the eventuality of death.

The death of a child in the twentieth century shocks us all. We have grown used to an order of events in which the elderly pre-decease the young. The death of a child threatens our certainties and reminds us of our own mortality. Whole communities may be touched, and some individuals will find solace in formal religion, while others will be left angry, confused and frightened. Just as changes in the exosystems and macrosystems (Bronfennbrenner, 1979) can impinge on the child in her microsystems, sickness in the child will produce major reactions in the child's family and considerable ripples in the school and community. The sickness of some may have an even wider influence[12.2], both raising questions for those in political power and challenging the values of cherished social institutions.

CONCLUSION

The sick child, whether their illness is self-limiting, chronic or life-threatening, will spend most of their time in their own home. The care will be largely delivered by family, but may involve a variety of professionals and support workers, who may, or may not collaborate. The care on offer is influenced by wider psychological, social, professional and political ideas. The care of the child affects siblings, peers and the wider community – no man, or child, is an island.

Endnotes

12.1 Beverly Allitt was a general trained enrolled nurse at Grantham and Kesteven Hospital. In 1991 she was instrumental in causing the death of four children and causing harm to others. The ensuing Inquiry (Department of Health, 1994a) highlighted poor practice in terms of appointment and monitoring of ill health of staff, and identified shortcomings in the quality of medical and nursing staff on the paediatric wards. Referring back to *The Welfare of Children and Young People in Hospital* (Department of Health, 1991), it recommended that there should be at least two RSCNs or child branch-educated nurses on duty on the paediatric ward, for 24 hours day.

12.2 In 1995, child B, a leukaemia sufferer, was refused a second transplant operation by Cambridge Health Authority. The case went to the High Court and the Appeal Court, challenging the authority's right to make the decision. A benefactor stepped in, providing the £75,000 needed for further treatment. The child appeared to go into remission, but later died in 1996. The case and the child's death were widely reported in the media, attracting attention as an example of rationing in the NHS.

References

Armstrong, D. (1983): *The Political Anatomy of the Body.* Cambridge: Cambridge University Press.

Atwell, J.D. and Gow M. A. (1985): Paediatric Trained District Nurse in the Community: Expensive Luxury or Economic Necessity? *British Medical Journal* **291**, 227–9.

Audit Commission (1993): *Children First.* London: HMSO.

Audit Commission (1994): *Seen but not Heard.* London: HMSO.

Bignold, S., Ball, S. and Cribb, A. (1994): *Nursing Children with Cancer: the Work of the Paediatric Oncology Nurse Specialist.* London: Department of Health.

Bronfenbrenner, U. (1979): *The Ecology of Human Development.* Cambridge, MA: Harvard University Press.

Campbell, S. and Summersgill, P. (1993): Keeping it in the Family: Defining and Developing Family-centred Care. *Child Health,* **1**, 17–20.

Central Statistical Office (1996): *Social trends.* London: HMSO.

Child Accident Prevention Trust (1991): *Preventing Accidents to Children: a Training Resource for Health Visitors.* London: Child Accident Prevention Trust.

Cowley, S. (1993): Collaboration in Health Care: the Education Link. *Health Visitor Journal* **67**, 13–17.

Department of Health (1991): *The Welfare of Children and Young People in Hospital.* London: HMSO.

Department of Health (1994a): *The Independent Inquiry Relating to Deaths and Injuries on the Children's Ward, Grantham and Kesteven Hospital, During the Period February to April 1991 (The Clothier Report).* London: HMSO.

Department of Health (1994b): *Response by the Secretary of State for Health to the Detailed Recommendations of the Independent Inquiry relating to Deaths and Injuries on the Children's Ward, Grantham and Kesteven Hospital, During the Period February to April 1991. (The Clothier Report).* London: HMSO.

Department of Health and Social Security (1959): *The Welfare of Children in Hospital. The Platt Report.* London: HMSO.

Department of Health and Social Security (1976): *Fit for the Future. The Court Report.* London: HMSO.

Dominica, F. (1990): Hospice: a Philosophy of Care. In Baum, J.D., Dominica, F. and Woodward, F. (eds), *Listen my Child has a lot of Living to do.* Oxford: Oxford University Press, 3–5.

Fitzpatrick, R. (1991): Society and Changing Patterns of Disease. In Scambler, G. (ed.), *Sociology as Applied to Medicine.* London: Ballière Tindall, 3–17.

Freidson, E. (1970): *Profession of Medicine.* New York: Dodd, Mead and Company.

Goldman, A. and Baum ,D. (1994): Provision of Care. In Goldman, A. (ed.), *Care of the Dying Child.* Oxford: Oxford Medical Publications, 107–14.

Hall, D.M.B. (1996): *Health for all Children,* 3rd edn. Oxford: Oxford University Press.

Hannay, D.R. (1979): *The Symptom Iceberg: a Study of Community Health.* London: Routledge and Kegan Paul.

Heggarty, H. (1994): Good Beginnings. In Hill, L. (ed.), *Caring for Dying Children and their Families.* London: Chapman and Hall, 1–15.

Leathard, A. (1991): *Health Care Provision: Past Present and Future.* London: Chapman and Hall.

Lessing, D. and Tatman, M.A. (1991): Paediatric Home Care in the 1990s. *Archives of Disease in Childhood* **66**, 994–996.

Mikkelson, J. (1993): Sibling Care. In Glasper, E.A. and Tucker, A. (eds), *Advances in Child Health Nursing.* Harrow: Scutari Press, 141–53.

Parsons, T. (1951): *The Social System.* Glencoe, IL: Free Press.

Phillips, T. (1994): The Professions Working Together; Learning to Collaborate. In Lindsay, B. (ed.), *The Child and Family: Contemporary Nursing Issues in Child Health and Care.* London: Ballière Tindall, 160–73.

Robertson, J. and Robertson, J. (1989): *Separation and the very Young.* London: Free Association Press.

Stacey, M. (1988): *The Sociology of Health and Healing.* London: Routledge.

Stein, A. and Wooley, H. (1990): An Evaluation of Hospice Care. In Baum, J.D., Dominica, F. and Woodward, F. (eds), *Listen my Child has a lot of Living to do.* Oxford: Oxford University Press, 66–90.

Waterworth, S. (1992): Long-term Effects of Cancer on Children and their Families. *British Journal of Nursing* **1**, 373–77.

Wuest, J. and Stern, P. (1990): The Impact of Fluctuating Relationships with the Canadian Health Care System on Family Management of Otitis Media with Effusion. *Journal of Advanced Nursing* **15**, 556–63.

Further reading

Baum, J.D. , Dominica, F. Sr and Woodward, R.N. (1990): *Listen my Child has a lot of Living to do.* Oxford: Oxford University Press.

Belson, P. (1993): Children in Hospital. *Children and Society* **7**, 196–210.

Cowley, S. (1993): Collaboration in Health Care: the Education Link. *Health Visitor Journal* **67**, 13–17.

Department of Health and Social Security (1959): *The Welfare of Children in Hospital. The Platt Report.* London: HMSO.

Goldman, A. (1994): *Care of the Dying Child.* Oxford: Oxford Medical Publications.

Hill, L. (ed.) (1994): *Caring for Dying Children and their Families.* London: Chapman and Hall.

McFadyen, A. (1994): *Special-care Babies and their Developing Relationships.* London: Routledge.

Phillips, T. (1994): The Professions Working Together; Learning to Collaborate. In Lindsay, B. (ed.), *The Child and Family: Contemporary Nursing Issues in Child Health and Care.* London: Ballière Tindall, 160–73.

Stewart, A. and Dent, A. (1994): *At a Loss. Bereavement Care when a Baby Dies.* London: Ballière Tindall.

Children in developing countries

Jayne Taylor

This chapter aims to:

- explore the experiences of children in developing countries using the declaration of the Rights of the Child as a framework;
- focus upon the holistic needs of children in developing countries with particular emphasis on life expectancy and health, education and wealth;
- examine ways in which international aid is focused in the developing world.

Introduction

All children have rights: the right to protection, to education, to food and medical care, and to much more. Every child, no matter where he or she lives, has the right to grow up feeling safe and cared for: a simple thought, which few would openly challenge. But, sadly, the reality is quite different.

(Audrey Hepburn, In United Nations International
Children's Emergency Fund, 1989)

In 1959 the United Nations made a declaration of the Rights of the Child – a set of 10 principles which apply to *all* children, regardless of where they live, their race, colour, sex or religion. These principles are still as relevant and necessary in the 1990s as they were when they were first written. The world has changed during this time, and the lives of millions of children throughout the world have been affected by change in some way. However, perfection is still a long way ahead.

The inclusion of this chapter on the lives of children in developing countries is justified on two grounds. First, it adds a truly international perspective to the study of early childhood, and enables the reader to gain some insight into the everyday existence of those children who live in less developed parts of the world. Secondly, it perhaps allows the reader to reflect on the relativity of disadvantage which has been referred to throughout the rest of the book.

This does not mean to say that we in any way condone the despair, neglect and poverty in which some children exist in this country. Rather, we wish to put this existence into a context. Those of us who are concerned with and have an interest in children during their early years are moved by the plight of disadvantaged children wherever they live, regardless of their religious affiliation, ethnicity, culture or creed. We recognise that children have rights such as those set out in the declaration of the Rights of the Child, and we recognise that children are special.

This chapter explores the lives of children in the less developed world from an holistic perspective, with the ultimate aim of enabling the reader to develop a broader view of those early years.

Definitions

It is important that we begin by clarifying what we mean by the developing countries, before we can explore more fully the lives of children who live there. At one time the term the *Third World* was used synonymously with the developing world, with countries being classified according to their economic or 'civilised' level as being first, second, third or fourth. Countries such as the UK, most of Europe, the USA and Australia were included in the First World category, the former Eastern Bloc countries were defined within the Second World category, the Third World category included countries within Southern Asia, South America and Africa, and the Fourth World category included specific tribal peoples such as the African Bushmen, the Australian Aborigines and the South American Indians.

Clearly, however, there were problems in utilising such broad categories. In the first place, the terms first, second, third and fourth imply some hierarchical classification, suggesting that first is 'better' than second, second is 'better' than third, and so on. Secondly, critics also argued that the terminology was essentially ethnocentric, and did not acknowledge that because something is inherently different this does not make it better or worse.

The World Health Organisation and the World Bank choose to classify countries according to the gross national product (GNP) per capita (the total wealth of a country divided by its population) as an indication of social and economic development. Countries are categorised as low-income economies, middle-income economies or high-income economies. However, there are also weaknesses within this system. First of all, the GNP is not a sensitive measure in cultures where goods and services are exchanged without financial accreditation. Secondly, the GNP does not account for depreciation of resources. If a country undertakes to sell its natural resources, its GNP will rise in the short term, but the real wealth of a country is gradually reduced rather than increased. Finally, the GNP does not give an indication as to how a country spends its wealth, e.g. in terms of the provision of health, education and welfare, particularly for children. Gray (1993) reports that in some low-economy countries, for example, spending on militia exceeds spending on health and education.

The term *developing countries* is therefore a preferable terminology, particularly when considered alongside the United Nations development measure referred to as the Human Development Index (United Nations, 1991), which accounts for life expectancy, education and wealth. However, the words 'developing' and 'development' do also suggest a hierarchy and imply that something is not yet fully formed and will eventually develop. Inadvertently it also suggests that being fully developed is a wholly desirable attribute, and yet we are aware from the readings throughout this text that not all children who live in a developed world experience the ideal. Poverty, ill health and cruelty exist for children in the UK and other western 'developed' countries, and their lives are far from ideal. It is also true to say that some children residing in the developing world have lives that are enriched by cultures and pleasures which children in the West will never be fortunate enough to experience.

As we have mentioned above, we prefer the term 'developing countries' when considered along with the Human Development Index which will form the framework for the rest of the discussion within this chapter. However, we do acknowledge that this is not an ideal classification system which universally reflects the reality of growing up and living in different parts of the world.

The health of children

The Rights of the Child – Principle 4

> *The child shall enjoy the benefits of social security. He shall be entitled to grow and develop in health; to this end special care and protection shall be provided both to him and to his mother, including adequate pre-natal and post-natal care. The child shall have the right to adequate nutrition, housing, recreation and medical services.*

Throughout this text we have discussed the need to take an holistic perspective when considering children during the early years. This approach is also adopted by the United Nations in its Human Development Index in recognition that it is the tripartite combination of life expectancy, education and wealth that contributes to our experiences of life. In many respects these three components are interwoven, and certainly each will influence the other two. However, for the purposes of clarity we shall discuss each in turn before considering the overall picture at the end of the chapter. We shall therefore commence our discussion by looking at life expectancy and health in relation to children in developing countries.

It is interesting to reflect for a moment on the major causes of death among populations within the developed world, and to make comparisons with the developing world. In developed countries the major causes of death are circulatory and degenerative diseases, followed by cancers. Many of these causes are attributable either directly or indirectly to life-style, e.g. diet, smoking, lack of exercise, alcohol. In the developing world the picture has historically been very different, with the major causes of death being infectious and parasitic diseases (Lopez, 1993). Indeed, it is a similar scenario to that which existed in the UK during the last century, although the causal organisms are different (see also Chapters 5 and 8). However, there are evident changes in terms of mortality in developing countries, with HIV- and AIDS-related deaths affecting both the child and adult populations of many countries, particularly in Africa (Peer, 1993). Smoking-related deaths are also likely to increase over the next few decades due to a rise in tobacco use.

In terms of child mortality, approximately 250 000 children die in the developing world each week (Child-to-Child Trust, 1993). Six million children die each year from the effects of measles, pertussis, tetanus and malaria. Other major causes of child mortality in developing countries are diarrhoea and starvation (approximately 8 million children die each year from these two causes). These and other diseases lead to marked differences between developed and developing countries in terms of life expectancy at birth and infant mortality rates (the numbers of deaths in the first year of life per 1000 live births).

Life expectancy

Life expectancy is a useful indicator, although the lack of data generated within some countries in relation to death registrations does lead to some doubt as to its usefulness as an entirely reliable indicator. What is evident from basic indicators is that a child born in 1992 in Japan, which currently leads the world league tables, has a life expectancy of 79 years, which is almost double that of a child born in Uganda (life expectancy 42 years – the world's lowest). Life expectancy at birth in the UK for the same year was 76 years.

However, there are a number of factors which may influence life expectancy at birth which will be discussed later in this chapter. For example, war, drought and crop failure can have a marked impact on statistics such as those mentioned above.

Infant mortality

The infant mortality rate (IMR) is one of the most reliable indicators of the health of a country because it is relatively easy to measure, even in countries without sophisticated registration systems, by asking appropriate samples of the adult population about the numbers of children born live who have sub-sequently died. There is also a positive correlation between infant mortality and adult mortality . What the infant mortality rate for a country cannot do is give an indication about variations within countries at a given point in time – it will only allow for comparisons to be made between countries and within countries *over* time. However, these are both useful comparisons, particularly the latter, which is a good indicator of progression. For example, Niger currently has the highest infant mortality rate, of 191 per 1000 live births. This IMR is the same as it was 30 years ago, whereas Mali, which had the highest IMR 30 years ago now has an IMR of 122 and has fallen to tenth in the global infant mortality tables (i.e. still high, but nevertheless improved).

Infant mortality rates are attributable to similar causes to those mentioned above in relation to child mortality. However, there are other factors which lead to early childhood deaths which are less significant during later child-hood. These factors are generally associated with the perinatal period. For example, it is estimated that moderate to severe birth asphyxia will affect nearly 4 million infants each year (Costello, 1994), and almost 25 per cent of these children will die as a result. The reasons for birth asphyxia are many, and include factors associated with maternal health prior to birth, such as having many children, heavy work and poor maternal nutrition, intrapartum factors such as maternal haemorrhage and cord prolapse, and postnatal factors such as hypothermia which, even in hot climates, is exacerbated by washing but not drying babies after birth. Sadly, many of these deaths could be prevented if mothers and their babies in developing countries had access to trained personnel and incubators, and if the hazards of some traditional practices, such as rubbing babies with mustard oil and not breast-feeding for the first 3 days of life, were avoided. However, effectively conveying such messages to relatively isolated people is extremely difficult, particularly in countries where illiteracy is common among women. Traditional practices frequently have cultural or religious significance, and prevention of such practices requires a consistent and innovative approach to health promotion. The difficulties are compounded by the fact that many mothers may be unable to access medical services, or deliberately choose not to access such services because of a misconception that medicine and hospitals are for the ill. They are therefore not an entirely accessible population. Given all of these difficul-ties, there *are* examples of cases where whole communities have taken acc-ount of such issues. Quezon City, in the Philippines, campaigned to become the 'first mother-baby friendly city', and mobilised the entire community – government, health professionals, women and men – towards positive part-nerships in child bearing.

A further issue which is also of great importance in relation to infant mortality is son preference. The extent to which this contributes to infant mor-tality is unknown, as governments are clearly unwilling (or unable) to publi-cise selective abortion rates for female fetuses, or the extent to which female infanticide is practised. In 1995 and 1996 the broadcasting on television of *The Dying Rooms* documentaries brought this hidden problem vividly to the forefront of UK society by focusing on the abandonment and killing of female children in China, as a result of the 'one child only policy', combined with the traditional view of a patriarchal society which values male children more highly than female children. Many female children are apparently placed in understaffed orphanages where they spend their short lives physically restrained, without affection, play or education. This clearly contravenes the declaration of the Rights of the Child.

The Rights of the Child – Principle 2

The child shall enjoy special protection, and shall be given opportunities and facilities, by law and by other means, to enable him to develop physically, mentally, morally, spiritually and socially in a healthy and normal manner and in conditions of freedom and dignity. In the enactment of laws for this purpose the best interests of the child shall be of paramount consideration.

Child morbidity

Where child mortality is attributed to particular causes, it is usually the cases that child morbidity can be attributed in a similar way. For example, diarrhoea and malnourishment are significant causes of illness among children, as well as being major causes of mortality. Large-scale education about the benefits of oral rehydration (which re-establishes the body's fluid and electrolyte balance) has taken place in the developing world, and such treatment is both cheap and easy to administer. However, many children continue either to die or to be severely affected by diarrhoea, often because of the underlying disease, or because they do not receive adequate help.

Another cheap and easily administered measure which can prevent acute enteritis and other childhood mortality and morbidity is to discourage bottle-feeding in favour of breast-feeding (United Nations International Children's Emergency Fund, 1990). Kelly (1993) discusses the evidence from Iraq and Africa which suggests that breast-fed children, even when their mothers may be malnourished themselves, had less diarrhoea-related illness than bottle-fed babies. However, the bottle-feeding industry is large and commercially lucrative, and Palmer (1987, 1994) and Baby Milk Action (1993) suggest that the baby milk industry continues to discourage breast-feeding through the advertising (both covert and overt) of their products.

HIV- and AIDS-related illnesses also affect many, many children, although it is possible that the preliminary estimates made at the start of the pandemic in the 1980s – that half a million people would die of AIDS in Africa each year by the year 2000 – now seem unlikely. That is not to say that HIV and AIDS are not important issues in the developing world, as clearly they are significant for a number of reasons. First, there are many children who are HIV-positive, who have had the virus transmitted to them either vertically (from mother to baby *in utero* or during birth), from contaminated blood products, from infected needles, through sexual contact or via breast milk. Diarrhoea is a predominant symptom and death occurs rapidly, often because of prevailing social conditions. Secondly, children are affected when their parents or carers are HIV-positive or become ill with or die of AIDS-related disease. The stigma associated with HIV and AIDS is as apparent in the developing world, as it is in the developed world and many children suffer because they are associated with the disease – even though they themselves may not be HIV-positive. Thirdly, the HIV/AIDS issue has had a further 'knock-on' effect which is affecting children in developing countries, as scarce research funding into killer diseases such as malaria has been diverted to AIDS prevention.

Other significant causes of child morbidity can be attributed to perinatal factors. We mentioned in the previous section that nearly a million children die of birth asphyxia each year. There are also over 3 million children who survive but are disabled by epilepsy, mental retardation, cerebral palsy and learning difficulties (Costello, 1994). These children clearly require special health care and education as set out in the declaration of the Rights of the Child.

The Rights of the Child – Principle 5

The child who is physically, mentally of socially handicapped shall be given the special treatment, education and care required by his particular condition.

Traditionally, however, children with such handicaps have been placed in large institutions in urban areas, which are a consequence of colonial influence, with the British system of providing care for these children being transposed to different areas of the world, regardless of their relevance to local culture (Serpell and Nabuzoka, 1991). Such institutions served only to isolate these children from their families and their culture, and whilst their health and development may have been optimised, it was virtually impossible for them ever to be integrated back into their own societies in later years. The current view is that children should be provided with home-based care by utilising a system of people who can provide intervention. If possible, there should be a family member who, with professional support, education and back-up, can provide therapy. Some developing countries have introduced a tier of workers (front-line workers) who operate between the professionals and the family. Other countries aim to provide day-care with specialist input, with the children being enabled to remain with their families for the rest of the time (Serpell and Nabuzoka, 1991). This philosophy is in line with the declaration of the Rights of the Child.

The Rights of the Child – Principle 6

The child, for the full and harmonious development of his personality, needs love and understanding. He shall, wherever possible, grow up in the care and under the responsibility of his parents, and in any case in an atmosphere of affection and of moral and material security; a child of tender years shall not, save in exceptional circumstances, be separated from his mother. Society and public authorities shall have the duty to extend particular care to children without a family and those without adequate means of support. Payment of state and other assistance towards the maintenance of children of large families is desirable.

Even diseases which are relatively minor in developed countries, or which have been eradicated, carry high mortality and morbidity in developing countries. One example of such a disease is measles, which it should theoretically be possible to eradicate, or at least effectively to control, if total immunisation could be achieved. Unfortunately, despite large-scale vaccination programmes (Bloom, 1990), we are a long way from achieving this objective. Child morbidity in developing countries, including measles, is heavily influenced by a number of factors which, if overcome, could have a significant impact upon the health of children. These include:

- poor sanitation and water supply;
- lack of education about control and spread of disease;
- overcrowded housing/large families;
- deficient health care systems;
- environmental conditions;
- lack of immunisation policies;
- poverty;
- war;
- national debt;
- bottle-feeding (rather than breast-feeding);
- malnutrition.

Improving, maintaining and promoting the health of children in the developing world is a complex and difficult problem which is hampered by many factors. However, improvements have been and continue to be made. Methods of health intervention and promotion are at last being adapted that are suitable and appropriate for the cultures which they aim to support. This has happened because objective systems of evaluation have been set up, which are the key to success. We can only hope that the days of building large urban institutions for children with severe learning disabilities, or of imposing westernised, didactic health promotion campaigns, or of donating incubators for babies which are unsuitable for the climate and cannot be mended when they break down, are over.

The education of children

The Rights of the Child – Principle 7

The child is entitled to receive education, which shall be free and compulsory, at least in the elementary stages. He shall be given an education which will promote his general culture, and enable him on a basis of equal opportunity to develop his abilities, his individual judgement, and his sense of moral and social responsibility, and to become a useful member of society. The best interests of the child shall be the guiding principle of those responsible for his education and guidance; that responsibility lies in the first place with his parents. The child shall have full opportunity for play and recreation, which should be directed to the same purpose as education; society and the public authorities shall endeavour to promote the enjoyment of this right.

The *World Declaration on Education for All* was issued in 1990 by the United Nations International Children's Emergency Fund (UNICEF), and reiterates Principle 7 of the declaration of the Rights of the Child. As we mentioned earlier, it is extremely difficult to separate life expectancy, education and wealth, because each of these is dependent upon and influences the others. For example, with regard to health and life expectancy we have considered how a lack of education, particularly literacy, can affect health promotion. We have also discussed how children with severe learning disabilities were effectively removed from their own cultures and placed in urban institutions, thus depriving them of education which would promote their 'general culture'. Life expectancy, health and education are also influenced by the wealth of a country, or by the unequal distribution of wealth within a country, just as the wealth of a country will influence health care and education systems.

Education in the developing world aims to achieve similar outcomes to education in the developed world. Children require educational opportunities that will enable them to acquire the skills of literacy, numeracy, oral expression and problem-solving, as well as to develop skills, knowledge, values and attitudes appropriate to their culture. Education of children is also important for the future economy of developing countries. Being able to train professionals such as doctors, nurses, engineers and teachers enables a country to decrease its dependence on the developed world (Peer, 1993), and can help to increase the quality of life of individuals and families.

However, there are still many children in the developing world who are deprived of education, or who receive only a limited education for a short period of time. The United Nations International Children's Emergency Fund (UNICEF) compared literacy rates between the developing world and the developed world, and found that in the developed world literacy rates are almost 100 per cent, in Latin America the rate is approximately 75 per cent, in

Asia it is about 25 per cent (UNICEF, 1993). There is also a marked gender difference in illeteracy rates, with 66 per cent of the illiterate people being female. Whilst looking at literacy rates does give a 'snapshot' view of a particular country, it does not provide detailed information about the education systems within countries, or about the levels of education within those systems. Literacy, whilst clearly being very important, is only one outcome measure, and there are many more. It is also possible that many children who *do* receive education remain illiterate because the quality of education is so poor. Other children remain illiterate because they *do not* receive education in any form.

The United Nations Education, Scientific and Cultural Organisation (UNESCO) was set up with the aim of restoring education systems following the Second World War. It now operates in partnership with governments to enable them to put educational policies into practice, including the provision of education for adults as well as for children. A great deal of progress has been made where governments are committed to education in terms of providing primary education (UNESCO, 1991; Peer, 1993). However, in very poor countries this may mean very large classes of children (Barker, 1994) and severely restricted learning and teaching resources, making teaching very difficult. In many countries there are gender differences in the extent to which education is received. In Bangladesh, for example, about 60 per cent of children start school, but the majority are boys, who may only receive a couple of years of schooling in any case. UNESCO (1991) has identified that, despite improvements over two decades, there continues to be a need for good teachers and financial resources devoted to education. They also recognise the need for parents and local communities to be involved in decision-making about their children's education, so that they may feel an increased sense of commitment to education.

In other countries where the government is not committed to education, or where there is war, education provision can be non-existent for some children.

In some countries the education provision varies considerably, with certain children being excluded from the education system altogether. For example, there are over 30 million children world-wide, colloquially known as 'street children', who have been forced to live and work on the streets of large cities for a number of reasons (Independent Commission on International Humanitarian Issues, 1986). This growing urban tragedy is more prevalent in, but not solely confined to, developing countries. For example, in parts of South America, such as Brazil, Mexico and Colombia, the number of children who roam the streets of large cities is an ever present problem, with very young children being forced to work to live – some shining shoes or washing cars, whilst others turn to prostitution as a means of earning money. In some places these children are seen as being no more valuable than vermin, and are hunted down and murdered by adults wishing to clear them from the streets. They receive no formal education, and have often been 'written off' by the societies in which they live. The ICIHI report wrote of these children:

The street offers its children the spectacle of society without integration into its values; proximity, but not participation. It becomes symbolic of their distress. It replaces school, and has a very different syllabus. It belongs to everybody and nobody, and puts everyone on the same footing. It cancels out the past and makes the future uncertain: only the present moment counts.

(Independent Commission on International Humanitarian
Issues, 1986, p.37)

Clearly the experiences of these children are dire, and the increase in the numbers of such children is an embarrassment to many governments world-wide, particularly in the developed world. The fact that very young children should be forced to call the streets their home and work from a very early age is an appalling situation which is totally in conflict with the declaration of the Rights of the Child.

The Rights of the Child – Principle 9

The child shall be protected against all forms of neglect, cruelty and exploitation. He shall not be the subject of traffic, in any form. The child shall not be admitted to employment before an appropriate minimum age; he shall in no case be caused or permitted to engage in any employment which would prejudice his health or education, or interfere with his physical, mental or moral development.

However, the situation is not, entirely negative for street children and other children in developing countries. A variety of projects world-wide are improving education for children – some under the auspices of UNESCO and others independent of them. One example of such a project is the 'Bosconia/ La Florida counselling project' which aims to contact street children and gradually build relationships with them, and teach them primarily to want to learn (Independent Commission on International Humanitarian Issues, 1986). Another example is provided by the Bangladesh Rural Advancement Committee (BRAC)-supported schools, which are funded by a number of donors, including the World Bank and the Canadian Government (Barker, 1994). Many BRAC-supported schools are targeted mainly at girls, and aim to improve literacy among the female population of Bangladesh. Unfortunately, difficulties with regard to attendance persist, particularly in rural communities at busy times of the year such as planting and harvest, and the schools tend to close down during these periods.

Wealth

The final measure accounted for by the Human Development Index (United Nations, 1991), referred to at the beginning of this chapter, is wealth. We mentioned previously some of the difficulties in considering wealth in that measures such as the GNP do not account for how a country spends its wealth, or the extent to which countries are using, selling or destroying a country's natural resources. However, there are very great differences in the living standards of people, including children, in different countries, and large-scale poverty is evident in the developing world, associated with hunger and mass misery.

In 1980 the Brandt report (Brandt, 1980) highlighted many of these issues and claimed that change must take place if 'mankind wants to survive'. The report made recommendations to improve poverty within the developing world, including:

- emergency programmes for the poorest countries;
- an end to mass hunger;
- support for family planning programmes;
- the channelling of funding formerly for weapons to more peaceful ends;
- the more efficient use of an individual country's commodities to increase earnings;
- an increase in overseas aid;
- the introduction of an international income tax to divert monies from the richest to the poorest countries;
- reform of the international monetary system;
- the setting up of a World Development Fund to distribute resources raised;
- educating public opinion about international co-operation.

One of the key areas addressed within the report was the North-South divide, with the richest countries being located in the northern hemisphere and the poorest in the southern hemisphere. The difficulties experienced within the poorer countries are often compounded by political instability and war, land which is unsuitable for growing essential crops, and massive debt.

Political instability and war

Political instability and war have many effects on civilians, including children. Not only does the infrastructure of a country stagnate, but it is also often destroyed. For example, the war in Somalia caused mass starvation, large cities such as Mogadishu were reduced to rubble, and for months on end electricity and water supplies were non-existent. Many children died of starvation or were injured or killed during the fighting. Others died because of disease associated with poor sanitation, and many more were orphaned and left Somalia as refugees. The problem with this and other conflicts, including more recently that in Rwanda, where large-scale 'ethnic cleansing' took place, is that when peace is restored, the difficulties of reuniting the many children who have been separated from their families are immense and often insurmountable. In many cases children are denied not only a nationality of their own but also even a name of their own, and are subject to racial discrimination. This contravenes the declaration of the Rights of the Child.

The Rights of the Child – Principle 3

The child shall be entitled from his birth to a name and nationality.

The Rights of the Child – Principle 10

The child shall be protected from practices which may foster racial, religious and any other form of discrimination. He shall be brought up in a spirit of understanding, tolerance, friendship among people, peace and universal brotherhood and in full consciousness that his energy and talents should be devoted to the service of his fellow men.

War also brings less obvious challenges. Whilst children are frequently denied education during times of war, the existing professionals within a country are also denied education. For example, Swinburne (1994) described the situation of health professionals in Sarajevo during the conflict there, and discussed the academic stagnation and difficulty in keeping up to date with developments.

The lack of advancement as a result of war has many detrimental effects on children (and adults), and whilst we have seen many examples of how developed countries have come to the aid of individual children in order to overcome the deficits of, for instance, medical technology as a result of war, there are many, many more children who do not receive such aid.

Developed countries, usually in collaboration with UNICEF and international charities such as the Red Cross, aim to provide assistance to civilians caught up in war. However, the problems faced by foreign workers in developing countries during times of war are enormous (Gates, 1993). For example, the equipment they are used to dealing with in the developed world, which might be available in the field, is difficult to operate within war zones where electricity supplies may be unreliable or lacking. The types of wounds which health professionals encounter may also be unlike any that they have experienced before (Kerr and Volpe, 1993).

Food and hunger

Developing countries are seldom self-sufficient in terms of their food production for several reasons. First, they tend to be politically unstable, with unstructured agricultural policies. Secondly, the populations of these countries tend to exceed the capacity of farmers to grow sufficient crops. Thirdly, the land is frequently poor and only amenable to the growth of limited crops. Fourthly, the international commodities markets are often working against the individual farmer in developing countries. Finally, ecological changes within the world are resulting in seemingly natural disasters and crop failures which can in part be attributed to environmental damage caused within the country or as a consequence of practices in other countries.

At present only 11 per cent of the world's surface is farmed for crops, while a further 20 per cent is apparently cultivable. The development of new, high-yielding strains of wheat, corn and rice, and the development of fertilisers, herbicides, pesticides and irrigation techniques have contributed to what is known in the developed world as the *Green Revolution* – and bumper harvests have been the result. However, current methods of modern farming are not without problems. The chemicals needed to produce high-yield crops are derived from fossil fuels, mechanised farming also depletes energy resources, and the spraying of crops with pesticides can pollute both the atmosphere and the water supply.

There are differences in the types of crops which can be successfully grown in different parts of the world. In many parts of the developing world, environmental variation is such that there tends to be an over-reliance on single crops. If the main crop fails, the results are catastrophic in terms of human life and the country's economic infrastructure. A further problem arises when a country relies on a single crop and overproduces, which forces down the price of the commodity on the world market.

The distribution of the world's food supply has given rise to some speculation in recent years. If the global harvest was to be shared out, there would easily be enough food to feed everyone. Famines are the result of complexities relating to politics, economics, war and problems of storage and distribution. One short-term response to starvation in the developing world is to transport stockpiled surplus food to the places where it is needed most. In the long term, however, this does nothing to help farming in developing countries. Pouring surplus cheap and free food into developing countries lowers food prices, and can lead to less food being grown locally as it becomes financially non-viable to continue to farm. Except in emergency situations, the general view is that the most successful strategy involves enabling the development of appropriate technology, transportation systems, education programmes and administration systems.

The problems of mass starvation were vividly brought to the attention of the developed world in the 1980s by 'Band Aid' and the work of Bob Geldof, who was moved to action after seeing a news report about starvation in Ethiopia in 1984. Geldof visited Ethiopia and, on his return, organised 'Band Aid' – a massive musical extravaganza and other projects which raised millions of pounds for Africa. The importance of the aid to Africa was that it was channelled into projects which aimed to solve the longer-term problems of feeding vast populations, rather than just dumping excess food from the developed world.

Following Geldof's success, the General Agreement on Tariffs and Trade (GATT) drew up Article XXXVI, which attempted to discriminate positively in favour of developing countries in terms of export, access to world markets, financial support, and the elimination of barriers and custom duties, as well as introducing measures to stabilise world markets (General Agreement on Tariffs and Trade, 1986). These longer-term policies can only benefit those in developing countries, but the compounding factors mentioned above will probably always mean that organisations such as UNICEF will need to provide emergency food aid to the developing world. When this need arises, the declaration of the Rights of the Child must be taken into consideration.

The Rights of the Child – Principle 8

The child shall in all circumstances be among the first to receive protection and relief.

Debt

Many developing countries struggle continually under huge foreign debt. They are forced to take drastic measures to repay both the debt and the resulting interest which accumulates on it (Jenkins, 1987), and consequently less money is available to solve the current problems within these countries, including education and child health.

There is international recognition of the fact that the cycle of debt in which some countries have found themselves must be broken, whether it be by the cancellation of debt or the re-scheduling of debt. There is also recognition of the fact that, to some extent, blame for the current financial situation can be laid at the door of developing countries, and as such they should take some responsibility for helping to resolve the problems. Glasman (1994) reports on projects which have shied away from the traditional 'top-down' approach to lending (i.e. to governments), in favour of 'directing loans to boost the informal economy of the poor'. This type of philosophy has long being advocated in a limited way with the 'barefoot bank' in Bangladesh, which lends small amounts of money for the purchase of basic equipment (Peer, 1993).

There is no easy answer to the debt problem in the developing world. Certainly the GATT Article XXXVI mentioned above may in the long term have some positive effects, but these will only be limited and cannot replace what is really required. It is perhaps ironic that it is often those developed countries who give the most in terms of free aid who have lent money to developing countries in the first place, and to whom debt is therefore owed. The question that springs to mind is whether, if the debt were to be cancelled, those developing countries would need foreign aid in the quantities currently required.

CONCLUSION

This chapter has focused upon three key elements of childhood experience, although there are clearly many others that are vitally important. Many children growing up in the developing world suffer disadvantage in the form of poverty, poor health and limited educational opportunities, and many never reach adulthood.

However, there is hope for children in the developing world, and it does give us at least some satisfaction to know that there is international recognition that investment in today's children will bring benefits to tomorrow's societies, although it is important to realise that 'the creation of a supportive, social, economic, and physical environment . . . requires vision and political will' (Levin, 1989, p.153). Policies aimed at helping children in the developing world must be culturally sensitive and appropriate, consistently carried out, child friendly and above all they must be evaluated fully in order to provide evidence of their efficacy.

The declaration of the Rights of the Child outlines the principles which should be afforded to all children. We have referred to nine of the 10 principles throughout this chapter, and conclude with the first principle,

The Rights of the Child – Principle 1

The child shall enjoy all the rights set forth in this Declaration. All children, without any exception whatsoever, shall be entitled to these rights, without distinction or discrimination on account of race, colour, sex, language, religion, political or other opinion, national or social origin, property, birth or other status, whether of himself or of his family.

References

Baby Milk Action (1993): *It's Not Just 'Over There'*. Update 12:2. Cambridge: Baby Milk Action.

Barker, A. (1994): *Bangladesh*. Oxford: Heinemann.

Bloom, B.R. (1990): Vaccines for the Third World. *World Health* **June/July/August**, 13–5.

Brandt, W. (1980): *North–South: a Programme for Survival*. London: Pan.

Child-to-Child Trust (1993): *Children for Health*. London: Child-to-child Trust in Association with UNICEF.

Costello, A.M. De L. (1994): *Perinatal Asphyxia in less Developed Countries*. Paper Presented at Symposium at Queen Charlotte's Hospital, London, March 21 1994.

Gates, E. (1993): Nursing Under Fire. *Nursing Times* **89**, 26–7.

General Agreement on Tariffs and Trade (GATT) (1986): *Trade and Development Article XXXVI*. Geneva: GATT.

Glasman, D. (1994): Spending Power to the People. *The Guardian* **April 27**, 15.

Gray, A. (1993): *World Health and Disease*. Milton Keynes: Open University Press.

Independent Commission on International Humanitarian Issues (1986): *Street Children: a Growing Urban Tragedy. Report for the Independent Commission on International Humanitarian Issues*. London: Weidenfeld and Nicolson.

Jenkins, J. (1987): *Contemporary Moral Issues*. Oxford: Heinemann Educational.

Kelly, M. (1993): Infant Feeding in Emergencies. *Disasters* **17**, 111–21.

Kerr, A. and Volpe, G. (1993): Theatre of War. *Nursing Times* **89**, 28–30.

Levin, L.S. (1989): Health for Today's Youth, Hope for Tomorrow's World. *World Health Forum* **10**, 151–7.

Lopez, A.D. (1993): Causes of Death in the Industrialised and the Developing Countries. In Jamieson, D.T. and Moseley, H. (eds), *Disease Control Priorities in Developing Countries*. New York: Oxford University Press.

Palmer, G. (1990): *Politics of Breast-feeding*. London: Pandora.

Palmer, G. (1994): *The Politics of Breast-feeding*. Paper Presented at Symposium at Queen Charlotte's Hospital, London, 21 March 1994.

Peer, C. (1993): *Examining Global Issues*. Oxford: Heinemann.

Serpell, R. and Nabuzoka, D. (1991): Early Intervention in Third World countries. In Mitchell, D. and Brown, R. (eds), *Early Intervention Studies for Young Children with Special Needs*. London: Chapman and Hall, 93–126.

Swinburne, C. (1994): War Babies. *Nursing Times* **90**, 23.

United Nations (1959): *Universal Declaration of the Rights of the Child*. New York: United Nations.

United Nations (1991): *United Nations Development Programme*. Human Development Report. Oxford: Oxford University Press.

United Nations Educational, Scientific and Cultural Organization (1991): *World Education Report*. Paris: UNESCO.

United Nations International Children's Emergency Fund (1989): Foreword. In *For every child*. London: Hutchinson.

United Nations International Children's Emergency Fund (1990): *World Declaration on Education for All*. New York: UNICEF.

United Nations International Children's Emergency Fund (1993): *State of the World's Children*. New York: UNICEF.

14 Perspectives on early childhood research

Jayne Taylor

This chapter aims to:

- explore the value of research to the early years professional;
- discuss methodological issues in early years research;
- examine ethical considerations involved in undertaking research using child subjects.

Introduction

Imagine two staff nurses watching two women enter a children's ward. Both women are of a similar age and appearance. One is dressed in casual attire, whist the other is wearing a smart business suit. Each women holds a suitcase and the hand of a small boy. Both boys are about to be admitted to hospital. One of them, when passing the open door of the playroom, looks up at his mother, and on receiving her assent he runs to join the children who are playing there. His mother smiles and continues to walk towards the nurses. The other boy clutches his mother's hand very tightly and starts to cry very softly.

One of the nurses tuns to the other:

Nurse 1: I wonder why two seemingly similar children in a similar situation react so differently.

Nurse 2: There could be a hundred and one reasons.

Nurse 1: Yes, but if we could find out why, we could help little chaps like this one – he's so frightened. Imagine the ward full of happy, playing kids!

Nurse 2: Bliss!

Similar scenes are undoubtedly played out in nurseries, playgroups, schools, hospitals and crèches each time a group of new children arrives on the scene. The individual difference as well as the similarities which exist between children have both puzzled and fascinated professionals, and given them the motivation and material to enable them to delve into the complex world of the child through research. Many answers to countless questions have been discovered through investigation, but many questions remain unanswered, and indeed always will. Children change as society progresses, and they need to develop new behaviours in order to adapt to a complex and demanding world. There will always be questions which can be addressed through research, and as answers to existing questions are found, new and different questions will emerge.

We have included this chapter within the book for two main reasons. First, we wish to present a text that will support the training of early years professionals, and research awareness, at the very least, is an expectation of most if not all training programmes. Secondly, we have included this chapter because, as a writing team, we are firmly committed to the notion of research as a valuable asset in the advancement of practice. Early years professionals should be able to use other people's research intelligently by developing their own critical reading skills and, where necessary, undertake research themselves. They should work from an established knowledge base which they understand, and seek to advance knowledge and theory through research.

The chapter begins by exploring the value of research to practice, and then moves on to examine different approaches and methodologies which have specific relevance to the study of children. We shall also focus on the ethical implications of undertaking research which involves children, with particular reference to early years professionals working within health settings. However, we must emphasise that we cannot cover all aspects of research methodology within the scope of one chapter. There are many excellent books which do this, and we have included a selection in the further reading section at the end of the chapter.

The value of research in the early years

In Chapter 1 we discussed why the study of early childhood is important, with reference to its value as an emerging discipline in its own right, and also to the need for professionals to be able to map the childhood/adulthood continuum and explore the influence of children of childhood experience on adult behaviour.

Throughout the other chapters in this volume we have referred to work of researchers who have undertaken research for both purposes, although clearly there are fewer works which follow the progress of children into adulthood, because of the methodological challenges such an approach entails. It is because of the contributions of all of these researchers that we have the body of knowledge relating to the early years which exists today.

Drawing upon previous research serves a number of purposes. It can, for example, enable the investigation of a particular problem through the study of literature and lead to greater understanding of a particular phenomenon, which can in turn lead to changes in and advancement of practice. It can also predicate further empirical study of a particular area by informing the future researcher of existing work, tried and tested methodologies, and the problems, pitfalls and potential limitations of a specific approach. Existing research can enable researchers to replicate and approach in a similar or different setting, but can also inform them so that they do not unnecessarily undertake work which has already been done. Studying previous research in a particular area is almost always prerequisite of future research-based activity. We shall explore this in more detail.

Using existing knowledge to inform practice

Look again at the vignette presented at the beginning of this chapter. The first nurse is making an assumption that the two children are *similar*. They may indeed be of a similar age and be similar in their looks. What the nurse does not know, however, at this stage is that the 'happy' child has been into hospital before, although never to this particular ward. His mother has spent a great deal of time preparing him for this admission, including borrowing books about hospitals from the library and engaging the help of the child's nursery-school teacher. At nursery all of the children in the little boy's class have been investigating hospitals and have built a small toy ward. They have a nurse's uniform and a doctor's coat. The little boy's experience of being a patient has been utilised to the full, and he has been able to impress friends with his superior knowledge! His mother also brought him to the 'Saturday Club' held at the hospital the previous week. This club is for all pending admissions, so that the children and parents have the opportunity to become familiar with the environment and some of the equipment. The little boy had taken a ride on a trolley which was made to look like Thomas the Tank Engine, and had listened to his own heartbeat via a stethoscope. The other little boy had done none of these things, and was only told he was to be admitted to hospital the day before.

The nurse is also making assumptions about the mothers of these two children. The mother of the happy child feels comfotable in the hospital setting. She is familiar with the environment, hospital routines and procedures. The suitcase she carries contains her belongings as well as those of her child because she will be staying in hosptial with her son throughout his admission. The case also contains what she describes as her 'hospital survival kit', consisting of magazines, a good book, some ear-plugs, chocolate, orange juice, coffee and a comfortable tracksuit.

The mother of the unhappy child, by contrast, feels very uncomfortable. Her only experience of hospital, other than when she gave birth to her son, was as a small child. Her memories are unhappy – separation from her parents, pain, being in a ward with very elderly ladies, smells, unpleasant noises, and someone dying. Her childhood ordeal has given her a persistent fear of hospitals, and she has avoided telling her son about his admission for as long as possible because she knows she cannot cope with his questions. She is not going to stay overnight with him, although she knows she ought to do so. The guilt that she feels about this is making her even more tense. All she wants to do is hand her son over to the nurse as quickly as possible and leave.

The second nurse was right – there are potentially a 'hundred and one' reasons why these children behave differently. However, by talking to both mothers and visiting the library, the nurses will identify the most likely reasons for the differences in behaviour. They can narrow down the reasons for the differences by studying and understanding previous research. They may, for example, find the following.

- Mothers who have had negative experiences of hospital as children are less likely to visit or stay with their children than non-fearful mothers. The fear of mothers is more likely to lead to stressful reactions in the child (see Muller *et al.*, 1992). The fearful mothers tend to be reluctant to have contact with hospital staff.
- Encouraging a mother (or parent) to stay with a child during hospitalisation reduces the social discontinuity between hospital and home which can distress young children (Miron, 1990).
- Preparation for the experiences of hospital can help young children to cope and reduce stress (see Smith, 1996). Preparation should involve parents (Rodin, 1983) and nurseries and playgroups, etc. (Jolly, 1981). The use of leaflets and books is an excellent way of introducing children to hospitals in a non-threatening manner (Carter, 1988).
- Pre-admission visits to the hospital can also reduce anxiety in children during hospitalisation (Marriner, 1988: Kiely, 1989). Using play as a way of introducing some of the equipment that children will encounter can be extremely beneficial (Crocker, 1980: Smallwood, 1988).

As a result of reading about previous research in this area, it may be possible to change practice so that mothers such as the mother of the unhappy child can be helped in positive ways to cope with their fears.

Using research to inform practice is the first (and an essential) step towards making progress, and as professionals we should strive to ensure that each and every part of our practice is informed by research. In the scenario described above, the nurses would have been able to find, through thorough and systematic searching of the literature, that there are research findings which can inform practice in this particular field.

Developing critical reading skills

The use of literature to inform practice is not entirely straightforward. Undertaking a literature review in itself can be complex, and involves library skills which take time to develop. Most of us only use libraries in a very superficial way, and it is only when we become familiar with a library that we can begin to use it to its full potential. In addition, the increasing use of databases, CD-ROM and the Internet have revolutionised our ability to access material quickly.

However, when material has been identified it may, in some fields, reveal conflicting views about certain topics. This is particularly so when the area being researched is new. You may recall, for example, the contrasting information which emerged during the early 1980s about the transmission of human immunodeficiency virus (HIV), which led to a certain amount of panic. It was only as more research was undertaken and reliable data emerged about the virus that some of the previous literature was shown to be incorrect.

It is important that early years professionals are able to make informed decisions about when research is reliable and valid, so that they do not make changes to practice on the basis of 'bad' research. There are clearly a number of ways of learning critical reading skills and there are many good books which can help (see the further reading section at the end of this chapter). There are also many professional training programmes which require students to undertake supervised research themselves, and whilst the value of this has been questioned (Department of Health, 1993), it is a good way of learning to understand the somewhat mystical language of research and developing skills which will help with critical reading. It is to research activity that we shall now turn.

Undertaking research with children

We have stated previously that this chapter is not intended to give a step-by-step guide to undertaking research – that would be neither possible nor appropriate. The main intention is to focus upon aspects of research involving children which are *different* to those which involve adults, so that the early years professional undertaking research may more ably transfer knowledge designed to apply to adult subjects to children in early years settings. Those areas of research methodology where there seem to be a few tangible differences (e.g. identification of problems, question formation) are not discussed. However, we shall commence with a few very broad principles which apply when undertaking research with children.

Overarching principles

As you have read throughout this book, children are not small adults. They perceive events differently to adults, their understanding of experience is different to that of adults, and the social contexts within which they exist are different to those of adults. Children are very special and deserve special consideration. They are also fascinating becasue of the way in which they rapidly develop physically, socially, psychologically and emotionally, and because of their ways of knowing and understanding.

The researcher who wishes to study children, particularly during the early years, is faced with a wealth of potential, as well as a few methodological 'headaches'! For example, traditional methods of collecting data may be inappropriate or even impossible because of the child's stage of development. Imagine the stupidity of asking a group of 2-year-olds to complete a questionnaire!

The early years researcher must possess those vital qualities which are essential to early years workers in all settings, namely well-developed skills of observation (see Chapter 1), knowledge of child development, a liking for children, patience and an ability to communicate through a variety of media. In many ways young children themselves can provide the researcher with an apt role model! From the first days of life children set out on a voyage of discovery. They explore, investigate, examine, categorise experiences, draw conclusions and seek to extend the boundaries of their knowledge. A very early text (Murray and Brown Smith, 1922) discusses the philosophy of Froebel (see also the introductory chapter), which summarises this point admirably. He wrote that:

> Like things must be ranged together, unlike things separated . . . The child loves all things that enter his small horizon and extend his little world. To him the least thing is a new discovery, but it must not come dead into the little world, nor lie dead therein, lest it obscure the small horizon and crush the little world. Therefore the child would know why he loves this thing, he would know all its properties. For this reason he examines the object on all sides; for this reason he tears and breaks it; for this reason he puts it in his mouth and bites it. We reprove the child for naughtiness and foolishness; and yet he is wiser than we who reprove him.

(Murray and Brown Smith, 1992, p. 47)

The thorough way in which children investigate new experiences or seek to find solutions, the way in which they systematically approach problems and extend the boundaries of their knowledge – these are the principles of undertaking research with young children.

Methodological differences

When engaging upon early years research, the researcher needs to employ all of the skills and knowledge referred to above in order to ensure that the research yields results which are both reliable and valid. Three of the main problems, which are interelated, are sampling, data collection and ethical implications (which will be discussed separately in the next section of this chapter).

Samples are the foundation of research and provide the researcher with the medium to answer research questions through data collection. A sample is anything which is smaller than a full population, and samples are used because it is rarely possible to study an entire population (although this does happen sometimes, e.g. the United Kingdom 10-yearly Population Census, or Graham and Rutter's Isle of Wight Study (see Rutter and Hersov, 1985, for various reviews). The basis of sampling involves two general laws, the first being that a relatively large, randomly selected sample will represent the characteristics of the sample population, and the second being that larger groups of data are more highly stable than smaller groups of data.

The importance of sampling during early childhood relates to the homogeneity of groups of children. You will recall the discussion in various chapters so far in this book about children's development, particularly in terms of their cognition and their social development. It is extremely difficult to identify an homogenous group of children because age is a relatively poor predictor of cognitive and social development. Therefore bias in sampling is a problem faced by many early years researchers. There are ways of overcoming bias, but the researcher must be aware that a group of intellectually intact pre-school children (spanning a 5-year period from 0–5 years) is likely to be a far less homogenous group than a group of intellectually intact adults (spanning, for example, a 5-year period from 34–39 years).

However, many early years researchers are not concerned with being able to generalise their results across populations, but *are* concerned with their own practice in their own familiar settings. Samples which are 'convenient' may be biased and non-random, and regardless of the size of the sample, bias will remain in evidence. This presents no difficulty so long as it is recognised and acknowledged that the results cannot be generalised beyond the sample.

The second main problem relating to undertaking research during the early years concerns data collection. We have already mentioned the difficulty of using questionnaires among groups of young children. Similar difficulties are equally evident when using other self-report methods, such as rating scales. However, as with other data collection methods, modification can enable their use. For example, collecting data about post-operative pain using a numerical rating scale with young children may prove very unsuccessful, but by adapting the scale and using pictures of 'smiley' faces (see Whaley and Wong, 1991), or photographs as in the 'Oucher Scale' (Beyer and Aradine, 1987), success can be achieved. Using colour to symbolise levels of response is also a useful means of collecting data from children (see, for example, Sandberg *et al.*, 1993, who used colour-coded post-boxes). Similarly, a questionnaire designed to elicit information from hospitalised patients was modified by the author for use on the children's wards to include a 4-point scale which included the headings 'yuk', 'a bit yuk', 'O.K.' and 'yummy', instead of the adult version of 'not very good', 'all right', 'good' and 'very good'.

Observation is one of the most important data-collection methods for the early years researcher, and indeed it is one of the most important skills of the early years professional as was discussed in Chapter 1. One particular observation technique derived from ethology, which involves the observation of children in their natural settings is particularly useful. Observer effects (i.e. changes in behaviour caused by the intrusiveness of the observer within the situation) are problematic, but young children tend to adapt relatively quickly to the presence of, for example, a new adult within their nursery class. Observer effects can be minimised, therefore, by allowing the children being studied to adapt to the presence of the researcher (e.g. Hawthorn, 1975), or by the researcher blending into the natural setting of the child.

Researchers using observation as a data-collection tool frequently need to adapt their methods to suit the cognitive level of the child. Whereas researchers using adult subjects may be able to ask their subject to use complex skills, early years researchers will use observation of the medium of play and toys in order to collect data (see for example, Smallwood, 1988: Cummings and El-Sheikh, 1991: Egeland and Kreutzer, 1991).

Interviews involving young children can also be problematic for the early years researcher, particularly in terms of the reliability of data. We have stressed many times that children and adults percieve experiences in different ways (Bower, 1977), and the reporting of interview data may lead to inaccuracies because of the *interpretation* of a child's language by the researcher. Children may, in fact, use quite complex language, but have limited understanding of the meaning of their words (see Luria and Yudovich, 1959, for a fascinating and detailed record of children's conversation), and they may be paraphrasing words that they have heard adults using, or they may understand but not have the language acquisition to be able to verbalise adequately. Others may pronounce words in strange ways, or use 'pet' words which stand for something completely different! (see also Chapter 9). However, it is important to stress that it is valuable to seek information directly from children, rather than relying on data from adults *about* children. Compas and Phares (1991) explore this issue and suggest that wide variations may exist between the reportings of teachers, parents and the children themselves in relation to specific data.

The need for small-scale studies

Well-designed research on a small scale, using small convenient samples and data-collection methods which are appropriate to the child's level of understanding, provides the building blocks of professional knowledge because such research contributes to the generation of theory and, ultimately, to the advancement of practice. Much of the existing knowledge we work with today was originally derived from small beginnings. Axline's (1964) study of Dibs provided the basis for further study in the field of play therapy, and even Piaget himself formulated many of his early working hypotheses through close observation of his own three children! However, whether the research is on a small or large scale, whether it uses observation, questionnaires, interviews or other forms of data collection, it is always necessary to give due consideration to the ethical implications of undertaking research. It is to this important area that we shall now turn.

Ethical implications of research involving children

All researchers have a responsibility to analyse the ethical implications of their work, whether they work in the health services, the educational sector, social services or elsewhere. However, this responsibility is greatly amplified when the research being undertaken can be linked to the health or illness of children. According to Brykczynska (1989), responsibility becomes a 'moral obligation' because of the need to maintain a covenant relationship with the 'patient', and clearly when the patient is a child that moral obligation becomes even more acute.

There are, however, some types of research which will carry stronger ethical implications that others and, as a starting point, researchers should always define very clearly what the child will be asked to do in order to participate in the research. If the research is *invasive*, either physiologically, psychologically or socially, then its moral acceptability should be questioned. This applies not only to health care workers but to *all* researchers using child subjects, because of the potential detrimental effects on the child. Brkczynska clarifies this point further:

> *Invasiveness is not only about a concept of physiological invasiveness; children sharing ideas about life at home, for the benefit of the researcher, can become just as upset at the insistent questions of researchers, as children having blood taken.*

> (Brykczynska, 1989, p. 121)

Brkczynska (1989) goes on to discuss how both of these examples involve invading the private world of the child and, because children do not perceive events in the same way as adults, seemingly *harmless* experiences can be potentially *harmful* to the child. This poses difficulties for the researcher, parents and others (e.g. members of ethical committees, research supervisors, managers who control access to physical environments) who have to make an informed judgement about the potential effects of involving a child or group of children. This problem has long been recognised, but there is no easy answer, although we shall explore further criteria which can be utilised. However it is useful to remember the words used in the Platt Report:

> *It is never safe to assume that a child will be afraid of an experience that an adult regards as frightening, or conversely that an experience which has no terrors for an adult will have none for a child.*

> (Platt, 1959, p. 28)

One of the main criteria which should be applied relates to whether the research is *therapeutic* or *non-therapeutic*. Dimond (1996) defines therapeutic research as that which takes place when 'the subject stands to receive direct benefit from the research which is undertaken as part of his or her treatment' (p. 123). Non-therapeutic research is defined as research conducted without 'any direct or indirect benefit to the data subject' (p. 123).

Therapeutic research is evidently less contentious than non-therapeutic research which, when it involves children, is only acceptable so long as ethical principles and ethical codes are adhered to, and if there will be direct benefit to other children, and provided that the research has obtained the assent of children and the consent of parents (Brykczynska, 1989). It is perhaps prudent always to ask whether it is absolutely necessary to use children at all, or is it possible to obtain the information required from adult subjects (Dimond, 1996), although it is worth mentioning that the level of agreement between parents and children concerning their individual interpretation of experiences is not always high (Compas and Phares, 1991; Sandberg *et al.*, 1993). However, if children must be used, then the researcher must ensure that the correct procedures and protocols are followed to protect the rights of the child.

Post-war codes of ethics

Following the Second World War and the War Crimes Trial in Nuremberg, and as a direct result of the atrocities which were carried out during the war under the guise of 'research', the Nuremberg code was declared in 1946 as a set of guidelines which should govern the behaviour of those undertaking research on human subjects. This code, and others which have since been developed, have application to working with child subjects particularly as many of the atrocities which made the design of such codes necessary involved child subjects. Doctor Josef Mengele, Chief Medical Officer of Auschwitz-Brikenau Concentration Camp, involved many children, usually twins, in inhumane research in an attempt to discover the secret of multiple births so that the Aryan *Ubermensch* (super-race) could be multiplied at a faster rate than normal and world power achieved (Vigorito, 1992). Segal (1992) documents that this research included cruel, scientifically senseless and sometimes lethal methods carried out in atrocious conditions, resulting in needless suffering and the early death of innocent children.

The War Crimes Trial, and particularly what became known as the 'medical case', brought to light may issues surrounding experimentation on human subjects, and the need to ensure that the 'safety rails' such as the Hippocratic Oath, which should protect human subjects, cannot be removed again (Neuhaus, 1992). The Nuremberg code (Nuremberg Military Tribunals, 1949), the Universal Declaration of Human Rights (United Nations, 1948) the Declaration of Helsinki (World Medical Association, 1964, amended in 1975, 1983 and 1989), the European Commission Directive 91/507/EEC (European Commission, 1991) and other profession-specific codes such as the Royal College of Nursing's code (Royal College of Nursing, 1993) have all been developed because of the recognition of the vulnerability of human beings and the need to preserve and protect human rights. Derived from, and incorporated within, the various codes mentioned above are the basic ethical principles upon which all research should be based:

- respect for persons and their autonomy;
- justice and fair treatment;
- honesty and truthfulness;
- beneficence;
- non-maleficence

(after Brykczynska, 1989)

Whilst it is not possible to explore these principles further, there are many excellent texts which do so and are cited in the further reading section at the end of this chapter.

Consent issues

It has already been mentioned above that the assent of children involved in research (if they are able to give such assent) and the consent of those with parental responsibility should be sought prior to their involvement in the research (Brykzynska, 1989). This is particularly important in that the Children Act (1989) (Department of Health, 1989) purports that there should be participation on the part of children in making decisions in cases where they have sufficient intelligence and maturity (although deciding upon what constitutes *sufficient* is open to interpretation). Dimond (1996) suggests that mentally competent 16-and 17-year-olds should give informed consent to their own involvement in research. Children below the age of 16 years should be asked to consent if they have sufficient understanding to do so. However, Dimond advises that the consent of parents should be sought as well, particularly if the risks involved are considered to be significant.

CONCLUSION

This chapter has focused on two main areas. First, it is important to emphasise that research is of great value to all of us who work with children. It is research which has enabled us to develop those theories which underpin our practice, and it is important that we are able both to access previous research and to develop skills so that we may critically read and intelligently use previous research. It also enables us to undertake further research and to build upon the existing body of knowledge so that the boundaries of practice can be extended.

However, it is important to recognise that undertaking early years research is not straightforward, and we may need to adapt and modify methodologies so that the design of the research is appropriate to the age and cognitive and social development of the child. Undertaking research with child subjects also involves additional

ethical considerations which have been discussed in the last section of this chapter.
Research involving children can be problematic, but the rewards of systematically
study in the complex world of the child make the efforts of the researcher very
worthwhile.

References

Axline, V. (1964): *Dibs in Search of Self*. Harmondsworth: Penguin.

Beyer, J. and Aradine, C.R. (1987): Patterns of Pediatric Pain Intensity: a Methodological Investigation of a Self-report Scale. *Clinical Journal of Pain* **3**, 130–41.

Bower, T. (1977): *The Perceptual World of the Child*. London: Fontana/Open Books.

Bryczynska, G.M. (1989): Ethical Considerations in Paediatric Nursing Research. In
Ethics in Paediatric Nursing. London: Chapman and Hall, 119–41.

Carter, M. (1988): *You and Your Child in Hospital*. London: National Association for
the Welfare of Children in Hospital.

Compas, B.E. and Phares, V. (1991): Stress During Childhood and Adolescence:
Sources of Risk and Vulnerability. In Cummings, E.M., Greene, A.L. and Karraker, K.H.
(eds), *Life-span Developmental Psychology: Perspectives on Stress and Coping*. Hillsdale, NJ:
Lawrence Erlbaum Associates, 111–30.

Crocker, E. (1980): Reactions of Children to Health Care Encounters. In Robinson,
G.C. And Clark, H.F. (eds), *The Hospital Care of Children: a Contemporary Issue*. New
York: Univeristy Press, 90–110.

Cummings, E.M. and El-Sheikh, M. (1991): Children's Coping with Angry Environments: a Process-oriented Approach. In Cummings, E.M., Greene, A.L. and Karraker, K.H. (eds), *Life-span Developmental Psychology: Perspectives on Stress and Coping*.
Hillsdale, NJ: Lawrence Erlbaum Associates, 131–50.

Department of Health (1989): *The Children Act*. London: HMSO.

Department of Health (1993): *Report of the Taskforce on the Strategy for Research in
Nursing, Midwifery and Health Visiting*. London: HMSO.

Dimond, B. (1996): Legal issues. In De Raeve, L. (ed.), *Nursing Research: and Ethical
and Legal Appraisal*. London: Ballière Tindall, 118–37.

Egeland, B. and Kreutzer, T. (1991): A Longitudinal Study of the Effects of Maternal
Stress and Protective Factors on the Development of High-risk Children. In Cum-
mings, E.M., Greene, A.L. And Karraker, K.H. (eds), *Life-span Developmental Psychology:
Perspectives on Stress and Coping*. Hillsdale, NJ: Lawrence Erlbaum Associates, 61–84.

European Commission (1991): *European Commission Directive 91/507/EEC*. Brussels:
European Commission.

Hawthorn, P. (1975): *Nurse I want my Mummy!* London: Royal College of Nursing.

Jolly, J. (1981): *The Other Side of Paediatrics*. London: Macmillan.

Kiely, T. (1989): Preparing Children for Admission to Hospital. *Nursing Series* **3**: 42–4.

Luria, A.R. and Yudovich, F. (1959): *Speech and the Development of Mental Processes in
the Child*. Harmondsworth: Penguin.

Marriner, J. (1988): A Children's Tour. *Nursing Times* **84**, 39–40.

Miron, J. (1990): What Children think about Hospitals. *The Canadian Nurse* **86**, 23–5.

Muller, D.J., Harris, P.J., Wattley, L. and Taylor, J.D. (1992): *Nursing Children: Psychology, Research and Practice*, 2nd edn. London: Chapman and Hall.

Murray, E.R. and Brown Smith, H. (1922): *The Child under Eight*. London: Edward
Arnold.

Neuhaus, R.J. (1992): The Way They Were, The Way We Are. In Caplan, A.L. (ed.), *When
Medicine went Mad: Bioethics and the Holocaust*. Totowa, NJ: Humana Press, 211–32.

Nuremberg Military Tribunals (1949): *Nuremberg Code*. Washington, DC: US Government Printing Office.

Platt, H. (1959): *The Welfare of Children in Hospital: Report of the Committee on Child Health Services.* London: HMSO.

Rodin, J. (1983): *Will this Hurt?* London: Royal College of Nursing.

Royal College of Nursing (1993): *Ethics Related to Research in Nursing.* London: Royal College of Nursing.

Rutter, M. and Hersov L. (eds) (1985): *Child and Adolescent Psychiatry: Modern Approaches, 2nd edn.* Oxford: Blackwell Scientific Publications.

Sanberg, S., Rutter, M., Giles, S. et al. (1993): Assessment of Psychosocial Experiences in Childhood: Methodological Issues and Illustrative Findings. *Journal of Child Psychology and Psychiatry* **34**, 879–97.

Segal, N.L. (1992): Twin Research at Auschwitz-Birkenau: Implications for the use of Nazi Data Today. In Caplan, A.L. (ed.), *When Medicine went Mad: Bioethics and the Holocaust.* Totowa, NJ: Humana Press, 281–300.

Smallwood, S. (1988): Preparing Children for Surgery. *Association of Operating Room Nursing Journal* **47**, 177–85.

Smith, P. (1996): General Concepts in Child Care. In McQuaid, L., Huband, S. and Parker, E. (eds), *Children's Nursing.* New York: Churchill Livingstone, 141–52.

Vigorito, S.S. (1992): A Profile of Nazi Medicine: the Nazi doctor – his Methods and Goals. In Caplan, A.L. (ed.), *When Medicine went Mad: Bioethics and the Holocaust.* Totowa, NJ: Humana Press, 9–14.

Whaley, L.F. and Wong, D.L. (1991): *Nursing Care of Infants and Children,* 4th edn. St Louis, MO: Mosby.

World Medical Association (1964) (amended in 1975, 1983 and 1989): *Declaration of Helsinki. World Medical Assembly.* Helsinki: World Medical Association,

United Nations (1948): *Universal Declaration of Human Rights.* New York: United Nations.

Further reading

Beauchamp, T.L. and Childress, J.F. (1989): *Principles of Biomedical Ethics,* 3rd edn. New York: Oxford University Press.

Burgess, R. (1948): *In the Field.* London: George Allen and Unwin.

Cohen, L. and Manion, L. (1994) *Research Methods in Education,* 4th edn. London: Routledge.

Oppenheim, A.N. (1992): *Questionnaire Design and Attitude Measurement,* new edn. London: Pinter.

Polit, D.F. and Hungler, B.P. (1993): *Nursing Research: Principles and Methods,* 5th edn. Philadelphia, PA: Lippincott.

Yin, R.K. (1989): *Case Study Research: Design and Methods.* Newbury Park, CA: Sage.

Managing self and others

Caroline Jeffree and Graham Fox

This chapter aims to:

- explore the knowledge of self and the nature of relationships;
- examine communication, assertiveness and stress;
- discuss working in groups and teams, and the concept of leadership.

Introduction

This chapter recognises that in early years settings, as in many others, good care is intrinsically entwined with good management (Briggs, 1972). The concept of 'care' in this instance extends to facilitation of the growth and development – whether physical, emotional or cognitive – of young children in a variety of settings, be they nurseries, playgroups, hospital or school. In order to become a good manager, there is a requirement for both personal and professional development to take place. This development enables the early years practitioner to become equipped with the essential knowledge and skills to become effective both intra- and inter-personally in order objectively to assess and enhance their own performance and that of others within Early Years Settings. It is hoped that this chapter will act as a foundation for these skills, both theoretically and practically, whilst also making links to related theory in other chapters.

The sequencing of this chapter is designed to lead the reader in a logical manner from knowledge and management of self to relating to and managing others. Working with young children and their families is very people-centred work, and as Hochschild (1983) and Smith (1992b) have identified this type of work involves much 'emotional labour'.

Relating to and working with children and adults in early years settings is physically and emotionally demanding, and the stresses involved in such work are increasing because of the political, social and ethical issues that impinge upon it (Rodd, 1994).

In order to operate successfully in such a climate, a high degree of self-awareness is required which will form the basis for building relationships and learning communication and assertiveness skills. These abilities may in turn be applied in order to utilise self more effectively in various positions within

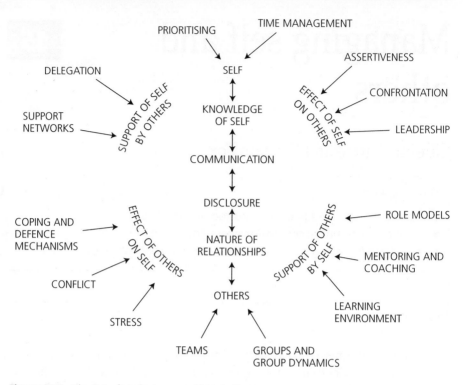

Figure 15.1   The interface between self and others.

groups and teams, and in relating to peers, parents and children as an early years practitioner.

Figure 15.1 illustrates how the sequencing of this chapter may be represented diagrammatically, indicating how the various topics are interrelated.

The nature of relationships

From the time we are born, or even before, we are aware of others around us and we quickly learn how we may affect them and how they affect us – in other words we become aware of the existence of the relationships which form part of life's experience from birth to death.

Working as an early years practitioner involves the formation of professional relationships with children, parents, co-workers and managers. These relationships may be of long or short duration. Whatever their length, the quality of these relationships is important to the work of the early years practitioners, and the way in which they relate to others has significant consequences for all concerned (Duldt *et al.*, 1984).

Relationships may be viewed as being divided into two main types:

- social relationships – with friends, acquaintances, family and strangers (see also Chapter 7);

- professional relationships – which involve professional and lay people, or professionals and professionals.

What sets the professional relationship apart from the purely social relationship are the parameters that encompass it. These parameters include specialised knowledge, training and expertise (Blane, 1991), as well as the norms of behaviour expected of a professional person. These behavioural norms include both non-verbal aspects, such as dress, deportment, etc., and verbal skill in relating to the other person. Rodd (1994), noting that many professions have recognised the advantages of interpersonal and management skills training, urges that this is taken up by those in the early childhood field.

Both social and professional relationships are built on trust and sharing. Although the balance of the sharing is altered in the professional relationship where appropriate, sharing is exercised in order to build rapport and trust with the client. Duldt *et al.* (1984) identify relationships as having three primary diversions:

- the degree of involvement invested in that relationship;
- the emotional tone or feelings present;
- the amount of interpersonal control exercised – that is, the extent to which one person or the other is dominant within the relationship.

For the early years professional, the degree of involvement will depend upon the length of the relationship as well as the nature of that relationship. For instance, nursing a child with a chronic illness over many months or years would, in all likelihood, lead to a very different relationship to one in which a child is one of many in a nursery or playgroup. The level of emotional involvement will consequently be higher or lower.

Knowledge of self

One of our most important relationships, yet one that is often neglected, is that which we have with our 'selves' – but who or what are we? We experience being 'different things to different people' because of the roles we hold and our relationship to them. How may we discover what self is, and what makes us the way we are?

It is difficult to arrive at a definition of self. Kagan *et al.* (1986) suggest that the self is at the core of the adult personality, which is formed as a result of childhood and adolescent experience. This view supports a psychoanalytical perspective which argues that childhood experiences affect and shape the self (Burnard, 1993). Alternatively, there is the view that we gain our sense of identity from the way in which others react to us. Identity is therefore inextricably linked to the roles we play and the combination of roles that we occupy. It is also a lifelong process of developing self as we mature, grow and adopt new roles (Kagan *et al.*, 1986).

Both of these perspectives on the development of self-identity are relevant to early years settings. If self is predetermined by experiences during childhood, then the role of the early years practitioner in those experiences is crucial. Working in early years settings may produce experiences that closely mirror others we have had – perhaps as children, or as parents. Unless we become self-aware of what drives us, these past experiences and the emotions that they arouse may block our relationships (Kagan *et al.*, 1986).

Self-awareness can relate to any or all of the following:

- personal identity – who am I? how did I get to be who I am?
- internal events – physical and emotional feelings, values and beliefs;
- external events – behaviour, speech, social interaction and cultural experiences;
- our sense of self as 'agent' – how in control we feel over our life and the influence we have on others (Kagan *et al.*, 1986).

In the process of becoming more self-aware it is important to distinguish between what Laing (1959) calls 'true self' and 'false self'. True self is the inner private self, whereas false self is the outer self which is often pretending, or acting out a role (Burnard, 1985). In relationships that involve helping people it is important to present authenticity of self – the state of true and honest presentation of being. Rogers (1961) considers this genuineness, or 'what you see is what you get' as being essential in helping relationships.

Communication

The early years practitioner requires the appropriate communication skills to meet the needs of children and parents from differing backgrounds, as well as other professionals. Many early years practitioners will understand and adjust to the developmental needs of children when communicating with them (Rodd, 1994). However, communicating with adults and fellow practitioners may prove more demanding. It is important for good management, care and education that messages are conveyed clearly and accurately. Often we only have one chance to convey our message so that it is correctly understood, and it is therefore important that we get it right first time.

Communication may be conceptualised as an ongoing process in which two or more people engage in verbal or non-verbal interactions during which all of those involved are aware of the reactions of the others. During this process, behaviours, feelings and meanings are exchanged (Duldt *et al.*, 1984).

The dynamic nature of this process is dependent on four factors:

- an intact physiology – in order to receive the message, decode and return it;
- listening skills – in order to hear the message clearly;
- attending skills – to focus on the message and sender;

- observational skills – to assess factors such as mood, or hidden meaning behind words.

Communication has two major components:

- non-verbal;
- verbal.

Non-verbal and verbal communication are of little use if the four prerequisites for communication outlined above are not present.

An intact physiology enables us to receive the message clearly. The toddler whose development is not complete experiences difficulty, as will the child or adult with learning difficulties, deafness or blindness.

Listening is an important skill which, if we are to understand what is said rather than just hearing, it needs to be worked at. In order to listen actively we need to take account of three aspects of listening:

- the linguistic aspect – the words that are spoken;
- the para-linguistic aspect – the tone and rate of speech;
- the non-verbal aspect – the gestures and facial expressions that accompany speech.

In order to listen actively we also need to attend and observe – not to do so is to risk misreading the message or appearing offhand or unconcerned.

Barriers to effective attending include:

- personal feelings – attitudes, stress, tiredness;
- social circumstances – hierarchy, power;
- environmental influences – noise, lack of time;
- cultural aspects – differing norms of behaviour and values may all interfere with our ability to listen effectively.

Argyle (1988) has identified that non-verbal communication, or the way in which our body conveys messages to others, is at the heart of human social behaviour. Non-verbal communication is composed of:

- physical appearance;
- gestures/facial appearance;
- proximity – how near we get to the other person;
- para-language – speed, tone, etc;
- touch.

Whereas verbal communication appears to be the dominant way of communicating in our society, non-verbal communication has a great impact, and may often reveal the real message behind the words. From childhood we are taught to 'watch what we say', but we are not taught to monitor our body language. We therefore develop more control over our verbal than our non-verbal communication (Dickson *et al.*, 1989). It is this control that allows us to give one message whilst feeling another – for instance, the response 'I'm alright' when this is far from true. For early years practitioners the ability to 'read' this hidden message is an important skill, as it may indicate, for example, stress in an employee, distress in a parent, or pent-up anger and frustration in a colleague. If we are able to help in these situations, we must first be able to recognise the non-verbal message. We may then take the appropriate action to manage the situation.

The intentional use of non-verbal information is also very useful. It may enhance self-presentation, giving an aura of self-confidence and self-esteem. Relationships with and the management of others may be improved, for example, with the use of a kindly smile or a touch of the hand. Gestures and dress also relay non-verbal messages to those around us and can, for example, enhance assertiveness skills (see also the next section for further discussion).

The functions of non-verbal communication are therefore:

- to replace speech;
- to complement the verbal message;
- to regulate and control the flow of communication;
- to provide feedback;
- to help define relationships between people;
- to convey emotional states.

(Dickson *et al.*, 1989, pp. 72–3)

The above list shows how important the non-verbal component of communication is for the professional working in early years settings, and how good use of non-verbal communication skills may enhance management and practice by increasing assertiveness and reducing stress.

Assertiveness

The ability to be assertive appears to be a skill that a person learns, and not a characteristic that is innate. Assertiveness is dependent on both the situation and the people involved. For example, it may be far easier to be assertive when confronting a colleague of the same grade than when confronting the boss. The skill of assertion involves verbal and non-verbal responses and some personal risk. Assertiveness is often regarded as an unwanted attribute by people who see it only in terms of its use in conflict situations, and hence often confuse assertion with aggression. So what is assertiveness, and how may the acquisition of such a skill help the early years practitioner to manage self and others more effectively?

Burnard (1993) describes the assertive person as 'one who can state clearly and calmly what he/she wants to say, does not back down in the face of disagreement and, if necessary, is prepared to repeat what he/she has to say' (p.53). This quotation does, however, miss an important quality of assertiveness – that of valuing the other's opinion. In contrast to aggressive behaviour, assertive behaviour involves both the genuine presentation of self and positive regard for the other person. Aggression is only concerned with getting one's own way. Assertiveness is positioned at the mid-point between aggression and submission (or passivity). The submissive or passive stance allows others to 'trample' one's rights and feelings underfoot, whereas assertive behaviour enhances individual rights. In early years settings this enhancement of rights must improve the care of children, the motivation of professionals and the self-esteem of all concerned.

Those working in the professions that are characterised by caring and educating, such as those found in early years settings, often find the practice of assertiveness difficult (Rodd, 1994). This may be because professionals in care-related jobs have a misconception of what assertiveness actually is, and it may also be related to gender socialisation in what are essentially female dominated professions. Female children are not encouraged to develop assertive skills from birth, as boys more commonly are. However, the ability to assert oneself skilfully is crucial to effective interpersonal functioning in many situations (Dickson *et al.*, 1989).

How then may we learn to be more assertive when relating to others? First, we need to become more self-aware, reflecting on our emotional and behavioural reaction to others in varying situation. Secondly, we need to become aware, through this reflective process, of our individual 'blocks' to becoming assertive. These may be caused by factors related to culture, social influences, personality and self-esteem, and Rodd (1994) has indicated that low self-esteem plays a major part in poor assertiveness skills. Thirdly, by developing and using verbal and non-verbal communication skills effectively we will be able to convey our messages assertively.

Non-verbal messages may be made more assertive by the use of:

- eye contact – a direct gaze sends the message that you mean what you say;
- facial expression – this must match what is being said in order to avoid ambiguity;
- body posture – upright yet relaxed;
- gestures – spontaneous, natural, non-aggressive movements;
- tone of voice – volume, inflection, well-modulated without whining or bullying, neither too loud nor too soft.

Verbal messages may be enhanced by the use of:

- clear, specific, direct statements – stating what is felt without 'wrapping it up';
- use of 'I' statements – taking responsibility for and owning what you say.

It may be seen that assertiveness will be improved by practising self-awareness, identifying blocks and improving interpersonal skills. This may be represented diagrammatically as shown in Figure 15.2.

The ability to act assertively enhances both our personal and our professional lives – our rights are preserved and our professional development enhanced as early years practitioners.

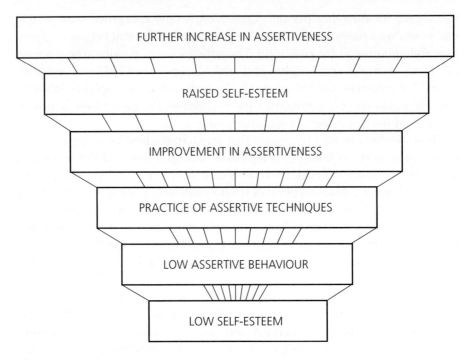

Figure 15.2   A diagrammatical representation of the improvement of assertiveness as a result of practising assertive techniques.

Stress

Stress appears to be an ever-increasing factor in the lives of most people. This can be attributed to a number of factors, e.g. twentieth-century living, change in the family, an increase in the number of single parent families, an increase in the divorce rate, and the rise in the number of women who go out to work as well as caring for their families (Cox, 1983). These factors impinge on all sections of society at a personal level. For many profession-als there has been an increase in expectation of responsibility, standards and quality of service offered. At the same time, there is an ongoing cutting of resources in terms of both staff and equipment (Smith, 1992a). Those working in Early Years Settings are not exempt. The extent to which we are affected by stress is a very individual matter, but the level of stress that we experience determines our effectiveness in both our personal and our pro-fessional lives.

Stress is a difficult concept to define. It is a dynamic, interactional process that accumulates over time. Bailey (1986) describes it as occurring when the balance of the demands in our lives is perceived as being greater than the capacity that we have to meet those demands. Lazarus and Folkman (1984) suggest that stress is a process that takes place as individuals encounter and adjust to environmental circumstances that may be internal (e.g. physical illness), or external (e.g. bereavement) which destabilise our physical and/or emotional functioning, or threaten to do so.

Stress is therefore individually perceived and dealt with, and it may be experienced as acute or chronic. Acute stress might be felt when we sit examinations or go for a job interview. It is transient, whereas chronic or long-term stress emanates from ongoing situations which stress us, such as continuous unrealistic expectations by our employers, or role conflict. All too often stress is seen only in a negative light, but many life events that are regarded as 'happy occasions', such as births, weddings, etc., carry a stress component (Holmes and Rahe, 1967).

Paradoxically, the type of person who is most vulnerable to stress is exactly the type that employers seek, being an idealistic, committed, enthusiastic, dedicated, energetic perfectionist who does not like to compromise and who has difficulty in turning down requests. Therefore it behoves those who are managing in early years settings to ensure that they are aware of what stress is and how to mediate its effects upon their staff and themselves.

Possible causes of stress for those working in early years settings may be:

- related to unrealistic management expectations;
- the increased level of responsibility placed on individuals without consequent staff development;
- dealing with angry parents and disruptive children;
- coping with ethical decisions, e.g. cases involving abuse;
- physical tiredness resulting from working with children;
- the often noisy environment.

When an individual is suffering from stress, he or she may exhibit signs which can be physical (e.g. insomnia, headaches, digestive upsets), cognitive (e.g. inability to make decisions), emotional (e.g. worrying excessively about trivial matters, crying or flying into a rage), or behavioural (e.g. constantly being late for work or absent, working obsessively, increasing alcohol consumption or smoking).

If these warning signs are not recognised, the stress levels may rise to the extent that 'burn-out' or exhaustion occurs and the person affected can no longer operate at any level.

To be able to identify those under stress, or stress in ourselves, is a start, but we also need to be able to manage it. Different ways of mediating stress are represented in Figure 15.3.

Predictability allows the person to anticipate the stress and so gather his or her physical and emotional resources in order to cope with it.

Having control over a stressful situation helps us feel less stressed – we can make choices about how we can handle a situation, rather than allowing the situation to control us. It is important to interpret or find a meaning for the stresses that we experience, as this allows us to rationalise the event. For example, disruptive behaviour by a child in playgroup may be explained

Figure 15.3   Different ways of mediating stress.

because he or she has a new sibling. Such knowledge allows the early years practitioner to cope more effectively with the child's behaviour.

Defence mechanisms such as denial and projection are used to distance the reality of the stressful situation, and are therefore self-deceiving and only useful in the short term.

Coping mechanisms, such as objectivity and logical analysis, are conscious ways of trying to adapt to stress and anxiety in a positive and constructive manner. These coping skills have often been learned in previous stressful situations and are then re-employed or adopted in the new situation.

Social support helps us to alleviate stress by calling on the emotional and practical help of family, friends and professions, to share the stressful burden. For example, the support that an early years practitioner is able to offer a troubled colleague or parent may enable that parent to find a solution for the stressful situation and then to employ coping mechanisms in order to gain control over the situation.

Indeed individuals, especially those in leadership positions in early years settings, can do much to mediate the stress of others by:

- being aware of stress factors;
- communicating effectively;
- providing adequate information and discussing uncertainty;
- encouraging assertiveness so that individual rights are enhanced and professionals feel in control;
- enhancing the natural coping mechanisms of individuals.

Perhaps the most important strategy in the above list is that of communication – lack of communication is the root cause of much stress in many organisations, including early years settings.

Groups and teams

As we have already discussed, it is important for the early years practitioner to develop strong relationships with individuals in order to carry out his or her work effectively, and this includes working successfully as a member of a group or team. Groups and teams have many similarities, although Nicholson (1992) suggests they differ in that team members have a common aim and every member co-operates and shares his or her experiences in order to maximise the efficiency of the provision. For the purposes of this chapter, however, the terms 'groups' and 'teams' will be used synonymously unless otherwise stated.

All groups, if they are to operate effectively, must have two dimensions, namely the 'task' and the 'process' (sometimes referred to as the socio-emotional dimension). The task concerns the job to be done or the problem to be resolved, etc., while the process concerns the way in which it is done, that is, how the people working in the group bring their knowledge, skills and qualities together (Tuckman, 1965). In an early years setting the range of people who constitute a group can be very diverse. The group may consist of professionals from various disciplines, lay people, parents or children, and all of these individuals must feel that their presence and contribution are valued and help to bring about an appropriate outcome.

Just because a number of people come together to work with children or to manage an initiative or activity, it should not be expected that they will automatically form a close-knit team from the outset. In the introductory chapter the philosophy of holism and the multidisciplinary approach to working with young children and families were discussed. Whilst each professional brings his or her own particular expertise to the early years setting, so long as all members of the group share the underpinning philosophy of holism, in time they can learn in harmony for the benefit of the child and his or her family. The dynamics of the group will need to mature, by going through a number of stages, in order to reach the 'performing' or 'harmonious' level of competence (Tuckman, 1965).

Whether people work together for a few hours, many months or years, it is important that they become a cohesive team as quickly as possible. The leading professional in the group is of paramount influence in this process, and it will be his or her responsibility to take group members through the stages of 'forming', 'storming', and 'norming' to 'performing' as effectively as possible. Equally, once the group has come to the end of its life, or there has been a significant change in its membership, it may be the leader's responsibility to manage the 'mourning' stage, perhaps by supporting, for example, a family to be self-sufficient and able to function without the support of the group.

The task, or in this case the provision of optimum 'educare', is the main reason why a group or team is formed in the first place. Until the participants operate in a co-ordinated and supportive way with one another, and with the children and their families, they are unlikely to achieve a significant outcome. As the group moves through the development stages, the focus of activity will move from being mainly individual and group-orientated at the forming stage, to focusing on achieving the group's stated aims and outcomes when performing (Tuckman, 1965). Chapter 11 discusses the goals and processes for achieving quality in early years provision.

Groups and teams develop characteristics and lives of their own. Equally, the people who make up the group take on, or demonstrate, behaviours or roles (Mullins, 1996). When there is disharmony within a group, individuals or sub-groups may project blame on to the group as a whole, or on to each other by 'scapegoating'. In extreme cases, members may 'take flight' if they feel unable to cope with a particular situation, by talking light-heartedly, intellectualising or changing the subject.

Members of a group take on different and usually complementary roles. For example, there may be 'ideas people' (the Plant), the 'dissector and analyser of ideas' (the Monitor-Evaluator) or someone who injects urgency into the situation and 'chivvies' the others along (the Complete-Finisher). Belbin (1981) has provided a full discussion of the eight roles that constitute the 'ideal' group. In the real world it is very unlikely that the early years practitioner will find an ideal group, i.e. one containing each role type. It will therefore be extremely important for group leaders to be able to identify those roles which are present and, if necessary to 'adopt' others themselves.

Leadership

Leadership is a dynamic process whereby a person 'leads' a number of other individuals, (a group or team) to an agreed set of aims and/or objectives, such as those referred to in Chapter 11 with regard to early years provision. There are five basic types of leader.

- The *charismatic leader* becomes a leader as a result of personal qualities or traits, e.g. Billy Graham, Martin Luther King.
- The *traditional leader* has the right of leadership by virtue of birth, e.g. a king, tribal leader.
- The *situational leader* is in the right place at the right time, e.g. when the original leader leaves the organisation. Leadership in such cases may be temporary and short-term.
- The *appointed leader* is a leader by virtue of his or her role, and may not possess the qualities looked for in a leader, e.g. a manager or supervisor who has been promoted because of technical rather than 'people' skills.

• The *functional leader* secures a leadership position by virtue of what he or she does or has achieved. The functional leader will adapt his or her behaviour according to the developing needs of the situation.

According to Adair (1979), the functional leader is the type most likely to succeed. He argues that, because the dynamics of a situation are continually in flux (that is, the relationship between the task, the individual and the group is constantly changing), the leader, who is at the centre of the system, needs to be able to adapt accordingly. In addition to change *within* a given situation, external factors can also influence stability, because no group can act in a vacuum. Therefore the leader and group need to be able to operate effectively regardless of the tensions and pressures acting on them from outside.

Rodd (1994) suggests that the key elements of effective leadership involve the ability to:

• provide vision and communicate it;
• develop a team culture;
• set goals and objectives;
• monitor and communicate achievements;
• facilitate and encourage the development of individuals.

Equally, there are different approaches that can and at times must be adopted when undertaking the 'leader' role. An individual may have a preference for a particular leadership style, e.g. autocratic, democratic or *laissez-faire*. However, he or she may need to adopt any one of these styles depending on the prevailing circumstances. For example, where a child's safety is at risk the appropriate style might be 'autocratic', whereas during discussions about stalls to be included at a summer fair a *laissez-faire* approach would be more appropriate. All professional practitioners, whatever their area of specialism, need to adopt an action-centred, flexible approach to leadership if they are to be truly effective.

Groups are often formed and leaders selected because it has been decided that the task can best be achieved by this means. Within a task there are many activities which only the leader can perform. However, there are often, opportunities for leaders to delegate parts of the task to colleagues. Delegation is defined as 'the assignment of duties . . . accompanied by the devolution of authority necessary to implement decisions' (Bennet, 1994, pp.249–50). Delegating is often a strategy for survival on the part of the leader, although it should be recognised that, whilst one can *authorise* another to carry out a task on one's behalf, the *responsibility* for its successful completion remains in the hands of the delegator. Tasks can be delegated for a number of reasons, e.g. to enable the delegator to carry out higher-priority tasks because the task is more suited to the knowledge and skills of the colleague, or to aid the personal and/or professional development of a colleague. Delegation should not be undertaken in order to off-load boring, tedious, unrewarding tasks, but to empower and enhance job satisfaction and reward.

As we have mentioned above, responsibility cannot be delegated. It is therefore important that there is control over the colleague during the execution of the task, although it is neither appropriate nor desirable to have the delegator 'breathing down the neck' of the colleague whilst he or she undertakes the task. It is far better to ensure that the task and 'terms of reference' have been thoroughly communicated, and then to 'control by exception' – that is, to identify critical areas or stages, of the task and check personally that the colleague is working within defined limits at these times. The frequency of such control points will be dependent upon the duration of the task, its complexity, and the ability and experience of the colleague.

In addition to the benefits referred to above, delegation will give the leader more time. Time is one of the absolutes of life – it is either used or lost, and can never be retrieved. Working in what is often referred to as a 'people' business, it is very easy for time to be wasted, not by inefficiency but by the demands made by other people. Better management of time does not happen by accident. It is rather like dieting – good intentions are of no use, and only a positive frame of mind and realistic targets will achieve success. You may find it helpful to consider:

- the job – what is important or urgent? What are the priorities? Whose are they?
- how time is currently spent – what activities are valuable, doubtful or useless?

When these areas have been looked at, it is necessary to compare each with the 'Priority Mountain' (Figure 15.4).

The Priority Mountain advocates a number of questions which the leader should ask of him- or herself.

- Is this something I must do?
- Is it something I can delay?
- Can I delegate this task to someone else?
- Is the task so unimportant that it can be dumped?

Figure 15.4 The Priority Mountain.

When the priorities and their levels of ranking have been established, the most appropriate action can then be taken.

One of the reasons for delegating mentioned earlier was to advance the personal or professional development of colleagues. Opportunities for development can also be enhanced by the leader creating a learning environment and mentor culture within the workplace. People learn best by 'doing' (Gibbs, 1988). This does not mean 'stumbling' along by trial and error, but engaging in practice which is supported by underpinning knowledge, reflection and feedback. This is discussed in relation to early years provision in Chapter 11. Kolb (1984) and Honey and Mumford (1986) call this process *experiential learning*. Experiential learning is a continuous cyclical process which involves reflection, conceptualisation, experimentation and practice. It is the model upon which the concept of *lifelong learning* is based – a concept which should be advocated by all managers and leaders who wish to see the continual growth of their staff.

Experiential and lifelong learning do not happen automatically – they need to be managed and supported. The work environment must be conducive to learning, that is, it must be one in which:

- the linking of theory and practice is encouraged, and current research is critically evaluated;
- there are facilities for learning;
- people have the time and space to 'reflect' and 'experiment';
- there are personnel available with appropriate personal and professional knowledge and skills to provide guidance and mentorship.

The term 'mentor' derives from Greek mythology and means one who is a father figure, role model, counsellor, trusted adviser, encourager or challenger. The person being supported is often referred to as the 'protégé' (from the French, 'to protect'). Therefore a mentor needs to be someone who will help the individual to 'develop' in a 'protected', non-threatening environment. The mentor must possess a high level of intra- and interpersonal skills, and be committed to helping to develop similar skills in others. He or she must be able to communicate effectively and must have the trust and confidence of the protégé.

Through such a learning environment and mentor culture, a leader in any work situation, and particularly one which is heavily people-orientated, as in early years settings, should be able to enhance in his or her staff many of the skills and behaviours that have been articulated in this chapter.

CONCLUSION

It is hoped that this chapter has shown the reader how the successful management of self and others may be enhanced in order to improve the all-important interpersonal relationships within early years settings.

The skills and theoretical concepts described in this chapter represent the tip of the iceberg in relation to the totality of what may be learned. The chapter serves as a 'stepping-stone' to further learning, growth and development in the management of self and others. It has been necessary for the sake of clarity to present these topics as small 'chunks' but, by referring back to Figure 15.1, we are reminded that all of these skills and concepts are interrelated and interlinked. It is, therefore, only by cross-referencing the skills and concepts involved in managing self and others in a flexible manner that we may grow and develop both as individuals and as early years professionals.

References

Adair, J. (1979): *Action-centred Leadership*. London: Gower.

Argyle, M. (1988): *Bodily Communication*, 2nd edn, London: Meuthen.

Bailey, R. (1986): *Coping with Stress in Caring*. Oxford: Blackwell Scientific Publications.

Belbin, R.M. (1981): *Management Teams: why they Succeed or Fail*. London: Heinemann.

Bennett, R. (1994): *Organisational Behaviour*. Pitman, London.

Blane, D. (1991): Health Professions. In Scambler, G. (ed.), *Sociology as Applied to Medicine*. London: Bailliére Tindall.

Briggs, A. (1972): *Report of the Committee on Nursing*. London: HMSO.

Burnard, P. (1993): *Teaching Interpersonal Skills*. London: Chapman and Hall.

Cox, C. (1983): *Sociology. An Introduction for Nurses*. London: Butterworth.

Dickson, D.A, Hargie, O. and Morrow, N.C. (1989): *Communication Skills Training for Health Professionals: an Instructors Handbook*. London: Chapman and Hall.

Duldt, B.W., Giffen, K. and Patton, B.R. (1984): *Interpersonal Communication in Nursing*. Philadelphia, PA: F.A. Davis Co.

Gibbs, G. (1988): *Learning by Doing*. London: Further Education Unit.

Hochschild, A.R. (1983): *The Managed Heart: Commercialisation of Human Feeling*. Berkely, CA: University of California Press.

Holmes, T.H. and Rahe, R.H. (1967): The Social Maladjustment Rating Scale. *Journal of Psychosomatic Research* **11**, 213–18.

Honey, P. and Mumford, A. (1986): *Using your Learning Styles*, 2nd edn. Maidenhead: Peter Honey.

Kagan, C., Evans, J. and Kay, B. (1986): *A Manual of Interpersonal Skills for Nurses*. London: Harper and Row.

Kolb, D.A. (1984): *Experiential Learning – Experience as the Source of Learning and Development*. New Jersey: Prentice-Hall.

Laing, R.D. (1959): *The Divided Self*. Harmondsworth: Penguin.

Lazarus, R.S, Folkman, S. (1984): *Stress, Appraisal and Coping*. New York: Springs.

Mullins, L.J. (1996): *Management and Organisational Behaviour*, 4th edn. London: Pitman.

Nicholson, J. (1992): *How do you Manage? How to Make the Most of Yourself and your People*. London: BBC Books.

Rodd, J. (1994): *Leadership in Early Childhood*. Buckingham: Open University Press.

Rogers, C. (1961): *On Becoming a Person*. Boston, MA: Houghton Miffen.

Smith, F. (1992a): *Children Act (1989): Guide to Childminding and Day Care of under Eights in England and Wales*. London: NES Arnold.

Smith, P. (1992b): *The Emotional Labour of Nursing: How Nurses care*. London: Macmillan Press Ltd.

Tuckman, B.W. (1965): Development Sequence in Small Groups. *Psychological Bulletin* **63**, 384–99.

Working with young children and their families

Jayne Taylor

Introduction

We come to the study of early childhood with a personal set of experiences of our own childhood, of our education, of our professional practice (or intended practice), of other people's children and, perhaps, experiences of our own children. We also bring to our studies a perspective, and we will each have an agenda or a personal set of aims. For example, a student may ultimately wish to qualify as an early years teacher and will therefore focus his or her study upon education, or a student may wish to work as a children's nurse, in which case a health bias through the study of early childhood will be preferable. Other students may already have professional qualifications but wish to enhance their practice through further study.

What soon becomes apparent when studying early childhood is that the 'subject' chosen for study (that is, children and childhood) is vast, complex and strangely addictive. As mentioned above, we will have a personal agenda and may come to our studies wishing to focus specifically upon one aspect of childhood, such as, health or education or social policy. What we soon realise is that it is almost impossible to study discrete areas of early childhood without gaining a fundamental knowledge of other areas – which brings us back to our holistic perspective. In our introductory chapter we emphasised this point when we introduced the concept of educare, which does not attempt to separate these areas, recognising instead that for the child and the family these aspects of childhood are inextricably interwoven. Separation of these aspects of childhood does not reflect the real essence of childhood and family life, and it soon becomes apparent that there are a common set of skills and a baseline of knowledge which all early years workers require, as well as the necessity to understand the context of childhood and family life.

Whether you have read this book from cover to cover or delved into certain chapters, you will have noticed that the chapters fall generally into three types. There are those that examine the skills of the competent early years professional, such as Chapter 1 (Early Childhood Studies – first principles), Chapter 14 (Perspectives on early childhood research) and Chapter 15 (Managing self and others) These chapters highlight the essential skills which are common across specialisms; the first two discuss the scientific study of early childhood, whereas Chapter 15 focuses particularly on the skills of communication required by the early years profession, recognising that all such professionals need 'people' management skills. Working with children will also involve communicating with parents and significant others, and with other professionals. Rarely will an early years professional function in isolation from colleagues who are part of the same profession or from other professions.

Then there are those chapters which explore developmental aspects of childhood, including Chapter 2 (New beginnings: factors affecting health and eell-being in the infant), Chapter 7 (Growth and development), Chapter 4 (Personal, social and affective development), Chapter 7 (Children's relationships) and Chapter 9 (Play, language and learning). These chapters explore developmental processes and, because these are common to all children, we consider that knowledge relating to them is essential for all early years practitioners, regardless of specialism. Knowledge of play, for example, is pivotal to our understanding of childhood, our ability to communicate with children and a child's ability to communicate with us. Observing children at play can, if we have the requisite knowledge, tell us about the ways in which children perceive their worlds, about the nature of childhood itself, and about the child's stage of development. Knowledge, coupled with a well-developed ability to observe and assess, will allow the practitioner to see beyond the outer child and will enable understanding of the complex set of experiences which make up the life of the child. As Froebel says, 'play at first is just natural life'.

Then there are those chapters which examine issues relating to the context of child and family life, policy and provision, including Chapter 5 (Child in society), Chapter 6 (Social policy: the state, the family and young children), Chapter 11 (Early childhood education in pre-school settings), Chapter 8 (Child health) and Chapter 13 (Children in developing countries). With the exception of the last of these, all explore the development of factors and systems that influence the lives of children and their families. Chapter 13, which explores the lives of children in the Third World, takes an even broader view, examining issues relating to policy, education, health and health care provision.

Chapters 10 (Child protection, welfare and the law) and Chapter 12 (Multidisciplinary care of the sick child in the community) discuss issues which face children, families and early years practitioners during adversity. Whilst there are clearly many more issues that we could have included which focus on children who experience life events which lead to difficulties, we felt that these two areas are those which the early years practitioners are most likely to encounter during their everyday working lives. For these children, in particular, the holistic framework which has been a recurring theme throughout the book is of the utmost importance. The children who are the focus of these two chapters will have contact with a range of early years professionals, and communication and collaboration are essential for the provision of competent care.

This final chapter aims to look at these issues in the context of working with children and their families, by drawing together the themes which permeate the book. These themes are communication and collaboration, developmental issues, the family in context, and finally we shall return to the our principle theme, which is holism.

Communication and collaboration

As we mentioned above, the early years practitioner is unlikely to work in total isolation, regardless of his or her chosen specialism. Team-work is the norm when working with children and their families, whether it involves working with fellow professionals or across professional boundaries.

When I first began working as a health visitor, a discerning manager gave me an excellent piece of advice which was that, every day, before leaving work, I should ensure that a colleague would be able to take over my caseload without any difficulty – in case I was run over by a tram. Whilst it was unlikely that a tram would run me over (we had no trams in Great Yarmouth!), the advice was sound and taught me an important lesson. Working with children and families was the pleasant part of my work, and the aspect which had attracted me to health visiting in the first place. The record-keeping, communication of problems to the manager and referral to other agencies were the infrastructure of my practice and, whilst these were also the mundane and sometimes tedious aspects of the job, they were absolutely fundamental to my professional practice. This principle is as true today as it was then, even though the methods may have changed with parent-held records and data bases.

However, communicating with colleagues and other professionals is not always easy. In Chapter 15 the potential barriers to communication are discussed, and in professional practice these barriers operate at different levels. There may be barriers between the early years practitioner and the child and family, between colleagues working within the same sphere of practice, or between different professional groups.

Barriers which exist between the early years practitioner and the child and family may arise for a number of reasons. First, the practitioner may not be aware of the cognitive abilities of the child (or indeed of the family), and communication may be at an inappropriate level. This was discussed more fully in Chapter 9. Secondly, the ethnocentrism of the practitioner may mean that communication is inappropriate in terms of its content or delivery. Practitioners should take care not to impose values from their own calls, religion or culture upon families. Finally, there may be reasons why even appropriate communication is ineffective, e.g. because the child and family are in a state of denial (Rathbone, 1996). This is a relatively normal stage for families to pass through when they have to face bad news about the health and well-being of a child. It can also be apparent, however, when a parent is told about the deviant behaviour of a beloved (and normally good) child by a teacher, for example. Some parents will not seem to believe what is being said about the child because it is outside their own experience of him or her and cannot be aligned with their previous understanding and knowledge of that child's behaviour.

Barriers that exist between early years practitioners from within the same specialism can be particularly awkward, and were discussed fully in Chapter 15. These barriers tend to be of a personal nature, and should never be allowed to affect the care of children or families. However, there are occasions when a lack of communication about very simple matters will have detrimental effects. For example, if one practitioner gives a mother advice about how to wean her baby and a second practitioner (maybe inadvertently) contradicts this advice, the mother may become very confused, and in the end follows the advice of neither professional. The development of clear protocols and standards within organisations about what constitutes appropriate advice in a given situation can be extremely useful and beneficial to both the practitioner who gives the advice and the parent who receives it.

Barriers to communication that exist between professional groups can be very difficult to break down, and can also be potentially harmful to the child and family. For example, we have been given anecdotal evidence about children and families who have 'fallen through the net' and not received appropriate care in terms of family support, benefits and other tangible forms of care, because each professional group has assumed that the others have taken responsibility for care. There is also case-study evidence from some of the major child abuse inquiries which indicates that this does indeed happen, with devastating consequences. Corby writes:

Almost all the inquiries published since 1973 have highlighted failures of systems to act in a co-ordinated way and failures of individuals to co-operate and communicate effectively in events leading up to children's deaths.

(Corby, 1995, p.211)

Non-effective communication and collaboration are not always connected to a reticence on the part of professional groups to break down barriers, nor do they always result in no one group taking responsibility for care. In some instances the problems stem from too many groups wishing to take responsibility and ownership for care, which results in the child and family becoming 'swamped' by well-meaning practitioners. Take the example of a child who, after a long struggle against cancer, faces the final hours of life at home with her family. The child has known many professionals over a number of years who have been responsible for various aspects of her care. At this very private and special time for the family, their home begins to fill with these people who all feel that they have a part to play in the child's last hours. The reality, we are told, is that the parents are left comforting the deeply distressed professionals and making tea, rather than focusing on the needs of themselves and their child.

Such well-meaning but misdirected care is the result of a communication barrier between groups. Whilst we recognise that working with young children does involve emotional commitment on the part of the professional, difficult as it may be, there are times when we must relinquish care to other groups by effectively communicating and collaborating. Case-conferencing is one of the better ways of ensuring that each professional group is aware of its boundaries and responsibilities when more than one group is involved in the care of the child. It is not only applicable to child protection practices, but also to a range of other situations. The presence of the parents (and the presence of the child, if appropriate) should be encouraged at these discussions, and they should be listened to.

Effective communication and collaboration is thus vitally important in competent professional practice, and should form a major part of any training programme for early years professionals. As already mentioned, it is not something which is easy to accomplish, although it is perhaps true to say that some people appear to find it relatively more easy than others.

Understanding development

A second theme which underlies the competent care of children relates to an understanding and knowledge of, child development and those factors which influence such development. Professionals working with children must be aware of how children develop physically, psychologically, emotionally and socially, and several chapters within this book are devoted entirely to these aspects because we recognise the importance of this knowledge base.

Understanding development involves three distinct components which have been brought to the attention of the reader. First, there is the knowledge of normal patterns and sequences of growth and development. Such knowledge can be acquired in a number of ways, although we consider that the most effective way of learning about growth and development must always involve a combination of theory and integrated practice. A very simple example in relation to cognitive development and Piaget's theory of conservation is to ask students to try out some of the simpler experiments, such as manipulating rows of different-coloured buttons or rolling equally sized pieces of Plasticine into different shapes, with children of different ages. Students are usually entranced by the children who fail to conserve, and delighted by the responses of those who can!

The second component which is integral to the above discussion is observation, which was introduced in Chapter 1 and revisited in later chapters. Observation is an essential part of the role of all early years practitioners, and is vital for the acquisition of our knowledge of growth and development. Students who are new to the study of early childhood may occasionally feel that they already have a very well-developed sense of observation, and indeed some do. The majority, however, find that in reality their skills require considerable refinement, and are pleased with the wealth of data that their developed skill offers. As with gaining knowledge of developmental processes, the student can learn a great deal about the skill of observation by watching children at play. Froebel (in Murray and Brown Smith, 1922) made much of observation of children and of the benefits for the student of studying the child's own powers of observation, saying 'become a learner with the child' (p.101). Clutton Brock (in Murray and Brown Smith, 1922) wrote on a similar theme, but cautioned that when children observe, they do so in a different way to adults, because adults cannot observe without being influenced by other, interfering, events. He wrote that:

> *The child feels . . . delight among spring flowers; we can all remember how we felt it in the first apprehension of some new beauty of the universe . . . most of us remember too the indifference of our elders. They were not considering the lilies of the field; they did not want us to get our feet wet among them . . . parents and nurses (and teachers) have . . . to be aware that the child, when he forgets himself in the beauty of the world, is passing through a sacred experience which will enrich and glorify the whole of his life. Children, because they are not engaged in the struggle for life, are more capable of this aesthethic self-forgetfulness.*
>
> (Murray and Brown Smith, 1922, p.95)

The third component which is important for understanding growth and development, and which is integral to the other two components mentioned above, is assessment. Assessment, along with observation, was introduced to the reader in Chapter 1, and we have returned to it continually. Working with children during the early years is not a static process, but usually involves helping, enabling and facilitating the child to progress. In order to do this effectively, the practitioner – using his or her knowledge of growth and development and powers of observation – must engage in a process of assessment so that the child can be enabled in an appropriate and meaningful way. This principle is true in almost every setting, whether it be choosing an appropriate activity for a group of pre-school children in a nursery, or working with an individual child with learning disabilities on portage, which involves the setting of small, measurable goals following assessment. Assessment is also a fundamental part of the role and training of all early years practitioners, including teachers, nurses, midwives, health visitors, psychologists and social workers.

As with our other two components, learning assessment skills must involve practice as well as theory, so that students can apply their knowledge in a meaningful way.

The family

The third theme which permeates this book is the role of the family in childhood, which was introduced in Chapter 2 and revisited in other chapters, particularly in Chapters 5 and 7.

Early year practitioners may *only* work with the child as part of a family. For example, health visitors, social workers and midwives rarely, if ever, work with individual children in isolation from the family. Other practitioners, such as teachers and nursery nurses, may consider children to be their 'primary' clients, but realise that the child is part of a family which will influence the development, behaviour and personality of the child. In recognition of this, most organisations encourage parental participation in pre-school and school educational activities, in health care, in child protection work, etc.

The important message which we wish to bring to the attention of the reader is that it is not practicable to work with a child without considering the family context, because children do not grow up in vacuums, but are part of a living, interacting group that is far more influential upon the child's development than any other facet of childhood.

The family, above all others, will know the child and appreciate his or her uniqueness. They will be skilled in providing care and will understand the child's behaviour patterns. They may also hold the key which enables the practitioner to understand the individual child. To study a child outside the context of his or her family, or without at least acknowledging the power and influence of the family, is both narrow and mechanistic – and does not capture the true essence of childhood.

Sameroff (1989) discusses the concept of *codes* which influence behaviour within the family and, consequentially, the behaviour of the child. The first type of code he discusses is the *cultural code,* which organises a society's child-rearing system and regulates 'the fit between individuals and the social system' (p.25), so that individuals can fulfil an acceptable role within society. The second type of code is the *family code,* which determines behaviour within the family system and produces individuals who fulfil an acceptable role within the family. The third type of code is the *individual parent's code,* which originates from his or her own past experiences of family code. In other words, parents bring to the new family their own experiences of belonging to a different family, which will influence the interaction within the new family. This can clearly be a positive influence, but it can equally well be a negative one.

Sameroff (1989) also discusses regulations within society and the family which are different to the parental styles described in Chapter 7, but are certainly not disconnected from them. Sameroff writes that 'It is important to recognise the parent as a major regulating agency of child development, but it is equally important to recognise that parental behavior is itself embedded in regulatory contexts' Sameroff, 1989, p.26.

Regulations within the family include *macroregulations,* which provide the rules for a society and dictate the expected behaviour of individuals within each culture. *Miniregulations* are a second level of regulation, and regulate behaviour within the family. For example, miniregulations will operate in terms of how a family will discipline children, and how the family may view activities such as play and learning. The third type of regulation is *microregulations,* which Sameroff describes as 'momentary interactions between child and caregiver' (Samaroff, 1989, p.28). For example, a parent may make a seemingly insignificant gesture, such as the slight raising of an eyebrow, which the child will recognise as displeasure, but of which a stranger will be unaware.

Codes and regulations will clearly influence the child's development as well as the way in which they behave outside the family, their attitudes, values, beliefs and aims. If, as professionals in early years settings, we wish to view parents as equal partners, we must be aware of factors within the family which can influence the child, so that we can work with the parents.

Holism

The final and probably strongest theme which underpins this entire book is that of holism, which was first brought to the attention of the reader in the introductory chapter. We have strongly advocated the notion that each practitioner must work within an holistic framework, even though he or she may come to work with the child and family in a very specialised way. If our work has a purpose, and we wish to be successful in our work, we must focus upon the whole child. For example, consider a teacher who is working with a child on a particular subject, but who ignores the signs which indicate that the child is clearly distressed and anxious. If the child's distress is not managed, he or she is unlikely to learn from the teacher, because we know that anxiety is a barrier to learning. Far better that the teacher spends time trying to find out why the child is distressed, before instigating appropriate intervention.

Holism also involves recognition that the child is part of a family, a culture and a society, as we have discussed in the preceding section. Failure to recognise the child as part of a larger network will result in his or her experiences of life not being utilised to their full potential. Children learn best by being active, by discussing their thoughts and feelings in a variety of situations, and by experimenting with their newly acquired skills. Learning does not only occur in the nursery or classroom, but also takes place within the family, where the child is able to consolidate and experiment in his or her natural world.

Our first theme of communication and collaboration is also a fundamental part of holism. As we have stated before, we come to the study of early childhood from a particular perspective or specialism. Childhood, however, is so complex that the child will form relationships and interact with a number of practitioners. Some children, particularly those with a chronic illness or disability, are likely to interact with more practitioners than others. The important point to make here is that each practitioner should have a knowledge of the roles and responsibilities of the other professionals, and should communicate and collaborate effectively in order to break down actual or potential barriers which could be harmful to the well-being of the child and his or her family.

Finally, our aim in writing this book was to bring together professionals from a variety of backgrounds to write about aspects of our shared interest, namely children during the early years. Each writer has brought to the debate a specialist slant, but each has also considered the child within our holistic framework. We hope you have enjoyed it!

References

Corby, B. (1995): Interprofessional Co-operation and Interagency Co-ordination. In Wilson, K. And James, A. (Eds), *The Child Protection Handbook*. London: Ballière Tindall, 211–26.

Murray, E.R. and Brown Smith, H. (1922): *The Child under Eight*. London: Edward Arnold.

Rathbone, B. (1996): Developmental Perspectives. In Lindsay, B. and Elsegood, J. (eds), *Working with Children in Grief and Loss*. London: Ballière Tindall, 16–31.

Sameroff, A.J. (1989): Principles of Development and Psychopathology. In Sameroff, A.J. and Emde, R.N. (eds), *Relationship Disturbances in Early Childhood: a Developmental Approach*. New York: Basic Books, 17–32.

Index

Abstract thinking
  development 76–7
  play theories 167
Abuse *see* Child abuse
Academic study of early childhood
  10–11
Accidents
  morbidity patterns 228
  prevention 149
Accommodation, learning theory 157–8,
  165
Acts of Parliament *see* Legislation
Adaptation, learning through 74–5,
  157–8
Aesthetic needs, hierarchy of needs 53,
  56
Affective development 75
  abstract thinking 76–7
  care provision 82–3
  communication 79–80
  perception 75–6
  relationships 80–2
  role of play 77–9, 164, 168
Affective expression 79–80
AIDS, developing countries 248–9
Alcohol, in pregnancy 37, 38, 40
Allitt Inquiry 232
Anonymity, ethics 29
Antenatal care 41–2
Anti-discriminatory practice 217–18
Assertiveness 278–80
Assessing children 14–17, 294
  see also Observation of children
Assessment models, child abuse 192–4
Assimilation, learning theory 157, 165
Associationism 12–13
  see also Behaviourism; Empiricism
Asthma management 150–1
Attachment, mother–child 129–32, 135,
  230
Authoritarian parents 126
Authoritative parents 126–7

Behaviourism 12–13, 157, 161
Belonging, hierarchy of needs 53, 56

Biological theories, play 163–4
Bottle feeding 58, 62–3
  developing countries 248
  weaning from 63–6
Bowel care, stool consistency 63
Brandt report 254
Breast feeding 57–61, 63
  developing countries 248
  weaning from 63–6
Butler Act (Education Act 1944) 109, 111

Care providers
  1989 Children Act 108–9, 112
  division of labour at home 100–1,
    132–3
  holistic development and 80–3
  social policy 108–9, 112
  and women in the workplace 99, 100
  see also Early childhood studies;
    Management
Case conferences 293
Centile charts, physical growth 48–52
Charitable organisations, social policy 121
Check-lists, for assessment 21–3, 48
Child abuse 139–41, 172–98
  child neglect 180–2
  definitions 176–7, 178, 180, 182, 186
  education curriculum for
    professionals 174–5
  emotional abuse 177–80
  emotional neglect 139, 179–80
  learning about child protection 173–4
  multidisciplinary child protection
    189–91
  physical 139, 186–9
  psychological 139
  as a public issue 175–6, 187
  responding to 191–5
  and school health service 115
  sexual 140–1, 182–6
    definitions of abuse 176–7, 182
    secondary prevention 150
  social policy 187
Child Abuse Enquiry Reports 188–9, 194
Child Benefit 117–18

Child care
  1989 Children Act 108–9
  division of labour at home 100–1,
    132–3
  history 1–3
  holistic development and 80–3
  see also Educare; Management
Child development see Development
Child labour 89, 90–1, 144–5, 252–3
Child neglect 180–2
Child protection 172–98, 290–1
  abuse as a public issue 175–6
  child neglect 180–2
  curriculum for education in 174–5
  definitions of abuse 176–7, 178, 180,
    182, 186
  emotional abuse 177–80
  learning about 173–4
  multidisciplinary work 189–91
  physical abuse 186–9
  responding to abuse 191–5
  sexual abuse 182–6
Child Protection Register 176
  emotional abuse 178
Child Support Act (1991) 119–20
Child Support Agency (CSA) 120
Childbearing
  developing countries 247, 249
  health in 41–3
Child-centred ethos, educare 205,
  209
Child-centred families 101–2
Child-centred health care 231–2
Childminder service 112
Children Act (1948) 108
Children Act (1989) 108
  child abuse 176, 177
  child protection 173, 191, 192
  child-minder services 112
  educare 204, 209, 217
Children Come First 119–20
Children First 231–2
Children and Young Persons Act (1969)
  108
Chromosomal abnormalities 36–7
Cigarette smoking 37, 38, 40, 149
Codes, families 295
Cognitive development
  play/learning/language 154–71, 293
  theory overview 12–4
Cognitive needs, hierarchy 53, 56
Collaborative care, sick children 233–4,
  292–3, 296

Communication
  development of 79–80, 159–60
  see also Language development
  early years practitioners 276–8, 279,
    290, 291–3, 296
Community health services
  children's nurses 232–3
  foundations 107
  and hospital care 226–7, 229–32
  and outreach oncology nurses 239
  policy 115
Confidentiality, ethics 29
Consent issues, research 270
Conservation theory 293
Constructivism (interactionism) 12,
  13–14
  children in society 86, 89
  educare 205
  education 199
  language theories 160–2, 165–6, 168–9
  learning theory 157–9
  play theories 165–7
Coronary heart disease, prevention 149
Corporal punishment 187
  see also Physical abuse
Court Report 231
Cow's milk 58, 62
Cultural issues
  breast feeding 61
  childhood 5–6
  diet of pre-school children 67, 68
  discrimination 217–8, 255
  ethnocentrism 291
  play 77–8, 162
  preconception care 41
  for students of early childhood 29–30
  weaning 65, 66
Cytomegalovirus 36

Data collection, for research 266–7, 293–4
  see also Observation of children
Day care
  holistic development 82–3
  percentage of children in 100
  social policy 112
  and women in the workplace 99, 100
  see also Educare
Death
  books about 237
  children's understanding of 236–7
  in developing countries 246–8
  tertiary prevention 151–2
  see also Dying children

Debt, developing countries 257
Delegation 285–6, 287
Denial 291–2
Denver Development Screening test 48
Depression, postnatal 42
Developing countries 243–59, 290
  Brandt report 254
  causes of death 246–8
  child labour 252–3
  child morbidity 248–9
  debt 257
  definitions 244–5
  education 251–3
  food and hunger 248, 255–7
  handicapped children 249
  immunisation programmes 250
  infant mortality 246–8
  life expectancy 246, 251
  political instability 254–5
  Rights of the Child
    principle 1 258
    principle 2 248
    principle 3 255
    principle 4 245
    principle 5 249
    principle 6 250
    principle 8 257
    principle 9 253
    principle 10 255
  street children 252–3
  war 254–5
  wealth 244–5, 253–4
Development
  affective 72–84, 164
  assessment
    check-lists 22, 48
    data analysis 25–7
    health screening 46–7
    schedules 47–8, 49
  Maslow's hierarchy of needs 52–7
  personal 72–84
  physical
    antenatal care 41–2
    breast or bottle feeding 57–63
    growth 48–52, 63
    postnatal 42–3
    preconception care 40–2
    prenatal 33–5, 36–9, 147
  play/learning/language 154–71, 290
  pre-school education see Educare
  reasons for study of 45–6, 289, 293–4
  relationships 80–2, 124–42
  social 72–84, 164

Diabetes in pregnancy 36
Diaries, observation methods 24
Diarrhoea 248
Diet
  pre-school children 66–9
  preconceptional 40
  in pregnancy 37–8
  primary prevention 149
  schoolchildren 69
  weaning 64–6
  see also Feeding
Discrimination
  developing countries 255
  educare 217–18
Down's syndrome 36, 37
Drugs, use in pregnancy 37, 40
Dying children 151–2, 235–6
  children's understanding of death
    236–7
  education 239–40
  place of care 237–9
  professional communication 292–3
  relationships 239–40

Early Childhood Studies
  as academic discipline 10–11
  focus of 4–6
  holism 289–90
  personal agendas in 289
  reasons for studying 6–7, 293–4
  see also Research
Ecological theory, development 13
Economic issues see Socio-economic
  factors
Educare 199–224
  child-centred ethos 205, 209
  Children Act (1989) 204, 209, 217
  conversation 214–15
  curriculum 215–17
  discrimination 217–18
  educators' qualities 212–15
  Effective Early Learning Research
    Project 206–7, 208–9, 220
  equality of opportunity 217–18
  evaluating standards 205–6, 220–2
  fostering the right ethos 209–12
  HighScope programme 203, 205–6
  history 2, 3
  holistic principle 8, 209
  home–nursery collaboration 218–20
  learning in 204–5
  monitoring standards 220–2
  multidisciplinary work 209

Educare *cont.*
  outcomes 216–17
  play 212–14
  process evaluation 221
  process variables 206
  product evaluation 221
  quality issues 203–8, 220–2
  reasons for 201–3, 205–6
  relationships 210–11
  Rumbold Report 204, 205, 206, 208–209, 212, 213, 216, 217, 218–19
  Schools Curriculum and Assessment Authority 204–5, 208–9, 216–17
  self-esteem 211–12
  treatment variables 205
  use of term 3
  voucher scheme 204–205
Education Act (1870) 107
Education (Butler) Act (1944) 109, 111
Education Act (1981) 111
Education Act (1993) 111
Education (children)
  childhood as social construct 5
  compulsory elementary 91, 251
  developing countries 251–3
  history 1–3
  play theories 167–8
  policy 107, 109–12
  pre-school *see* Educare
  schools' health care role 149–51
  sick and dying children 151–52, 239–40
  visions of 199–201
Education (parents)
  antenatal care 42, 43
  preconceptional 40–2
Education (professionals) 3–4, 6–7, 10–11
  child protection 173–5
  developing countries 255
  see also Management; Research
Education Reform Act (1988) 111
Educators, pre-school 212–15, 220–2
Effective Early Learning Research Project 206–7, 208–9, 220
Egocentric speech 160–1
Embryonic development 33–5, 36, 38
Emotional abuse 177–80
Emotional development *see* Affective development
Emotional neglect 139, 179–80
Empiricism 12–13, 76, 156–7
Employment
  child labour 89, 90–1, 144–5, 252–3

women in the workplace 98–100
Empowerment
  care of sick children 234–5
  of patients 146
Enlightenment period 90
Equal opportunities, educare 217–18
Equilibration, learning theory 157, 158
Esteem, hierarchy of needs 53, 56
  see also Self-esteem
Ethical issues
  child observation 28–9
  research 268–70
Ethnocentrism 291
Ethology, mother–child relationships 129
Event sampling 20–1
Evolutionary theories, play 163–4
Experiential learning 287
Extended families 92–3, 95, 96–8

Families 294–6
  Children Act responsibilities 108–9
  codes 295
  communication with 291–3
  empowerment in care of sick children 234–5
  family-centred health care 231–2, 234
  holistic development 80–3
  home–nursery collaboration 218–20
  regulations 295–6
  relationships in 125
    dysfunctional families 127–8, 129
    family structures 127–8
    fathers 132–4
    mothers 129–32, 134–6
    and parenting styles 126–7
    siblings 81, 134–6
    well-functioning families 128
  sociological perspectives 92–3
    child-centred 101–2
    definitions 93–4
    division of labour 100–1
    family structures 94–8
    working women 98–100
  see also Child abuse
Family Credit 118
Family Income Supplement 118
Father–child relationship 132–4
Favouritism, siblings 136
Fear, mother–child attachment 130
Feeding
  breast or bottle 57–63, 248
  developing countries 248, 255–7
  pre-school children 66–9

Feeding *cont.*
  schoolchildren 69
  weaning 63–6
Feminism 86, 88, 100
Fetal alcohol syndrome 37
Fetal development 33–5, 36–8
Field notes, observation methods 24
Folic acid 40
Food supply, global 255–7
Formula milks 58, 62–3
Foster care 109
Frame analysis 169
Friends 136–8
  of dying children 239–40
Functionalism 86, 88, 92, 93

Game playing *see* Play
GATT 256–7
Gender issues 86, 88
  family division of labour 100–1
  literacy 252
  son preference 247–8
  women in the workplace 98–100
General Agreement on Tariffs and Trade
    256–7
Genetic abnormalities 36–7
Genetic counselling 41
Goat's milk 62
Government policy *see* Social policy
Gross national product (GNP),
    developing countries 244, 254
Groups, management 283–4
  see also Multidisciplinary teams
Growth, physical
  centile charts 48–52
  monitoring 63

Handicapped children *see* Special needs
  children
Health 143–53, 290
  antenatal care 41–2
  community services 107
    see also below sick children
  developing countries
    child morbidity 248–9
    and education 251
    food and hunger 248, 255–7
    handicapped children 249
    immunisation 250
    infant mortality 246–8
    life expectancy 246, 251
    Rights of the Child 245, 248, 249,
      250

  war 254, 255
  empowerment of patients 146
  history 2, 6, 91–2, 107, 144–6, 229–30
  holism 147–8
  hygienist movement 6
  partnerships in 148
  Patients' Charter 116, 146
  postnatal 42–3
  preconception care 40–2
  prenatal 33–5, 36–9, 147
  primary health care team 229
  primary prevention 148–9
  screening 46–7, 147, 149–50
  secondary prevention 149–50
  sick children 225–42, 290–1
    books about death 237
    chronic illness 228, 235–6
    collaborative care 233–4
    in the community 146–7, 151–2,
      226–7
    community nurses 232–3
    death 240
    education 151–2, 239–40
    empowerment of the family 234–5
    family-centered care 234
    friends 239–40
    glossary 228–9
    hospices 238
    hospital care 226–7, 229–32, 260,
      262–3
    lay referral system 226, 228
    life-limiting illness 228
    morbidity 228
    mortality 227–8, 240
    oncology 228, 239
    otitis media 229, 235
    outreach oncology nurses 239
    relationships 239–40
    research scenario 260, 262–3
    self-limiting illness 228
    serious illness 235–40
    siblings 237, 238, 239, 240
    sick role 225, 228
    terminal illness 229, 235–6, 292–3
    types of sickness 225–6
    understanding of death 236–7
  social policy 107, 115–16, 144–5
    and social security benefits 118, 119
    tertiary prevention 150–3
Hearing, screening 150
Height measurement 50
Herpes simplex 36
HighScope programme 203, 205–6

HIV, developing countries 248–9
Holism 8–9, 296
  health 147–8
  Human Development Index 245
  play 155, 168
  pre-school education 8, 209
Hospices 238
Hospital care 226–7, 229–32
  research scenario 260, 262–3
Housework 100–1
Housing Act (1985) 114
Housing (Homeless Persons) Act (1977)
  114
Housing policy 113–14, 119
Human Development Index 245, 253–4
Human rights, Nuremberg Code 269–70
  see also Rights of the Child
Hygiene, hierarchy of needs 53
Hygienist movement 6

Ideal self 211
Identity, self-knowledge 275–6
Illness see Health, sick children
Immunisation programmes 148–9
  developing countries 250
Income Support 118–19
Industrial period 90–1, 144–5
Infant mortality, developing countries
  246–8
  see also Mortality
Infections
  bottle feeding 63
  breast feeding 59
  developing countries 248–9, 250
  history 145
  immunisation 148–9, 250
  morbidity patterns 228
  otitis media 229, 235
  in pregnancy 36, 41
Intellectual development, abstract
  thinking 76–7
  see also Learning
Interactionism (constructivism) 12, 13–14
  children in society 86, 89
  educare 205
  education 199
  language theories 160–2, 165–6, 168–9
  learning theory 157–9
  play theories 165–7
Interpersonal skills
  assertiveness 278–80
  care provision and 80–2
  role of play 78–9, 168

see also Social development
Ipsative assessment 25
Iron deficiency 64, 66, 67

Kinship 94, 95, 97–8

LAD (Language Acquisition Device)
  161–2
Language development 154–71
  educare 214–15
  egocentric speech 160–1
  holism 155, 168
  and interviews with children 267
  issues in 159–61
  learning issues 156–7
  learning theories 157–9, 168–9
  linguistic determinism 160
  linguistic relativity 160
  observational data analysis 26–7
  play issues 162–3
  play theories 163–9
  theories of 12, 161–2, 168–9
  and thought 160–1
LASS (Language Acquisition Support
  System) 161–2
Lay referral system, illness 226, 228
Leadership 284–7
Learning 154–71
  educare
    child-centred ethos 209
    conversation 214–15
    curriculum 215–17
    educators' qualities 212–15
    equal opportunities 217–18
    home–nursery collaboration 218–20
    outcomes 216–17
    play 212–14
    quality 204–8, 220–2
    self-esteem 211–12
  experiential 287
  holistic perspective 155, 168, 296
  issues in 156–7
  language issues 159–61
  language theories 161–2, 168–9
  mentors 287
  play issues 162–3, 212–13
  play theories 163–9
  professional development 287
  theories of 157–9, 168–9, 212–13
Learning theory, language development
  161
Legislation
  Child Support Act (1991) 119–20

Legislation *cont.*
  Children Act (1948) 108
  Children Act (1989) 108
    child abuse 176, 177
    child protection 173, 191, 192
    child-minder services 112
    educare 204, 209, 217
  Children and Young Persons Act
    (1969) 108
  Education Act (1870) 107
  Education Act (1944) 109, 111
  Education Act (1981) 111
  Education Act (1993) 111
  Education Reform Act (1988) 111
  Housing Act (1985) 114
  Housing (Homeless Persons) Act
    (1977) 114
  National Health Service Act (1948) 115
  NHS and Community Care Act (1990)
    115–16
  Poor Law 106
  Poor Law Amendment Act (1889) 107
  Public Health Act (1847) 107
Libraries, use of 263–4
Life expectancy 246, 251
Linguistic determinism 160
Linguistic relativity 160
Listening skills 277
Literacy
  developing countries 251–2, 253
  educare 219
Literature reviews 263–4
Local authorities
  day-care provision 112
  housing policy 114
  social policy 108–9
Lone-parent families
  Child Support Act (1991) 119–20
  day-care provision 112
  family structures 95–6
  housing 114, 119
  social security benefits 118, 119
Love, hierarchy of needs 53, 56

Management 273–88
  assertiveness 278–80
  communication 276–8, 290, 291–3, 296
  delegation 285–6, 287
  experiential learning 287
  groups 283–4
  importance of 273–4
  knowledge of self 275–6
  leadership 284–7

  mentors 287
  nature of relationships 274–5
  professional development 287
  of self 273–4
  self–others interface 274
  stress 280–3
  teams 283–4
  time 286
Marxism 86, 88, 92, 100
Maslow's hierarchy of needs 52–7
Maternal bonding 130
McMillan sisters 2, 6, 167–8
Means-tested benefits 117, 118–19, 120
Measles, developing countries 250
Medieval period 89–90
Men
  developing countries 247–8
  division of labour at home 100–1, 132–3
  father–child relationship 132–4
Mentors 287
Metacognition 167
Metacommunication 167, 169
Metarepresentation 167, 169
Milk, infant feeding 57–63
Morbidity
  developing countries 248–9
  patterns 228
Mortality
  cultural relativism 5
  death of a child 240
  developing countries 246–8
  holistic perspective 147–8
  infant welfare movement 145
  patterns 227–8
  primary prevention 149
Mothers
  developing countries 247
  hospital research scenario 260, 262–3
  mother–child relationships 129–32,
    134–6
  see also Families; Parents
Multidisciplinary teams
  child protection 189–91
  communication and collaboration
    233–4, 291–3, 296
  educare 209
  management 283–4
  sick children in the community 233–4,
    292–3, 296

Narrative reports 18–19
National Children's Bureau, values and
  principles 30

National Health Service, social policy
   115–16
National Oracy Project 214
Nativism 12, 156
   language development 12, 161
   perceptual development 76
Needs, Maslow's hierarchy of 52–7
Neglect 180–2
   emotional 139, 179–80
Neonates
   attachment 130
   developing countries 247
   factors affecting health 32–44
   fathers' involvement 132
NHS, social policy 115–16
NHS and Community Care Act (1990)
   115–16
Non-verbal communication 79, 158–9,
   277–8, 279
Nuremberg Code 269–70
Nursery education
   history 2, 3
   social policy 109–11, 112
   voucher scheme 110–11, 204–5
   see also Pre-school education
Nutrition
   bottle feeding 58, 62–3, 248
   breast feeding 57–61, 63, 248
   developing countries 248, 255–7
   hierarchy of needs 52, 53, 57
   and physical growth 52, 63
   pre-school children 66–9
   preconceptional 40
   in pregnancy 37–8
   primary prevention 149
   schoolchildren 69
   vegetarians 65, 67, 68
   weaning 63–6

Object permanence 130
Observation of children 14–28, 266–7,
   293–4
   check-lists 21–3
   data analysis 24–8
   diaries 24
   ethical issues 28–9
   event sampling 20–1
   field notes 24
   narrative reports 18–19
   observer effects 267
   time sampling 19–20
   verbatim reporting 23
Olson model, family structures 127–8, 129

Oncology 228, 239
Oracy Project 214
Otitis media 229, 235
Outreach oncology nurses 239

Paediatric specialists, need for 232
Parents
   child protection 173, 191
   Children Act (1989) responsibilities
      108–9, 173, 191
   consent issues 270
   education policy 111–12
   empowerment in care of sick children
      234–5
   home–nursery collaboration 218–20
   influences on infant health 33,
      36–43
   parent–child relationships 81, 134
      father–child 132–4
      mother–child 129–32, 134–6
   styles of parenting 126–7
      child neglect 181
      emotional neglect 179–80
   see also Child abuse; Families
Partnerships in child health 148
Patients' Charter 116, 146
Perceptual development 75–6
Permissive parents 126
Personal development 75
   abstract thinking 76–7
   care provision 82–3
   communication 79–80
   perception 75–6
   relationships 80–2
   role of play 77–9
Physical abuse 139, 186–9
Physical development 290
   antenatal care 41–2
   breast or bottle feeding 57–63
   postnatal 42–3
   preconception care 40–2
   prenatal 33–5, 36–9, 147
Physical growth
   centile charts 48–52
   monitoring 63
Plato 1
Platt Report 230–1, 232, 268
Play 77–9, 154–71, 290
   definitions 162–3
   in educare 212–14
   fathers' role 132–3
   holism 155, 168
   language issues 159–61

Play *cont.*
  language theories 161–2, 168–9
  learning issues 156–7
  learning theories 157–9, 168–9, 212–13
  theories of 163–9
Play groups *see* Pre-school education
Policymaking *see* Social policy
Political instability 254–5
Poor Law 106
Poor Law Amendment Act (1889) 107
Post-traumatic stress disorder (PTSD)
  184–5
Poverty *see* Socio-economic factors
Practice theory, play 164
Pre-school education 199–224
  child-centred ethos 205, 209
  Children Act (1989) 204, 209, 217
  conversation 214–15
  curriculum 215–17
  discrimination 217–18
  educators' qualities 212–15
  Effective Early Learning Research
    Project 206–7, 208–9, 220
  equality of opportunity 217–18
  evaluating standards 205–6, 220–2
  fostering the right ethos 209–12
  HighScope programme 203, 205–6
  holistic approach 209
  home–nursery collaboration 218–20
  monitoring standards 220–2
  multidisciplinary work 209
  outcomes 216–17
  play 212–14
  process evaluation 221
  process variables 206
  product evaluation 221
  quality issues 203–8, 220–2
  reasons for 201–3, 205–6
  relationships 210–11
  Rumbold Report 204, 205, 206, 208–9,
    212, 213, 216, 217, 218–19
  Schools Curriculum and Assessment
    Authority 204–5, 208–9, 216–17
  self-esteem 211–12
  treatment variables 205
Preconception care 40–2
Pregnancy
  antenatal care 41–2
  fetal development 33–5, 36–8, 43, 147
  postnatal care 42–3
  preconception care 40–2
Preventive approach, child health
  148–52

Primary health care
  policy 115
  team 229
Primary prevention, health 148–9
Principles, early childhood studies 29–30
Priority mountain 286
Psychoanalysis, play 164–5, 168
Psychological abuse 139
Psychological theories
  learning 157–9
  overview 12–14
  social *see* Relationships
Public Health Act (1847) 107

Quality issues, educare 203–8, 220–2

Rating scales, design 266
Rationalism (nativism) 12, 156
  language development 12, 161
  perceptual development 76
Recapitulation theory, play 164
Reflective practice 27
Regulations, families 295–6
Relationships 80–2, 124–42
  abusive 139–41
  dying children 239–40
  dysfunctional families 127–8, 129
  early years practitioners 274–5
    communication 291–3, 296
    knowledge of self 275, 276
  family 125
  family structures 127–8
  father–child 132–4
  friends 136–8
  importance in educare 210–11
  mothers 129–32, 134–6
  parenting styles 126–7
  siblings 81, 134–6
  well-functioning families 128
Research 260–72
  consent 270
  critical reading skills 263–4
  data collection 266–7, 293–4
  ethics 268–70
  interviews 267
  knowledge informing practice 262–3
  methodologies 265–7
  Nuremberg Code 269–70
  principles 264–5
  sampling 265–6
  scale of studies 267–8
  therapeutic 268–9
  value of 261–2

Rights of the Child 243
  principle 1 258
  principle 2 248
  principle 3 255
  principle 4 245
  principle 5 249
  principle 6 250
  principle 7 251
  principle 8 257
  principle 9 253
  principle 10 255
Rubella 36, 41
Rumbold Report 3, 110–11
  educare 204, 205, 206, 208–9
    curriculum 216
    discrimination 217
    educators' qualities 212
    home–nursery collaboration 218–19
    play 213

Safety
  accident prevention 149
  hierarchy of needs 53, 56
Sampling
  observation methods 19–20
  research methodology 265–6
Schema theory 169
Schemas, Piagetian theory 157–8
School health service 115, 145
  immunisation 148–9
Schools, role in child health 149–52
Schools Curriculum and Assessment
  Authority (SCAA) 204–5, 208–9, 216–17
Script theory 168–9
Secondary prevention 149–50
Security, hierarchy of needs 53, 56
Seen But Not Heard 232
Self
  false 276
  interface with others 274
  knowledge of 275–6
  management of 273–4
  true 276
Self-actualisation 53, 56
Self-awareness 275–6
  assertiveness 279
Self-efficacy 211
Self-esteem
  assertiveness 278, 279
  hierarchy of needs 53, 56
  pre-school education 211–12
Self-image 211
Self-respect 211

Separation protest 130
Sex-role development 133–4
Sexual abuse 140–1, 182–6
  definitions of abuse 176–7, 182
  secondary prevention 150
Sexually transmitted diseases 36
  developing countries 248–9
Siblings
  of a dying child 237, 238, 239, 240
  relationships 81, 134–6
Sick children *see* Health, sick children
Single parent families *see* Lone-parent
    families
Smoking
  in pregnancy 37, 38, 40
  teachers 149
Social construct
  'child abuse' term as 177
  childhood as 5–6
  see also Sociological perspectives
Social development 72–5
  abstract thinking 76–7
  care provision 80–3
  communication 79–80
  perception 75–6
  relationships 80–2
  role of play 77–9, 164, 168
  see also Relationships
Social Fund 119
Social housing 113–14, 119
Social interactionism
  language acquisition 160–2, 165–6,
    168–9
  play theories 165–7
Social learning, mother–child
  relationships 129–30
Social policy 105–23, 290
  child abuse 187
  Child Support Act (1991) 119–20
  day care 112
  education 107, 109–12
  foundations 106–7
  health care 107, 115–16, 144–5
  housing 113–14, 119
  local authorities 108–9
  principle objectives 105
  rights and interests of the child
    108–9
  social security 116–20
  voluntary sector 121
Social referencing 79
Social security system 116–20
Social support, new mothers 42–3

Socio-economic factors
　children in history 89–91
　fetal health 38, 43
　lone-parent families 96
　poverty confused with neglect 181
　poverty in developing countries
　　244–5, 253–4, 257
　pre-school children's diet 67, 68–9
　social security 116–20
　weaning 65–6
Sociological perspectives 85–102, 290
　child defined 87–8
　child-centred families 101–2
　children in history 89–92
　division of labour 100–1
　family defined 92–4
　family functioning 98–102
　family structures 94–8
　sociology explained 85
　variety of 86–7, 88–9
　working women 98–100
Soya milk 62
Special needs children
　developing countries 249
　education 109, 111
Speech see Language development
Starvation 256–7
State policymaking see Social policy
Stools, consistency of 63
Street children 252–3
Stress 280–3
Structural functionalism 86, 88, 92, 93
Surplus energy theory, play 163
Survival, hierarchy of needs 52–3, 57

Teamwork see Multidisciplinary teams
Teratogens 37
Terminally ill children 151–2, 229, 235–6
　children's understanding of death 236–7
　education 239–40
　place of care 237–9
　professional communication 292–3
　relationships 239–40
Tertiary prevention, health 150–3
Third World 244
Time management 286
Time sampling 19–20
Tobacco smoking
　in pregnancy 37, 38, 40
　teachers 149
TORCH 36
Toxoplasma gondii 36
Trade, developing countries 256–7

United Nations
　Human Development Index 245, 253–4
　Rights of the Child see Rights of the
　　Child
　UNESCO 252
　UNICEF 251–2

Vaccination programmes 148–9
　developing countries 250
Values, for early years professionals/
　students 29–30
Vegetarianism 65, 67, 68
Verbatim reporting 23
Violence, child abuse 186–9
Vitamin D deficiency 67
Voluntary sector, social policy 121
Voucher scheme, nursery education
　110–11, 204–5

War, effects of 254–5
Wealth, developing countries 244–5,
　253–4, 257
　see also Socio-economic factors
Weaning 63–6
Weight measurement 48–52
Welfare of Children in Hospital (Platt
　Report) 230–1, 232, 268
Welfare of Children and Young People in
　Hospital 230–2
Welfare policy see Social policy
Women
　developing countries 247–8
　division of labour at home 100–1
　mother–child relationship 129–32,
　　134–6
　pregnancy
　　antenatal care 41–2
　　fetal development 33–5, 36–8, 43
　　postnatal care 42–3
　　preconception care 40–2
　in the workplace 98–100
Work
　child labour 89, 90–1, 144–5, 252–3
　division of labour at home 100–1,
　　132–3
　women in the workplace 98–100
Workhouses 106–7
Working Together, child abuse 177, 178, 189
World Bank 244
World Health Organization 244

Zone of proximal development (ZPD)
　159, 166